DFR	Decreasing failure rate
IFRA	Increasing failure rate on the average
DFRA	Decreasing failure rate on the average

Chapter 4   Parametric Lifetime Models

λ	Scale parameter
$\sim$	Is distributed as
κ	Shape parameter
$\Gamma(y)$	Gamma function
$I(y, x)$	Incomplete gamma function
$\chi^2(n)$	Chi-square distribution with n degrees of freedom
α	Significance level
$\chi^2_{n,\alpha}$	$1 - \alpha$ Fractile of the chi-square distribution with n degrees of freedom
$T_{(i)}$	Order statistic i
a, b	Location parameters
γ, δ	Shape parameters

Chapter 5   Specialized Models

k	Number of risks
$C_1, \ldots, C_k$	Causes of failure
X_j	Net lifetime j
$q_j(a, b)$	Net probability of failure from risk j in $[a, b]$
Y_j	Crude lifetime j
$Q_j(a, b)$	Crude probability of failure from risk j in $[a, b]$
π_j	Probability of failure from risk j
$S(x_1, \ldots, x_k)$	Joint survivor function for the net lives
m	Number of populations in a mixture model
p_l	Mix parameters
$f_l(t \mid \theta_l)$	Population probability density functions
θ_l	Parameters for distribution l
q	Number of covariates
$\mathbf{z}$	$q \times 1$ Vector of covariates
$\psi(\mathbf{z})$	Link function
$S_0(t)$	Baseline survivor function
$f_0(t)$	Baseline probability density function
$h_0(t)$	Baseline hazard function
$H_0(t)$	Baseline cumulative hazard function
β	$q \times 1$ Vector of regression coefficients
T_0	Lifetime under baseline conditions

Continued on back endpapers

RELIABILITY

RELIABILITY
Probabilistic Models
and Statistical Methods

Lawrence M. Leemis

Department of Mathematics
College of William and Mary

 Prentice-Hall, Englewood Cliffs, New Jersey 07632

Library of Congress Cataloging-in-Publication Data

Leemis, Lawrence M.
  Reliability : probabilistic models and statistical methods /
Lawrence M. Leemis.
      p.   cm. — (Prentice Hall international series in industrial
and systems engineering)
  Includes bibliographical references and index.
  ISBN 0-13-720517-1
  1. Reliability (Engineering)   I. Title.   II. Series.
TA169.L43 1995   94-23068
620'.00452—dc20 CIP

Acquisitions editor: *Marcia Horton*
Editorial/production supervision: *Raeia Maes*
Cover design: *Wendy Alling Judy*
Manufacturing manager: *William Scazzero*

 © 1995 by Prentice-Hall, Inc.
A Simon & Schuster Company
Englewood Cliffs, New Jersey 07632

Printed in the United States of America

10 9 8 7 6 5 4 3 2 1

ISBN 0-13-720517-1

Prentice-Hall International (UK) Limited, *London*
Prentice-Hall of Australia Pty. Limited, *Sydney*
Prentice-Hall Canada Inc., *Toronto*
Prentice-Hall Hispanoamericana, S.A., *Mexico*
Prentice-Hall of India Private Limited, *New Delhi*
Prentice-Hall of Japan, Inc., *Tokyo*
Simon & Schuster Asia Pte. Ltd., *Singapore*
Editora Prentice-Hall do Brasil, Ltda., *Rio de Janeiro*

For Jill, Lindsey, and Mark

Contents

Preface   **xiii**

1 Introduction   1

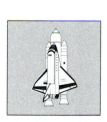

1.1 Definition of Reliability   2

1.2 Case Study   5

1.3 Overview   7

1.4 Further Reading   12

1.5 Exercises   14

2 Coherent Systems Analysis   15

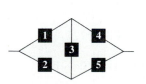

2.1 Structure Functions   15

2.2 Minimal Path and Cut Sets   23

2.3 Reliability Functions   27

2.4 System Reliability Bounds   36

2.5 Further Reading   37

2.6 Exercises   39

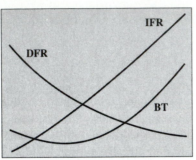

3   Lifetime Distributions   45

3.1   Distribution Representations   45

3.2   Discrete Distributions   55

3.3   Moments and Fractiles   59

3.4   System Lifetime Distributions   62

3.5   Distribution Classes   64

3.6   Further Reading   68

3.7   Exercises   69

4   Parametric Lifetime Models   78

4.1   Parameters   78

4.2   Exponential Distribution   81

4.3   Weibull Distribution   88

4.4   Gamma Distribution   91

4.5   Other Lifetime Distributions   94

4.6   Further Reading   101

4.7   Exercises   102

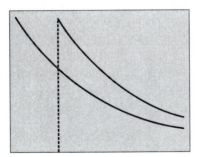

5   Specialized Models   108

5.1   Competing Risks   109

5.2   Mixtures   117

5.3   Accelerated Life   121

5.4   Proportional Hazards   125

5.5   Further Reading   128

5.6   Exercises   129

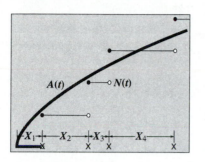

6 Repairable Systems   133

6.1   Introduction   134

6.2   Point Processes   136

6.3   Availability   147

6.4   Birth–Death Models   154

6.5   Further Reading   156

6.6   Exercises   157

7 Lifetime Data Analysis   160

7.1   Point Estimation   161

7.2   Interval Estimation   166

7.3   Likelihood Theory   172

7.4   Asymptotic Properties   179

7.5   Censoring   181

7.6   Further Reading   186

7.7   Exercises   187

8 Parametric Estimation for Models Without Covariates   189

8.1   Sample Data Sets   189

8.2   Exponential Distribution   191

8.3   Weibull Distribution   215

8.4   Further Reading   220

8.5   Exercises   222

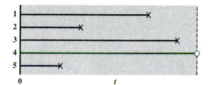

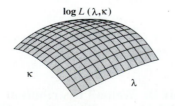

9 Parametric Estimation for Models with Covariates 228

9.1 Model Formulation 228

9.2 Accelerated Life 230

9.3 Proportional Hazards 238

9.4 Further Reading 247

9.5 Exercises 249

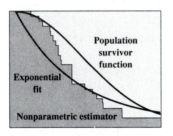

10 Nonparametric Methods and Model Adequacy 252

10.1 Survivor Function Estimation 253

10.2 Life Tables 261

10.3 Kolmogorov–Smirnov Test: All Parameters Known 265

10.4 Kolmogorov–Smirnov Test: Parameters Estimated from Data 273

10.5 Further Reading 275

10.6 Exercises 276

Appendix A: Exponential Distribution Properties 279

Appendix B: Gamma and Incomplete Gamma Functions 286

Appendix C: A Result in Competing Risks Theory 288

Appendix D: Weibull Distribution Initial Parameter Estimation 291

**Appendix E: Extreme Value Distribution
    Parameter Estimation   294**

**Appendix F: A Result for Discrete
    Lifetime Distributions   297**

References   299

Index   308

Preface

The goal of this text is to give an elementary introduction to the probabilistic models and statistical methods used by reliability engineers. These models and methods can be applied, for example, to electrical or mechanical systems. This text is appropriate for a one-semester advanced undergraduate or a graduate-level course in reliability engineering. The text should give students enough background to read most reliability journal articles and more advanced reliability texts. A second course in reliability might consider topics not presented in detail here, such as accelerated testing (Nelson, 1990), Bayesian models (Martz and Waller, 1982), coherent systems (Barlow and Proschan, 1981), covariate effects on survival (Cox and Oakes, 1984; Kalbfleisch and Prentice, 1980; Lawless, 1982), reliability networks (Shier, 1991), or repairable systems (Ascher and Feingold, 1984).

The background for this text is a calculus-based course in probability and statistics, as well as familiarity with Markov models for the chapter on repairable systems. A student completing a course using this textbook should have an intuitive understanding of probabilistic models and statistical methods associated with lifetimes and should be able to apply these methods to reliability problems. A number of interesting topics have been left out to keep the size of the text manageable. The text is not just a collection of results and proofs. It contains explanations of how the mathematical models and results apply to engineering design and the analysis of lifetime data sets. Proofs and derivations are included if they are simple or aid in understanding results.

I have found that students sometimes have difficulty differentiating between probabilistic models and statistical methods. To address this problem, there is a separation between probability models (Chapters 2–6) and statistical methods (Chapters 7–10).

The notation largely parallels that from the literature. In some cases this means that a variable may have two different meanings. The variable n, for instance, is commonly used to denote the number of components in a system and the number of items placed on test. Some of the standard reliability notation that occasionally confuses students (such as using μ as a repair rate) has been altered. Boldface is used for vectors. The notation, with the exception of that in the Further Reading and Exercises sections, is defined in the notation list printed on the endpapers in the order in which it is presented.

Most of the examples and many of the exercises in the text have tractable, or closed-form, answers. These have been chosen for the sake of brevity and simplicity and do not imply that this will always be the case when performing a reliability analysis. A few intractable exercises have been included to allow the student to practice using numerical methods to arrive at a solution to a problem. Symbolic algebra languages and subprograms for high-level programming languages have made the distinction between tractable and intractable expressions less important. A solutions manual is available to instructors by writing the publisher.

Students who spend time reading reliability literature or other textbooks will soon find out that there are no standard parameterizations for the popular parametric distributions such as the Weibull distribution. An effort has been made to keep most of the parameterizations consistent throughout, yet expose students to these differences by parameterizing the exponential distribution by its failure rate in Chapters 4 and 8 and by its mean in Chapter 7.

To improve readability, all references are given at the end of each chapter in a Further Reading section. One paragraph is devoted to each section in the chapter that references topics that may be of interest. This Further Reading section is not intended to be a complete literature review of the current topic, so many excellent references do not appear here. For example, hundreds of articles have been published on the Weibull distribution. Therefore, most of the references are to other textbooks and a few selected articles.

This is intended to be a classroom text, and hence there are a number of exercises at the end of each chapter. Continual review of the subjects covered early in the text through homework exercises is encouraged. To this end, the earlier chapters in the textbook have more exercises than the later chapters. This allows an instructor to have review exercises later in the course for material covered early in the course.

Actuarial science, biostatistics, and reliability engineering share a common interest: determining the distribution of a lifetime and the associated probabilities. Actuaries are interested in the lifetimes of people and emphasize the use of life tables in determining these probabilities. Biostatisticians are interested in the lifetimes of organisms and emphasize the effect of covariates on these lifetimes. Reliability engineers are interested in system lifetimes and tend to emphasize system structure (that is, the way the components comprising the system relate to one another). I believe that it is healthy for students taking a first course in any of these three fields to understand the basic models and methods from all three disciplines. Although the emphasis in this text is on reliability engineering, the models and methods described in this text apply equally well to all three areas of application.

Since censored data analysis requires a variety of statistical techniques, the number of data sets used in the text has been kept to a minimum to ensure that students do not get the techniques and the data sets confused. The data sets have been drawn from a variety of fields, such as biostatistics, in order to emphasize the applicability of these models to nonreliability situations. The data set used most often in the text consists of ball bearing failure times. Several examples using various techniques are given to indicate beyond a shadow of a doubt that these ball bearings have an increasing hazard function. Likewise, the data set involving covariates that is used most often in the text involves a study concerning a drug called 6-mercaptopurine. Many analysis techniques are used to show that this drug is effective in prolonging the remission times of leukemia patients.

There are many different ways that the material in the text can be presented. Chapters 2 and 3, with the exceptions of Sections 3.4 and 3.5, can be transposed. The shortest path through the text, which might be appropriate for a one-quarter course, is 1, 2.1, 3 (excluding 3.4 and 3.5), 4, 7, 8, 10. This shortest path emphasizes lifetime data analysis.

I appreciate the help of the students at the University of Oklahoma and the College of William and Mary who have class tested the text and made helpful suggestions. In particular, Ralph Boedigheimer, Pam Burch, CB Eagye, Amy Goldberg, Anuradha Maria, Jen Mauser, Sabra Nelson, Bryan Norman, Karen Prosser, Aminur Rahman, Hussein Saber, Li-Hsing Shih, and Mark Waltensperger have made substantial improvements. In addition, Ralph Evans has made numerous contributions to the portions of the manuscript that have been used in the Annual Reliability and Maintainability Symposium. Careful reviews from four anonymous referees have also improved the presentation. Thanks also goes to Mike Taaffe and the students at the University of Minnesota and to Tom Landers and the students at the University of Arkansas for class testing the text.

Lawrence M. Leemis

1

Introduction

Recent tragedies such as the Space Shuttle *Challenger* accident, the Chernobyl and Three Mile Island nuclear power plant accidents, and aircraft catastrophes highlight reliability problems in design. This textbook describes probabilistic models for reliability design problems and statistical techniques that can be applied to a data set of lifetimes. Although the majority of the illustrations in this text come from engineering problems, these techniques may be applied to problems in actuarial science and biostatistics.

Reliability engineers, actuaries, and biostatisticians are all interested in lifetimes. A reliability engineer may study the lifetimes of products used in the marketplace. The interest may be in the failure time of a light bulb (a nonrepairable item) or a drill press (a repairable item). An actuary might be interested in the distribution of the lifetime of a person in order to determine the appropriate premium for a life insurance policy. A biostatistician might analyze the survival times of cancer patients in order to compare the effectiveness of treatment techniques, such as radiation and chemotherapy.

Reliability engineers concern themselves with lifetimes of inanimate objects, such as light bulbs, microprocessors, or drill bits. They usually regard a complex system as a collection of components when performing an analysis. These components are arranged in a structure (simple examples include series and parallel structures) that allows the system state to be determined as a function of the component states. Interest in reliability and quality control has been revived by a more competitive international market and increased consumer expectations.

Actuaries are usually employed by insurance companies to determine premiums and payment schedules for policies. They often use *life tables* to determine the appropriate premium for a particular individual. Life tables are used to determine the probability of death as a function of age for an individual. Factors such as medical history and occupation of an individual affect this probability. These tables need to be updated annually as medical science advances and new diseases arise. Actuaries need to understand the time value of money when determining the appropriate rate schedule for a policy, since payments are often made over several years.

Biostatisticians are interested in the lifetimes of organisms. These may be the lifetimes of patients undergoing treatment for a disease or laboratory animals in an experiment. Biostatisticians often investigate the effects of *covariates* on lifetimes. Simple examples of covariates include the gender, age, and weight of a patient. To account for these covariates, many probabilistic lifetime models that they use include covariates and associated regression coefficients that alter the distribution of the failure time.

Literature on reliability tends to use *failure*, actuarial literature tends to use *death*, and point process literature tends to use *epoch* to describe the event at the termination of a lifetime. Likewise, reliability literature tends to use *system*, *component*, or *item*, actuarial literature uses *individual*, and biostatistical literature tends to use *organism* as the object of a study. To avoid switching terms, *failure* of an *item* will be used as much as possible throughout the text, since the emphasis is on reliability. The concept of failure time (or lifetime or survival time) is very general, and the models and statistical methods presented here apply to any nonnegative random variable (for example, the response time at a computer terminal).

To complicate things further, the three different fields have developed their own notation, so the notation used here will not necessarily match the notation in the literature. Whenever possible, existing notation from the reliability literature will be used.

1.1   DEFINITION OF RELIABILITY

Before considering the analysis of lifetime data (Chapters 7 through 10), probabilistic models for lifetimes will be introduced (Chapters 2 through 6). Many of these models have their basis in reliability theory. As shown in Chapter 3, the concept of reliability generalizes to a survivor function when time dependence is introduced. The definition for reliability is given next. The paragraphs following the definition expand on those words italicized in the definition.

Definition 1.1   The *reliability* of an *item* is the *probability* that it will *adequately perform* its specified *purpose* for a specified *period of time* under specified *environmental conditions*.

The definition implies that the object of interest is an *item*. The definition of the item depends on the purpose of the study. In some situations, we will consider an item to be an interacting arrangement of components; in other situations, the component level of detail in the model is not of interest. Assume, for example, that a computer terminal (the item of interest) consists of three components: a keyboard, CRT, and other electronic components. The object of the study may be the terminal (ignoring the individual components), or the item may be modeled as an arrangement of the three components.

The modeler needs to carefully define what the item of interest is and the level of detail to be considered when analyzing that item.

In addition to the question of resolution (that is, how to decompose the system into components), the modeler must determine an external boundary for the item. This external boundary determines what is to be considered part of the item and what is to be considered part of the environment around the item for modeling purposes.

Reliability is defined as a *probability*. Thus, the axioms of probability apply to reliability calculations. In particular, this means that all reliabilities must be between 0 and 1 inclusive, along with spinoffs from the probability axioms. For example, if two independent components have 1000-hour reliabilities of p_1 and p_2, and system failure occurs when either component fails, then the 1000-hour system reliability is $p_1 p_2$.

Adequate performance for an item must be stated unambiguously. A *standard* is used to determine what is considered adequate performance. A ball bearing, for example, may be performing adequately if wear has not changed its diameter outside of the range 3 ± 0.001 mm. This tolerance is an example of a specification that delineates adequate performance from inadequate performance.

Specifying the adequate performance of an item implies knowledge of when it fails, since, when it fails, it is no longer adequately performing. If the item of interest is an automobile, an appropriate performance level might be that the car is mobile. If this is the case, the automobile is still functioning if the radio is broken or the muffler falls off. The performance of an item is related to the mathematical model used to represent the condition of the item. The simplest model for an item is a binary model, in which the item is in either the functioning or failed state. This model is easily applied to a fuse, but more difficult to apply to items that gradually degrade over time, such as a drill bit. To apply a binary model to an item that degrades gradually, a threshold value must be determined to separate the functioning and failed states. To summarize, failure needs to be unambiguously defined in order to build a mathematical model for an item.

The definition of reliability also implies that the *purpose* or intended use of the item must be specified. It is common to produce several grades of one particular consumer good. A drill, for example, may have one grade for a weekend handyman and another for a contractor. Although these two grades of drills have identical functions, their reliabilities differ since they are designed for light and heavy usage.

Definition 1.1 also indicates that *time* is involved in reliability, which implies five consequences. First, the units for time need to be specified (for example, minutes, hours, years) by the modeler in order to perform any analysis. Second, many lifetime models use the random variable T (rather than X, which is common in classical statistics) to represent the failure time of the item. Third, time need not be taken literally. The number of miles may represent time for an automobile tire, the number of flips may represent time for a light switch, the number of cycles may represent time for a ball bearing, and the number of whacks may represent time for a stapler. Fourth, we must specify a time duration associated with a reliability. To say that an item has a reliability of 0.8 is meaningless. This reliability for the item is valid for a particular time value, such as 1000 hours. Finally, determining what should be used to measure the lifetime of an item may not be obvious. Many analysts have considered whether continuous operation or on/off cycling is more effective for items such as motors or computers. If a light bulb, for example, is to operate continuously, the number of hours burned should be used for the lifetime. If the light bulb is turned on and off, as most are, the number of hours burned may not be appropriate. If a comparison of the number of hours burned by bulbs burned continuously and bulbs burned intermittently showed a shorter burning lifetime for those burned intermittently, the modeler can assume that the shock of lighting and extinction decreases the light bulb's life. The modeler must account for these differences in order to compare light bulbs used continuously with those used intermittently. One solution is to consider the "age" of the light bulb to be a function of the number of hours burned and the number of illuminations so that all light bulbs will have equivalent age regardless of the number of illuminations. This example may be oversimplified, but it indicates that there may be more to defining a lifetime than just the amount of time spent functioning.

The last aspect of the definition of reliability is that *environmental conditions* must be specified. Conditions such as temperature, humidity, and turning speed all affect the lifetime of a machine tool. The 20,000-mile reliability of a subcompact car is different if it is used for highway driving or to tow a trailer down city streets. Environmental conditions associated with the lifetime of a person might be the city in which they live and whether they smoke. Included in environmental conditions is the preventive maintenance to be performed on the item. Although preventive maintenance may be costly, it is usually effective in prolonging the lifetime of the item and hence increasing the reliability.

Reliability is often misunderstood. A single grenade, for example, that explodes when it should might erroneously be called 100% reliable. This is inaccurate since a reliability of 100% implies that each grenade of this type will explode when it should. The true reliability of these grenades might be 0.9999 (or 99.99%) and we just happened to toss one that worked.

Reliability is also often confused with quality. The primary difference between these two terms is that reliability incorporates the passage of time, whereas quality does not, since it is a static descriptor of an item. Two transistors of equal quality sit side by side on a shelf. One of these transistors will be used in a television set, the other in a cannon launch environment. Both transistors are of identical quality, but the first one has a higher reliability since it will operate in a less stressful environment.

High reliability implies high quality, although the converse is not necessarily true. Consider two automobile tires, each of high quality. One was produced in 1957, the other in 1995. Although each was produced with the most stringent quality control procedures available, their reliabilities will be different due to technology changes introduced between 1957 and 1995, such as steel-belted radials. The 60,000-mile reliability of the tire produced in 1995 will be higher than the reliability of the 1957 tire. Technology advances in the 38 years between the manufacture of the two tires may come in the form of improved design (for example, tread or steel belts), components (for example, rubber), or processes (for example, manufacturing advances). *Some* quality improvements (for example, improved tread design) improve the reliability of the tire, while others (for example, improved white wall design) will not.

Figure 1.1   Six-component series arrangement of O-rings.

1.2   CASE STUDY

This section consists of a rather sketchy case study involving the O-rings on the solid rocket motors on the Space Shuttle. Large, complex systems such as the Space Shuttle are often divided into *subsystems* to simplify reliability calculations. The Space Shuttle system consists of four subsystems: the *orbiter* that contains the crew and the controls, the *external liquid-fuel tank* that contains fuel for the main engines on the orbiter, and two *solid rocket motors* that are used to boost the Space Shuttle into orbit. The emphasis here is on the reliability of the solid rocket motors, since the Rogers Commission Report concluded that O-ring failure on the joints in these motors caused the tragic *Challenger* accident on January 28, 1986.

The two solid rocket motors are each shipped to the Kennedy Space Center in four pieces. Each assembled solid rocket motor contains three joints, for a total of six joints for the entire Space Shuttle. These joints are referred to as field joints, and it is critical to seal the small gap that is left between each of the parts of the motor. O-rings, which measure 37.5 feet in diameter and are 0.28 inch thick, are used to seal the gaps in the field joints. All six O-rings must operate in order to avoid having the propellant escape from the solid rocket motor, so the O-rings form a six-component series system, as indicated by the *block diagram* in Figure 1.1. Series system arrangements for components as critical as O-rings are risky since failure of any one component results in catastrophic failure. A common technique used by design engineers to improve the reliability of a series system is to include a redundant component (also known as a secondary or backup component) that will take over if the first component fails. The designers of the solid rocket motors added a secondary O-ring to back up the primary O-ring. This results in a total of 12 O-rings arranged as shown in Figure 1.2. This technique is highly effective if the components that are being placed in parallel fail independently of one another.

In 1977, before the first shuttle flight in 1981, NASA discovered a problem known as field joint rotation that indicated that the failure of the primary and secondary O-rings may not be independent. Soon after ignition, the pressure and temperature inside the solid rocket motor increase rapidly. This causes the O-rings, along with some putty used to protect them, to "seat" and seal the field joint. The sides of the motor's metal casing also tend to bulge under the heat and pressure, and it was discovered that this bulge

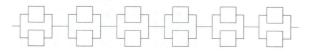

Figure 1.2   Twelve-component arrangement of O-rings.

caused a rotation between the pieces of the motor. This rotation causes a widening of the gap that the primary and secondary O-rings were intended to seal. Unfortunately, this wider gap affects both the primary and secondary O-rings, so the assumption of independent failures was not justified. Thus, the reliability of each field joint will not be as high as would be calculated assuming independence.

Prior to the *Challenger* accident, there were 24 shuttle flights. On 23 of these flights, the solid rocket motors were recovered from the ocean for inspection and possible reuse. There was concern that an environmental variable, temperature at launch, might influence the reliability of the field joints. This was particularly important since there was a forecast of 31°F for the morning of the launch of the *Challenger*, the coldest launch temperature to date. Table 1.1 gives the flight number, joint temperature at launch, and number of field joint failures, sorted by temperature, for the 23 flights. In a 3-hour teleconference between the manufacturer of the solid rocket motors and NASA officials on the evening prior to the accident, it was concluded that the previous launch temperature data were not conclusive on predicting primary O-ring failure. The Rogers Commission, appointed by President Reagan after the accident, believed that a mistake was made in the analysis of the O-ring failure data. The original analysis left out the

TABLE 1.1   O-RING FIELD JOINT FAILURES

Flight	Temperature (° Fahrenheit)	Failures
51-C	53	3
41-B	57	1
61-C	58	1
41-C	63	1
STS-1	66	0
STS-6	67	0
51-A	67	0
51-D	67	0
STS-5	68	0
STS-3	69	0
STS-2	70	1
STS-9	70	0
41-D	70	1
51-G	70	0
STS-7	72	0
STS-8	73	0
51-B	75	0
61-A	75	2
51-I	76	0
61-B	76	0
41-G	78	0
51-J	79	0
51-F	81	0

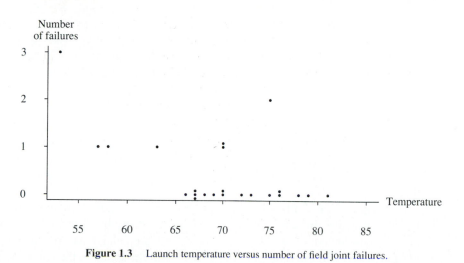

Figure 1.3   Launch temperature versus number of field joint failures.

flights with zero failures because it was believed that these flights did not contribute any information about the effect of temperature on failure. Figure 1.3 shows a plot of the data in Table 1.1, revealing that there is a U shape when the flights with zero failures are excluded, but a trend is more apparent when the flights with zero failures are included. Tied data pairs have been offset.

After the accident, an analysis by three statisticians concluded that the effect of temperature was indeed significant. They estimated the launch reliability to be 0.87 or less when the temperature was 31°F and concluded that postponement of the flight until the temperature reached 60°F would have increased the launch reliability to 0.98 or less. The analysis presented here concerns the O-rings only, and, of course, thousands of other electrical, mechanical, and software system components must also function for the Space Shuttle to operate properly.

1.3   OVERVIEW

This text is divided into two sections. Chapters 2 through 6 discuss probability models for lifetimes, and the remaining chapters discuss methods related to data collection and inference.

Chapter 2 defines the structure and reliability functions. In this chapter, an item, often referred to as a *system*, is assumed to be a collection of *n components*. The structure function determines whether the system is functioning, given the states of the components. Two of the simplest structures are the series and parallel systems. A series system functions if all its components function. A parallel system functions if one or more components function. The design for the O-rings on the Space Shuttle described in the previous section is a combination of series and parallel arrangements. Block diagrams of three-component series, parallel, and complex arrangements are shown in

Figure 1.4   Block diagrams.

Figure 1.4. The reliability function, on the other hand, is used to determine the system reliability, given the component reliabilities. These calculations are often known as *static* reliability calculations since the item is considered at only one particular point in time.

Chapter 3 generalizes the work in Chapter 2 as random lifetimes are considered. In particular, five different representations for the distribution of the failure time of an item are considered: the survivor, density, hazard, cumulative hazard, and mean residual life functions. The survivor and hazard functions are arguably the two most popular of the five because they express the probability of surviving to time t and the risk at time t, respectively. A sample survivor function and corresponding hazard function are shown in Figure 1.5. This particular hazard function shape is known as a bathtub-shaped hazard function and is appropriate for modeling human lifetimes. In addition, some electrical and mechanical items also follow a bathtub-shaped hazard function. These five representations apply to individual components, as well as systems of components. Since system reliability is now expressed as a function of time, these calculations are known as *dynamic* reliability calculations.

Chapter 4 investigates several popular parametric models for the lifetime distribution of an item. The *exponential distribution* is examined first due to its importance as the only continuous distribution with the memoryless property, which implies that a used item that is functioning has the same failure distribution as a new item. Just as the normal distribution plays a central role in classical statistics due to the central limit theorem, the exponential distribution is central to the study of the distribution of lifetimes, since it is the only continuous distribution with a constant hazard function. Figure 1.6 shows the

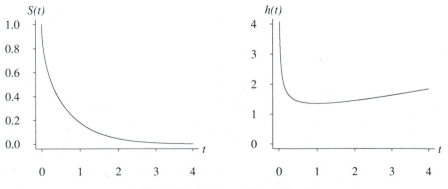

Figure 1.5   Survivor and hazard functions.

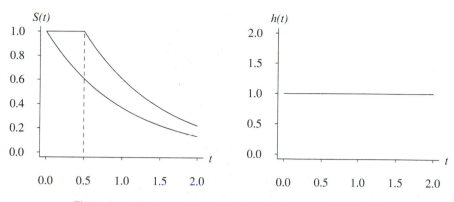

Figure 1.6   Survivor and hazard functions for the exponential distribution.

survivor function and hazard function for a lifetime with the exponential distribution. The fact that the survivor function of an item that has survived to time t_0 has the same shape as a new item is evidence that the exponential distribution has the memoryless property. The exponential distribution has the drawback that it is appropriate for modeling the lifetime of a limited number of items, mainly electrical components. More flexible lifetime distributions, such as the Weibull and gamma distributions, are outlined in this chapter. Each of these distributions has mathematical properties that make it appropriate for modeling certain types of failure mechanisms, such as fatigue or wear-out.

Chapter 5 presents models that have been devised to overcome the limitations of many of the parametric lifetime models presented in Chapter 4. In particular, most of the lifetime distributions presented in Chapter 4 have hazard functions that are monotonic (that is, increasing or decreasing for all t). Competing risks and mixtures are two models that can easily achieve a nonmonotonic hazard function, as well as be applied to situations involving multiple causes of failure and multiple populations of items. The hazard functions in Figure 1.7 for a calculator show three competing risks for the lifetime of the calculator: manufacturing defects, dropping the calculator, and wear-out failures. Covariates (for example, age or gender of a person in a medical setting) often need to be included in a lifetime model. We would certainly not want to use the same lifetime model on a drill bit working at two different turning speeds. Two models that are useful ways to include these covariates in a lifetime model are the accelerated life and proportional hazards models. In the previous section, the temperature at launch was believed to be a covariate that influenced the survival of the O-rings.

Models for repairable systems, which are often encountered in reliability systems, are introduced in Chapter 6. Many systems, such as aircraft, have repairable components. Failures for these systems will either be detected in routine inspection and maintenance, be eliminated during an overhaul of the aircraft, or cause catastrophic failure. These models are effective for determining the *availability* of a particular item. Figure 1.8 shows graphs associated with the availability of an aircraft; state 1 denotes available and state 0 denotes unavailable. The left-hand graph is associated with a single realization of the repair record for an aircraft, and the right-hand graph is a probability model

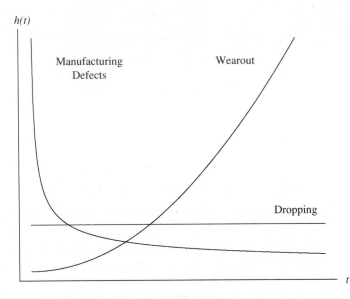

Figure 1.7   Competing risks for a calculator.

that may be associated with this type of aircraft. The left-hand graph shows the times when the aircraft is available. For this particular realization, three failures are shown where the aircraft goes from state 1 to state 0. The graph of the availability function $A(t)$ shows the availability approaching a steady-state value as t increases. This implies that, although the availability of a new aircraft is typically higher initially, it eventually approaches a constant value.

The emphasis changes from developing probabilistic models for lifetimes to analyzing lifetime data sets in Chapter 7. One problem associated with these data sets is that of censored data. Data are censored when only a bound on the lifetime is known. This would be the case, for example, when conducting an experiment with light bulbs, and half of the light bulbs are still operating at the end of the experiment. Figure 1.9

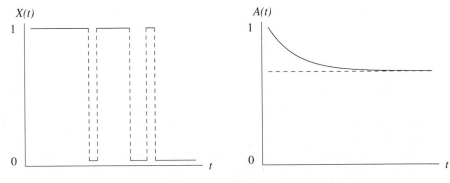

Figure 1.8   Aircraft availability graphs.

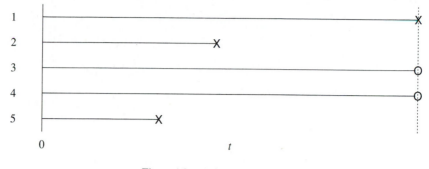

Figure 1.9   A right-censored data set.

shows the results of a life test of five light bulbs. Failures were observed for the first, second, and fifth light bulbs, and the other two are *right-censored* data values. Censored observations complicate the analysis of a data set. The properties of point and interval estimates for a parameter are reviewed in this chapter.

Chapter 8 surveys methods for fitting parametric distributions to data sets. Maximum likelihood parameter estimates are emphasized because they have certain desirable statistical properties. Figure 1.10 shows two diagrams that are useful in the analysis of a data set. The figure on the left shows the empirical and fitted survivor functions for an uncensored data set. The empirical survivor function is a step function that decreases by $1/n$ at each data value, where n is the sample size. The data are fitted to a parametric distribution by maximum likelihood and the fitted survivor function is the smooth curve. In this particular case, the data have been fitted to a Weibull distribution with scale parameter λ and shape parameter κ. In the figure on the right, a 95% confidence region for the parameters λ and κ indicates the accuracy of the estimates. The point in the center of the confidence region denotes the maximum likelihood estimators $\hat{\kappa}$ and $\hat{\lambda}$.

Chapter 9 presents techniques that can be used to estimate the effects of covariates on a particular lifetime distribution. The accelerated life and proportional hazards models have regression coefficients that need to be estimated for data sets containing covari-

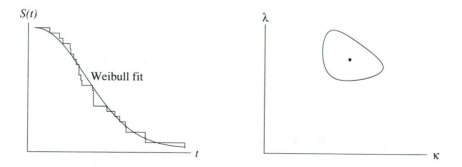

Figure 1.10   Fitting a parametric distribution to a lifetime data set.

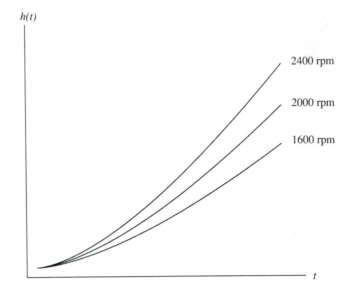

Figure 1.11   Hazard functions for several turning speeds of a drill bit.

ates. Maximum likelihood methods are used to estimate these coefficients. Figure 1.11 shows the hazard functions for the lifetime of a drill bit at several different turning speeds. The regression parameter in this case is the turning speed of the drill bit. Not surprisingly, the risk is higher at increased turning speeds.

Chapter 10 reviews some nonparametric methods for determining the lifetime of an item, including *life tables*, which are used by actuaries, and the Kaplan–Meier product-limit estimate, which is used as an estimate for the survivor function for a censored data set. An example of a product-limit estimate for a survivor function from a censored data set is shown in Figure 1.12. The downward steps in the survivor function correspond to observed failure times and the hash marks on the survivor function denote right-censoring times. The dashed lines are 95% confidence limits for the survivor function. Nonparametric methods are often used when there is no parametric distribution to accurately model the lifetime. Once a parametric model has been chosen to represent the failure time for a particular item, the adequacy of the model should be assessed. Goodness-of-fit tests for assessing how well a fitted lifetime distribution models the lifetime of the item are introduced. One popular test for continuous lifetime models is the Kolmogorov–Smirnov test, in which the largest difference between the fitted and empirical survivor functions is used as the test statistic.

1.4   FURTHER READING

The example in Section 1.1 concerning how to measure time for on/off cycling of a light bulb was taken from Kaufmann, Grouchko, and Cruon (1977, p. 5).* Dozens of reliabil-

---

*References are found at the end of the book.

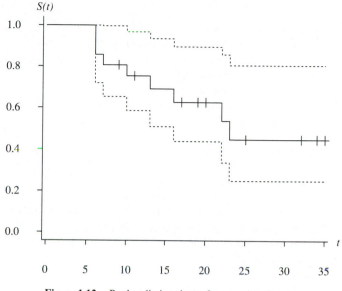

Figure 1.12   Product-limit estimate for a survivor function.

ity textbooks are available. One of the earliest is Shooman (1968). A classic reference in the reliability literature is Barlow and Proschan (1981). Another classic reference that contains more on statistical inference is Mann, Schafer, and Singpurwalla (1974). A third standard reference that emphasizes engineering design is Kapur and Lamberson (1977). A chapter overviewing the more mathematical aspects of reliability theory is provided by Shaked and Shanthikumar (1990). More recent textbooks devoted to reliability models and applications include Ascher and Feingold (1984), Bain and Engelhardt (1991), Billinton and Allan (1985), Birolini (1985), Colbourn (1987), Condra (1993), Crowder et al. (1991), Dhillon (1983), Dhillon (1984), Dovich (1990), Enrick (1985), Fleming and Harrington (1991), Foster et al. (1981), Fuqua (1987), Gertsbakh (1989), Goldberg (1981), Grosh (1989), Harr (1987), Henley and Kumamoto (1985), Jensen and Petersen (1982), Jones (1988), Kalbfleisch and Prentice (1980), Kececioglu (1991), Klaassen and van Peppen (1989), Klinger et al. (1990), Krishnamoorthi (1992), Lawless (1982), Lewis (1987), Lloyd and Lipow (1984), Martz and Waller (1982), Meeker and Hahn (1985), Miller (1981), Modarres (1993), Moura (1991), Musa et al. (1987), Nelson (1982, 1990), Neufelder (1993), O'Connor (1991), Ramakumar (1993), Rao (1992), Sander and Badoux (1991), Shier (1991), Sinha (1986), Sundararajan (1991), Thompson (1988), Tobias and Trindade (1986), Trivedi (1982), Ushakov and Harrison (1994), and Zacks (1992). Texts with less emphasis on the quantitative aspects of reliability include Doty (1985), Dummer and Winton (1990), and Moss (1985).

The information on the Space Shuttle case study is from Dalal et al. (1989), Hogg and Ledolter (1992, pp. 47–48), and Martz and Zimmer (1992). These authors draw a great deal of their information about the *Challenger* accident from the Rogers Commission report.

1.5 EXERCISES

1.1. Estimate the reliability for
(a) a 60-watt light bulb burned continuously for 1 year.
(b) an automobile used to commute 30 miles daily for 3 years with standard preventive maintenance performed regularly.
(c) a television set operated continuously for 10 years.

1.2. Reliability can be applied to the service industry, as well as to physical objects that are subject to failure. Four applications of reliability in the service industry, for example, are the following:
- Overnight package delivery: the package arrives by the prescribed time.
- Job shop: an order arrives to the customer by the prescribed due date.
- Accounting: meeting the April 15 deadline.
- Airline industry: a flight arrives on time.

List four additional applications of reliability in the service industry.

1.3. The accelerated life and proportional hazards models are concerned with the effect of covariates on a lifetime. What are appropriate covariates for
(a) a machine tool (for example, a drill bit)?
(b) an automobile (for an insurance policy)?
(c) a person (for a life insurance policy)?

1.4. Bring two products to the next class session: one that exemplifies good engineering design with respect to reliability and another that exemplifies poor engineering design with respect to reliability. Remember to differentiate between *utility* and reliability.

2

Coherent Systems Analysis

This chapter examines techniques for expressing the arrangement of components in a system and for determining its reliability. We assume that an item consists of n components, arranged into a *system*. Two key decisions that are always a part of the modeling process are (1) which elements of the system are excluded and included and (2) the level of detail to be represented by the components. If the item under study is an automobile, for example, the modeler needs to decide whether the entire electrical system should be modeled as a component, or whether the individual assemblies, such as the alternator or ignition, should be modeled as components. The first two sections in this chapter survey *structural properties* associated with a system of components, and the next two sections survey *probabilistic properties* associated with a system of components. *Structure functions* are used to relate the states of the individual components to the state of the system. A block diagram is often helpful in visualizing the way components are arranged. *Minimal path sets* and *minimal cut sets* are two other ways of specifying the arrangement of components in a system. *Reliability functions* are used to determine the system reliability at a particular point in time, given the component reliabilities at that time. *Reliability bounds* may be used to obtain an interval that contains the system reliability when there are many components and exact system reliability is difficult to compute.

2.1 STRUCTURE FUNCTIONS

A *structure function* is a useful tool in describing the way n components are related to form a system. The structure function defines the system state as a function of the component states. A *system* is assumed to be a collection of n *components*. In addition,

it is assumed that both the components and the system can either be functioning or
failed. Although this *binary assumption* may be unrealistic for certain types of components or systems, it makes the mathematics involved more tractable. The assumption
implies that component failure due to catastrophic causes is more readily modeled than
component failure due to gradual degradation. An electrical component that undergoes
drift or a mechanical component that undergoes *wear* must have a threshold value
defined that will place the state of the item into the functioning or failed states in order to
analyze the item using these techniques. A discussion of techniques to overcome the
binary assumption is given at the end of this chapter.

The functioning and failed states for both components and systems will be denoted
by 1 and 0, respectively, as shown in the following definition.

Definition 2.1   The state of component i, x_i is

$$x_i = \begin{cases} 0 & \text{if component } i \text{ has failed} \\ 1 & \text{if component } i \text{ is functioning} \end{cases}$$

for $i = 1, 2, \ldots, n$.

These n values can be written as a system state vector, $\mathbf{x} = (x_1, x_2, \ldots, x_n)$. Since there
are n components, there are 2^n different values that the system state vector can assume,
and $\binom{n}{j}$ of these vectors correspond to exactly j functioning components, $j =
0, 1, \ldots, n$. The structure function, $\phi(\mathbf{x})$, maps the system state vector $\mathbf{x}$ to 0 or 1, yield-
ing the state of the system.

Definition 2.2   The *structure function* ϕ is

$$\phi(\mathbf{x}) = \begin{cases} 0 & \text{if the system has failed when the state vector is } \mathbf{x} \\ 1 & \text{if the system is functioning when the state vector is } \mathbf{x}. \end{cases}$$

The most common system structures are the series and parallel systems, which are
defined in the following examples.

Example 2.1

A *series system* functions when all its components function. Thus $\phi(\mathbf{x})$ assumes the value 1
when $x_1 = x_2 = \cdots = x_n = 1$, and 0 otherwise. Therefore,

$$\phi(\mathbf{x}) = \begin{cases} 0 & \text{if there exists an } i \text{ such that } x_i = 0 \\ 1 & \text{if } x_i = 1 \text{ for all } i = 1, 2, \ldots, n \end{cases}$$

$$= \min \{x_1, x_2, \ldots, x_n\}$$

$$= \prod_{i=1}^{n} x_i.$$

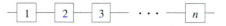

Figure 2.1   Series system block diagram.

These three different ways of expressing the value of the structure function are equivalent, although the third is preferred because of its compactness. Systems that function only when all their components function should be modeled as series systems. If a calculator, for example, is modeled as a system of four components (a keyboard, display, microprocessor, and battery), a series arrangement is appropriate since failure of any component results in system failure. *Block diagrams* are useful to visualize a system of components. The block diagram corresponding to a series system of n components is shown in Figure 2.1. Although there are similarities, a block diagram is not equivalent to an electrical wiring diagram. A block diagram is a graphic device for expressing the arrangement of the components to form a system. If a path can be traced through functioning components from left to right on a block diagram, then the system functions. The boxes represent the system components, and either component numbers or reliabilities are placed inside the boxes.

A second popular system structure is the parallel arrangement.

Example 2.2

A *parallel system* functions when one or more of the components function. Thus $\phi(\mathbf{x})$ assumes the value 0 when $x_1 = x_2 = \cdots = x_n = 0$, and 1 otherwise.

$$\phi(\mathbf{x}) = \begin{cases} 0 & \text{if } x_i = 0 \text{ for all } i = 1, 2, \ldots, n \\ 1 & \text{if there exists an } i \text{ such that } x_i = 1 \end{cases}$$

$$= \max \{x_1, x_2, \ldots, x_n\}$$

$$= 1 - \prod_{i=1}^{n} (1 - x_i).$$

As in the case of the series system, the three ways of defining $\phi(\mathbf{x})$ are equivalent. The block diagram of a parallel arrangement of n components is shown in Figure 2.2. A parallel arrangement of components is appropriate when all components must fail for the system to fail. Numerous examples of parallel systems exist. Kidneys are an example of a two-component parallel system, since many people live normal lives with a single kidney. Another two-component system is the brake system on an automobile that contains two reservoirs for brake fluid.

Series and parallel systems are special cases of k-out-of-n systems: the system functions if k or more of the n components function. A series system is an n-out-of-n system, and a parallel system is a 1-out-of-n system. A suspension bridge that needs only k of its n cables to support the bridge, an automobile engine that needs only k of its n cylinders to run, and a bicycle wheel that needs only k out of its n spokes to function are examples of k-out-of-n systems.

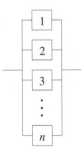

Figure 2.2   Parallel system block diagram.

Example 2.3

The structure function for a k-out-of-n system is

$$\phi(\mathbf{x}) = \begin{cases} 0 & \text{if } \sum_{i=1}^{n} x_i < k \\ 1 & \text{if } \sum_{i=1}^{n} x_i \ge k. \end{cases}$$

The block diagram for a k-out-of-n system is difficult to draw in general, but for specific cases it can be drawn by repeating components in the diagram. The block diagram for a 2-out-of-3 system, for example, is shown in Figure 2.3. The block diagram indicates that if all three, or exactly two out of three components (in particular 1 and 2, 1 and 3, or 2 and 3) function, then the system functions. The structure function for a 2-out-of-3 system is

$$\phi(\mathbf{x}) = 1 - (1 - x_1 x_2)(1 - x_1 x_3)(1 - x_2 x_3)$$

$$= x_1 x_2 + x_1 x_3 + x_2 x_3 - x_1^2 x_2 x_3 - x_1 x_2^2 x_3 - x_1 x_2 x_3^2 + (x_1 x_2 x_3)^2.$$

Some systems require a more complex arrangement of components than k-out-of-n systems. The next example illustrates how to combine series and parallel arrangements to determine the appropriate structure function for a more complex system.

Example 2.4

An airplane has four propellers, two on each wing. The airplane will fly (function) if at least one propeller on each wing functions. Find the structure function for this situation.

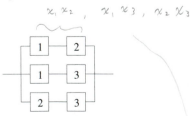

Figure 2.3   Two-out-of-three system block diagram.

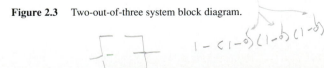

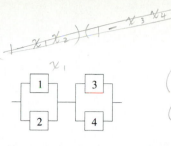

$$\left(1+x_1 x_2\right)\left(1-x_3 x_4\right)$$

x_1

$\left(1-(1-x_1)(1-x_2)\right)$

$\left(1-(\quad)(\quad)\right)$

Figure 2.4   Four-propeller subsystem block diagram.

(Note that, although many problems other than propeller failure could cause the airplane to fail, this example only considers propeller failure.)

In this case, the four propellers are denoted by components 1, 2, 3, and 4, with 1 and 2 being on the left wing and 3 and 4 on the right wing. For the moment, if the plane is considered to consist of two wings (not considering individual propellers), then the wings are arranged in series, since failure of the propulsion on either wing results in system failure. Each wing, however, can be modeled as a two-component parallel subsystem of propellers, since only one propeller on each wing is required to function. The appropriate block diagram for the system is shown in Figure 2.4. The structure function is the product of the structure functions of the two parallel subsystems:

$$\phi(\mathbf{x}) = [1 - (1 - x_1)(1 - x_2)]\,[1 - (1 - x_3)(1 - x_4)].$$

Example 2.5

A more complex example is given by the *bridge structure* shown in Figure 2.5. One way to determine the appropriate structure function is to draw the block diagram using repeated components. A moment's reflection on the block diagram reveals that the system functions if any one of the following sets of components functions:

$$\{1, 3, 5\} \qquad \{1, 4\} \qquad \{2, 3, 4\} \qquad \{2, 5\}.$$

These sets will be referred to as *minimal path sets* in the next section. Since one or more of these sets of components must function for the system to function, the block diagram may be rewritten as a parallel arrangement of these components in series, as shown in Figure 2.6. This system has the corresponding structure function

$$\phi(\mathbf{x}) = 1 - (1 - x_1 x_3 x_5)\,(1 - x_1 x_4)\,(1 - x_2 x_3 x_4)\,(1 - x_2 x_5).$$

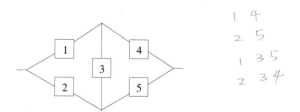

Figure 2.5   Bridge system block diagram.

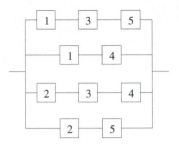

Figure 2.6   Alternative block diagram for a bridge system.

Unfortunately, many possible structure functions can be defined for a system. Consider a one-component system with structure function

$$\phi(x) = 1 - x,$$

which indicates that the system is functioning when the component has failed, and vice versa. This is not a very sensible structure function. To avoid studying structure functions that are unreasonable, a subset of all possible systems of n components, that is, *coherent systems,* has been defined. A system is coherent if $\phi(\mathbf{x})$ is nondecreasing in $\mathbf{x}$ [for example, $\phi(x_1, \ldots, x_{i-1}, 0, x_{i+1}, \ldots, x_n) \leq \phi(x_1, \ldots, x_{i-1}, 1, x_{i+1}, \ldots, x_n)$ for all i] and there are no irrelevant components. The condition that $\phi(\mathbf{x})$ be nondecreasing in $\mathbf{x}$ implies that the system will not upgrade if a component degrades. A component is *irrelevant* if its state has no impact on the structure function. In the two block diagrams in Figure 2.7, the state of component 2 does not influence the state of either system, so it is an irrelevant component and these are not coherent systems. Of the many theorems related to coherent systems, one that describes the relative merits of component and system redundancy is of particular merit. If a particular engineering design is not able to achieve a reliability goal, this theorem shows that it is wiser to use redundancy at the component level, as opposed to the system level.

Theorem 2.1   Let ϕ be the structure function for a coherent system of n components. For any state vectors $\mathbf{x}$ and $\mathbf{y}$,

$$\phi(1 - (1 - x_1)(1 - y_1), \ldots, 1 - (1 - x_n)(1 - y_n)) \geq 1 - [1 - \phi(\mathbf{x})][1 - \phi(\mathbf{y})]$$

and equality holds when

Figure 2.7   Noncoherent systems.

$$\phi(\mathbf{x}) = 1 - \prod_{i=1}^{n}(1 - x_i).$$

Proof Since $1 - (1 - x_i)(1 - y_i) \geq x_i$ for $i = 1, 2, \ldots, n$, and ϕ is nondecreasing (because the system is coherent), this implies that

$$\phi(1 - (1 - x_1)(1 - y_1), \ldots, 1 - (1 - x_n)(1 - y_n)) \geq \phi(\mathbf{x}).$$

Similarly,

$$\phi(1 - (1 - x_1)(1 - y_1), \ldots, 1 - (1 - x_n)(1 - y_n)) \geq \phi(\mathbf{y}).$$

Therefore, since the left-hand sides of these two inequalities are greater than or equal to the two right-hand sides,

$$\phi(1 - (1 - x_1)(1 - y_1), \ldots, 1 - (1 - x_n)(1 - y_n)) \geq \max\{\phi(\mathbf{x}), \phi(\mathbf{y})\}.$$

Since $\max\{\phi(\mathbf{x}), \phi(\mathbf{y})\}$ equals $1 - [1 - \phi(\mathbf{x})][1 - \phi(\mathbf{y})]$, the inequality in the theorem is true. When $\phi(\mathbf{x}) = 1 - \prod_{i=1}^{n}(1 - x_i)$, that is, a parallel arrangement, both sides of the inequality reduce to $1 - \prod_{i=1}^{n}(1 - x_i)(1 - y_i)$, so the theorem is proved.

This theorem is particularly important in design since it states that redundancy at the component level is more effective than redundancy at the system level, as illustrated in the following example.

Example 2.6

Consider the three-component coherent system with block diagram shown in Figure 2.8. If you were to procure another set of three components identical to these three, which arrangement of the six components shown in Figure 2.9 would be more effective? The block diagram on the left corresponds to component redundancy, while the block diagram on the right corresponds to system redundancy. Since the theorem states that component redundancy is always superior to system redundancy, the arrangement on the left is preferred. Component redundancy may create design problems (for example, in electrical systems where timing is important) and may not always be possible to achieve.

A final concept related to structure functions is the notion of *structural importance,* which measures the impact of each component on the structure function. Some components play a more important role in determining whether the system functions

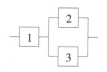

Figure 2.8   Three-component system.

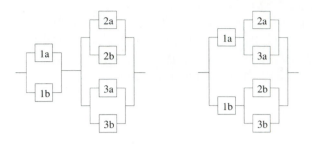

Figure 2.9   Component and system redundancy.

based on their position in the system. Consider again the block diagram shown in Figure 2.8. Which component would you consider the most important component in the system? You should have said that component 1 is the most important, since, if it has failed, the system has necessarily failed. This is not true of components 2 and 3. One way of stating this mathematically is that $\phi(1_i, \mathbf{x}) - \phi(0_i, \mathbf{x}) = 1$ for three of the four possible $\mathbf{x}$ values when $i = 1$, where the notation $\phi(1_i, \mathbf{x})$ denotes that x_i assumes the value 1, and the remaining components may assume any other values. More specifically, of the four state vectors corresponding to component 1 operating,

$$(1, 1, 1) \qquad (1, 0, 1) \qquad (1, 1, 0) \qquad (1, 0, 0),$$

the first three vectors correspond to a system that changes from operating to failed if component 1 fails. This leads to a formal definition for the structural importance of each component.

Definition 2.3   The *structural importance* of component i in a coherent system of n components is

$$I_\phi(i) = \frac{1}{2^{n-1}} \sum_{\{\mathbf{x} \mid x_i = 1\}} [\, \phi(1_i, \mathbf{x}) - \phi(0_i, \mathbf{x}) \,]$$

for $i = 1, 2, \ldots, n$.

The summation in this definition runs across all the 2^{n-1} state vectors $\mathbf{x}$ such that $x_i = 1$. The summation counts the number of these vectors for which $\phi(1_i, \mathbf{x}) - \phi(0_i, \mathbf{x}) = 1$. This summation gives more weight to those vectors for which the failing of component i results in system failure. Thus, for any coherent system, $0 < I_\phi(i) \le 1$ for $i = 1, 2, \ldots, n$.

Example 2.7

Compute the structural importance of all the components in Figure 2.8.

Since there are three components, there are $2^3 = 8$ possible system state vectors, and the summations used in calculating the structural importance run across four of these state vectors. To calculate the structural importance of component 1, $I_\phi(1)$, the summation will run over the state vectors $(1, 0, 0)$, $(1, 0, 1)$, $(1, 1, 0)$, and $(1, 1, 1)$, since all these vectors have $x_1 = 1$. Of these four vectors, $\phi(1_1, \mathbf{x}) - \phi(0_1, \mathbf{x}) = 1$ for the last three vectors listed. Therefore,

$$I_\phi(1) = \frac{1}{4}[(0-0) + (1-0) + (1-0) + (1-0)] = \frac{3}{4}.$$

To find the structural importance of component 2, the summation is taken over the vectors $(0, 1, 0)$, $(0, 1, 1)$, $(1, 1, 0)$ and $(1, 1, 1)$. In this case,

$$I_\phi(2) = \frac{1}{4}[(0-0) + (0-0) + (1-0) + (1-1)] = \frac{1}{4}$$

and, by symmetry,

$$I_\phi(3) = \frac{1}{4}.$$

These calculations show that component 1 is more important than either component 2 or 3 by virtue of its position in the system.

Structural importance may be useful to the design engineer who has the resources to improve one or more of the existing components in a system. Assuming that the goal is to upgrade those components with the largest impact on the system, the designer should make improvements on the components with the largest structural importance.

2.2   MINIMAL PATH AND CUT SETS

Structure functions define the arrangement of components in a system. Two other ways of expressing this arrangement are minimal path and cut sets. These sets can be used to express any coherent system as the parallel arrangement of series subsystems or the series arrangement of parallel subsystems.

Before defining a path vector, minimal path vector, and path set, inequality must be defined for vectors.

Definition 2.4 $\mathbf{x} < \mathbf{y}$ if and only if $x_i \leq y_i$ for $i = 1, 2, \ldots, n$, and $x_i < y_i$ for some i.

This definition indicates that the vector $\mathbf{x}$ is less than the vector $\mathbf{y}$ when all the elements of $\mathbf{x}$ are less than or equal to the corresponding elements of $\mathbf{y}$, and one or more elements of $\mathbf{x}$ are less than the corresponding elements of $\mathbf{y}$. The definitions of $>$, $\geq$, and $\leq$ for vectors are analogous.

Definition 2.5   A vector $\mathbf{x}$ is a *path vector* for a coherent system if $\phi(\mathbf{x}) = 1$.

Path vectors are sometimes referred to as *link vectors* and *tie vectors* by other authors. This definition indicates that out of the possible 2^n state vectors, those that correspond to a functioning system [that is, $\phi(\mathbf{x}) = 1$] are path vectors.

Definition 2.6   A path vector $\mathbf{x}$ is a *minimal path vector* for a coherent system if $\phi(\mathbf{y}) = 0$ for any $\mathbf{y} < \mathbf{x}$.

A minimal path vector is a path vector for which the failure of any functioning component results in system failure.

Example 2.8

Consider the three-component system with block diagram shown in Figure 2.8. Find the path vectors and minimal path vectors.

Out of the $2^3 = 8$ state vectors, only the vectors $(1, 1, 0)$, $(1, 0, 1)$, and $(1, 1, 1)$ correspond to a functioning system, so these are the path vectors. The minmal path vectors are $(1, 1, 0)$ and $(1, 0, 1)$, since the vector $(1, 1, 1)$ does not satisfy the definition for a minimal path vector [since there are two vectors $\mathbf{y} < \mathbf{x}$ such that $\phi(\mathbf{y}) = 1$].

Each minimal path vector for a coherent system structure has an associated *minimal path set* that consists of the component numbers corresponding to *functioning* components. The s path sets for a system are denoted by $P_1, P_2, \ldots, P_s$. The previous example has $s = 2$ minimal path sets: $\{1, 2\}$ and $\{1, 3\}$.

Cut vectors, minimal cut vectors, and minimal cut sets are defined analogously to the corresponding path concepts.

Definition 2.7   A vector $\mathbf{x}$ is a *cut vector* for a coherent system if $\phi(\mathbf{x}) = 0$.

Whereas path vectors correspond to a functioning system, cut vectors correspond to a failed system. Since all state vectors correspond to a functioning or failed system, the sum of the number of path vectors and the number of cut vectors for a system is 2^n.

Definition 2.8   A cut vector $\mathbf{x}$ is a *minimal cut vector* for a coherent system if $\phi(\mathbf{y}) = 1$ for any $\mathbf{y} > \mathbf{x}$.

A minimal cut vector is a cut vector for which the repair of any failed component results in a functioning system.

Example 2.9

Find the cut vectors and minimal cut vectors for the three-component system in Example 2.8.

Out of the eight state vectors, the five state vectors $(0, 0, 0)$, $(0, 0, 1)$, $(0, 1, 0)$, $(0, 1, 1)$, and $(1, 0, 0)$ correspond to a failed system, so these are the cut vectors. The minimal cut vectors are $(0, 1, 1)$ and $(1, 0, 0)$, since any vector $\mathbf{y}$ that is greater than these two vectors results in a functioning system.

Each minimal cut vector for a coherent system structure has an associated *minimal cut set* that consists of the component numbers corresponding to *failed* components. The k cut sets for a system are denoted by $C_1, C_2, \ldots, C_k$. Example 2.9 has $k = 2$ minimal cut sets: $\{1\}$ and $\{2, 3\}$.

We have now encountered four different ways to specify the arrangement of binary components to form a coherent system: a block diagram, a structure function $\phi(\mathbf{x})$, minimal path sets $P_1, P_2, \ldots, P_s$, and minimal cut sets $C_1, C_2, \ldots, C_k$. These four are equivalent in the sense that specifying one implies knowledge of the other three.

One purpose of defining minimal path and cut sets is to write any system as the parallel arrangement of series systems or the series arrangement of parallel systems. The derivation and examples to follow indicate how this can be done.

Let $P_1, P_2, \ldots, P_s$ be the s minimal path sets for a coherent system, and define

$$\alpha_j(\mathbf{x}) = \begin{cases} 1 & \text{if all components of } P_j \text{ are functioning} \\ 0 & \text{otherwise} \end{cases}$$

for $j = 1, 2, \ldots, s$. The variable $\alpha_j(\mathbf{x})$ indicates whether the components in the jth minimal path set are all functioning. An equivalent way of expressing this binary variable is

$$\alpha_j(\mathbf{x}) = \prod_{i \in P_j} x_i$$

for $j = 1, 2, \ldots, s$. The system operates if the components corresponding to one or more of the minimal path sets are operating. Hence, the structure function can be rewritten as

$$\phi(\mathbf{x}) = \begin{cases} 1 & \text{if } \alpha_j(\mathbf{x}) = 1 \text{ for } some \ j \\ 0 & \text{if } \alpha_j(\mathbf{x}) = 0 \text{ for } all \ j \end{cases}$$

$$= \max_j \alpha_j(\mathbf{x})$$

$$= \max_j \prod_{i \in P_j} x_i$$

$$= 1 - \prod_{j=1}^{s} \left(1 - \prod_{i \in P_j} x_i\right).$$

This equation indicates that if the minimal path sets are known, any coherent system may be written as the parallel arrangement of s banks of series subsystems.

Example 2.10

The system structure considered in the four previous examples has $s = 2$ minimal path sets: $P_1 = \{1, 2\}$ and $P_2 = \{1, 3\}$. The preceding equation indicates that the structure function can be written as

$$\phi(\mathbf{x}) = 1 - \prod_{j=1}^{2}\left(1 - \prod_{i \in P_j} x_i\right)$$

$$= 1 - (1 - x_1 x_2)(1 - x_1 x_3)$$

and the corresponding block diagram is shown in Figure 2.10. Although this block diagram

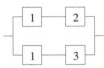

Figure 2.10   Three-component system as a parallel arrangement of series subsystems.

is not as succinct as the original, it is equivalent since the system fails if either component 1 fails or both components 2 and 3 fail.

This same idea can be applied to minimal cut sets as well. Let $C_1, C_2, \ldots, C_k$ be the k minimal cut sets for a coherent system, and define

$$\beta_j(\mathbf{x}) = \begin{cases} 1 & \text{if at least one component in the } j\text{th minimal cut set is functioning} \\ 0 & \text{otherwise} \end{cases}$$

for $j = 1, 2, \ldots, k$. An equivalent way of expressing $\beta_j(\mathbf{x})$ is

$$\beta_j(\mathbf{x}) = \max_{i \in C_j} x_i$$

$$= 1 - \prod_{i \in C_j} (1 - x_i)$$

for $j = 1, 2, \ldots, k$. The system fails if all components corresponding to one or more of the minimal cut sets have failed. Hence, the structure function can be rewritten as

$$\phi(\mathbf{x}) = \min_j \beta_j(\mathbf{x})$$

$$= \prod_{j=1}^{k} \beta_j(\mathbf{x})$$

$$= \prod_{j=1}^{k} [1 - \prod_{i \in C_j} (1 - x_i)].$$

The structure of this equation indicates that, once the minimal cut sets are known, any coherent system may be written as the series arrangement of k banks of parallel subsystems.

Example 2.11

The bridge structure, with block diagram shown in Figure 2.5, has $k = 4$ minimal cut sets: $C_1 = \{1, 2\}$, $C_2 = \{1, 3, 5\}$, $C_3 = \{2, 3, 4\}$, and $C_4 = \{4, 5\}$. A system of this type may arise in a communications network in which there are alternative ways of connecting devices, such as telephones or computer networks, if one link fails. The preceding equation indicates that the structure function can be written as

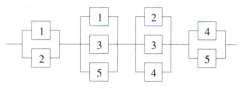

Figure 2.11   Bridge structure as a series arrangement of parallel subsystems.

$$\phi(\mathbf{x}) = \prod_{j=1}^{4} \left[1 - \prod_{i \in C_j} (1 - x_i) \right]$$

$$= [1 - (1 - x_1)(1 - x_2)] \, [1 - (1 - x_1)(1 - x_3)(1 - x_5)]$$

$$[1 - (1 - x_2)(1 - x_3)(1 - x_4)] \, [1 - (1 - x_4)(1 - x_5)].$$

The corresponding block diagram is shown in Figure 2.11.

In conclusion, these manipulations of the structure function allow any coherent system to be expressed as a parallel arrangement of s banks of series subsystems (often called redundant-series or parallel-series)

$$\phi(\mathbf{x}) = 1 - \prod_{j=1}^{s} \left(1 - \prod_{i \in P_j} x_i \right)$$

or as a series arrangement of k banks of parallel subsystems (often called series-redundant or series-parallel)

$$\phi(\mathbf{x}) = \prod_{j=1}^{k} [1 - \prod_{i \in C_j} (1 - x_i)].$$

2.3   RELIABILITY FUNCTIONS

All mathematical models for coherent systems of components presented so far are *deterministic*. This section introduces *probabilistic* models for coherent systems and, in particular, defines the reliability function.

Two additional assumptions need to be made for the analysis in this section. First, the n components comprising a system must be *nonrepairable.* Once a component changes from the functioning to the failed state, it cannot return to the functioning state. This assumption was not necessary in the previous section, since a structure function simply maps the component states to the system state. The structure function can be applied to a system with nonrepairable or repairable components since it is capable of determining the state of the system at any time t. The second assumption is that the components are independent. Thus, failure of one component does not influence the probability of failure of other components. This assumption is not appropriate if the components operate in a common environment where there may be "common-cause" failures. Although the independence assumption makes the mathematics simpler, the assumption should not be automatically used for every system. The independence assumption would not be satisfied, for example, on a suspension bridge, since the failure of one cable increases the load on the remaining cables.

Previously, x_i was defined to be the state of component i. Now X_i is a random variable with the same meaning.

Definition 2.9   The random variable denoting the state of component i, X_i, is

$$X_i = \begin{cases} 0 & \text{if component } i \text{ has failed} \\ 1 & \text{if component } i \text{ is functioning} \end{cases}$$

for $i = 1, 2, \ldots, n$.

These n values can be written as a random system state vector $\mathbf{X}$. The probability that component i is functioning at a certain time is given by $p_i = P[X_i = 1]$, which is often called the *reliability* of the ith component, for $i = 1, 2, \ldots, n$. These n values can be written as a reliability vector $\mathbf{p} = (p_1, p_2, \ldots, p_n)$. It should be noted that the reliability cannot be stated without also specifying the time at which the reliability applies. The reliability of a component, for example, should not be stated as simply 0.83, since no time is specified. It is equally ambiguous for a component to have a 5000-hour life without indicating a reliability for that time. Instead, it should be stated that the 5000-hour reliability is 0.83. Similarly, in a medical setting, it should not be stated that the probability of surviving prostate cancer is 0.76; rather, the 5-year survival probability is 0.76. This requirement of stating a time along with a reliability applies to systems as well as components.

The *system reliability, r,* is defined by

$$r = P[\phi(\mathbf{X}) = 1]$$

where r is a quantity that can be calculated from the vector $\mathbf{p}$, so $r = r(\mathbf{p})$. The function $r(\mathbf{p})$ is called the *reliability function.* In some of the examples in this section, the components have identical reliabilities (that is, $p_1 = p_2 = \cdots = p_n = p$). The notation $r(p)$ is used to indicate this.

Several techniques are used to calculate system reliability, and this section will illustrate five: definition, expectation, the path vector technique, the cut vector technique, and decomposition. Each technique has its advantages and disadvantages, which should be considered when applied to a particular system.

Definition of $r(\mathbf{p})$

The first technique for finding the reliability of a coherent system of n independent components is to use the definition of system reliability directly. Example 2.12 illustrates the use of the definition in calculating system reliability.

Example 2.12

The system reliability of a *series* system of n components is easily found using the definition of $r(\mathbf{p})$ and the independence assumption.

$$r(\mathbf{p}) = P[\phi(\mathbf{X}) = 1]$$

$$= P[\prod_{i=1}^{n} X_i = 1]$$

$$= \prod_{i=1}^{n} P[X_i = 1]$$

$$= \prod_{i=1}^{n} p_i.$$

The product in this formula indicates that system reliability is always less than the reliability of the least reliable component. As will be seen later, this "chain is only as strong as its weakest link" result indicates that improving the weakest component causes the largest increase in the reliability of a series system.

In the special case when all components are identical (such as a string of Christmas tree lights for which the failure of one bulb extinguishes all bulbs), $r(p) = p^n$, where $p_1 = p_2 = \cdots = p_n = p$. The plot in Figure 2.12 of component reliability versus system reliability for several values of n shows that highly reliable components are necessary to achieve reasonable system reliability, even for small values of n. The only encouraging news from this plot is that a small increase in component reliability nets a substantial increase in system reliability for a system with a large number of components.

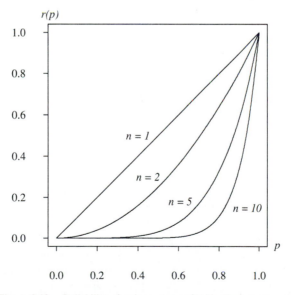

Figure 2.12   Reliability of series systems of n identical components.

Expected Value of $\phi(\mathbf{X})$

The second technique, *expectation,* is based on the fact that $P[\phi(\mathbf{X}) = 1]$ is equal to $E[\phi(\mathbf{X})]$, since $\phi(\mathbf{X})$ is a Bernoulli random variable. Consequently, the expected value of $\phi(\mathbf{X})$ is the system reliability $r(\mathbf{p})$, as illustrated in Example 2.13.

Example 2.13

Find the system reliability for a parallel system of n components using expectation.
Since the components are independent,

$$r(\mathbf{p}) = E[\phi(\mathbf{X})]$$

$$= E[1 - \prod_{i=1}^{n} (1 - X_i)]$$

$$= 1 - E[\prod_{i=1}^{n} (1 - X_i)]$$

$$= 1 - \prod_{i=1}^{n} E[1 - X_i]$$

$$= 1 - \prod_{i=1}^{n} (1 - p_i).$$

In the special case of identical components, this expression reduces to $r(p) = 1 - (1 - p)^n$. Figure 2.13 shows component reliability versus system reliability for a parallel system of n identical components. The "law of diminishing returns" is apparent from the graph when a

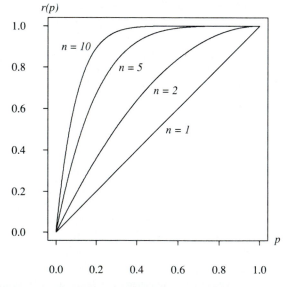

Figure 2.13   Reliability of parallel systems of n identical components.

fixed component reliability is considered. The marginal gain in reliability decreases dramatically as more components are added to the system.

There are two systems that appear to be similar to parallel systems on the surface, but that are not "true" parallel systems such as the one considered in Example 2.13. The first such system is a *standby system*. In a standby system, not all the components function at the same time, and components are switched to standby components upon failure. Examples of standby systems include bringing a spare pencil to an exam, keeping a spare tire in the trunk of a car, and having three power sources (utility company, backup generator, and batteries) for a hospital. In contrast, all components are functioning simultaneously in a true parallel system.

The second such system is a *shared-parallel system*. In a shared-parallel system, all components are on-line, but the component reliabilities change when one component fails. The lug nuts that attach a wheel to an automobile are an example of a five-component shared-parallel system. When one lug nut fails (that is, loosens or falls off), the load on the remaining functioning lug nuts increases. Thus, the static reliability calculations presented in this section are not appropriate for a wheel attachment system. In contrast, the failure of a component in a true parallel system does not affect the reliabilities of any of the other components in the system.

Both the standby and shared-parallel systems have the same structure function as a true parallel system:

$$\phi(\mathbf{x}) = 1 - \prod_{i=1}^{n} (1 - x_i).$$

Their structure functions are identical because the structure function only relates the state of the components to the state of the system. The reliability calculations for these systems are where the differences become apparent. The reliability calculations for a standby system involve the reliability of the switch (in terms of sensing failure and switching to the next component) and the sums of the random component lifetimes. The reliability calculations for a shared-parallel system involve random lifetimes that are dependent on the number of system failures.

Path Vector Technique

Since the expectation technique is difficult to use on some systems, the *path vector technique* can be used to calculate system reliability. Although the path vector technique is often very time consuming for large systems, it always works. To find the system reliability using the path vector technique, simply sum the probabilities corresponding to the path vectors for the system. Since mutually exclusive path vectors are used, the path vector probabilities and cut vector probabilities must sum to 1, since the number of path vectors plus the number of cut vectors totals 2^n. Thus, the path vector and cut vector techniques illustrate that system reliability and system unreliability (1 minus the system reliability) must sum to 1. The system reliability is

$$r(\mathbf{p}) = P[\mathbf{X} \text{ is a path vector}],$$

as illustrated by Example 2.14.

Example 2.14

Consider the 2-out-of-3 system, which we know, from Example 2.3, has structure function

$$\phi(\mathbf{X}) = 1 - (1 - X_1 X_2)(1 - X_1 X_3)(1 - X_2 X_3)$$

and path vectors (0, 1, 1), (1, 0, 1), (1, 1, 0), and (1, 1, 1). To use the path vector technique, the probabilities corresponding to each of these path vectors should be summed:

$$r(\mathbf{p}) = (1 - p_1)p_2 p_3 + p_1(1 - p_2)p_3 + p_1 p_2(1 - p_3) + p_1 p_2 p_3$$

$$= p_1 p_2 + p_1 p_3 + p_2 p_3 - 2 p_1 p_2 p_3.$$

Expectation can also be used to solve this problem. A naive (and incorrect) approach is to replace each X_i value in the structure function with the corresponding p_i value to arrive at the reliability function

$$r(\mathbf{p}) = 1 - (1 - p_1 p_2)(1 - p_1 p_3)(1 - p_2 p_3).$$

This approach is incorrect because the right-hand side of the structure function contains product terms (such as $X_1^2 X_2 X_3$), and $E[X_1^2] = p_1^2$ does not hold for a Bernoulli random variable X_1. Since $E[X_1] = E[X_1^2] = p_1$ for a Bernoulli random variable X_1, a correct method to determine the reliability function $r(\mathbf{p})$ for a 2-out-of-3 system using expectation is

$$r(\mathbf{p}) = E[\phi(\mathbf{X})]$$

$$= E[1 - (1 - X_1 X_2)(1 - X_1 X_3)(1 - X_2 X_3)]$$

$$= E[X_1 X_2 + X_1 X_3 + X_2 X_3 - X_1^2 X_2 X_3 - X_1 X_2^2 X_3 - X_1 X_2 X_3^2 + X_1^2 X_2^2 X_3^2]$$

$$= p_1 p_2 + p_1 p_3 + p_2 p_3 - p_1 p_2 p_3 - p_1 p_2 p_3 - p_1 p_2 p_3 + p_1 p_2 p_3$$

$$= p_1 p_2 + p_1 p_3 + p_2 p_3 - 2 p_1 p_2 p_3.$$

Cut Vector Technique

Analogous to the path vector technique, the *cut vector technique* gives the system reliability as

$$r(\mathbf{p}) = 1 - P[\mathbf{X} \text{ is a cut vector}].$$

As with the path vector technique, this method becomes rather inefficient as the number of components in the system grows.

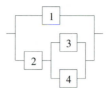

Figure 2.14   Four-component system.

Example 2.15

Consider the system with the block diagram shown in Figure 2.14. This system has five cut vectors:

$$(0, 0, 0, 0), \quad (0, 0, 0, 1), \quad (0, 0, 1, 0), \quad (0, 0, 1, 1), \quad (0, 1, 0, 0).$$

The reliability function can be found using the cut vector technique:

$$r(\mathbf{p}) = 1 - (1 - p_1)(1 - p_2)(1 - p_3)(1 - p_4)$$
$$- (1 - p_1)(1 - p_2)(1 - p_3)p_4 - (1 - p_1)(1 - p_2)p_3(1 - p_4)$$
$$- (1 - p_1)(1 - p_2)p_3 p_4 - (1 - p_1)p_2(1 - p_3)(1 - p_4).$$

Decomposition

The fifth and final method discussed in this text for finding the reliability of a coherent system of n components is *decomposition*. To use decomposition, identify a key component in the system and condition on the state of that key component. Using the conditioning argument (also known as the rule of elimination), the system reliability is

$$r(\mathbf{p}) = P[\text{system functions} \mid \text{key component functions}] \, P[\text{key component functions}]$$

$$+ \, P[\text{system functions} \mid \text{key component fails}] \, P[\text{key component fails}].$$

Defining system A with the key component replaced by a perfect component in the system of interest and system B with the key component replaced by a failed component in the system of interest, this is equivalent to

$$r(\mathbf{p}) = P[\text{system } A \text{ functions}] \, P[\text{key component functions}]$$

$$+ \, P[\text{system } B \text{ functions}] \, P[\text{key component fails}].$$

This expression can be rewritten as

$$r(\mathbf{p}) = r(1_i, \mathbf{p}) \, p_i + r(0_i, \mathbf{p}) \, (1 - p_i),$$

where i is the index of the key component and $r(1_i, \mathbf{p})$ denotes the reliability function when the ith component has reliability 1 and the other components have reliabilities

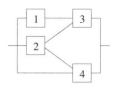

Figure 2.15   Four-component system.

$p_1, p_2, \ldots, p_{i-1}, p_{i+1}, \ldots, p_n$. Any component may be used as the key component, although it is usually easiest to choose one with a unique position in the block diagram, as illustrated in Example 2.16.

Example 2.16

Consider the system with the block diagram shown in Figure 2.15. Using component 2 as the key component, the systems A and B are shown in Figure 2.16. System A corresponds to the original system with component 2 replaced by a perfect component (note that component 1 is irrelevant in this system and hence is dropped from the diagram), and system B corresponds to the original system with component 2 replaced by a failed component. Using the decomposition formula, the system reliability is

$$r(\mathbf{p}) = [1 - (1 - p_3)(1 - p_4)] \, p_2 + [1 - (1 - p_1 p_3)(1 - p_4)](1 - p_2).$$

Four comments follow concerning the methods presented in this section. First, one advantage all five techniques share is that they yield the *exact* system reliability. Unfortunately, however, these techniques often become cumbersome as the number of components increases. To that end, a number of *reliability bounds* have been developed, two of which are introduced in Section 2.4.

Second, the systems that are considered in this section have *binary, independent* components. One way to relax the binary assumption is to consider systems that have more than two (for example, functioning, partially functioning, and failed) component states and system states. These multistate systems have path and cut sets defined analogously to binary systems. Another way to relax the binary assumption is to allow components and systems to assume continuous values. A model of this type allows a machine to operate at, for instance, 63% capacity, rather than being either "up" or "down." The independence assumption can be relaxed by having all components operate in a common environment or by using multivariate models to describe failure times. In the Further Reading section at the end of this chapter, references on models incorporating multiple states, continuous states, and dependent components are cited.

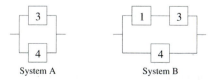

Figure 2.16   Systems A and B conditioned on the state of component 2.

Third, the system reliability calculations performed in this section are particularly important to designers when considering alternative system designs. The preliminary analysis of a particular configuration of components to form a system should be evaluated in light of the performance, schedule, marketability, cost, and reliability of the system.

Fourth, once the reliability function is known, the *reliability importance* of each component in the system can be calculated. Whereas structural importance, defined earlier, indicated the relative importance of a component in the system due to its position in the system, reliability importance combines position and reliability to indicate the relative importance of components with respect to the system reliability.

Definition 2.10   The *reliability importance* of component i in a coherent system of n components is

$$I_r(i) = \frac{\partial r(\mathbf{p})}{\partial p_i}$$

for $i = 1, 2, \ldots, n$.

This definition for reliability importance emphasizes the impact of the ith component on system reliability. The component with the largest reliability importance is that component for which an increase in its reliability corresponds to the largest increase in the system reliability. An equivalent definition for reliability importance is found by differentiating both sides of the decomposition technique formula for computing system reliability with respect to p_i:

$$I_r(i) = r(1_i, \mathbf{p}) - r(0_i, \mathbf{p})$$

for $i = 1, 2, \ldots, n$. The reliability importance of component i satisfies

$$0 < I_r(i) < 1 \qquad i = 1, 2, \ldots, n$$

for a coherent system composed of $n > 1$ components. Assuming that reliability improvement costs are comparable, it is always wisest to aim reliability improvement efforts at the component(s) with the highest reliability importance.

Example 2.17

Consider a series arrangement of n components with reliabilities $p_1, p_2, \ldots, p_n$. The reliability importance of the ith component is

$$I_r(i) = \frac{\partial r(\mathbf{p})}{\partial p_i} = \frac{\partial}{\partial p_i} \prod_{j=1}^{n} p_j = \prod_{j \neq i} p_j$$

for $i = 1, 2, \ldots, n$. This formula reveals (not surprisingly) that in a series system the component with the greatest reliability importance is the component with the smallest reliability. This is another version of the "a chain is only as strong as its weakest link" view of series systems and indicates to the design engineer that the greatest change in system reliability can be attained by improving the least reliable component.

2.4 SYSTEM RELIABILITY BOUNDS

This section illustrates two system reliability bounds. These bounds are useful for analyzing systems of many components for which the methods of the previous section are too cumbersome. Although there are a multitude of methods for bounding the system reliability, only two simple methods are outlined here. The first method states that all coherent systems of n components must have a system reliability that is between that of a series system of n components and a parallel system of n components. Often called *trivial bounds*, a coherent system is compared to the worst (series) and best (parallel) possible component arrangements.

Theorem 2.2   If ϕ is a coherent system of independent components, then

$$\prod_{i=1}^{n} p_i \le r(\mathbf{p}) \le 1 - \prod_{i=1}^{n} (1 - p_i).$$

Equivalently, from a design point of view, the worst possible system arrangement is a series system, and the best possible system arrangement is a parallel system. These bounds typically carry little practical value. For example, if each of four identical components has a reliability of 0.9 for a particular time value, Theorem 2.2 implies that $0.6561 \le r(\mathbf{p}) \le 0.9999$, which does not yield a lot of information about the reliability of the system. A better method for bounding the reliability when the minimal path and minimal cut sets are known is as follows.

Theorem 2.3   If ϕ is a coherent system of independent components with minimal path sets $P_1, P_2, \ldots, P_s$, and minimal cut sets $C_1, C_2, \ldots, C_k$, then

$$\prod_{j=1}^{k} [1 - \prod_{i \in C_j} (1 - p_i)] \le r(\mathbf{p}) \le 1 - \prod_{j=1}^{s} [1 - \prod_{i \in P_j} p_i].$$

Example 2.18 illustrates the use of these reliability bounds on a small system.

Example 2.18

Consider the coherent system with block diagram given in Figure 2.14. This system has $s = 3$ minimal path sets,

$$\{1\}, \qquad \{2, 3\}, \qquad \{2, 4\},$$

and $k = 2$ minimal cut sets,

$$\{1, 2\}, \qquad \{1, 3, 4\}.$$

Using Theorem 2.3, bounds on the system reliability are

$$\prod_{j=1}^{2} [1 - \prod_{i \in C_j} (1 - p_i)] \le r(\mathbf{p}) \le 1 - \prod_{j=1}^{3} [1 - \prod_{i \in P_j} p_i]$$

$$[1 - \prod_{i \in C_1} (1 - p_i)][1 - \prod_{i \in C_2} (1 - p_i)] \le r(\mathbf{p}) \le 1 - [1 - \prod_{i \in P_1} p_i][1 - \prod_{i \in P_2} p_i][1 - \prod_{i \in P_3} p_i]$$

$$[1 - (1 - p_1)(1 - p_2)][1 - (1 - p_1)(1 - p_3)(1 - p_4)] \le r(\mathbf{p}) \le 1 - [1 - p_1][1 - p_2 p_3][1 - p_2 p_4].$$

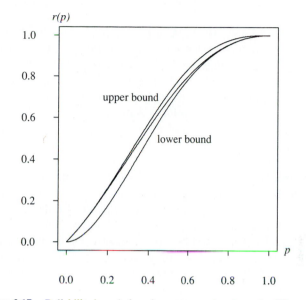

Figure 2.17   Reliability bounds for a four-component system using Theorem 2.3.

When all the components are identical, these reliability bounds reduce to

$$[1 - (1 - p)^2][1 - (1 - p)^3] \leq r(p) \leq 1 - [1 - p][1 - p^2]^2.$$

Using Example 2.15, the exact reliability for this system with identical components is

$$r(p) = 1 - (1 - p)^4 - 3(1 - p)^3 p - (1 - p)^2 p^2.$$

The upper and lower bounds, as well as the exact system reliability, are plotted in Figure 2.17. The bounds of Theorem 2.3 do a significantly better job of bounding the reliability of the system than the bounds of Theorem 2.2.

2.5   FURTHER READING

This chapter emphasizes the evaluation of system reliability based on the assumption of independent, binary components with known reliabilities. Current system design practices are significantly more complicated than those presented here and involve concurrently considering reliability, maintainability, and supportability. Many of the tools presented here, however, are valuable in increasing the reliability of a system of components. Early work in this area was done by Moore and Shannon (1956) and Birnbaum et al. (1961). The proof of Theorem 2.1, comparing component and system redundancy, is given in Barlow and Proschan (1981, p. 8) and extended in Ross (1993, p. 421). A similar result is obtained by letting ϕ be the structure function for a coherent system of n components. For any state vectors $\mathbf{x}$ and $\mathbf{y}$,

$$\phi(x_1 y_1, x_2 y_2, \ldots, x_n y_n) \leq \phi(\mathbf{x})\phi(\mathbf{y})$$

and equality holds when $\phi(\mathbf{x}) = \prod_{i=1}^{n} x_i$. Barlow and Proschan also give an excellent treatment of structure and reliability functions. Three other good sources on structure and reliability functions are Colbourn (1987), Kaufmann et al. (1977), and Shier (1991). Event trees, fault trees, and failure modes and effects analysis (FMEA) are approaches for considering the arrangement of components in a system (Barlow and Proschan, 1981). *Consecutive k-out-of-n* systems are a generalization of *k-out-of-n* systems when the components are arranged linearly. The system functions when all sequences of k consecutive components function (Chan et al., 1988). The binary coherent systems outlined in this chapter may be generalized to multistate coherent systems in which the components and system can assume more than just two states or to continuous systems for which $\mathbf{x}$ and $\phi(\mathbf{x})$ can assume values between 0 and 1. The multistate problem grew out of reliability problems encountered in electronics with two different failure modes: open and short circuit (see von Alven, 1964, pp. 216–223, 248–249; Billinton and Allan, 1985, p. 116; Dhillon, 1983, p. 31; Grosh, 1989, p. 159; and Kapur and Lamberson, 1977, p. 55, for examples). El-Neweihi et al. (1978), Ross (1979), and Barlow and Wu (1978) are three of the first papers to define a multistate coherent system. Hudson and Kapur (1983) and Boedigheimer (1992) review the multistate literature. Work on continuous systems has been done by Baxter (1984) and Block and Savits (1984).

The development of minimal path sets and minimal cut sets follows that of Ross (1993, pp. 414–417). Other sources that have discussions on minimal path and cut sets include Barlow and Proschan (1981), Colbourn (1987), Crowder et al. (1991), Gertsbakh (1989), Grosh (1989), Kaufmann et al. (1977), Shier (1991), Sundararajan (1991), and Zacks (1992).

Two other techniques for determining system reliability are the delta-star method (Dhillon, 1983, p. 38) and modular decomposition (Barlow and Proschan, 1981, p. 17). A chart containing some popular system arrangements and their reliability functions is contained in von Alven (1964, p. 245), which is where the terms series-parallel and parallel-series are found. The example in Section 2.3 using the lug nuts on an automobile tire is in Kapur and Lamberson (1977, p. 59). Martz and Waller (1982, pp. 143–146) discuss standby systems with perfect switching, imperfect switching, and shared-load systems. All the textbooks cited in the previous paragraph also have sections on reliability functions. Other textbooks that examine reliability functions and their evaluation are Halpern (1978), Henley and Kumamoto (1981), Kececioglu (1991), Lewis (1987), Smith (1976), Tobias and Trindade (1986), and Trivedi (1982). Iyer (1992) discusses reliability importance and considers dependent components. The case of dependent components is covered in several articles in the literature. One way to introduce dependence of component failure times in a common environment is to use either the proportional hazards or accelerated life models, which will be outlined in Chapter 5. A second way to introduce dependence is through a parametric distribution, two of the most popular of which are given by Freund (1961) and Marshall and Olkin (1967).

The proof of the reliability bounds given in Section 2.4 is in Barlow and Proschan (1981, p. 35), along with several other bounds. Many other procedures are available for determining bounds on the reliability function. Some of these procedures are given in Ball and Provan (1982), Barlow and Proschan (1981), Colbourn (1987), Gertsbakh (1989), Ross (1993), and Shier (1991).

2.6   EXERCISES

Use the block diagrams in Figure 2.18 for the following questions.

2.1.   Give the structure function for system A
   (a) using just minimums and maximums.
   (b) algebraically.

2.2.   Give the structure functions for systems B and C.

2.3.   Draw the block diagrams for the coherent systems having structure functions
   (a) $\phi(\mathbf{x}) = x_1 x_2 (1 - (1 - x_3)(1 - x_4))$.
   (b) $\phi(\mathbf{x}) = (1 - (1 - x_1)(1 - x_2 x_3)(1 - x_4)) x_5$.
   (c) $\phi(\mathbf{x}) = x_1 x_2 + x_1 x_3 + x_2 x_3 - x_1^2 x_2 x_3 - x_1 x_2^2 x_3 - x_1 x_2 x_3^2 + (x_1 x_2 x_3)^2$.

2.4.   (Ross, 1993, p. 449) Show that the relationship

$$\phi(\mathbf{x}) = x_i \phi(1_i, \mathbf{x}) + (1 - x_i) \phi(0_i, \mathbf{x})$$

is true for any coherent structure function $\phi(\mathbf{x})$ and any $i = 1, 2, \ldots, n$.

2.5.   Olivia is giving a concert. Her "system" consists of a microphone, an amplifier, and two speakers. If the microphone, amplifier, or both of the speakers fail, Olivia's "system" fails since her concert-goers can no longer hear her. Draw a block diagram for the system.

2.6.   Draw block diagrams corresponding to component and system redundancy for system A.

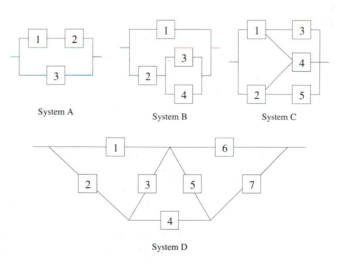

System A

System B

System C

System D

Figure 2.18

2.7. Draw a block diagram and give a structure function for a 2-out-of-4 system.

2.8. Find the structural importance of each component in system A.

2.9. Find the structural importance for each component in an n-component
   (a) series system.
   (b) parallel system.

2.10. (Barlow and Proschan, 1981, p. 7) Draw block diagrams and list the corresponding mini-mal path sets of all the distinct coherent systems (do not include those that are just permuta-tions of components) of
   (a) two components (*hint*: there are two of these).
   (b) three components (*hint*: there are five of these).
   (c) four components.

2.11. A coherent system S has a *dual system*, $\overline{S}$, whose structure function is

$$\overline{\phi}(\mathbf{x}) = 1 - \phi(\mathbf{1} - \mathbf{x}),$$

where $(\mathbf{1} - \mathbf{x}) = (1 - x_1, 1 - x_2, \ldots, 1 - x_n)$.
   (a) Draw the block diagram of the dual system corresponding to system A.
   (b) For system A, show that a minimal path set for A is a minimal cut set for $\overline{A}$ and a mini-mal cut set for A is a minimal path set for $\overline{A}$.
   (c) What is the dual of an n-component parallel system?
   (d) What is the dual of a k-out-of-n system?

2.12. (Kaufmann et al., 1977, p. 65) If S is a coherent system of n components, U_k is the number of path vectors having exactly k operating components, and V_k is the number of cut vectors having exactly k failed components, then

$$U_k + V_{n-k} = \binom{n}{k} \qquad k = 1, 2, \ldots, n.$$

Show that this is true for system B with $k = 2$.

2.13. Find the minimal path sets and minimal cut sets for system D.

2.14. Draw the block diagrams for system C written as the parallel arrangement of series subsys-tems and as the series arrangement of parallel subsystems.

2.15. For the system defined by the block diagram in Figure 2.19, is the vector (1, 0, 1, 1, 1, 1, 0, 0, 1, 1, 1) a path vector? Is it a minimal path vector? Explain why it is or is not a minimal path vector.

2.16. Find the minimal path sets and minimal cut sets for a parallel system of n components.

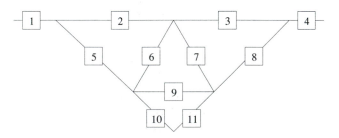

Figure 2.19

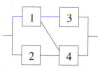

Figure 2.20

2.17. Find $\phi(\mathbf{x})$ and draw a block diagram without repeated components for the coherent system with minimal path sets $\{1, 2, 4\}$, $\{1, 3, 4\}$, and $\{1, 5\}$.

2.18. Draw a block diagram for the system whose minimal cut sets are the same as the minimal path sets for the system in Figure 2.20.

2.19. Redraw the block diagram shown in Figure 2.21 as the parallel arrangement of series subsystems and as the series arrangement of parallel subsystems.

2.20. What is the minimum number of identical components, each with reliability 0.2, that must be placed in parallel to achieve a system reliability of 0.999?

2.21. What is the component reliability of each of n identical components in a series system if the system reliability is 0.8?

2.22. Find p_3 in system A to achieve a system reliability of 0.76 if
(a) $p_1 = 0.8$, $p_2 = 0.4$.
(b) $p_1 = 0.9$, $p_2 = 0.9$.

2.23. Make a plot of n (from 1 to 10) on the horizontal axis versus $r(p)$ (from 0 to 1) on the vertical axis for a *series* system of identical components having component reliabilities $p = 0.99, 0.95, 0.90$. Make a similar plot for *parallel* systems of identical components, but this time make the plot for component reliabilities $p = 0.20, 0.50, 0.90$.

2.24. Make a plot of p (on the horizontal axis) versus $r(p)$ (on the vertical axis) for a 2-out-of-3 system of identical components.

2.25. Find the reliability of system C by using the decomposition technique by conditioning on the state of component 4.

2.26. Find the reliability of the system with the block diagram shown in Figure 2.22 by using decomposition and conditioning on the state of component 1.

Figure 2.21

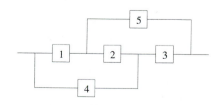

Figure 2.22

Figure 2.23

2.27. (Barlow and Proschan, 1981, p. 27) Show that $I_\phi(i) = I_r(i)$ for $i = 1, 2, \ldots, n$ if $p_j = 0.5$ for all $j \neq i$ for component 2 of system A.

2.28. Consider a 2-out-of-3 system with $p_1 < p_2 < p_3$. Which component has the highest reliability importance?

2.29. Which configuration of identical components shown in Figure 2.23 has higher reliability? Why? Do *not* calculate $r(\mathbf{p})$.

2.30. Set up, but do not solve, an expression for finding the appropriate component reliabilities required to achieve a system reliability of r in a 2-out-of-3 system with identical components.

2.31. Give an expression that, when solved, gives the component reliabilities required to achieve a system reliability of r in a k-out-of-n system with identical components.

2.32. Express the reliability of the two systems of ab identical components whose block diagrams are shown in Figure 2.24. Assume that each component has reliability p.

2.33. Find the reliability importance of each component in system A.

2.34. A three-component series system has reliability importances of m_1, m_2, and m_3 for components 1, 2, and 3, respectively. Solve for p_1, p_2, and p_3 in terms of m_1, m_2, and m_3.

2.35. Find the reliability importance for each component in a parallel system of n components.

2.36. Crowder et al. (1991, p. 186) give a general expression for the reliability of a coherent system of n components as

$$r(\mathbf{p}) = \sum_{\text{all } \mathbf{x}} [\phi(\mathbf{x}) \prod_{i=1}^{n} \{ p_i^{x_i}(1 - p_i)^{1 - x_i} \}].$$

Which of the five methods for finding exact system reliability does this particular expression most closely match?

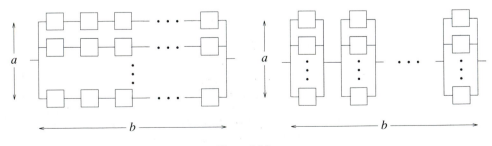

Figure 2.24

2.37. Consider the five possible arrangements of components in a coherent system of three components. Do not consider systems that are just permutations of components. If the components are independent and have identical reliabilities p, determine the system reliability for each arrangement and rank the arrangements from the least reliable to the most reliable.

2.38. Consider a two-component series system with reliabilities $p_1 = 0.6$ and $p_2 = 0.9$. The goal for system reliability is 0.95. The components in the system are independent. Component-level redundancy is used to increase system reliability. How many components of each type should be used to meet the system reliability goal with the minimum total number of components?

2.39. An engineer is considering two competing designs for a system that consists of n identical components, each with reliability p for a prescribed time. The first is a parallel design (a 1-out-of-2 system) and the second is a 2-out-of-4 design. Which design should the engineer choose? (*Hint*: Your design choice may depend on p.)

2.40. Using two different methods, find reliability bounds for system A. Plot these two bounds for identical components where the horizontal axis is component reliability p and the vertical axis is system reliability $r(p)$.

2.41. Find a reliability bound for system B.

2.42. Some authors shorten the notation for a parallel system by defining

$$\coprod_{i=1}^{n} x_i = 1 - \prod_{i=1}^{n}(1 - x_i)$$

and $x_1 \coprod x_2 = 1 - (1 - x_1)(1 - x_2)$. Thus $\sum_{i=1}^{n}$, $\prod_{i=1}^{n}$, and $\coprod_{i=1}^{n}$ are operators across indexes, and $+, \times$, and $\coprod$ are the corresponding operators on two arguments.
(a) Write the structure function for system B in terms of this notation.
(b) Rewrite the second reliability bound given in Section 2.4 in terms of this notation.

2.43. Reliability can be parameterized by strength and stress, rather than time, for mechanical items. Let the random variable S denote the *strength* of an item and the random variable s denote the *stress* applied to the item at a particular point in time. In this case, the reliability of the item is the probability that strength exceeds stress; that is,

$$r = P[S > s].$$

(a) Give two equivalent expressions (by changing the limits of integration) for r, given that the joint probability density function for strength and stress is $f(S, s)$.
(b) Find r when strength is normally distributed with a mean of μ_S and variance σ_S^2, and stress is normally distributed with a mean of μ_s and variance σ_s^2, independent of strength. Find a numerical value for r when $\mu_S = 103,800$ psi, $\sigma_S = 3300$ psi, $\mu_s = 98,100$ psi, and $\sigma_s = 1900$ psi. Assume that stress and strength are independent.
(c) Find r when strength has the normal distribution and stress has the exponential distribution. Assume that stress and strength are independent.

2.44. Consider a smoke alarm that has two modes of failure: catastrophic failure (or failure by open) occurs when the alarm does not beep when there is smoke present, and failure by short occurs when the alarm beeps when there is no smoke present. The 10,000-hour reliability of each *component* in the smoke alarm is 0.999, with a failure by open probability of 0.0009 and a failure by short probability of 0.0001. To minimize the probability of system failure by open, n of these components are arranged in parallel. Find the number of components in the parallel system that maximizes system reliability.

2.45. As in the movie *War Games*, a defense system is always concerned with two types of failure: failure to launch the weapons when the weapons should be launched, and launching the weapons when they should not be launched. Relate this problem to the bimodal failure model and discuss possible solutions to the problem. Go into as much detail as you think appropriate.

2.46. Three diodes are arranged as shown in the block diagram for system A. Assuming that each diode can undergo open or short failure (with q_{is} being the probability that component i fails short and q_{io} being the probability that component i fails open for $i = 1, 2, 3$), find the system reliability.

3

Lifetime Distributions

Up to this point, reliability has only been considered at one particular instance of time. Reliability is generalized to be a function of time in this chapter, and various lifetime distribution representations that are helpful in describing the evolution of the risks to which an item is subjected over time are introduced. In particular, five lifetime distribution representations are presented: the *survivor* function, the *probability density* function, the *hazard* function, the *cumulative hazard* function, and the *mean residual life* function. These five representations apply to both continuous (for example, a light bulb) and discrete (for example, a computer program that is run weekly) lifetimes. *Moments* and *fractiles* are useful ways to summarize the survival pattern of an item, although they do not completely define a distribution (as the five lifetime distribution representations do). The representations can be used to describe the distribution of systems, as well as components. Survivor functions and reliability functions are combined to give the distribution of system failure time once component failure time distributions and the arrangement of the components are known. Finally, some *distribution classes* are defined using the lifetime distribution representations that classify an item based on how it ages.

3.1 DISTRIBUTION REPRESENTATIONS

This section introduces five functions that define the distribution of a continuous, non-negative random variable T, the lifetime of an item. The five representations are not the only ways to define the distribution of T. Other methods include the moment generating function $E[e^{sT}]$, the characteristic function $E[e^{isT}]$, and the Mellin transform $E[T^s]$. The five representations used here have been chosen because of their intuitive appeal, their usefulness in problem solving, and their popularity in the literature. In the next section, these functions are applied to discrete distributions.

Survivor Function

The first lifetime distribution representation is the *survivor function*, $S(t)$. The survivor function is a generalization of reliability. Whereas reliability is defined as the probability that an item is functioning at one particular time, the survivor function is the probability that an item is functioning at any time t:

$$S(t) = P[T \geq t] \qquad t \geq 0.$$

It is assumed that $S(t) = 1$ for all $t < 0$. A survivor function is also known as the reliability function [since $S(t)$ is the reliability at time t] and the complementary cumulative distribution function (since $S(t) = 1 - F(t)$ for continuous random variables, where $F(t) = P[T \leq t]$ is the cumulative distribution function). All survivor functions must satisfy three conditions:

$$S(0) = 1 \qquad \lim_{t \to \infty} S(t) = 0 \qquad S(t) \text{ is nonincreasing.}$$

There are two interpretations of the survivor function. First, $S(t)$ is the probability that an individual item is functioning at time t. This is important, as will be seen later, in determining the lifetime distribution of a system from the distribution of the lifetimes of its individual components. Second, if there is a large population of items with identically distributed lifetimes, $S(t)$ is the expected fraction of the population that is functioning at time t.

The survivor function is useful for comparing the survival patterns of several populations of items. The graph in Figure 3.1 is a plot of $S_1(t)$ and $S_2(t)$, where $S_1(t)$ corresponds to population 1 and $S_2(t)$ corresponds to population 2. Since $S_1(t) \geq S_2(t)$ for all t values, it can be concluded that the items in population 1 are superior to those in population 2 with regard to reliability.

The conditional survivor function, $S_{T \mid T \geq a}(t)$, is the survivor function of an item that is functioning at time a:

$$S_{T \mid T \geq a}(t) = \frac{P[T \geq t \text{ and } T \geq a]}{P[T \geq a]} = \frac{P[T \geq t]}{P[T \geq a]} = \frac{S(t)}{S(a)} \qquad t \geq a.$$

Figure 3.2 shows the original survivor function $S(t)$ and the conditional survivor function $S_{T \mid T \geq a}(t)$ when $a = 0.5$. Since the conditional survivor function is rescaled by the factor $S(a)$, it has the same shape as the remaining portion of the original survivor function. The conditional survivor function is useful for comparing the survival experience of a group of items that has survived to time a. Examples include manufactured items surviving a burn-in test and cancer patients surviving 5 years after diagnosis and treatment. The conditional survivor function is of particular interest to actuaries. For example, if a 43-year-old woman is purchasing a 1-year term life insurance policy, an estimate of $S_{T \mid T \geq 43}(44)$ is required to determine an appropriate premium for the policy.

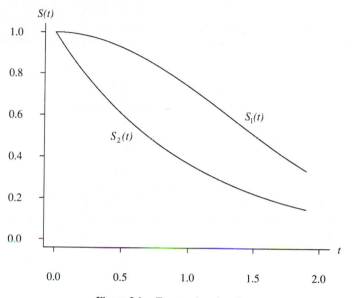

Figure 3.1   Two survivor functions.

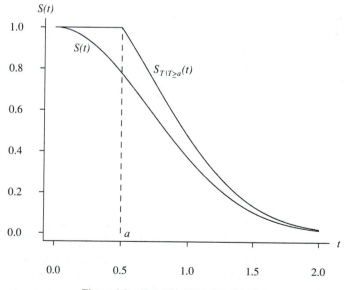

Figure 3.2   Conditional survivor function.

Probability Density Function

The second lifetime distribution representation, the *probability density function*, is defined by $f(t) = -S'(t)$, where the derivative exists and has the probabilistic interpretation

$$f(t)\Delta t = P[t \le T \le t + \Delta t]$$

for small Δt values. Although the probability density function is not as effective as the survivor function in comparing the survival patterns of two populations, a graph of $f(t)$ indicates the likelihood of failure for any t. The probability of failure between times a and b is calculated by an integral:

$$P[a \le T \le b] = \int_a^b f(t)\,dt.$$

All probability density functions for lifetimes must satisfy two conditions:

$$\int_0^\infty f(t)\,dt = 1 \qquad f(t) \ge 0 \text{ for all } t \ge 0.$$

It is assumed that $f(t) = 0$ for all $t < 0$. The probability density function shown in Figure 3.3 illustrates the relationship between the cumulative distribution function $F(t)$ and the survivor function $S(t)$ for a continuous lifetime. The area to the left of time t_0 is $F(t_0)$ and the area to the right of t_0 is $S(t_0)$.

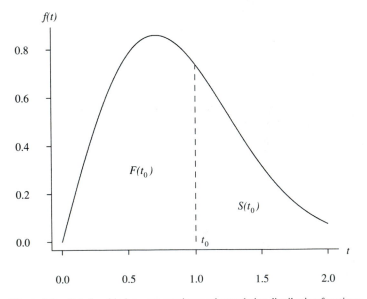

Figure 3.3   Relationship between survivor and cumulative distribution functions.

Hazard Function

The *hazard function, h(t)*, is perhaps the most popular of the five representations for life-time modeling due to its intuitive interpretation as the amount of *risk* associated with an item at time t. A second reason for its popularity is its usefulness in comparing the way risks change over time for several populations of items by plotting their hazard functions on a single axis. A third reason is that the hazard function is a special case of the intensity function for a nonhomogeneous Poisson process, which will be discussed in Chapter 6. A hazard function models the occurrence of one event, a failure, whereas the intensity function models the occurrence of a sequence of events over time. The hazard function goes by several aliases: in reliability it is also known as the hazard rate or failure rate; in actuarial science it is known as the force of mortality or force of decrement; in point process and extreme value theory it is known as the rate or intensity function; in vital statistics it is known as the age-specific death rate; and in economics its reciprocal is known as Mill's ratio.

The hazard function can be derived using conditional probability. First, consider the probability of failure between t and $t + \Delta t$:

$$P[t \leq T \leq t + \Delta t] = \int_{t}^{t+\Delta t} f(\tau)d\tau = S(t) - S(t + \Delta t).$$

Conditioning on the event that the item is working at time t yields

$$P[t \leq T \leq t + \Delta t \mid T \geq t] = \frac{P[t \leq T \leq t + \Delta t]}{P[T \geq t]} = \frac{S(t) - S(t + \Delta t)}{S(t)}.$$

If this conditional probability is averaged over the interval $[t, t + \Delta t]$ by dividing by Δt, an average rate of failure is obtained:

$$\frac{S(t) - S(t + \Delta t)}{S(t)\Delta t}.$$

As $\Delta t \to 0$, this becomes the instantaneous failure rate, which is the hazard function

$$h(t) = \lim_{\Delta t \to 0} \frac{S(t) - S(t + \Delta t)}{S(t)\Delta t}$$

$$= \frac{-S'(t)}{S(t)}$$

$$= \frac{f(t)}{S(t)} \qquad t \geq 0.$$

Thus, the hazard function is the ratio of the probability density function to the survivor function. Using the previous derivation, a probabilistic interpretation of the hazard function is

$$h(t)\Delta t = P[t \leq T \leq t + \Delta t \,|\, T \geq t]$$

for small Δt values, which is a conditional version of the interpretation for the probability density function. All hazard functions must satisfy two conditions:

$$\int_0^\infty h(t)\, dt = \infty \qquad h(t) \geq 0 \text{ for all } t \geq 0 .$$

Example 3.1

Consider the Weibull distribution defined by the survivor function

$$S(t) = e^{-(\lambda t)^\kappa} \qquad t \geq 0$$

with positive scale parameter λ and positive shape parameter κ. Find the hazard function.

By differentiating the survivor function with respect to t and negating, the probability density function is

$$f(t) = \lambda \kappa (\lambda t)^{\kappa - 1} e^{-(\lambda t)^\kappa} \qquad t \geq 0 ,$$

and the hazard function is

$$h(t) = \frac{f(t)}{S(t)} = \lambda \kappa (\lambda t)^{\kappa - 1} \qquad t \geq 0.$$

Figure 3.4 shows that the hazard function for $\lambda = 1$ and several κ values is constant if $\kappa = 1$, increasing if $\kappa > 1$ and decreasing if $\kappa < 1$.

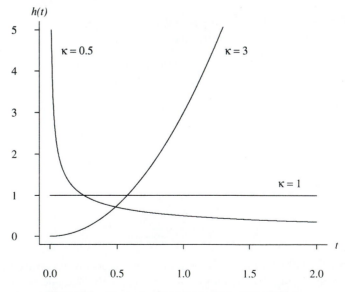

Figure 3.4   Hazard functions for the Weibull distribution.

The *units* on a hazard function are typically given in failures per unit time. In Example 3.1, if $\lambda = 0.01$, $\kappa = 1$ and time is measured in hours, then $h(t) = 0.01$ *failures per hour.* Manufactured items are often so reliable that to avoid hazard functions such as $h(t) = 0.00000128$ failures per hour the units are changed so that the hazard function may be expressed as $h(t) = 1.28$ failures per 10^6 hours. Another way to avoid writing too many leading zeroes is to change the units to years, where 1 year equals 8760 hours.

The shape of the hazard function indicates how an item ages. The intuitive interpretation as the amount of *risk* an item is subjected to at time t indicates that when the hazard function is large the item is under greater risk, and when the hazard function is small, the item is under less risk. The three hazard functions plotted in Figure 3.5 correspond to an increasing hazard function (labeled IFR for increasing failure rate), a decreasing hazard function (labeled DFR for decreasing failure rate), and a bathtub-shaped hazard function (labeled BT for bathtub-shaped failure rate).

The increasing hazard function is probably the most likely situation of the three. In this case, items are more likely to fail as time passes. In other words, items wear out or degrade with time. This is almost certainly the case with mechanical items that undergo wear or fatigue. It can also be the case in certain biomedical experiments. If T is the time until a tumor appears after the injection of a substance into a laboratory animal and the substance makes the tumor more likely to appear as time passes, the hazard function associated with T is increasing.

The second situation, the decreasing hazard function, is less common. In this case, the item is less likely to fail as time passes. Items with this type of hazard function improve with time. Some metals work-harden through use and thus have increased

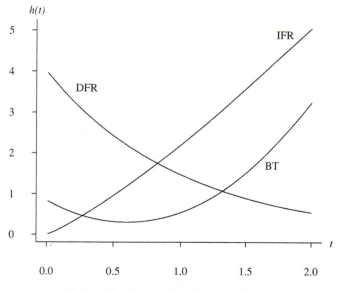

Figure 3.5   Common hazard function shapes.

strength as time passes. Another situation for which a decreasing hazard function might be appropriate for modeling is in working the bugs out of computer programs. Bugs are more likely to appear initially, but the likelihood of them appearing decreases as time passes.

The third situation, a bathtub-shaped hazard function, occurs when the hazard function decreases initially and then increases as items age. Items improve initially and then degrade as time passes. One situation where the bathtub-shaped hazard function arises is in the lifetimes of manufactured items. Often manufacturing, design, or component defects cause early failures. The period in which these failures occur is sometimes called the *burn-in* period. If failure is particularly catastrophic, this part of the lifetime will often be consumed by the manufacturer in a controlled environment. The time value during which early failures have been eliminated may be valuable to a producer who is determining an appropriate warranty period. Once items pass through this early part of their lifetime, they have a fairly constant hazard function, and failures are equally likely to occur at any point in time. Finally, as items continue to age, the hazard function increases without limit, resulting in *wear-out* failures. The three paragraphs that follow give examples of applications of the bathtub-shaped hazard function.

The bathtub-shaped hazard function can be envisioned for calculators; the burn-in period corresponds to the first few weeks of use when manufacturing, design, or component defects arise. Wear-out failures occur after a few years of use when the buttons are about ready to fall off. Failures due to calculators being dropped occur throughout the life of a calculator. If these failures are equally likely at any time, the hazard function will be increased by a constant that reflects the probability of dropping the calculator for all time values.

The bathtub-shaped hazard function also arises in the lifetimes of people. In this case, the early failures are known as *infant mortality* deaths and occur during the first few years of life. After this time, the hazard function has a very gentle increase through the teen-age years and into adulthood. Finally, *old age* deaths occur during the later years of life. The magnitude of the hazard function depends on factors such as the standard of living and medical services available. Also, occupation (for example, flower arranger versus stunt man) and life-style (for example, eating habits, sleeping habits, smoking habits, stress level) affect a lifetime distribution. The hazard function is used in actuarial science; the appropriate premium for a life insurance policy is based on probabilities associated with the lifetime distribution. The lowest life insurance premiums are usually for children who have survived the infant mortality part of their lifetimes.

The bathtub-shaped hazard function may also apply to human performance tasks, such as vigilance, monitoring, controlling, and tracking. In these situations, the lifetime T is the time to the first error. If the bathtub model applies, the burn-in period corresponds to *learning*, and the wear-out period corresponds to *fatigue*.

Care must be taken to differentiate between the hazard function for a *population* and the hazard function for an individual *item* under consideration. To use human lifetimes as an illustration, consider the following question: do two healthy 7-year-old boys living in the same town necessarily have the same hazard function? The answer is no. The reason is that all people are born with genetic predispositions that will influence their risk as they age. So, although a hazard function could be drawn for all 7-year-old boys living in that particular town, it would be an aggregate hazard function representing the population, and individual boys may be at increased or decreased risk. This is why life insurance companies typically require a medical exam to determine whether an individual is at higher risk than the rest of the population. The common assumption in most probabilistic models and statistical analyses is that of independent and identically distributed random variables, which in this case are lifetimes. This assumption is not always valid in reliability since items are typically manufactured in diverse conditions (for example, humidity, temperature, and raw materials).

Cumulative Hazard Function

The fourth lifetime distribution representation, the *cumulative hazard function, $H(t)$*, can be defined by

$$H(t) = \int_0^t h(\tau)\, d\tau \qquad t \geq 0.$$

The cumulative hazard function is also known as the integrated hazard function. All cumulative hazard functions must satisfy three conditions:

$$H(0) = 0 \qquad \lim_{t \to \infty} H(t) = \infty \qquad H(t) \text{ is nondecreasing.}$$

The cumulative hazard function is valuable for variate generation in Monte Carlo simulation, implementing certain procedures in statistical inference, and defining certain distribution classes.

Mean Residual Life Function

The last lifetime distribution representation, the *mean residual life* function, $L(t)$, is defined by

$$L(t) = E[T - t \mid T \geq t] \qquad t \geq 0.$$

The mean residual life function is the expected *remaining life*, $T - t$, given that the item has survived to time t. The unconditional mean of the distribution, $E[T]$, is a special case given by $L(0)$. To determine a formula for this expectation, the conditional probability density function is needed

$$f_{T \mid T \geq t}(\tau) = \frac{f(\tau)}{S(t)} \qquad \tau \geq t.$$

This conditional probability density function is actually a family of probability density functions (one for each value of t), each of which has an associated mean

$$E[T \mid T \geq t] = \int_t^\infty \tau\, f_{T \mid T \geq t}(\tau)\, d\tau = \int_t^\infty \tau \frac{f(\tau)}{S(t)}\, d\tau.$$

Since the mean residual life function is the expected *remaining* life, t must be subtracted, yielding

$$L(t) = E[T - t \mid T \geq t] = \int_t^\infty (\tau - t) \frac{f(\tau)}{S(t)} \, d\tau = \int_t^\infty \tau \frac{f(\tau)}{S(t)} \, d\tau - t = \frac{1}{S(t)} \int_t^\infty \tau f(\tau) d\tau - t.$$

All mean residual life functions associated with distributions having a finite mean must satisfy three conditions:

$$L(t) \geq 0 \qquad L'(t) \geq -1 \qquad \int_0^\infty \frac{dt}{L(t)} = \infty.$$

Example 3.2

Consider the exponential distribution defined by the survivor function

$$S(t) = e^{-\lambda t} \qquad t \geq 0$$

with positive scale parameter λ. Find the mean residual life function.

By differentiating the survivor function with respect to t and negating, the probability density function is

$$f(t) = \lambda e^{-\lambda t} \qquad t \geq 0.$$

Using the survivor function and the probability density function, the mean residual life function is

$$L(t) = \frac{1}{S(t)} \int_t^\infty \tau f(\tau) d\tau - t = e^{\lambda t} \int_t^\infty \tau \lambda e^{-\lambda \tau} d\tau - t = \frac{1}{\lambda} \qquad t \geq 0$$

by using integration by parts. This indicates that regardless of the age of the item the mean remaining lifetime is always $1/\lambda$.

The five distribution representations are equivalent in the sense that each completely specifies a lifetime distribution. Any one lifetime distribution representation implies the other four. Algebra and calculus can be used to find one lifetime distribution representation given that another is known. For example, if the survivor function is known, the cumulative hazard function can be determined by

$$H(t) = \int_0^t h(\tau) d\tau = \int_0^t \frac{f(\tau)}{S(\tau)} \, d\tau = -\log S(t),$$

where log is the natural logarithm (log base e). The matrix in Table 3.1 shows that any

TABLE 3.1   LIFETIME DISTRIBUTION REPRESENTATION RELATIONSHIPS

	$f(t)$	$S(t)$	$h(t)$	$H(t)$	$L(t)$
$f(t)$	$\bullet$	$\displaystyle\int_t^\infty f(\tau)d\tau$	$\dfrac{f(t)}{\displaystyle\int_t^\infty f(\tau)d\tau}$	$-\log\left[\displaystyle\int_t^\infty f(\tau)d\tau\right]$	$\dfrac{\displaystyle\int_t^\infty \tau f(\tau)d\tau}{\displaystyle\int_t^\infty f(\tau)d\tau} - t$
$S(t)$	$-S'(t)$	$\bullet$	$\dfrac{-S'(t)}{S(t)}$	$-\log S(t)$	$\dfrac{1}{S(t)}\displaystyle\int_t^\infty S(\tau)d\tau$
$h(t)$	$h(t)e^{-\int_0^t h(\tau)d\tau}$	$e^{-\int_0^t h(\tau)d\tau}$	$\bullet$	$\displaystyle\int_0^t h(\tau)d\tau$	$\dfrac{\displaystyle\int_t^\infty e^{-\int_0^\tau h(y)dy}\,d\tau}{e^{-\int_0^t h(\tau)d\tau}}$
$H(t)$	$H'(t)e^{-H(t)}$	$e^{-H(t)}$	$H'(t)$	$\bullet$	$e^{H(t)}\displaystyle\int_t^\infty e^{-H(\tau)}d\tau$
$L(t)$	$\dfrac{1+L'(t)}{L(t)}e^{-\int_0^t \frac{1+L'(\tau)}{L(\tau)}d\tau}$	$e^{-\int_0^t \frac{1+L'(\tau)}{L(\tau)}d\tau}$	$\dfrac{1+L'(t)}{L(t)}$	$\displaystyle\int_0^t \frac{1+L'(\tau)}{L(\tau)}d\tau$	$\bullet$

of the four other lifetime distribution representations (given by the columns) can be found if one of the representations (given by the rows) is known.

Example 3.3

Given $h(t) = 18t$, find $f(t)$.

Using the $(h(t), f(t))$ element of the matrix,

$$f(t) = h(t)\, e^{-\int_0^t h(\tau)\,d\tau} = 18t\, e^{-\int_0^t 18\tau\,d\tau} = 18t\, e^{-9t^2} \qquad t \ge 0,$$

which is a special case of the Weibull distribution with $\lambda = 3$ and $\kappa = 2$.

3.2   DISCRETE DISTRIBUTIONS

Many of the concepts that apply to continuous distributions also apply to discrete distributions. Discrete failure time distributions are applied less frequently than continuous distributions since there are fewer situations for which failures can only occur at discrete points in time.

A situation for which time might be modeled discretely is software reliability. The modeler must determine whether time should be modeled continuously (for example, an operating system) or discretely (for example, a monthly payroll program). If time is measured discretely and the time values correspond to the run number, the run number when failure occurs is the failure time. It can be argued that there is no such thing as a "bug" in a program, and programs just do what they are instructed to do. This philosophy indicates that there is not a problem with the program when it fails, but rather that there is a problem in the data that caused the failure to occur. In either case, the program or the data should be modified so that the program will not fail. The failure rate for a new computer program is usually decreasing over time, since bugs generally become less likely with subsequent runs.

It is not always clear whether a discrete or continuous model should be used. The modeler should consider whether failure can occur at any moment in time (for example, fuse failure, machine breakdown, or fatigue failure for systems operating continuously in time) or only upon demand (for example, a motor that doesn't start, a switch that fails to open, or automobile brakes that fail).

The five lifetime distribution representations apply to discrete distributions as well as continuous distributions. The probability density function will be replaced by the probability mass function, and the names of the other four representations will remain the same. Assume that the nonnegative discrete random variable T may assume the values $t_1, t_2, \ldots$, where $0 \leq t_1 < t_2 < \cdots$. The probability mass function is

$$f(t_j) = P[T = t_j] \qquad j = 1, 2, \ldots,$$

so the survivor function is the left-continuous [that is, for all t and $\varepsilon > 0$, $\lim_{\varepsilon \to 0}[S(t - \varepsilon) - S(t)] = 0$], nonincreasing step function

$$S(t) = P[T \geq t] = \sum_{j \mid t_j \geq t} f(t_j) \qquad t \geq 0.$$

The probability mass function has nonzero mass at the time values $t_1, t_2, \ldots$, while the survivor function is defined for all nonnegative t values. The hazard function is also defined at the discrete points in time $t_1, t_2, \ldots$, and the magnitude of the hazard function is still interpreted as the *risk* at time t_j. Also, since time is discrete, the hazard function is no longer derived as a limit:

$$h(t_j) = P[T = t_j \mid T \geq t_j] = \frac{P[T = t_j]}{P[T \geq t_j]} = \frac{f(t_j)}{S(t_j)} \qquad j = 1, 2, \ldots.$$

A dilemma is encountered when attempting to define the cumulative hazard function when time is discrete. Two possible, but different, choices for the definition are

$$H(t) = -\log S(t) \qquad t \geq 0,$$

or

$$H(t) = \sum_{j \mid t_j \leq t} h(t_j) \qquad t \geq 0.$$

The first definition parallels the relationship established in the continuous case, and the second definition accumulates the hazard function as it evolves over time. The first definition will be used, although the two are very close when the probability mass function values are small. Thus, the cumulative hazard function, $H(t) = -\log S(t)$, is a left-continuous, nondecreasing step function. The mean residual life function is defined as before:

$$L(t) = E[T - t \,|\, T \geq t] \qquad t \geq 0,$$

which is calculated by

$$L(t) = \frac{1}{S(t)} \left[\sum_{j \mid t_j \geq t} t_j \, f(t_j) \right] - t \qquad t \geq 0.$$

Since the mean residual life function is defined for all $t \geq 0$, and everything in the expression except t is constant between mass function values, the mean residual life function decreases with a slope of -1 at all time values for which there is no mass.

Example 3.4

Consider the geometric distribution defined by the probability mass function

$$f(t_j) = p(1 - p)^{j-1} \qquad j = 1, 2, \ldots.$$

The geometric distribution models the trial number of the first failure in repeated independent Bernoulli trials, where p is the probability of failure on each trial. Find the survivor function, hazard function, cumulative hazard function, and mean residual life function. Note that $t_j = j$ for this distribution.

The survivor function is

$$S(t) = P[T \geq t] = \sum_{j \mid t_j \geq t} f(t_j) = \sum_{j \mid t_j \geq t} p(1 - p)^{j-1} \qquad t \geq 0.$$

Letting k be the smallest j such that $t_j \geq t$ (that is, the lower limit of the summation), this expression simplifies to

$$S(t) = p(1 - p)^{k-1} + p(1 - p)^{k} + \cdots$$

$$= (1 - p)^{k-1} \qquad t \geq 0,$$

which is a left-continuous step function with decreasing step sizes. The hazard function is

$$h(t_j) = \frac{f(t_j)}{S(t_j)} = \frac{p(1 - p)^{j-1}}{(1 - p)^{j-1}} = p \qquad j = 1, 2, \ldots.$$

Since the hazard function is independent of time, the geometric distribution is memoryless from one t_j value to the next. The geometric distribution is the only discrete distribution with the memoryless property. The cumulative hazard function is

$$H(t) = -\log S(t) = -(k-1)\log(1-p) \qquad t \geq 0$$

where k is the smallest j such that $t_j \geq t$. Finally, several steps of algebra yield the mean residual life function:

$$L(t) = E[T - t \mid T \geq t] = \frac{1}{p} - (t - \lfloor t \rfloor) \qquad t \geq 0$$

where $\lfloor t \rfloor$ is the greatest integer less than t. A graph of the mean residual life function will have a sawtooth appearance, as shown in the diagrams of the five lifetime distribution representations shown in Figure 3.6 for $p = 0.4$.

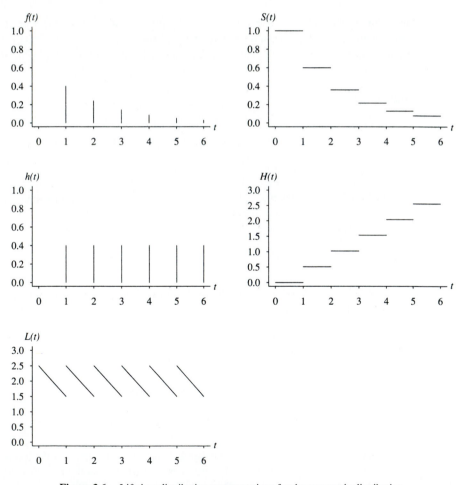

Figure 3.6   Lifetime distribution representations for the geometric distribution.

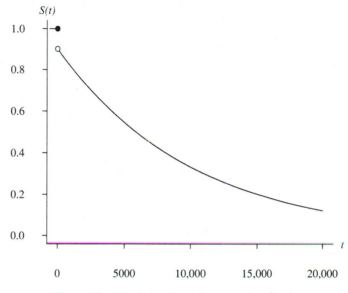

Figure 3.7   Mixed discrete-continuous survivor function.

Situations exist that are appropriately modeled by a mixed discrete–continuous distribution. Upon manufacturing a fuse, for example, 10% of the fuses may fail immediately due to manufacturing defects, while the remainder have an exponential time to failure with a mean of 10,000 hours. In this particular situation, the survivor function is $S(t) = 0.9\, e^{-t/10,000}$ for $t > 0$ having a discrete jump at $t = 0$, as shown in Figure 3.7.

3.3   MOMENTS AND FRACTILES

Once a lifetime distribution representation for a particular item (which may be a component or an entire system) is known, it may be of interest to compute a moment or a fractile of the distribution. Moments and fractiles contain less information than a lifetime distribution representation, but they are often useful ways to summarize the distribution of a random lifetime. Examples of these performance measures include the mean time to failure, $E(T)$, the median, $t_{0.50}$, and the 95th percentile of a distribution, $t_{0.95}$. The random lifetime T is assumed to be a continuous nonnegative random variable in this section. Analogous formulas exist for discrete lifetimes.

A formula for the expectation of some function of the random variable T, say $u(T)$, is

$$E[u(T)] = \int_{0}^{\infty} u(t)\, f(t)\, dt.$$

The most common measure associated with a distribution is its *mean*, or first moment,

$$\mu = E[T] = \int_0^\infty tf(t)\, dt = \int_0^\infty S(t)\, dt$$

where the last equality is proved using integration by parts and is based on the assumption that $\lim_{t \to \infty} tS(t) = 0$. The mean is a measure of the central tendency or average value that a lifetime distribution assumes and is known as the center of gravity in physics. It is often abbreviated by MTTF (mean time to failure) for nonrepairable items. For repairable items that can be completely renewed by repair, it is often abbreviated by MTBF (mean time between failures). Two other measures of central tendency are the *median* [the value m satisfying $S(m) = 0.5$] and the *mode* (the time value at which the probability density function achieves a maximum). Another value associated with a distribution is its *variance*, or second moment about the mean,

$$\sigma^2 = V[T] = E[(T - \mu)^2] = E[T^2] - (E[T])^2,$$

which is a measure of the dispersion of a lifetime distribution. The positive square root of the variance is known as the *standard deviation*, which has the same units as the random variable T. One drawback of using the variance or standard deviation to measure the dispersion of a distribution is that these quantities depend on the *scale* (for example, hours or minutes) of measurement used. One way to overcome this scale problem is to consider the coefficient of variation

$$\gamma = \frac{\sigma}{\mu},$$

which is dimensionless. Two problems associated with the coefficient of variation are that it assumes different values for populations having identical variability, but different means, and it is undefined when $\mu = 0$, although this is typically not an issue with lifetime distributions. Another moment of interest is the standardized third central moment, often called the *skewness*:

$$\gamma_3 = E\left[\left(\frac{T - \mu}{\sigma}\right)^3\right],$$

which is a measure of the symmetry of a distribution. Finally, the *kurtosis*, or the standardized fourth central moment, is defined by

$$\gamma_4 = E\left[\left(\frac{T - \mu}{\sigma}\right)^4\right],$$

which is a measure of the peakedness or the tail behavior of a distribution.

Fractiles of a distribution are the times to which a specified proportion of the items survives. The definition of the pth fractile of a distribution, t_p, (often called the pth quantile or $100p$th percentile) satisfies

$$F(t_p) = P[T \le t_p] = p,$$

or, equivalently,

$$t_p = F^{-1}(p).$$

Example 3.5

The exponential distribution has survivor function

$$S(t) = e^{-\lambda t}, \qquad t \ge 0.$$

Find the mean, variance, skewness and the pth fractile of the distribution.

The mean can be found by integrating the survivor function from 0 to infinity:

$$\mu = E[T] = \int_0^\infty S(t)\, dt = \int_0^\infty e^{-\lambda t}\, dt = \frac{1}{\lambda}.$$

Since the probability density function is $f(t) = -S'(t) = \lambda e^{-\lambda t}$ for $t \ge 0$, the second moment is

$$E[T^2] = \int_0^\infty t^2 f(t)\, dt = \int_0^\infty t^2 \lambda e^{-\lambda t}\, dt = \frac{2}{\lambda^2},$$

using integration by parts twice. Therefore, the variance is

$$\sigma^2 = V[T] = E[T^2] - (E[T])^2 = \frac{2}{\lambda^2} - \frac{1}{\lambda^2} = \frac{1}{\lambda^2}.$$

The skewness is most easily computed by cubing the argument in the definition:

$$\gamma_3 = E\left[\left(\frac{T - \mu}{\sigma} \right)^3 \right] = \sigma^{-3} \left[E[T^3] - 3\mu E[T^2] + 3\mu^2 E[T] - \mu^3 \right].$$

Since $E[T^3] = 6\lambda^{-3}$ for the exponential distribution, the skewness is

$$\gamma_3 = \lambda^3 \left[6\lambda^{-3} - 6\lambda^{-3} + 3\lambda^{-3} - \lambda^{-3} \right] = 2.$$

Finally, the pth fractile of the distribution, t_p, is found by solving

$$1 - e^{-\lambda t_p} = p$$

for t_p. This yields $t_p = -\frac{1}{\lambda} \log(1 - p)$.

Fractiles can be useful in the analysis of the costs associated with warranties, as illustrated in Example 3.6.

Example 3.6

An automobile manufacturer knows that the distribution of the time to the first failure of a particular engine in average driving conditions follows a Weibull distribution with $\lambda = 0.0000077$ and $\kappa = 1.22$, where time is measured in miles. Find the warranty period that would allow 1% of the engines to fail during the warranty period.

To find $t_{0.01}$, the cumulative distribution function for the Weibull distribution should be equated to 0.01:

$$1 - e^{-(\lambda t_{0.01})^{\kappa}} = 0.01.$$

Solving this equation for $t_{0.01}$ yields a warranty period of

$$t_{0.01} = \frac{1}{\lambda} \left[-\log 0.99 \right]^{1/\kappa} = \frac{1}{0.0000077} \left[-\log 0.99 \right]^{1/1.22} = 2992.$$

Thus, a warranty period of 3000 miles results in approximately 1% of the engines requiring maintenance or replacement during the warranty period. This information, along with the average cost for the company to handle a warranty claim, is an important consideration in determining a price for an automobile that includes the cost of servicing warranty claims.

3.4   SYSTEM LIFETIME DISTRIBUTIONS

To this point, the discussion on the five lifetime representations $S(t)$, $f(t)$, $h(t)$, $H(t)$, and $L(t)$ has assumed that the variable of interest is the *lifetime* of an *item*. For systems of components, both the individual components and the system have random lifetimes whose lifetime distributions can be defined by any of the five lifetime distributions. This section integrates reliability functions from Chapter 2 and the lifetime distribution representations from this chapter, which allows a modeler to find the distribution of the system lifetime, given the distributions of the component lifetimes. The component lifetime representations are denoted by $S_i(t)$, $f_i(t)$, $h_i(t)$, $H_i(t)$, and $L_i(t)$, for $i = 1, 2, \ldots, n$, and the system lifetime representations are denoted by $S(t)$, $f(t)$, $h(t)$, $H(t)$, and $L(t)$.

The survivor function is a time-dependent generalization of reliability from Chapter 2. Whereas reliability always needs an associated time value (for example, the 1000-hour reliability is 0.8), the survivor function gives the reliability at any time t, as shown in the plot of $S(t)$ in Figure 3.8.

To find the reliability of a system at any time t, the component survivor functions should be used as arguments in the reliability function:

$$S(t) = r(S_1(t), S_2(t), \ldots, S_n(t)).$$

Once $S(t)$ is known, it is straightforward to determine any of the other four lifetime representations, moments, or fractiles, as illustrated in the following examples.

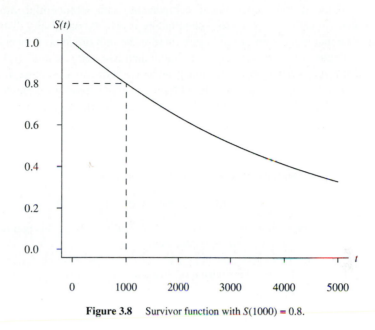

Figure 3.8   Survivor function with $S(1000) = 0.8$.

Example 3.7

Two independent components are arranged in series. The lifetimes of the two components have hazard functions

$$h_1(t) = 1 \quad \text{and} \quad h_2(t) = 2 \quad t \geq 0.$$

Find the survivor and hazard functions for the system lifetime.

The first step in finding the system survivor function is to find the survivor functions of the two components. Using Table 3.1, the survivor functions are

$$S_1(t) = e^{-t} \quad \text{and} \quad S_2(t) = e^{-2t} \quad t \geq 0.$$

Since the reliability function for a two-component series system is $r(\mathbf{p}) = p_1 p_2$, the system survivor function is

$$S(t) = S_1(t) S_2(t)$$
$$= e^{-t} e^{-2t}$$
$$= e^{-3t} \quad t \geq 0,$$

which can be recognized as the survivor function for an exponential distribution with $\lambda = 3$. To find the hazard function for the system, Table 3.1 can again be used to determine that

$$h(t) = 3 \quad t \geq 0.$$

Thus, if two independent components with exponential times to failure are arranged in series, the time to system failure is also exponentially distributed with a failure rate that is the sum of the failure rates of the individual components. This result can be generalized to series systems with more than two components. If the lifetime of component i in a series system of n independent components has an exponential distribution with failure rate λ_i, then the system lifetime is exponentially distributed with failure rate $\sum_{i=1}^{n} \lambda_i$. The next example considers a parallel system of components having exponential lifetimes.

Example 3.8

Two independent components have hazard functions

$$h_1(t) = 1 \quad \text{and} \quad h_2(t) = 2 \qquad t \geq 0.$$

If the components are arranged in parallel, find the hazard function of the time to system failure and the mean time to system failure.

As before, the survival functions of the components are $S_1(t) = e^{-t}$ and $S_2(t) = e^{-2t}$ for $t \geq 0$. Since the reliability function for a two-component parallel system is $r(\mathbf{p}) = 1 - (1 - p_1)(1 - p_2)$, the system survivor function is

$$S(t) = 1 - (1 - S_1(t))(1 - S_2(t))$$

$$= 1 - (1 - e^{-t})(1 - e^{-2t})$$

$$= e^{-t} + e^{-2t} - e^{-3t} \qquad t \geq 0.$$

To find the hazard function for the system, the relationship $h(t) = -S'(t)/S(t)$ is used:

$$h(t) = \frac{e^{-t} + 2e^{-2t} - 3e^{-3t}}{e^{-t} + e^{-2t} - e^{-3t}} \qquad t \geq 0.$$

To find the mean time to system failure, the system survivor function is integrated from 0 to infinity:

$$\mu = \int_0^{\infty} S(t)dt = \int_0^{\infty} (e^{-t} + e^{-2t} - e^{-3t})dt = 1 + \frac{1}{2} - \frac{1}{3} = \frac{7}{6}.$$

The mean time to failure of the stronger component is 1 and the mean time to failure of the weaker component is 1/2. The addition of the weaker component in parallel with the stronger only increases the mean time to system failure by 1/6. This is yet another illustration of the law of diminishing returns for parallel systems.

3.5 DISTRIBUTION CLASSES

Various *distribution classes* have been defined to distinguish sets of distributions from one another by certain properties of their failure time distributions. Although many classifications have been suggested by researchers, only four of them are discussed in this section: IFR (increasing failure rate), DFR (decreasing failure rate), IFRA (increasing failure rate on the average), and DFRA (decreasing failure rate on the average). An interesting result concerning the distribution of the system lifetime when all the components of a coherent system have IFRA distributions is given.

One simple way of classifying a lifetime distribution for a nonrepairable item is based on whether the hazard function increases for all t.

Definition 3.1   A lifetime distribution is IFR (DFR) if $h(t)$ is nondecreasing (nonincreasing) in t.

The loose usage of the term *increasing* in IFR (since IFR distributions have *nondecreasing* hazard functions) allows a distribution with a constant hazard function, the exponential distribution, to serve as a boundary between the two classes. The exponential distribution's hazard function $h(t) = \lambda$ is both nondecreasing and nonincreasing for all t, so it belongs to both the IFR and DFR classes. As shown in the Venn diagram in Figure 3.9, this definition of IFR and DFR classifies all lifetime distributions into one of four sets: a constant hazard function (that is, the intersection of IFR and DFR), strictly increasing hazard functions, strictly decreasing hazard functions, and other hazard functions (such as bathtub-shaped hazard functions).

A question of interest relating to distribution classes is the effect of various operations on lifetimes belonging to a class. One effect that can be observed is whether the distribution classifications are retained after an operation is performed on the lifetimes, often called *closure*. Assume that $T_1, T_2, \ldots, T_n$ are independent lifetimes that belong to a distribution class such as IFR. There are several choices for operations to be performed on these random lifetimes. One possibility is to consider their sum $T = T_1 + T_2 + \cdots + T_n$ and ask if T still belongs to the same distribution class as $T_1, T_2, \ldots, T_n$. This model would be appropriate, for example, if the interest was in modeling the lifetime of a system of n identical devices used in a passive standby system in which each failed item is immediately replaced with another item upon failure. A second possibility is to consider a *mixture* of the n random variables:

$$S(t) = p_1 S_1(t) + p_2 S_2(t) + \cdots + p_n S_n(t),$$

where $p_1 + p_2 + \cdots + p_n = 1$, and T_i has survivor function $S_i(t)$, for $i = 1, 2, \ldots, n$.

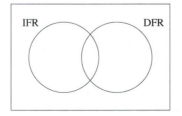

Figure 3.9   Venn diagram for IFR and DFR distribution classes.

This model would be appropriate for an item selected from one of n populations with survivor functions $S_1(t), \ldots, S_n(t)$, where the probability of selection from population i is p_i, and an item is not identified with respect to the population that it came from. As a third example of an operation, let $T_1, T_2, \ldots, T_n$ be the lifetimes of n components in the same distribution class in a coherent system with lifetime T. Again, a question of interest is whether or not the system lifetime is in the same distribution class as the component lifetimes. Finally, a distribution class may be closed with respect to scale. For example, if T is in a particular distribution class, and kT, where k is a positive constant, is also in the class, then the class is closed with respect to scale.

The question that will be examined for the rest of this section is whether the system lifetime of a coherent system of n components, each having IFR distributions, is IFR itself. Stated another way, if all components in a coherent system degrade (wear out) with time, does the system degrade with time? Although intuition indicates that the answer is *yes*, it will be seen by a simple counterexample that the answer is *no*. A class can be defined, however, that is preserved under the formation of coherent systems. This class is IFRA.

Example 3.9

We have already encountered an example of the formation of a coherent system of two components with IFR distributions in Example 3.8. In that case, the two components with hazard functions

$$h_1(t) = 1 \quad \text{and} \quad h_2(t) = 2 \qquad t \geq 0,$$

were placed in parallel. Since both of these hazard functions are nondecreasing, both components belong to the IFR class. As shown in Example 3.8, the hazard function for T, the system lifetime, is

$$h(t) = \frac{e^{-t} + 2e^{-2t} - 3e^{-3t}}{e^{-t} + e^{-2t} - e^{-3t}} \qquad t \geq 0.$$

This hazard function plotted over time is shown in Figure 3.10. Surprisingly, the hazard function is not monotonic! This runs against intuition, since we would expect that a system of components that do not improve with time would have a hazard function that increases for all t.

The reason for the fact that the system lifetime in Example 3.9 is not also IFR is explained in terms of mixture distributions. The system lifetime in question has two events of interest: the first component failure and the second component failure, which results in system failure. Let $X_1 = \min\{T_1, T_2\}$ be the time to the first failure, and let $X_2 = \max\{T_1, T_2\} - X_1$ be the time between the first and second failures, as shown in Figure 3.11. The system lifetime T is the sum of X_1 and X_2. Since X_1 is the minimum of an exponential with $\lambda = 1$ and an exponential with $\lambda = 2$, X_1 is also an exponential random variable with $\lambda = 3$, as shown in Example 3.7.

The distribution of X_2, the time between the first and second failures, is independent of X_1 since the surviving component has an exponential distribution that is

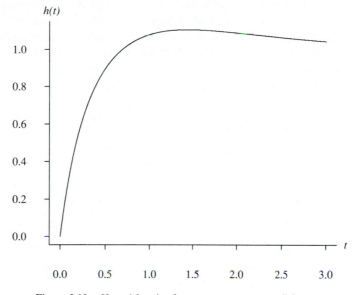

Figure 3.10   Hazard function for a two-component parallel system.

memoryless (see Chapter 4). The distribution of X_2 is a mixture of two random variables. The probability that component number 1 (the better component) is the first to fail (that is, $P[T_1 < T_2]$) is $1/3$. This may be found either by computing a double integral over the joint probability density function of T_1 and T_2 or by determining the distribution of $T_1 - T_2$ and computing the probability that this random variable is negative. The derivation of this result is given in Section 5.1. Therefore, the survivor function of X_2 is the mixture

$$S_{X_2}(x_2) = \frac{1}{3} e^{-x_2} + \frac{2}{3} e^{-2x_2} \qquad x_2 \geq 0,$$

which has corresponding hazard function

$$h_{X_2}(x_2) = \frac{-S'_{X_2}(x_2)}{S_{X_2}(x_2)} = \frac{e^{-x_2} + 4e^{-2x_2}}{e^{-x_2} + 2e^{-2x_2}} \qquad x_2 \geq 0,$$

which decreases in x_2 and hence is in the DFR class.

Figure 3.11   Failure sequence for a two-component parallel system.

The derivation of the distributions of X_1 and X_2 given in the two previous paragraphs indicates why the system lifetime in Example 3.9 is not IFR. As time passes, it is more likely that one component has failed. If one component has failed, the remaining time to failure, X_2, has a mixture distribution that is DFR. This is why the hazard function for the system lifetime decreases for large values of t.

Since Example 3.9 has shown that the system lifetime of a coherent system of components all having IFR distributions is not necessarily IFR itself, the question of whether there is a distribution class that is closed under the formation of coherent systems arises. There is such a class, and it is called IFRA (increasing failure rate on the average). The components and the system in Example 3.9 are members of the IFRA class.

Definition 3.2   A failure time distribution is IFRA (DFRA) if $H(t)/t$ is nondecreasing (nonincreasing) in t.

There are many ways to classify distributions other than IFR, DFR, IFRA, and DFRA. These other distribution classes are based on properties of one of the lifetime distribution representations [for example, a distribution is IMRL (increasing mean residual life) if $L(t)$ is nondecreasing for all t]. References that discuss these other distribution classes are given in the next section.

3.6   FURTHER READING

As indicated in the section on lifetime distribution representations, there are many more ways than $S(t)$, $f(t)$, $h(t)$, $H(t)$, and $L(t)$ to define the distribution of a lifetime. Other possibilities include the Mellin transform (Moschopoulos, 1983), the moment generating function (Hogg and Craig, 1995), the total time on test transform (Barlow, 1979, and Csorgo et al., 1986), and the density quantile function (Parzen, 1979). The existence conditions on the mean residual life function are given in Swartz (1973). Practically all the textbooks on reliability, biostatistics, or actuarial science discuss the lifetime distribution representations given in Section 3.1.

A discussion of the lifetime distribution representations for discrete distributions is given in Cox and Oakes (1984), Kalbfleisch and Prentice (1980), and Lawless (1982). There are added problems when a lifetime distribution has a *mixed* distribution (part discrete and part continuous), which are addressed by these authors. Kalbfleisch and Prentice (1980, p. 8) give the survivor function for a mixed distribution as

$$S(t) = e^{-H_C(t)} \prod_{j \mid t_j < t} (1 - h_D(t_j)) \qquad t \geq 0,$$

where $H_C(t)$ is the cumulative hazard function for the continuous part of the distribution and $h_D(t)$ is the hazard function for the discrete part of the distribution.

All texts on survival analysis include a discussion of moments. Cox and Oakes (1984) include a plot of the coefficient of variation versus the skewness for several popular distributions. This plot is useful in discriminating among several distributions for modeling a lifetime. Other authors have also plotted the skewness against the kurtosis in order to discriminate among several distributions for modeling a lifetime. A review of the interpretation of the kurtosis is given in Balanda and MacGillivray (1988). Two inequalities are useful when only one or two moments of a distribution are known. The *Markov inequality* (Trivedi, 1982, p. 223) states that

$$S(t) = P[T \geq t] \leq \frac{\mu}{t}$$

when μ is finite. *Chebyshev's inequality* (Trivedi, 1982, p. 226) states that

$$P[|T - \mu| < k\sigma] \geq 1 - \frac{1}{k^2}$$

for finite μ and σ and any $k > 0$.

Barlow and Proschan (1981), Crowder et al. (1991), Gertsbakh (1989), Goldberg (1981), Grosh (1989), Henley and Kumamoto (1981), Kapur and Lamberson (1977), Kaufmann et al. (1977), Kececioglu (1991), Klaassen and van Peppen (1989), Klinger et al. (1990), Lewis (1987), Zacks (1992), and others include discussions on determining the lifetime distribution of a system from the lifetime distributions of the components.

There is a multitude of lifetime distribution classes such as IFR (increasing failure rate), IFRA (increasing failure rate on the average), NBU (new better than used), NBUE (new better than used in expectation), NBAFR (new better than used average failure rate), DMRL (decreasing mean residual life), and HNBUE (harmonic new better than used in expectation). There is a corresponding complementary class for each mentioned above (DFR, DFRA, NWU, NWUE, NWAFR, IMRL, and HNWUE). These classes are referenced in Abouammoh (1988), Barlow and Proschan (1981), and Loh (1984). Ross (1993) gave the explanation of why the system lifetime of a parallel system of two IFR components is not itself IFR. The IFRA closure theorem is given in Barlow and Proschan (1981). Proschan (1963) uses the fact that a mixture of exponential items has a DFR distribution in the analysis of airplane air-conditioner failure times.

One important topic that has not been presented here is *reliability growth*. An item may have an initial distribution for its time to failure that improves as the item undergoes refinement in design and changes in components due to experience gained in the use of the item. Reliability growth references are given in the Further Reading section of Chapter 6, since these models are typically applied to repairable systems.

3.7 EXERCISES

3.1. Show that $f(0) = h(0)$ for a continuous lifetime T.

3.2. Richard is going on a 1-hour space walk. He has a choice between two life-support systems. Life-support system 1 has a Weibull lifetime with $\lambda = 1$ and $\kappa = 2$, and life-support system 2 has a Weibull lifetime with $\lambda = 1$ and $\kappa = 3$. Assuming that time is measured in hours and the Weibull survivor function is

$$S(t) = e^{-(\lambda t)^\kappa} \qquad t \geq 0; \lambda > 0, \kappa > 0,$$

which life-support system should Richard choose? Explain your reasoning.

3.3. Richard is going on another 1-hour space walk. He has a choice between two *used* life-support systems. Life-support system 1 has a Weibull lifetime with $\lambda = 1$ and $\kappa = 2$, and the Weibull survivor function is

$$S(t) = e^{-(\lambda t)^\kappa} \qquad t \geq 0; \lambda > 0, \kappa > 0.$$

Life-support system 1 has been used for 1 hour without failure. Life-support system 2 has an exponential lifetime with $\lambda = 2$, and the survivor function for the exponential distribution is

$$S(t) = e^{-\lambda t} \qquad t \geq 0; \lambda > 0.$$

Life-support system 2 has been used for 3.17 hours without failure. Assuming that time is measured in hours, which life-support system should Richard choose? Explain your reasoning.

3.4. Let $t^* > 0$ be the mode value for a continuous lifetime T. Show that $h'(t^*) = [h(t^*)]^2$.

3.5. The probability that an item will survive a 1000-hour mission is 0.4. If the item is operating 800 hours into the mission, the probability of surviving the remaining 200 hours of the mission is 0.85. What is the probability that the item survives the initial 800 hours of the mission?

3.6. Figure 3.12 shows the hazard function for a continuous random variable measured in hours. (a) Find $S(4)$. (b) Find $S(10)$. (c) Find $f(10)$.

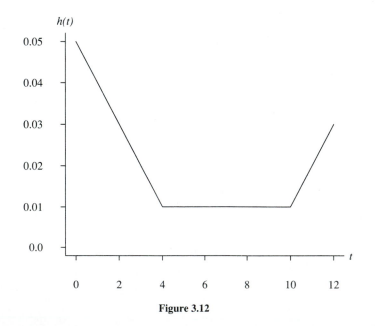

Figure 3.12

3.7. A component has a mean residual life function

$$L(t) = 3t + 1 \qquad t \geq 0.$$

Find the probability that the component survives to time 14.

3.8. Draw the survivor function corresponding to the probability density function shown in Figure 3.13. Use a straight edge whenever the function is linear. The rectangles and triangle on the probability density function all have an area of $1/3$.

3.9. Consider the hazard function

$$h(t) = \alpha + e^{\beta t} \qquad t \geq 0.$$

What conditions must the parameters α and β meet for $h(t)$ to be a legitimate hazard function for a random lifetime T?

3.10. The hazard function for pilots during a flight is bathtub shaped. Explain what is meant by this statement. Will the hazard function integrate to infinity? Refer to the issues raised in Exercise 3.9.

3.11. Consider the Weibull distribution defined by

$$S(t) = e^{-(\lambda t)^{\kappa}} \qquad t \geq 0.$$

Find the conditional survivor function.

3.12. Show that the appropriate way to find $h(t)$, given that $L(t)$ is

$$h(t) = \frac{1 + L'(t)}{L(t)} \qquad t \geq 0.$$

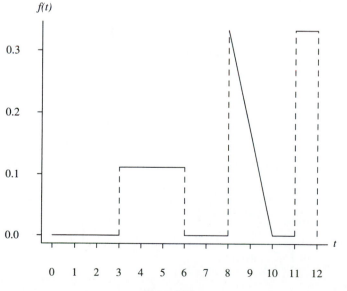

Figure 3.13

3.13. The Weibull distribution has survivor function

$$S(t) = e^{-(\lambda t)^{\kappa}} \qquad t \geq 0.$$

Find the probability density function, the hazard function, the cumulative hazard function, and the mean residual life function. Simplify the mean residual life function so that it is expressed in terms of the gamma function and the incomplete gamma function, which are described in Appendix B.

3.14. (Cox and Oakes, 1984, p. 46) Let the random lifetime T have a continuous survivor function $S(t)$, and cumulative hazard function $H(t)$, and $X = \min\{T, c\}$, where c is a constant. Show that $E[H(X)] = 1 - S(c)$.

3.15. The expected value of the residual life,

$$L(t) = E[T - t \mid T \geq t],$$

is only one measure that can be derived from the distribution of the residual life. Others include the variance of the residual life or a fractile of the residual life.

    (a) Find the variance of the residual life of an item with an exponential lifetime having survivor function $S(t) = e^{-\lambda t}$ for $t \geq 0$.

    (b) Find the median of the residual life of an item with an exponential lifetime.

    (c) Find the median of the residual life of an item with a Weibull lifetime having survivor function $S(t) = e^{-(\lambda t)^{\kappa}}$ for $t \geq 0$.

3.16. Find the five distribution representations for a random variable T that is uniformly distributed between 0 and 1. Plot each on a separate axis.

3.17. An economist named Pareto modeled the distribution of incomes by the probability density function

$$f(t) = \frac{\lambda^{\kappa} \kappa}{t^{\kappa + 1}} \qquad t \geq \lambda,$$

for positive parameters λ and κ.

    (a) Find $S(t)$, $h(t)$, $H(t)$, and $L(t)$.

    (b) Plot all these functions when $\lambda = 3$ and $\kappa = 4$.

    (c) Find the Mellin transform, $E[T^{s}]$.

    (d) Muth (1977, p. 415) suggests replacing an item when $L(t)/L(0) = q$, where q is some small fraction. Find the t value in the Pareto distribution where $L(t)/L(0) = 0.15$. Explain the intuition behind Muth's replacement policy.

3.18. (Swartz, 1973) For a continuous random lifetime with a finite mean, show that

    (a) $L'(t) \geq -1$.

    (b) $S(t) = \dfrac{L(0)}{L(t)} e^{-\int_0^t \frac{1}{L(\tau)} d\tau}$.

    (c) $\displaystyle\int_0^{\infty} \frac{dt}{L(t)}$ diverges.

3.19. (Lawless, 1982, p. 44) If T is a continuous random lifetime, show that

$$\lim_{t \to \infty} L(t) = \lim_{t \to \infty} \left(-\frac{d}{dt} \log f(t) \right)^{-1}$$

where $L(t)$ is the mean residual life function and $f(t)$ is the probability density function.

3.20. (Barlow, 1979) The total time on test transform for a continuous, nonnegative random variable T is defined by

$$H_{F^{-1}}(u) = \int_0^{F^{-1}(u)} S(t)\,dt$$

where $S(t)$ is the survivor function and $F^{-1}(u)$ is the inverse cumulative distribution function. Find the total time on test transform for the exponential distribution

$$f(t) = \lambda e^{-\lambda t} \qquad t \geq 0,$$

and the Pareto distribution

$$f(t) = \frac{\lambda^\kappa \kappa}{t^{\kappa+1}} \qquad t \geq \lambda.$$

Note that the lower limit for the total time on test transform for the Pareto distribution will be λ.

3.21. Gaver and Acar (1979, p. 106) give the hazard function

$$h(t) = \frac{a}{t+\alpha} + bt + \lambda \qquad t \geq 0;\, a > 0,\, \alpha > 0,\, b > 0,\, \lambda > 0.$$

What is the survivor function for such a distribution?

3.22. Show that for a discrete lifetime distribution

$$H(t) = -\log S(t) = -\sum_{j|t_j < t} \log(1 - h(t_j)).$$

3.23. For the discrete distribution with positive parameter c and probability mass function

$$f(t) = 1 \qquad t = c$$

where $c > 0$, find and graph the survivor function, the hazard function, the cumulative hazard function, and the mean residual life function.

3.24. Show that the geometric distribution has the memoryless property at its mass values.

3.25. Construct a 4×4 transition matrix that determines any one of $f(t)$, $S(t)$, $h(t)$, or $H(t)$ from any of the others for a discrete lifetime distribution. If the expression is not in closed form, write an expression that, when solved, will yield the required lifetime distribution representation.

3.26. Show that the mean residual life for the geometric distribution is

$$L(t) = \frac{1}{p} - (t - \lfloor t \rfloor).$$

3.27. Define the discrete random variable $N = \lceil T \rceil$, where T has a continuous lifetime distribution with constant hazard function $h(t) = \lambda$, the exponential distribution. This would be appropriate when the interest is in the cycle number of failure for an exponential component.

(a) What type of distribution does N have?

(b) Find $E[N]$.

3.28. Find the probability mass function $f(t)$ for the mean residual life function plotted in Figure 3.14. Note that $L(0) = 3.8$ and all lines have a slope of -1.

3.29. Let T be a random lifetime with cumulative hazard function

$$H(t) = \begin{cases} kt & 0 \le t \le 1, \\ t^2/2 & t > 1, \end{cases}$$

where k is a positive constant. Find the value of k such that T is strictly continuous.

3.30. A light bulb on a sign at a movie theater is turned off 1 second then on 1 second alternately. The lifetime of the light bulb is a mixed discrete–continuous distribution with a hazard function as shown in Figure 3.15, where time is measured in seconds. The discrete portions of the lifetime distribution occur at the illumination times $t = 1, 3, 5, \ldots$, and the continuous portions occur on the intervals $(1, 2)$, $(3, 4)$, $(5, 6)$, $\ldots$. Draw $S(t)$ on $(0, 6)$ and find $S(5)$.

3.31. Show that $E[T] = \int_0^\infty t f(t)\, dt$ can also be found by $E[T] = \int_0^\infty S(t)\, dt$ for any continuous nonnegative random variable T with a finite mean. Assume that $\lim_{t \to \infty} t\, S(t) = 0$.

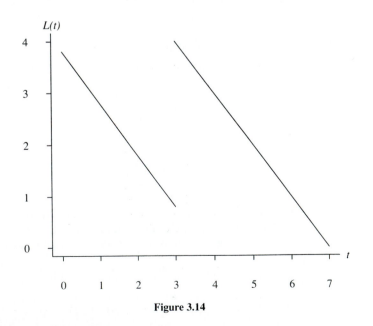

Figure 3.14

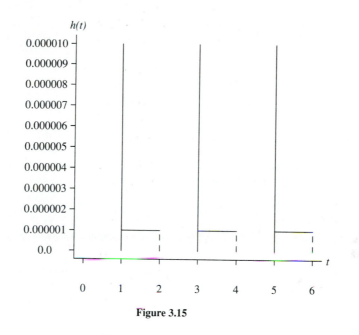

Figure 3.15

3.32. Let $T_{(1)}, T_{(2)}, \ldots, T_{(n)}$ be order statistics from a population with survivor function $S(t)$. Find $P[T_{(i)} \geq t]$ and $E[T_{(i)}]$ for $i = 1, 2, \ldots, n$.

3.33. Consider a series system of n independent components, each with a uniform time to failure between 0 and θ.
  (a) Find the median of the system lifetime distribution.
  (b) Find the expected system lifetime.

3.34. A manufacturer receives 10,000 components, each with a lifetime distribution with probability density function

$$f(t) = \frac{4}{t^5} \qquad t \geq 1.$$

What is the expected number of components that will still be functioning at $t = 3$? What is the variance of the number of components that will still be functioning at $t = 3$?

3.35. A population of nonrepairable items has a time to failure that follows the survivor function $S(t)$. If the items are burned in for b time units at typical operating conditions, find
  (a) an expression for the fraction of items that fail during the burn-in test.
  (b) an expression for the median residual lifetime of those items that survive the burn-in test.

3.36. Consider a system of three components with exponential lifetimes arranged as shown in Figure 3.16. If the first component lifetime is exponential with mean $1/\lambda_1$, the second component lifetime is exponential with mean $1/\lambda_2$, and the third component lifetime is exponential with mean $1/\lambda_3$, find the system survivor function and the expected system lifetime.

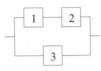

Figure 3.16

3.37. Two components are arranged in parallel. The first component has an exponential time to failure and the second has a Weibull time to failure. Find the survivor function and hazard function for the system time to failure. The survivor functions for the exponential and Weibull distributions are

$$S(t) = e^{-\lambda_1 t} \quad \text{and} \quad S(t) = e^{-(\lambda_2 t)^{\kappa}} \qquad t \geq 0,$$

where the subscripts have been added to differentiate between the two scale parameters λ_1 and λ_2.

3.38. Three exponential components are arranged as shown in Figure 3.17. The first component has a constant hazard function $h_1(t) = 0.00001$ failure per hour and the second component has a constant hazard function $h_2(t) = 0.00002$ failure per hour. What must the constant hazard function of the third component, $h_3(t) = \lambda_3$, be to achieve a 1-year system reliability of 0.98.

3.39. (Ross, 1993, p. 455) Assume that component 1 has a $U(0, 1)$ lifetime distribution and that component 2 has a $U(0, 2)$ lifetime distribution. Find the expected time to system failure if the two components are arranged in series.

3.40. Show that the mean time to failure of a parallel system of n identical components, each with an exponential time to failure with mean $1/\lambda$, is

$$\frac{1}{\lambda}\left(1 + \frac{1}{2} + \frac{1}{3} + \cdots + \frac{1}{n}\right).$$

3.41. (Ross, 1993, pp. 435–436) Show that if each component in an n-component coherent system has the same IFR lifetime distribution then the system life will be IFR if $pr'(p)/r(p)$ is a decreasing function of p.

3.42. (Ross, 1993, p. 454) The survivor function for the remaining lifetime of an item that has survived to time a is

$$S_{T-a|T \geq a}(t) = P[T - a \geq t | T \geq a], \qquad t \geq 0.$$

Figure 3.17

A distribution is IFR if this survivor function decreases in a for all t. Show that this definition is equivalent to the definition of IFR based on the hazard function $h(t)$.

3.43. Show that IFR implies IFRA.

3.44. Show that the condition

$$H(t + x) \geq H(t) + H(x) \qquad \text{for any } t \geq 0, \, x \geq 0,$$

implies that an item is NBU. An item is NBU if

$$S(t + x) \leq S(t) \, S(x) \qquad \text{for any } t \geq 0, \, x \geq 0.$$

This condition, which implies that the cumulative hazard functions are *superadditive*, indicates that the cumulative risk for an item that has been on one long mission (of duration $t + x$) is greater than that for two individual missions (of duration t and x), which implies that wear-out is occurring.

3.45. A lifetime is in the NBU class if $S(t + x) \leq S(t) \, S(x)$ for any nonnegative t and x. A lifetime is in the NBUE class if $L(t) \leq L(0)$ for any nonnegative t. Show that NBU implies NBUE. (*Hint*: One way to start is to integrate both sides of the NBU definition from 0 to ∞ with respect to x.)

3.46. Three statistically identical components each have Weibull lifetimes. The three components are arranged in a system that functions if component 1 and either component 2 or 3 function.

(a) Draw the block diagram for this system.

(b) Find the expected time to system failure.

(c) Write a program that calculates the expected time to system failure by numerically integrating the survivor function. Test the program when the components have scale parameters equal to 1 and shape parameters equal to 0.5.

(d) Write a program that estimates the expected time to system failure using Monte Carlo simulation (use the inverse-cdf technique to generate component lifetimes). Test the program when the components have scale parameters equal to 1 and shape parameters equal to 0.5. Use 100,000 system lifetimes.

4

Parametric Lifetime Models

The survival patterns of a drill bit, a fuse, an automobile, and a cat are vastly different. One would certainly not want to use the same failure time distribution with identical parameters to model these diverse lifetimes. This chapter describes several distributions that are commonly used to model lifetimes. To cover all the distributions currently in existence would require an entire textbook, so detailed discussion is limited to the exponential, Weibull, and gamma distributions.

A discussion of parameters that is pertinent to all distributions is given in Section 4.1. Section 4.2 reviews the exponential distribution, which is the simplest distribution for modeling lifetimes, since it is the only continuous distribution with a constant hazard function. This is followed by two sections on generalizations of the exponential distribution, the Weibull and gamma distributions. Section 4.5 discusses other lifetime distributions.

4.1 PARAMETERS

Three types of parameters are used in the distributions described in this chapter: location, scale, and shape. Parameters in a lifetime distribution allow modeling of such diverse applications as a light bulb failure time, patient postsurgery survival time, and automobile failure time by a single lifetime distribution (for example, the Weibull distribution).

Location (or *shift*) parameters are used to shift the distribution to the left or right along the time axis. If c_1 and c_2 are two values of a location parameter for a lifetime

78

distribution with survivor function $S(t; c)$, then there exists a real constant α such that $S(t; c_1) = S(\alpha + t; c_2)$. A familiar example of a location parameter is the mean of the normal distribution.

Scale parameters are used to expand or contract the time axis by a factor of α. If λ_1 and λ_2 are two values for a scale parameter for a lifetime distribution with survivor function $S(t; \lambda)$, then there exists a real constant α such that $S(\alpha t; \lambda_1) = S(t; \lambda_2)$. A familiar example of a scale parameter is λ in the exponential distribution. The probability density function always has the same shape, and the units on the time axis are determined by λ.

Shape parameters are appropriately named since they affect the shape of the probability density function. Shape parameter values may determine whether a distribution belongs to a particular distribution class such as IFR or DFR. A familiar example of a shape parameter is κ in the gamma distribution.

In summary, location parameters *translate* survival distributions along the time axis, scale parameters *expand* or *contract* the time scale for survival distributions, and all other parameters are shape parameters.

In Chapter 3, existence conditions for the lifetime distribution representations [for example, for the survivor function, $S(0) = 1$, $\lim_{t \to \infty} S(t) = 0$ and $S(t)$ is nonincreasing] were categorically stated as true. For modeling purposes, these existence conditions can be violated. For example, consider the survivor function

$$S(t) = \begin{cases} 1 & t \le c \\ a + (b-a)\, S_0\, (t-c) & t > c \end{cases}$$

where $0 < a < b < 1$ and $S_0(t)$ is a survivor function satisfying the three existence conditions. One such survivor function is given in Figure 4.1. In this case, $\lim_{t \to \infty} S(t) = a$. The location parameter c (also known as the minimum life, shift, threshold, or guarantee parameter) can be used to model warranty periods $(c > 0)$, where the item cannot fail (from the consumer's point of view), or failure before use $(c < 0)$, which may be appropriate for a battery that fails on the shelf before purchase. In a mechanical reliability model, for which time is modeled by the stress required for an item to fail, a stress value less than c will not cause failure. A nonzero value for c alters the mean of the distribution by c time units, whereas other moments, such as the variance, skewness, and kurtosis, remain unaffected by the translation. The parameter a accounts for items that will never fail. This may be appropriate for items that are used on a mission of fixed duration or items that are so reliable that it can be assumed that they do not fail for all practical purposes. The parameter b is used to account for items that fail immediately when put into service (that is, a discrete value at $t = c$), such as a light bulb filament that never burns at all. The fraction $1 - b$ is the percentage of items failing at time c. More generally, there may be several discontinuities in $S(t)$ corresponding to points in time where stresses occur (for example, illuminating and extinguishing a light bulb). The survivor function $S_0(t)$ corresponds to the lifetime distribution of those components that do not fail immediately and are not of the type that effectively never fail.

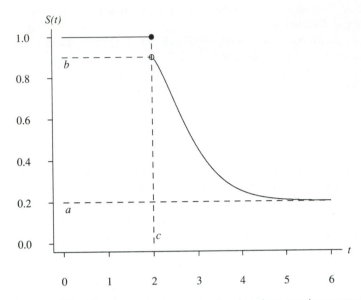

Figure 4.1   Mixed discrete–continuous survivor function where some items never fail.

Example 4.1

Consider the following survivor function.

$$S(t) = \begin{cases} 1 & t \leq 90 \\ 0.3 + 0.5\,e^{-0.01(t-90)} & t > 90. \end{cases}$$

In this case, 30% of the items in the population never fail, and 20% of the items fail at time 90. Since $S_0(t) = e^{-0.01t}$, the lifetime distribution of items that fail after time 90 is exponential, with $\lambda = 0.01$, as shown in the survivor function in Figure 4.2.

In the remaining sections, all distributions are presented in their simplest form ($a = 0$, $b = 1$, and $c = 0$). Nontrivial a, b, and c parameters can be used to model more complicated situations.

A finite time horizon may also lead to a violation of the existence conditions for $S(t)$, $f(t)$, $h(t)$, $H(t)$, or $L(t)$. Human performance tasks, such as a pilot taking a flight or an anesthesiologist administering anesthetic to a patient, may be modeled by a bath-tub-shaped hazard function since there is more risk at the beginning or end of the task. Since failure is extremely unlikely during one particular flight or surgery and the time horizon being considered is finite, the hazard function will not integrate to infinity between times 0 and the end of the task. Airline travel and surgery would not be very popular if it did integrate to infinity.

This chapter examines properties associated with the distributions that are introduced. The *distribution classes* (for example, IFR, DFR, and bathtub-shaped hazard function) that can be assumed by a particular distribution are important in determining

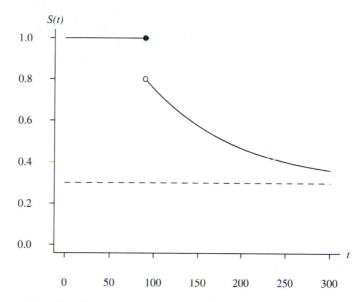

Figure 4.2   Mixed discrete–continuous survivor function with $a = 0.3$, $b = 0.8$, and $c = 90$.

the types of survival patterns that can be assumed. Other properties include the *self-reproducing property* (the minimum of lifetimes from a distribution is from the same parametric family as the individual lifetimes), the *residual property* (the remaining lifetime of a functioning item belongs to the same parametric family as a new item), and the *convolution property* (the sum of lifetimes from a particular family is from the same parametric family).

4.2   EXPONENTIAL DISTRIBUTION

Just as the normal distribution plays an important role in classical statistics because of the central limit theorem, the exponential distribution plays an important role in reliability and lifetime modeling since it is the only continuous distribution with a constant hazard function. The exponential distribution has often been used to model the lifetime of electronic components and is appropriate when a used component that has not failed is statistically as good as a new component. This is a rather restrictive assumption. Moreover, the exponential distribution is presented first because of its simplicity. Two-parameter distributions, which are more complex but can model a wider variety of situations, are presented in subsequent sections. The exponential distribution has a single positive scale parameter λ, often called the *failure rate,* and the five lifetime distribution representations are

$$S(t) = e^{-\lambda t} \qquad f(t) = \lambda e^{-\lambda t} \qquad h(t) = \lambda \qquad H(t) = \lambda t \qquad L(t) = \frac{1}{\lambda}$$

for all $t \geq 0$, and are plotted in Figure 4.3 for $\lambda = 1$ and $\lambda = 2$.

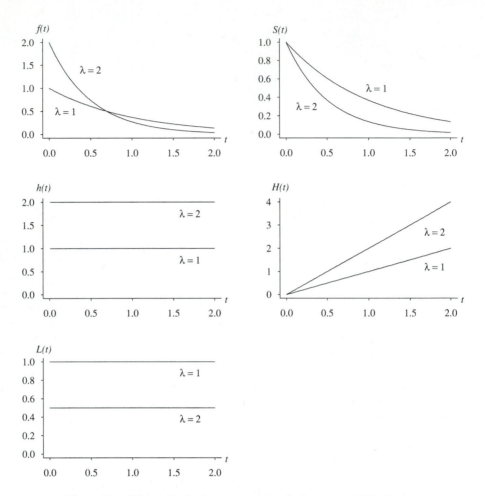

Figure 4.3   Lifetime distribution representations for the exponential distribution.

The following 11 probabilistic properties of the exponential distribution are useful in understanding how it is unique and how it should be applied. In all the properties, it is assumed that the nonnegative lifetime T has the exponential distribution with parameter λ, which denotes the number of failures per unit time. The symbol $\sim$ means "is distributed as." Proofs of these properties are contained in Appendix A.

Property 4.1   (memoryless property) If $T \sim$ exponential(λ), then

$$P[T \geq t] = P[T \geq t + s \mid T \geq s] \qquad t \geq 0; \ s \geq 0.$$

As shown in Figure 4.4 for $\lambda = 1$ and $s = 0.5$, this result indicates that the conditional survivor function for the lifetime of an item that has survived to time s is identical

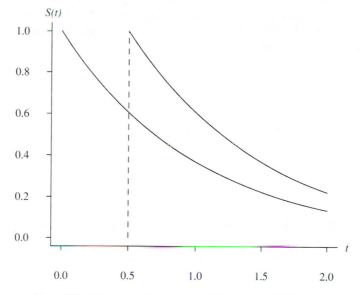

Figure 4.4   The memoryless property of the exponential distribution.

to the survivor function for the lifetime of a brand new item. This used-as-good-as-new assumption is very strong. Consider whether the exponential distribution should be used to model the lifetime of a candle with an expected burning time of 5 hours. If several candles are sampled, we could imagine a bell-shaped probability density function for candle lifetimes, centered around 5 hours. The exponential lifetime model is certainly not appropriate in this case, since a candle that has burned for 4 hours does not have the same lifetime distribution as a brand new candle. This same argument can be used to reason that the exponential lifetime model should not be applied to mechanical components that undergo wear (for example, bearings) or fatigue (structural supports) or electrical components that contain an element that burns away (filaments) or degrades with time (batteries). An electrical component for which the exponential lifetime assumption may be justified is a fuse. A fuse is designed to fail when there is a power surge that causes the fuse to burn out. Assuming that the fuse does not undergo any weakening or degradation over time and that power surges that cause failure occur with equal likelihood over time, the exponential lifetime assumption is appropriate, and a used fuse that has not failed is as good as a new one.

The exponential distribution should be applied judiciously since the memoryless property restricts its applicability. It is usually misapplied for the sake of simplicity since the statistical techniques for the exponential distribution are particularly tractable, or small sample sizes do not support more than a one-parameter distribution.

Property 4.2   The exponential distribution is the only continuous distribution with the memoryless property.

This result indicates that the exponential distribution is the only continuous lifetime distribution for which the conditional lifetime distribution of a used item is identical to the original lifetime distribution. The only discrete distribution with the memoryless property is the geometric distribution.

Property 4.3   If $T \sim$ exponential(λ), then $\lambda T \sim$ exponential(1).

An exponential random variable with $\lambda = 1$ is often called a *unit* exponential random variable. This particular exponential distribution is important for random variate generation, as indicated in the next result.

Property 4.4   If T is a continuous nonnegative random variable with cumulative hazard function H, then $H(T) \sim$ exponential(1).

This result is mathematically equivalent to the probability integral transformation, which states that $F(T) \sim U(0, 1)$, resulting in the inverse-cdf technique for generating random variates for Monte Carlo simulation: $T \leftarrow F^{-1}(U)$, where $U \sim U(0, 1)$. Using Property 4.4, lifetime variates are generated by

$$T \leftarrow H^{-1}(-\log(1-U))$$

since $-\log(1-U)$ is a unit exponential random variate.

Example 4.2

Assuming an item has the Weibull distribution with survivor function

$$S(t) = e^{-(\lambda t)^\kappa}   t > 0,$$

find an equation to convert $U(0, 1)$'s to Weibull variates.

The cumulative hazard function for the Weibull distribution is

$$H(t) = -\log S(t) = (\lambda t)^\kappa,$$

which has inverse

$$H^{-1}(y) = \frac{y^{1/\kappa}}{\lambda}.$$

Variates can be generated by

$$T \leftarrow \frac{1}{\lambda}[-\log(1-U)]^{1/\kappa},$$

where U is uniformly distributed between 0 and 1.

Figure 4.5 indicates how the technique generates a variate from the cumulative hazard function. The value of $-\log(1-U)$, the unit exponential random variate, is

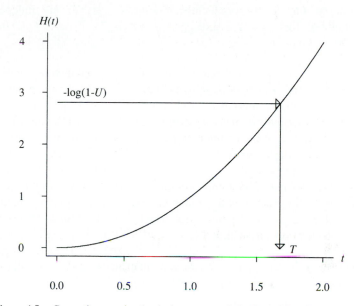

Figure 4.5   Generating a variate by the inverse cumulative hazard function technique.

indicated on the vertical axis, and the corresponding random variate T is indicated on the horizontal axis.

The next result gives a general expression for the sth moment of an exponential random variable.

Property 4.5   If $T \sim$ exponential(λ), then

$$E[T^s] = \frac{\Gamma(s+1)}{\lambda^s} \qquad s > -1,$$

where $\Gamma(\alpha) = \int_0^\infty x^{\alpha-1} e^{-x} \, dx.$

More information is given on the gamma function, $\Gamma(\alpha)$, and other related functions in Appendix B. When s is a nonnegative integer, this expression reduces to $E[T^s] = s!/\lambda^s$. By setting $s = 1, 2, 3,$ and 4, the mean, variance, coefficient of variation, skewness, and kurtosis can be obtained:

$$E[T] = \frac{1}{\lambda} \qquad V[T] = \frac{1}{\lambda^2} \qquad \gamma = 1 \qquad \gamma_3 = 2 \qquad \gamma_4 = 9.$$

Since the coefficient of variation is 1, a quick check for exponentiality from a data set is to see if the ratio of the sample standard deviation to the sample mean is approximately 1.

Property 4.6   (self-reproducing) If T_1, T_2, ..., T_n are independent, $T_i \sim$ exponential(λ_i), for $i = 1, 2, \ldots, n$, and $T = \min\{T_1, T_2, \ldots, T_n\}$, then $T \sim$ exponential($\sum_{i=1}^{n} \lambda_i$).

This result indicates that the minimum of n exponential random lifetimes also has the exponential distribution. This is important in two applications. First, if n independent exponential components, each with exponential times to failure, are arranged in series, the distribution of the system failure time is also exponential with a failure rate equal to the sum of the component failure rates. When the n components have the same failure rate λ, the system lifetime is exponential with failure rate $n\lambda$. Second, when there are several independent, exponentially distributed *causes* of failure competing for the lifetime of an item (for example, failing by open or short circuit for an electronic item or death by various diseases for a human being), the lifetime can be modeled as the minimum of the individual lifetimes from each cause of failure. This second application will be expanded upon in Section 5.1.

Property 4.7   If T_1, T_2, ..., T_n are independent and identically distributed exponential(λ) random variables, then $2\lambda \sum_{i=1}^{n} T_i \sim \chi^2(2n)$, where $\chi^2(2n)$ denotes the chi-square distribution with $2n$ degrees of freedom.

This property is useful for determining a confidence interval for a λ based on a data set of n independent exponential lifetimes. With probability $1 - \alpha$,

$$\chi^2_{2n, 1-\alpha/2} < 2\lambda \sum_{i=1}^{n} T_i < \chi^2_{2n, \alpha/2},$$

where the left- and right-hand sides of this inequality are the $\alpha/2$ and $1 - \alpha/2$ fractiles of the chi-square distribution with $2n$ degrees of freedom. Rearranging this expression yields a $100(1 - \alpha)\%$ confidence interval for λ:

$$\frac{\chi^2_{2n, 1-\alpha/2}}{2 \sum_{i=1}^{n} T_i} < \lambda < \frac{\chi^2_{2n, \alpha/2}}{2 \sum_{i=1}^{n} T_i}.$$

Property 4.8   If T_1, T_2, ..., T_n are independent and identically distributed exponential(λ) random variables, $T_{(1)}$, $T_{(2)}$, ..., $T_{(n)}$ are the corresponding order statistics (the observations sorted in ascending order), $G_k = T_{(k)} - T_{(k-1)}$ for $k = 1, 2, \ldots, n$, and if $T_{(0)} = 0$, then

(a) $P[G_k \geq t] = e^{-(n-k+1)\lambda t}$ $t \geq 0;\ k = 1, 2, \ldots, n.$

(b) G_1, G_2, ..., G_n are independent.

This property is best interpreted in terms of a life test of n items with exponential(λ) lifetimes. The items placed on the life test are *not* replaced with new items when they fail. The ith item fails at time $t_{(i)}$, and $G_i = t_{(i)} - t_{(i-1)}$ is the time between the $(i-1)$st and ith failure, for $i = 1, 2, \ldots, n$, as indicated in Figure 4.6 for $n = 4$. The result states that these gaps (G_i's) are independent and exponentially distributed. The proof of the result relies on Properties 4.1 and 4.6 of the exponential distribution, which implies that when the ith failure occurs the time until the next failure is the minimum of $n - i$ independent exponential random variables.

Property 4.9   If $T_1, T_2, \ldots, T_n$ are independent and identically distributed exponential(λ) random variables and $T_{(r)}$ is the rth order statistic, then

$$E[T_{(r)}] = \sum_{k=1}^{r} \frac{1}{(n-k+1)\lambda}$$

and

$$V[T_{(r)}] = \sum_{k=1}^{r} \frac{1}{[(n-k+1)\lambda]^2}$$

for $r = 1, 2, \ldots, n$.

The expected value and variance of the rth-ordered failure are simple functions of n, λ, and r. The proof of this result is straightforward, since the gaps between order statistics are independent exponential random variables from the previous property, and the rth ordered failure on a life test of n items is the sum of the first r gaps. This result is useful in determining the expected time to complete a life test that is discontinued after r of the n items on test fail.

Property 4.10   If $T_1, T_2, \ldots$ are independent and identically distributed exponential(λ) random variables denoting the interevent times for a point process, then the *number* of events in the interval $(0, t]$ has the Poisson distribution with parameter λt.

This property is related to the memoryless property and can be applied to a component that is subjected to shocks occurring randomly over time. It states that if the time between shocks is exponential(λ) then the number of shocks occurring by time t has the Poisson distribution with parameter λt. This result also applies to the failure time of a cold standby system of n identical exponential components in which nonoperating units do not fail and sensing and switching are perfect. The probability of fewer than n failures by time t (the system reliability) is

$$\sum_{k=0}^{n-1} \frac{(\lambda t)^k}{k!} e^{-\lambda t}.$$

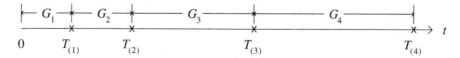

Figure 4.6   Order statistics and gap statistics.

Property 4.11   If $T \sim$ exponential(1), then $Y = \log T$ has survivor function

$$S_Y(y) = e^{-e^y} \qquad -\infty < y < \infty.$$

When developing statistical procedures for parametric distributions, many analysts prefer to work with the logarithm of the lifetime and then transform it back to the original distribution. This result gives the survivor function for the logarithm of a unit exponential random variable, which has support on $(-\infty, \infty)$. The random lifetime Y has a distribution that is a special case of the extreme value distribution, which will be defined in the next section.

The exponential distribution, for which the item under study does not age in a probabilistic sense, is the simplest of the lifetime models. Two other distributions that are generalizations of the exponential, the Weibull and the gamma, are presented in the next sections. They are more flexible for modeling, although more complex mathematically.

4.3   WEIBULL DISTRIBUTION

The exponential distribution is limited in applicability because of the memoryless property. The assumption that a lifetime has a constant failure rate is often too restrictive or inappropriate. Mechanical items typically degrade over time and hence are more likely to follow a distribution with a strictly increasing hazard function. The Weibull distribution is a generalization of the exponential distribution that is appropriate for modeling lifetimes having constant, strictly increasing, and strictly decreasing hazard functions. The first four lifetime distribution representations for the Weibull distribution are

$$S(t) = e^{-(\lambda t)^\kappa} \qquad f(t) = \kappa \lambda^\kappa t^{\kappa-1} e^{-(\lambda t)^\kappa} \qquad h(t) = \kappa \lambda^\kappa t^{\kappa-1} \qquad H(t) = (\lambda t)^\kappa,$$

for all $t \geq 0$, where $\lambda > 0$ and $\kappa > 0$ are the scale and shape parameters of the distribution. The hazard function approaches zero from infinity for $\kappa < 1$, is constant for $\kappa = 1$, the exponential case, and increases from zero when $\kappa > 1$. One other special case occurs when $\kappa = 2$, commonly known as the Rayleigh distribution, and the hazard function is a line with slope $2\lambda^2$. When $3 < \kappa < 4$, the probability density function resembles that of a normal probability density function, and the mode and median of the distribution are equal when $\kappa = 3.26$. The mean residual life function is not as mathematically tractable as the other four representations. It is given by

$$L(t) = \frac{1}{S(t)} \int_t^\infty S(\tau) d\tau$$

$$= e^{(\lambda t)^\kappa} \int_t^\infty e^{-(\lambda \tau)^\kappa} d\tau$$

$$= \frac{e^{(\lambda t)^{\kappa}}}{\lambda \kappa} \int_{(\lambda t)^{\kappa}}^{\infty} u^{1/\kappa - 1} e^{-u} \, du$$

$$= \frac{e^{(\lambda t)^{\kappa}}}{\lambda \kappa} \Gamma\left(\frac{1}{\kappa}\right) \left[1 - I\left(\frac{1}{\kappa}, (\lambda t)^{\kappa}\right) \right],$$

where

$$I(y, x) = \frac{1}{\Gamma(y)} \int_{0}^{x} u^{y-1} e^{-u} \, du$$

is the incomplete gamma function with $y > 0$ and $x > 0$, as described in Appendix B.

The *characteristic life* of the Weibull distribution is a special fractile defined by $t_c = 1/\lambda$. All Weibull survivor functions pass through the point $(1/\lambda, e^{-1})$, regardless of the value of κ, as shown in Figure 4.7 for $\lambda = 1$. Also, since $H(t) = -\log S(t)$, all Weibull cumulative hazard functions pass through the point $(1/\lambda, 1)$, regardless of the value of κ.

Using the expression

$$E[T^r] = \frac{r}{\kappa \lambda^r} \Gamma\left(\frac{r}{\kappa}\right),$$

for $r = 1, 2, \ldots$, the mean, variance, coefficient of variation, skewness, and kurtosis for the Weibull distribution are

$$\mu = \frac{1}{\lambda} \Gamma\left(1 + \frac{1}{\kappa}\right) = \frac{1}{\lambda \kappa} \Gamma\left(\frac{1}{\kappa}\right),$$

$$\sigma^2 = \frac{1}{\lambda^2} \left\{ \Gamma\left(1 + \frac{2}{\kappa}\right) - \left[\Gamma\left(1 + \frac{1}{\kappa}\right)\right]^2 \right\} = \frac{1}{\lambda^2} \left\{ \frac{2}{\kappa} \Gamma\left(\frac{2}{\kappa}\right) - \left[\frac{1}{\kappa} \Gamma\left(\frac{1}{\kappa}\right)\right]^2 \right\},$$

$$\gamma = \frac{\left\{ \frac{2}{\kappa} \Gamma\left(\frac{2}{\kappa}\right) - \left[\frac{1}{\kappa} \Gamma\left(\frac{1}{\kappa}\right)\right]^2 \right\}^{1/2}}{\frac{1}{\kappa} \Gamma\left(\frac{1}{\kappa}\right)},$$

$$\gamma_3 = \left\{ \frac{2}{\kappa} \Gamma\left(\frac{2}{\kappa}\right) - \left[\frac{1}{\kappa} \Gamma\left(\frac{1}{\kappa}\right)\right]^2 \right\}^{-3/2} \left\{ \frac{3}{\kappa} \Gamma\left(\frac{3}{\kappa}\right) - \frac{6}{\kappa^2} \Gamma\left(\frac{1}{\kappa}\right) \Gamma\left(\frac{2}{\kappa}\right) + 2\left[\frac{1}{\kappa} \Gamma\left(\frac{1}{\kappa}\right)\right]^3 \right\},$$

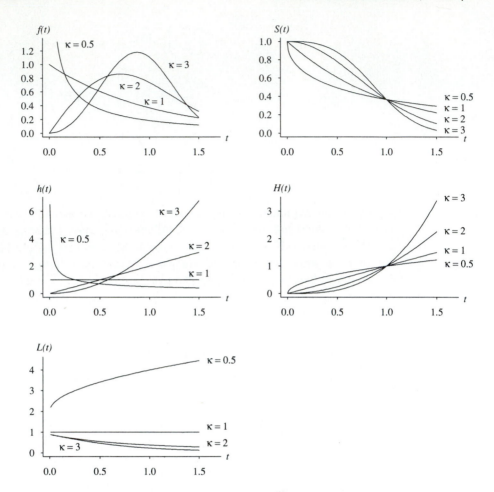

Figure 4.7   Lifetime distribution representations for the Weibull distribution.

$$\gamma_4 = \left\{ \frac{2}{\kappa}\Gamma\left(\frac{2}{\kappa}\right) - \left[\frac{1}{\kappa}\Gamma\left(\frac{1}{\kappa}\right)\right]^2 \right\}^{-2} \left\{ \frac{4}{\kappa}\Gamma\left(\frac{4}{\kappa}\right) - \frac{12}{\kappa^2}\Gamma\left(\frac{1}{\kappa}\right)\Gamma\left(\frac{3}{\kappa}\right) \right.$$

$$\left. + \frac{12}{\kappa^3}\left[\Gamma\left(\frac{1}{\kappa}\right)\right]^2\Gamma\left(\frac{2}{\kappa}\right) - \frac{3}{\kappa^4}\left[\Gamma\left(\frac{1}{\kappa}\right)\right]^4 \right\}.$$

Example 4.3

The lifetime of a certain type of spring used continuously under known operating conditions has the Weibull distribution with $\lambda = 0.0014$ and $\kappa = 1.28$, where time is measured in hours. (Estimating the parameters for the Weibull distribution from a data set is one of the topics of Chapter 8, but the parameters are assumed to be known for this example.) What is the mean time to failure, the probability a spring will operate for 500 hours, and the probability that a spring that has operated for 200 hours without failure will operate another 500 hours?

The mean time to failure is

$$\mu = E[T] = \frac{1}{(0.0014)(1.28)} \Gamma\left(\frac{1}{1.28}\right) = 661.8 \text{ hours.}$$

The probability that a spring will operate for 500 hours is

$$S(500) = e^{-[(0.0014)(500)]^{1.28}} = 0.531.$$

To calculate the conditional probability that a used spring lasts another 500 hours requires a conditional survivor function. The conditional survivor function for a spring that has operated for 200 hours is

$$S_{T|T \geq 200}(t) = \frac{S(t)}{S(200)} = \frac{e^{-(0.0014t)^{1.28}}}{e^{-[(0.0014)(200)]^{1.28}}} \qquad t \geq 200.$$

So the probability that the spring lasts another 500 hours is $S_{T|T \geq 200}(700) = 0.459$. It is not surprising that this survival probability is slightly lower than the probability that a new spring survives 500 hours. Since the shape parameter $\kappa = 1.28$ is greater than 1, the spring's lifetime is in the IFR class, which means that the spring degrades over time.

For calculating parameter estimates for the Weibull distribution from a data set, the logarithms of the data values are sometimes used to solve numerical stability difficulties. If T has the Weibull distribution, then $Y = \log T$ has the *extreme value distribution*. The survivor function for the extreme value distribution is

$$S(y) = e^{-e^{\frac{y-u}{b}}} \qquad -\infty < y < \infty,$$

where $u = -\log \lambda$ and $b = 1/\kappa$ are the location and scale parameters of the distribution.

The Weibull distribution has the self-reproducing property. If $T_1, T_2, \ldots, T_n$ are component lifetimes having the Weibull distribution with the same shape parameters, then the minimum of these values has the Weibull distribution. More specifically, if $T_i \sim \text{Weibull}(\lambda_i, \kappa)$ for $i = 1, 2, \ldots, n$, $\min\{T_1, T_2, \ldots, T_n\} \sim \text{Weibull}(\sum_{i=1}^{n} \lambda_i, \kappa)$.

4.4   GAMMA DISTRIBUTION

The gamma distribution is a second important generalization of the exponential distribution. The probability density function for the gamma distribution is

$$f(t) = \frac{\lambda}{\Gamma(\kappa)} (\lambda t)^{\kappa-1} e^{-\lambda t} \qquad t \geq 0,$$

where λ and κ are positive scale and shape parameters, respectively. When $\kappa = 1$, the gamma distribution is equivalent to the exponential distribution. It is often difficult to differentiate between Weibull and gamma distributions based on plots of their probability density functions, since the shapes of these plots are similar. The differences between these two distributions become apparent when their hazard functions are compared. The cumulative distribution function for a gamma random variable is

$$F(t) = \int_0^t \frac{\lambda}{\Gamma(\kappa)} (\lambda \tau)^{\kappa-1} e^{-\lambda \tau} \, d\tau$$

$$= \frac{1}{\Gamma(\kappa)} \int_0^t \lambda (\lambda \tau)^{\kappa-1} e^{-\lambda \tau} \, d\tau$$

$$= \frac{1}{\Gamma(\kappa)} \int_0^{\lambda t} x^{\kappa-1} e^{-x} \, dx$$

$$= I(\kappa, \lambda t) \qquad t \geq 0,$$

where I is the incomplete gamma function, defined in Appendix B. The survivor function is $S(t) = 1 - I(\kappa, \lambda t)$. The reason that the gamma distribution is less popular in modeling than the Weibull is partially due to the intractability of the survivor function.

The hazard function is the ratio of the density function to the survivor function. As shown in Figure 4.8 for $\lambda = 1$ and various values of κ, the shape of the hazard function differs from that of the Weibull distribution, particularly for large t values. The distribution is in the IFR class if $\kappa > 1$, the DFR class if $\kappa < 1$, and both classes if $\kappa = 1$, the exponential case. For all κ values, $\lim_{t \to \infty} h(t) = \lambda$, indicating that a lifetime with a gamma distribution will have an exponential tail. Thus, if an item survives far enough into the right-hand tail of the probability density function, the distribution of the remaining time to failure is approximately exponentially distributed by the memoryless property.

The cumulative hazard function and mean residual life functions

$$H(t) = -\log S(t) \qquad L(t) = \frac{1}{S(t)} \int_t^\infty S(\tau) d\tau$$

are also mathematically intractable and must be evaluated numerically. Using the expression

$$E[T^r] = \frac{\kappa(\kappa+1)(\kappa+2)\cdots(\kappa+r-1)}{\lambda^r},$$

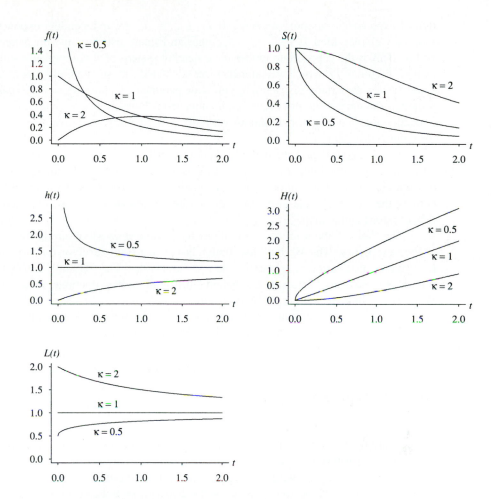

Figure 4.8   Lifetime distribution representations for the gamma distribution.

for $r = 1, 2, \ldots$, the moments of a gamma random variable are

$$E[T] = \frac{\kappa}{\lambda} \qquad V[T] = \frac{\kappa}{\lambda^2} \qquad \gamma = \kappa^{-1/2} \qquad \gamma_3 = 2\kappa^{-1/2} \qquad \gamma_4 = 3 + \frac{6}{\kappa}.$$

Two special cases of the gamma distribution are of interest. When the shape parameter κ is a positive integer, a gamma random variable has the *Erlang* distribution. The Erlang distribution has closed-form density and survivor functions. When $\kappa = n$,

$$f(t) = \frac{\lambda}{(n-1)!} \, (\lambda t)^{n-1} \, e^{-\lambda t} \qquad S(t) = \sum_{k=0}^{n-1} \frac{(\lambda t)^k}{k!} \, e^{-\lambda t}$$

for $t \geq 0$ and a positive integer n. The Erlang distribution's origins include the convolution of exponential random variables. If $T_1, T_2, \ldots, T_n$ are independent exponential(λ) random variables, then $T_1 + T_2 + \cdots + T_n$ has an Erlang distribution with parameters λ and n. This is the appropriate model for a standby system of n components with exponential lifetimes in which components are switched on sequentially upon failures. Equivalently, the Erlang distribution with scale parameter λ and integer shape parameter n models the time of the nth event in a homogeneous Poisson process with rate λ. More generally, the sum of gamma random variables with identical scale parameters also has the gamma distribution.

The second special case is the *chi-square* distribution. When $\lambda = 1/2$ and $\kappa = n/2$, where n is a positive integer referred to as the degrees of freedom, the random variable T has the chi-square distribution. The chi-square distribution is used for inference concerning the variance in classical statistics and inference concerning the exponential distribution for lifetime data.

The Weibull and gamma distributions have some interesting similarities in terms of their properties. The Weibull distribution has closed-form survivor function, whereas the gamma distribution survivor function is intractable. The Weibull distribution has intractable moments, whereas the gamma distribution has tractable moments. The Weibull distribution has the self-reproducing property when the shape parameters are constant, whereas the gamma distribution does not. The Weibull does not have the convolution property, whereas the gamma distribution does when the scale parameters are constant.

4.5   OTHER LIFETIME DISTRIBUTIONS

Although the exponential, Weibull, and gamma distributions are popular lifetime models, they are limited in their modeling capability. For example, if it were determined that an item had a bathtub-shaped hazard function, none of these three models would be appropriate unless a piecewise model over segments of the lifetime were used. Several other models that may be used to describe the distribution of a continuous lifetime T are surveyed in this section.

The distributions for the nonnegative random variable T described here have three types of parameters: location parameters, denoted by a, b, and μ; scale parameters, denoted by λ and σ; and shape parameters, denoted by κ, γ, and δ. All distributions have support on $[0, \infty)$ except for the uniform and Pareto distributions.

The one-parameter models that are summarized in this section are the exponential (λ) and Muth (κ) distributions. The two-parameter models are the Weibull (λ, κ), gamma (λ, κ), uniform (a, b), log normal (μ, σ), log logistic (λ, κ), inverse Gaussian (λ, μ), exponential power (λ, κ), Pareto (λ, κ), and Gompertz (δ, κ) distributions. The three-parameter models are the Makeham (δ, κ, γ), IDB (δ, κ, γ), and generalized Pareto (δ, κ, γ) distributions. The n-parameter models are the hypoexponential ($\lambda_1, \lambda_2, \ldots, \lambda_n$) and hyperexponential ($\lambda_1, \lambda_2, \ldots, \lambda_n$) distributions.

The shapes of the representations, particularly the hazard function, are useful in determining the appropriate distribution to use to model a lifetime. One-, two-, three-, and n-parameter lifetime distributions are described consecutively in the following paragraphs.

The one-parameter lifetime distributions defined here have their $f(t)$, $S(t)$, $h(t)$, and $H(t)$ functions given in Table 4.1. Certainly, the simplest lifetime distribution is the exponential distribution, with a positive scale parameter λ. As mentioned earlier, it is the only continuous distribution with a constant failure rate.

Muth developed a distribution with a single shape parameter κ ($0 < \kappa \leq 1$). Muth's distribution is asymptotically equivalent to the unit exponential distribution as $\kappa \to 0$ and has a hazard function that increases from $h(0) = 1 - \kappa$, for all κ.

The two-parameter lifetime distributions defined here have their lifetime distribution representations given in Table 4.2. As outlined earlier, the Weibull distribution, having positive scale parameter λ and positive shape parameter κ, is one of the most popular two-parameter lifetime models. The Weibull distribution includes the exponential distribution as a special case when $\kappa = 1$, and the hazard function increases from zero when $\kappa > 1$ and decreases from infinity when $\kappa < 1$.

The gamma distribution, as described in the previous section, has scale parameter λ and shape parameter κ. As with the Weibull distribution, the gamma distribution includes the exponential as a special case when $\kappa = 1$.

The uniform distribution is a simple two-parameter model. The main application of the uniform distribution is to approximate lifetime distributions over relatively small intervals. The uniform distribution has support on $[a, b]$ with location parameters a and b, where $0 \leq a < b$. The hazard function increases from $h(a) = 1/(b-a)$ to infinity. When $a = 0$ and $b = 1$, the uniform distribution can be used to generate random variates for Monte Carlo simulation by inversion of the cumulative distribution function based on the probability integral transformation.

The log normal distribution has a UBT [upside-down bathtub-shaped, or hump-shaped, where $h(t)$ increases initially and then decreases] hazard function. It is parameterized by μ and σ, since the logarithm of a log normal random variable is a normal random variable with mean μ and standard deviation σ. One historical reason that the log normal distribution has been less popular than the Weibull distribution is that its survivor function is not closed form. This is important for estimating parameters for right-censored data sets, although widespread numerical routines exist that can overcome this issue. The survivor function for a log normal random variable is

TABLE 4.1   ONE-PARAMETER UNIVARIATE LIFETIME DISTRIBUTIONS

Distribution	$f(t)$	$S(t)$	$h(t)$	$H(t)$	Parameters
Exponential	$\lambda e^{-\lambda t}$	$e^{-\lambda t}$	λ	λt	$\lambda > 0$
Muth	$(e^{\kappa t} - \kappa)e^{[-\frac{1}{\kappa}e^{\kappa t} + \kappa t + \frac{1}{\kappa}]}$	$e^{[-\frac{1}{\kappa}e^{\kappa t} + \kappa t + \frac{1}{\kappa}]}$	$e^{\kappa t} - \kappa$	$\frac{1}{\kappa}e^{\kappa t} - \kappa t - \frac{1}{\kappa}$	$0 < \kappa \leq 1$

TABLE 4.2   TWO-PARAMETER UNIVARIATE LIFETIME DISTRIBUTIONS

Distribution	$f(t)$	$S(t)$	$h(t)$	$H(t)$	Parameters
Weibull	$\kappa\lambda^\kappa t^{\kappa-1}e^{-(\lambda t)^\kappa}$	$e^{-(\lambda t)^\kappa}$	$\kappa\lambda^\kappa t^{\kappa-1}$	$(\lambda t)^\kappa$	$\lambda>0;\kappa>0$
Gamma	$\dfrac{\lambda(\lambda t)^{\kappa-1}e^{-\lambda t}}{\Gamma(\kappa)}$	$1-I(\kappa,\lambda t)$	$\dfrac{\lambda(\lambda t)^{\kappa-1}e^{-\lambda t}}{\Gamma(\kappa)[1-I(\kappa,\lambda t)]}$	$-\log(1-I(\kappa,\lambda t))$	$\lambda>0;\kappa>0$
Uniform	$\dfrac{1}{b-a}$	$\dfrac{b-t}{b-a}$	$\dfrac{1}{b-t}$	$-\log\left(\dfrac{b-t}{b-a}\right)$	$0\le a<b$
Log normal	$\dfrac{1}{\sigma t\sqrt{2\pi}}e^{\frac{-(\log t-\mu)^2}{2\sigma^2}}$	$\displaystyle\int_t^\infty f(\tau)d\tau$	$\dfrac{f(t)}{S(t)}$	$-\log S(t)$	$-\infty<\mu<\infty;\sigma>0$
Log logistic	$\dfrac{\lambda\kappa(\lambda t)^{\kappa-1}}{[1+(\lambda t)^\kappa]^2}$	$\dfrac{1}{1+(\lambda t)^\kappa}$	$\dfrac{\lambda\kappa(\lambda t)^{\kappa-1}}{1+(\lambda t)^\kappa}$	$\log[1+(\lambda t)^\kappa]$	$\lambda>0;\kappa>0$
Inverse Gaussian	$\sqrt{\dfrac{\lambda}{2\pi t^3}}\,e^{-\frac{\lambda}{2\mu^2 t}(t-\mu)^2}$	$\displaystyle\int_t^\infty f(\tau)d\tau$	$\dfrac{f(t)}{S(t)}$	$-\log S(t)$	$\lambda>0;\mu>0$
Exponential Power	$(e^{1-e^{\lambda t^\kappa}})e^{\lambda t^\kappa}\lambda\kappa t^{\kappa-1}$	$e^{(1-e^{\lambda t^\kappa})}$	$e^{\lambda t^\kappa}\lambda\kappa t^{\kappa-1}$	$e^{\lambda t^\kappa}-1$	$\lambda>0;\kappa>0$
Pareto	$\dfrac{\kappa\lambda^\kappa}{t^{\kappa+1}}$	$\left(\dfrac{\lambda}{t}\right)^\kappa$	$\dfrac{\kappa}{t}$	$\kappa\log\left(\dfrac{t}{\lambda}\right)$	$\lambda>0;\kappa>0$
Gompertz	$\delta\kappa^t e^{[-\delta(\kappa^t-1)/\log\kappa]}$	$e^{[-\delta(\kappa^t-1)/\log\kappa]}$	$\delta\kappa^t$	$\dfrac{\delta(\kappa^t-1)}{\log\kappa}$	$\kappa>1;\delta>0$

$$S(t)=1-\Phi\left(\frac{\log t-\mu}{\sigma}\right)\qquad t\ge0$$

where Φ is the cumulative distribution function for a standard normal random variable.

The log logistic distribution has scale parameter $\lambda>0$ and shape parameter $\kappa>0$. The hazard function is decreasing when $\kappa\le1$ and is UBT for $\kappa>1$. As with the exponential and Weibull distributions, its survivor function can be inverted in closed form, so variates can be generated by inversion for Monte Carlo simulation.

The inverse Gaussian distribution has a positive parameter μ and positive scale parameter λ. Similar to the log normal distribution, the inverse Gaussian distribution also has a UBT hazard function. The survivor function is not closed form, but can be written in terms of the cumulative distribution function for the standard normal distribution. The mean of the inverse Gaussian distribution is μ and the variance is μ^3/λ, so the parameter μ is not a true location parameter since it does more than just shift the location of the distribution.

The exponential power distribution has a positive scale parameter λ and a positive shape parameter κ. The exponential power distribution has two properties that make it unique. First, the hazard function increases exponentially for large t, whereas the Weibull hazard function increases polynomially. Second, the exponential power distribution is one of the few two-parameter distributions that has a hazard function that can assume a bathtub shape. The hazard function achieves a minimum at $[(1-\kappa)/(\lambda\kappa)]^{1/\kappa}$ when $\kappa < 1$. For $\kappa > 1$, the hazard function is increasing from zero to infinity, and for $\kappa = 1$ the hazard function increases from λ. The distribution has a characteristic life of $(1/\lambda)^{1/\kappa}$. The exponential power distribution's survivor function, which is $S(t) = e^{1-e^{\lambda t^\kappa}}$ for $t \geq 0$, can be inverted in closed form, so variates can be generated by inversion.

Pareto developed a distribution with support on $t \geq \lambda$, where $\kappa > 0$ is a shape parameter and $\lambda > 0$ is a scale parameter. The hazard function for the Pareto distribution decreases to zero from $h(\lambda) = \kappa/\lambda$.

The Gompertz distribution is a lifetime model that has been used to model adult lifetimes in actuarial applications. This distribution has positive shape parameters δ and κ. Gompertz assumed that Mill's ratio, the reciprocal of the hazard function, measures human resistance to death. He assumed this resistance decreases over time at a rate proportional to itself; that is,

$$\frac{d}{dt}\left[\frac{1}{h(t)}\right] = \kappa\left[\frac{1}{h(t)}\right]$$

where κ is a constant. The hazard function increases from $h(0) = \delta$. The solution to this separable differential equation is $h(t) = \delta\, e^{ct}$, where $e^c = \kappa$.

The three-parameter lifetime distributions defined here have their $f(t)$, $S(t)$, $h(t)$, and $H(t)$ functions given in Table 4.3. The Makeham distribution has three positive shape parameters and is a generalization of the Gompertz distribution with γ included in the hazard function. Whereas the Gompertz distribution describes lifetimes in terms of death from natural causes, the Makeham distribution takes into account the possibility of accidental deaths by including the extra parameter. The hazard function increases from $\delta + \gamma$.

The IDB (increasing, decreasing, bathtub) distribution is a three-parameter model that has a hazard function that can exhibit increasing $(\delta \geq \gamma\kappa)$, decreasing $(\delta = 0)$, and bathtub shapes $(0 < \delta < \gamma\kappa)$. The distribution has shape parameters $\delta \geq 0$, $\kappa \geq 0$, and $\gamma \geq 0$. Special cases of the IDB distribution are the Rayleigh distribution when $\gamma = 0$ and the exponential distribution when $\delta = \kappa = 0$.

TABLE 4.3   THREE-PARAMETER UNIVARIATE LIFETIME DISTRIBUTIONS

Distribution	$f(t)$	$S(t)$	$h(t)$	$H(t)$	Parameters
Makeham	$(\gamma+\delta\kappa^t)e^{-\gamma t-\frac{\delta(\kappa^t-1)}{\log\kappa}}$	$e^{-\gamma t-\frac{\delta(\kappa^t-1)}{\log\kappa}}$	$\gamma+\delta\kappa^t$	$\gamma t+\dfrac{\delta(\kappa^t-1)}{\log\kappa}$	$\delta>0;\ \kappa>1;\ \gamma>0$
IDB	$\dfrac{(1+\kappa t)\delta t+\gamma}{(1+\kappa t)^{\gamma/\kappa+1}}\,e^{-\delta t^2/2}$	$(1+\kappa t)^{-\gamma/\kappa}e^{-\delta t^2/2}$	$\delta t+\dfrac{\gamma}{1+\kappa t}$	$\dfrac{\delta}{2}t^2+\dfrac{\gamma}{\kappa}\log(1+\kappa t)$	$\delta\geq0;\ \kappa\geq0;\ \gamma\geq0$
Generalized Pareto	$(\gamma+\dfrac{\kappa}{t+\delta})(1+\dfrac{t}{\delta})^{-\kappa}e^{-\gamma t}$	$(1+\dfrac{t}{\delta})^{-\kappa}e^{-\gamma t}$	$\gamma+\dfrac{\kappa}{t+\delta}$	$\gamma t+\kappa\log(1+\dfrac{t}{\delta})$	$\delta>0;\ \gamma\geq0;\ \kappa\geq-\delta\gamma$

The generalized Pareto distribution is another three-parameter distribution with shape parameters δ, κ, and γ. It is able to achieve an increasing hazard function when $\kappa < 0$, a decreasing hazard function when $\kappa > 0$, and a constant hazard function when $\kappa = 0$. For all parameter values, $h(0) = \gamma + \kappa/\delta$ and $\lim_{t\to\infty} h(t) = \gamma$. The special cases of $\gamma = 0$ and $\kappa = -\delta\gamma$ result in the hazard functions

$$h(t) = \frac{\kappa}{t+\delta} \quad \text{and} \quad h(t) = \frac{\gamma t}{t+\delta}.$$

Finally, two n-parameter distributions are related to the exponential distribution. The first is the hypoexponential distribution. If $T_i \sim$ exponential(λ_i) for $i = 1, 2, \ldots, n$, then $T = T_1 + T_2 + \cdots + T_n$ has the hypoexponential distribution. The hypoexponential distribution collapses to the Erlang distribution with parameters λ and n when $\lambda = \lambda_1 = \lambda_2 = \cdots = \lambda_n$. The hypoexponential distribution is IFR for all values of its parameters.

The second n-parameter distribution is the hyperexponential distribution. If $T_i \sim$ exponential(λ_i) for $i = 1, 2, \ldots, n$, and T has probability density function

$$f_T(t) = p_1 f_{T_1}(t) + p_2 f_{T_2}(t) + \cdots + p_n f_{T_n}(t),$$

where $p_1 + p_2 + \cdots + p_n = 1$, then T has the hyperexponential distribution. The hyperexponential distribution collapses to the exponential distribution with failure rate λ when $\lambda = \lambda_1 = \lambda_2 = \cdots = \lambda_n$. The hyperexponential distribution is DFR for all values of its parameters.

Figure 4.9 shows how these distributions are related to one another. Each oval shows one lifetime distribution, listing its name, parameters, and range. Solid arrows connecting the distributions denote special cases and transformations. Dashed arrows denote limiting distributions, which typically arise as one of the parameters approaches 0 or infinity.

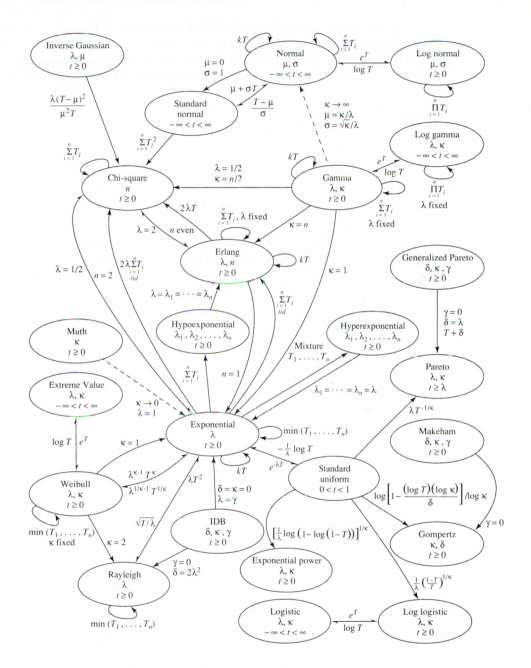

Figure 4.9   Relationships among continuous univariate lifetime distributions.

Table 4.4 contains a summary of the distribution classes to which the distributions belong. Double lines are used to separate the distributions by the number of parameters. For each class to which a distribution belongs, the corresponding set of parameter values is specified. The distribution classes that are considered are IFR, DFR, BT, and UBT.

TABLE 4.4   DISTRIBUTION CLASSES

Distribution	IFR	DFR	BT	UBT
Exponential	$\mathbf{YES}_{\text{all } \lambda}$	$\mathbf{YES}_{\text{all } \lambda}$	NO	NO
Muth	$\mathbf{YES}_{\text{all } \kappa}$	NO	NO	NO
Weibull	$\mathbf{YES}_{\kappa \geq 1}$	$\mathbf{YES}_{\kappa \leq 1}$	NO	NO
Gamma	$\mathbf{YES}_{\kappa \geq 1}$	$\mathbf{YES}_{\kappa \leq 1}$	NO	NO
Uniform	$\mathbf{YES}_{\text{all } a \text{ and } b}$	NO	NO	NO
Log normal	NO	NO	NO	$\mathbf{YES}_{\text{all } \mu \text{ and } \sigma}$
Log logistic	NO	$\mathbf{YES}_{\kappa \leq 1}$	NO	$\mathbf{YES}_{\kappa > 1}$
Inverse Gaussian	NO	NO	NO	$\mathbf{YES}_{\text{all } \lambda \text{ and } \mu}$
Exponential power	$\mathbf{YES}_{\kappa \geq 1}$	NO	$\mathbf{YES}_{\kappa < 1}$	NO
Pareto	NO	$\mathbf{YES}_{\text{all } \kappa}$	NO	NO
Gompertz	$\mathbf{YES}_{\text{all } \delta \text{ and } \kappa}$	NO	NO	NO
Makeham	$\mathbf{YES}_{\text{all } \delta \text{ and } \kappa}$	NO	NO	NO
IDB	$\mathbf{YES}_{\delta \geq \gamma\kappa}$	$\mathbf{YES}_{\delta = 0}$	$\mathbf{YES}_{0 < \delta < \gamma\kappa}$	NO
Generalized Pareto	$\mathbf{YES}_{\kappa \leq 0}$	$\mathbf{YES}_{\kappa > 0}$	NO	NO
Hypoexponential	$\mathbf{YES}_{\text{all } \lambda_1, \lambda_2, ..., \lambda_n}$	$\mathbf{YES}_{n = 1}$	NO	NO
Hyperexponential	$\mathbf{YES}_{\lambda_1 = \cdots = \lambda_n}$	$\mathbf{YES}_{\text{all } \lambda_1, \lambda_2, ..., \lambda_n}$	NO	NO

4.6   FURTHER READING

The preceding discussion about parameters in distributions is classical in the sense that the parameters are treated as constants. The Bayesian approach, in which parameters are treated as random variables, is emphasized in Mann et al. (1974), Martz and Waller (1982), and Sander and Badoux (1991).

The exponential, Weibull, and gamma distributions are covered in virtually all reliability textbooks. Hundreds of papers have been published on the Weibull distribution alone. Early references on the Weibull distribution include Fisher and Tippett (1928) and Weibull (1939, 1951). Rao (1992, p. 505) gives biographical information on Weibull. Weibull's work was not limited to the statistical analysis of failure; he also invented the ball bearing and electric hammer.

The various distributions considered in Section 4.5 that are typically not covered in many other reliability textbooks are Muth's distribution (Muth, 1977), the log normal distribution (Sweet, 1990), the exponential power distribution (Smith and Bain, 1975), the inverse Gaussian distribution (Chhikara and Folks, 1989; Edgeman, 1990; Schwarz and Samanta, 1991), the Pareto distribution (Miller, 1981), the Gompertz distribution (Jordan, 1967), the Makeham distribution (Jordan, 1967), the IDB distribution (Hjorth, 1980), the generalized Pareto distribution (Davis and Feldstein, 1979), and the hypoexponential and hyperexponential distributions (Trivedi, 1982). Relationships between the distributions and approximations to the distributions are reviewed in detail in Johnson and Kotz (1970) and by a diagram in Leemis (1986). Bowman and Shenton (1988) consider properties of estimators for the gamma distribution. A useful class of distributions for reliability modeling is known as the phase-type distributions (Neuts, 1981). In a phase-type model, the time to failure T is the time to absorption in a finite-state, continuous-time Markov chain. Fitting these models is considered by Johnson (1993). Some models use the physical deterioration of items as their basis. Bogdanoff and Kozin (1982) describe a cumulative damage model useful in modeling fatigue life, fatigue crack growth, and wear. A pure birth transition matrix models the amount of damage accumulated at any time. Crowder et al. (1991) reference the Burr distribution (p. 33) and the truncated normal distribution (p. 36). The generalized gamma distribution (Stacy, 1962) and the generalized F distribution (Prentice, 1975) include many of the distributions presented in this chapter as special and limiting cases. Either can be used as a lifetime model or to differentiate between competing models. Both of these models are presented in Kalbfleisch and Prentice (1980, pp. 27–29). Gaver and Acar (1979) consider general approaches for formulating lifetime distributions. This chapter has focused primarily on *univariate* lifetime distributions. Multivariate distributions are useful when there is an association between lifetimes, as in a shared-parallel system. Two popular extensions of the exponential model are the bivariate exponential models introduced by Marshall and Olkin (1967) and Freund (1961). Crowder et al. (1991, pp. 138–140) survey bivariate models.

4.7   EXERCISES

4.1. Show that the parameter λ in the Weibull distribution

$$S(t) = e^{-(\lambda t)^{\kappa}} \qquad t \geq 0$$

is a *scale* parameter (that is, find the appropriate constant α such that $S(\alpha t; \lambda_1, \kappa) = S(t; \lambda_2, \kappa)$) for any two shape parameters λ_1 and λ_2.

4.2. Find $E[T]$ for an item that has survivor function

$$S(t) = p e^{-\lambda t} \qquad t \geq 0; \, 0 < p < 1, \lambda > 0.$$

4.3. Show that

$$\int_0^\infty x^{z-1} e^{-\lambda x} dx = \lambda^{-z} \Gamma(z).$$

4.4. Show that $\Gamma(1/2) = \pi^{1/2}$.

4.5. If $T_1 \sim$ exponential(λ_1), $T_2 \sim$ exponential(λ_2), and T_1 and T_2 are independent, find $P[T_1 > T_2]$.

4.6. (von Alven, 1964) Assuming that components have exponential(λ) lifetimes, show that
   (a) the mean system lifetime of n identical exponential components arranged in series is $1/n\lambda$.
   (b) the mean system lifetime of four identical exponential components arranged in a series-parallel 2×2 arrangement (two banks of two-component parallel subsystems arranged in series) is $11/12\lambda$.

4.7. Find the skewness and kurtosis for an exponential random variable.

4.8. Let c_1 be the cost of each of n identical components. Let c_2 be the cost of system failure. The system is to be used on a 300-hour mission. Assuming that each component has an exponential time to failure with a failure rate of 0.005 failure per hour, find the number of components to be arranged in parallel to minimize costs.

4.9. Consider the three-component system depicted in Figure 4.10. Assume that component 1 has an exponential time to failure with a mean of 1000 hours, component 2 has an exponential time to failure with a mean of 2000 hours, and component 3 has an exponential distribution with a mean of 2500 hours. Your budget allows you to have five spares. Find the optimal number of spares of each type (for example, two spares of component 1, three spares of component 2, and no spares of component 3) that maximizes the system lifetime, assuming no delay in detecting and replacing a failed component. Give an estimate of the mean system lifetime (including the use of spares to extend the system life). Assume that spares are used upon *system* failure.

4.10. Three independent, exponential components comprise a 2-out-of-3 system. Give an expression for the system survivor function and the expected time to system failure.

4.11. A fuse has an exponential time to failure. The 1000-hour reliability of the fuse is 0.98. Find the mean residual life of the fuse if it is still operating after 567 hours of use.

Figure 4.10

4.12. What is the minimum number of identical exponential components, each with a failure rate of $\lambda = 0.0004$ failure per hour, that must be arranged in parallel to yield a mean time to failure of 7000 hours.

4.13. Which of the following properties are true for the exponential distribution?
(a) It is the only distribution with the memoryless property.
(b) It is in both the IFR and DFR classes.
(c) Coherent systems of exponential lifetimes have an exponential time to failure.
(d) It is in the NWU class.
(e) The minimum of 10 exponential random variables, each having a different failure rate, has the exponential distribution.
(f) $H(t)/t$ is constant.
(g) If n items (each with an exponential lifetime having a different failure rate) are put on test, the time between failures is exponential.
(h) The coefficient of variation, skewness, and kurtosis are the same for any failure rate.
(i) The natural logarithm of an exponential random variable has the extreme value distribution.
(j) It is a special case of the Weibull, gamma, and log normal distributions.

4.14. An item is to consist of three PNP germanium transistors and two germanium diode units operating at a stress ratio of 0.7. All transistors and diodes will operate at 30°C. In addition, there are five fixed composition resistors in the item operating at a stress ratio of 0.6 and an operating temperature of 50°C. Assume that this item is being used in a Naval undersea unsheltered environment. If failure occurs when any one of the components in this system fails, use MIL-HDBK-217 to find
(a) the probability density function for the system lifetime.
(b) the probability the system will survive to time 1000.

4.15. Find the failure rate of the transistor described next using MIL-HDBK-217. The NPN, silicon, group 1 transistor will be operating at 20°C. The stress ratio is 0.8, and the transistor will be used in a switch application in a cannon launch environment. The transistor will be encapsulated in plastic and has a power rating of 15 watts. The voltage stress, S_2, will be 40% and the complexity factor is dual (unmatched).

4.16. Consider a two-component parallel system of exponential components. If the failure rates of the two components are equal, find $\lim_{t \to \infty} h(t)$, where $h(t)$ is the system hazard function.

4.17. Consider a two-component series system of independent components. The first component has an exponential time to failure with $\lambda = 0.000006$ failure per hour. The second component has a Weibull time to failure with $\lambda = 0.000003$ and $\kappa = 1.364$.
(a) Plot the system survivor function.
(b) What is the probability that the system will survive 1000 hours?

4.18. For the Weibull random lifetime T, show that

$$P\left[T < \frac{1}{\lambda}\right] = 1 - \frac{1}{e},$$

regardless of the value of κ.

4.19. Show that if T is exponentially distributed then $(T/\lambda^{\kappa-1})^{1/\kappa}$ has the Weibull distribution.

4.20. Find the skewness and kurtosis of a Weibull random variable.

4.21. Find the value of the shape parameter in the Weibull distribution when the skewness is zero.

4.22. The system described by Figure 4.11 will be taken on a mission of fixed duration. Component 1 has a lifetime that is exponentially distributed with failure rate $\lambda_1 = 0.00001$, component 2 has a lifetime that is exponentially distributed with failure rate $\lambda_2 = 0.0005$, and component 3 has a lifetime that has the Weibull distribution with parameters $\lambda_3 = 0.0005$ and $\kappa = 2$. If time is measured in hours, find the component with the highest reliability importance if

(a) the mission duration is 10 hours.

(b) the mission duration is 5000 hours.

Write a short paragraph explaining your results.

4.23. Find the mode for an item with a lifetime following the Weibull distribution. For which parameter values is this value the mode? Find the probability that the item is still functioning at the mode value.

4.24. Find the value of the shape parameter in the Weibull distribution when the mode and median are equal.

4.25. What is the expected time to failure of a Weibull random variable with $\lambda = 2.7$ and $\kappa = 0.64$? What is the mean residual life of the item if it is still operating after 0.3 time unit? (*Hint*: To arrive at numerical answers for these questions, you need access to functions that calculate the gamma function and the incomplete gamma function.)

4.26. A design engineer wants an item with a 1-month reliability of 0.8. He designs the item and finds that the failure time has a Weibull distribution with parameters $\lambda = 8.33$ and $\kappa = 0.334$, with time measured in months. Unfortunately, he finds that the 1-month reliability is

$$S(1) = e^{-8.33^{0.334}} = 0.13,$$

which is clearly unacceptable. Fortunately, this Weibull distribution has a decreasing failure rate, so the designer knows that if he burns in the item, he can increase the items 1-month reliability. How long should the engineer burn the item in to achieve a 1-month reliability of 0.8 for items that survive the test? What fraction of the items placed on test will fail during the test?

4.27. Find the skewness and kurtosis of a gamma random variable.

4.28. Find the distribution of the sum of n independent gamma random variables, each with identical scale parameters.

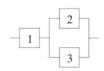

Figure 4.11

4.29. Show that the survivor function for an Erlang(λ, n) random variable is

$$S(t) = \sum_{k=0}^{n-1} \frac{(\lambda t)^k}{k!} e^{-\lambda t} \qquad t \geq 0.$$

4.30. Find the mean residual life for the gamma distribution with parameters $\lambda = 0.01$ and $\kappa = 2.5$ for $t = 5, 15, \ldots, 195$. Check to see that your solution is correct by assuring that all the $L(t)$ values lie between $L(0) = \kappa / \lambda$ and $\lim_{t \to \infty} L(t) = 1 / \lambda$. (*Hint:* You will need access to a function that computes the incomplete gamma function as well as a numerical integrator to compute the appropriate values.)

4.31. A particular type of semiconductor has an exponential lifetime distribution with a 1-year reliability of 0.98. If a passive standby system of four of these semiconductors (that is, a "cold" standby system with one component originally on-line and three spares), find the probability that the standby system of semiconductors survives a 3-year mission. Assume that sensing and switching are perfect and instantaneous upon failure.

4.32. Find the skewness and kurtosis of a Pareto random variable.

4.33. Find the skewness and kurtosis of a random variable that is uniformly distributed between 0 and 1.

4.34. Find the skewness and kurtosis of a log normal random variable. You may use the following result: $E[T^i] = e^{i\mu + \frac{1}{2}i^2\sigma^2}$, which is given in Johnson and Kotz (1970, p. 115).

4.35. Find $E[T^i]$ for $i = 1, 2, \ldots$ for a log logistic random variable.

4.36. Find the skewness and kurtosis of a log logistic random variable.

4.37. Find the parameter values when the coefficient of variation of a log logistic random variable is 1.

4.38. Make a plot of the coefficient of variation (horizontal axis) versus the skewness (vertical axis) for the U(0, 1), exponential, Weibull, gamma, Pareto, log normal, and log logistic distributions.

4.39. Make a plot of the skewness (horizontal axis) versus the kurtosis (vertical axis) for the U(0, 1), exponential, Weibull, gamma, Pareto, log normal, and log logistic distributions.

4.40. Let the lifetime of an item be defined by a special case of the log logistic distribution with survivor function

$$S(t) = \frac{1}{1 + \lambda t} \qquad t \geq 0; \lambda > 0.$$

If the item has been operating for a time units, find
(a) the probability it will last another r time units.
(b) the expected remaining time to failure.

4.41. Consider the three-component system given by Figure 4.12. Component 1 has an exponential distribution with $\lambda = 0.000036$ failure per hour, component 2 has a Weibull distribution with $\lambda = 0.000027$ and $\kappa = 1.24$, and component 3 has an exponential power distribution with $\lambda = 0.000018$ and $\kappa = 2.48$. Assuming that the failure times of the components are independent, use Monte Carlo simulation with 10,000 system lifetime variates to estimate
(a) the mean system lifetime.
(b) $t_{0.01}$ for the system lifetime.

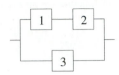

Figure 4.12

4.42. Find the five distribution representations for the exponential power distribution. Also, find the time value where the hazard function achieves a minimum. For which parameter values does the hazard function achieve a minimum? Investigate the properties of this distribution.

4.43. Find the five distribution representations for the IDB distribution. Investigate the properties of this distribution.

4.44. Consider the random variable X having the *logistic* distribution with location parameter η, positive scale parameter $\rho > 0$, and probability density function

$$f(x) = \frac{e^{(x-\eta)/\rho}}{\rho\left(1 + e^{\left(\frac{x-\eta}{\rho}\right)}\right)^2} \qquad -\infty < x < \infty.$$

Show that e^X has the log logistic distribution.

4.45. (Cox and Oakes, 1984, p. 31) Show that a plot of the coefficient of variation γ versus the skewness γ_3 for the log normal distribution is of the form

$$\gamma_3 = \gamma^3 + 3\gamma.$$

Also, for what values of σ does the log normal distribution have $\gamma < 1$?

4.46. Derive $\lim_{t \to \infty} h(t)$ for the log normal distribution.

4.47. For continuous lifetimes, it is usually assumed that the hazard function integrates to infinity. What if it does not? For example, if $h(t) = e^{-t}$, what are the corresponding survivor, density, cumulative hazard, and mean residual life functions? What is the interpretation of such a lifetime distribution? [*Hint*: A plot of $S(t)$ may help. Also, consider whether *all* lifetimes in a population must assume a finite value.]

4.48. Consider two components whose lifetimes T_1 and T_2 have the bivariate exponential distribution with parameters $\lambda_1 = 1$, $\lambda_2 = 2$, and $\lambda_{12} = 3$. An item that has the bivariate exponential distribution is subject to three types of shocks. The time of the first type of shock is exponentially distributed with a failure rate of λ_1, at which time component 1 fails. The time of the second type of shock is exponentially distributed with a failure rate of λ_2, at which time component 2 fails. The time of the third type of shock is exponentially distributed with a failure rate of λ_{12}, at which time both components 1 and 2 fail.
(a) Find $P[T_1 = T_2]$.
(b) If the components are arranged in series, find the system lifetime distribution.
(c) If the components are arranged in parallel, find the expected system lifetime.

4.49. For the following matrix of parameter values for the bivariate exponential distribution, use Monte Carlo simulation to estimate the correlation between T_1 and T_2 using 10,000 iterations. The bivariate exponential distribution is described in Exercise 4.48. Write a paragraph stating your conclusions.

	$\lambda_1 = \lambda_2$		
	1	2	4
$\lambda_{12} = 1$			
$\lambda_{12} = 2$			
$\lambda_{12} = 4$			

5

Specialized Models

Lifetime models for more complicated situations are presented in this chapter. There are several ways to combine and extend the continuous lifetime models outlined in Chapter 4 to increase their flexibility and generality. Four such models presented in this chapter are the *competing risks, mixtures, accelerated life*, and *proportional hazards* models.

Competing risks models are one way of combining several distributions to achieve a bathtub-shaped hazard function. In competing risks models, several "causes" of failure compete for the lifetime of an item. These models are also useful for analyzing the relationships between the causes of failure. *Mixtures* may also be used to achieve a bathtub-shaped hazard function by combining simpler lifetime distributions. Finite mixtures are appropriate for modeling situations when an item is drawn from one of several populations (for example, different manufacturing facilities). Continuous mixtures, or stochastic parameter models, are appropriate when there is a continuous variable that differentiates the populations (for example, the weight of an item). These models allow the parameters in the distributions discussed in Chapter 4 to be random variables (for example, an exponential lifetime with a failure rate having the gamma distribution). This assumption allows a large number of new distributions to be developed by having one lifetime distribution and a second distribution for the parameter. The *accelerated life* and *proportional hazards* models are appropriate for incorporating a vector of covariates that influence survival (for example, turning speed and feed rate for a drill bit) in a lifetime model.

5.1   COMPETING RISKS

In some situations, causes of failure may be grouped into k classes. A reliability engineer, for instance, might use failed open and failed short as a two-element competing risks model for the lifetime of a diode. Likewise, an actuary might use heart disease, cancer, accidents, and all other causes as a four-element competing risks model for human lifetimes. In *competing risks* analysis, an item is assumed to be subject to k competing risks (or causes) $C_1, C_2, \ldots, C_k$. Competing risks, often called *multiple decrements* by actuaries, can be viewed as a series system of components. Each risk can be thought of as a component in a series system in which system failure occurs when any component fails. Analyzing problems by competing risks may require the modeler to include an "all other risks" classification in order to study the effect of reduction or elimination of one risk. The origins of competing risks theory can be traced to a study by Daniel Bernoulli in the 1700s concerning the impact of eliminating smallpox on mortality for different age groups.

A second and equally appealing use of competing risks models is that they can be used to combine component distributions to form more complicated models. Although a distribution with a bathtub-shaped hazard function is often cited as an appropriate lifetime model, none of the four most popular lifetime distribution models (exponential, Weibull, gamma, and log normal) can achieve this shape. Competing risks models are one way of combining several distributions to achieve a bathtub-shaped lifetime distribution. As shown in Figure 5.1, if a DFR Weibull distribution is used to model manufac-

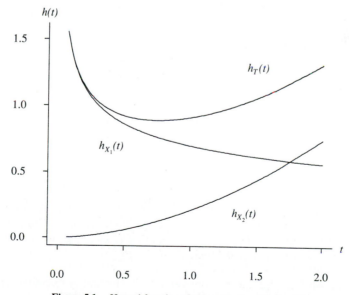

Figure 5.1   Hazard functions for a competing risks model.

turing defect failures and an IFR Weibull distribution is used to model wear-out failures, then a competing risks model ($k = 2$) will yield a bathtub-shaped hazard function.

Competing risks theory is complicated by the existence of *net* and *crude* lifetimes. When working with *net lifetimes* or *net probabilities*, the causes $C_1, \ldots, C_k$ are viewed individually; that is, risk C_j is analyzed as if it is the only risk acting on the population, $j = 1, 2, \ldots, k$. When working with *crude lifetimes* or *crude probabilities*, the lifetimes are considered in the presence of all other risks. The random variables associated with *net* and *crude* lifetimes are defined next.

Definition 5.1   Let the random variable X_j, having probability density function $f_{X_j}(t)$, survivor function $S_{X_j}(t)$, hazard function $h_{X_j}(t)$, cumulative hazard $H_{X_j}(t)$, and corresponding risk C_j, be the *net life* denoting the lifetime that occurs if only risk j is present, $j = 1, 2, \ldots, k$.

Unless all risks except j are eliminated, X_j is not necessarily observed. In this sense, each net lifetime is a *potential* lifetime that is observed with certainty only if all the other $k - 1$ risks are eliminated. The actual observed lifetime, T, is the minimum of $X_1, X_2, \ldots, X_k$. When the net lives are independent, the hazard function for the observed time to failure is $h_T(t) = \sum_{j=1}^{k} h_{X_j}(t)$, since $S_T(t) = \prod_{j=1}^{k} S_{X_j}(t)$ for a series system of k components.

The *net probability* of failure in $[a, b)$ from risk j, denoted by $q_j(a, b)$, is the probability of failure in $[a, b)$ from risk j if risk j is the only risk present, conditioned on survival to time a. So

$$q_j(a, b) = P[a \le X_j < b \mid X_j \ge a]$$

$$= 1 - P[X_j \ge b \mid X_j \ge a]$$

$$= 1 - \frac{S_{X_j}(b)}{S_{X_j}(a)}$$

$$= 1 - \frac{e^{-H_{X_j}(b)}}{e^{-H_{X_j}(a)}}$$

$$= 1 - e^{-\int_a^b h_{X_j}(t)\,dt}$$

for $j = 1, 2, \ldots, k$.

Crude lifetimes are more difficult to work with than net lifetimes since they consider each of the causes in the presence of all other causes. Crude lifetimes are observed when life data are collected in a competing risks model when all causes of failure are acting simultaneously in the population.

Definition 5.2   Let the random variable Y_j, having probability density function $f_{Y_j}(t)$, survivor function $S_{Y_j}(t)$, hazard function $h_{Y_j}(t)$, cumulative hazard $H_{Y_j}(t)$, and corresponding cause C_j, be the *crude life* denoting the lifetime conditioned on risk j being the cause of failure in the presence of all other risks, $j = 1, 2, \ldots, k$.

The *crude probability* of failure in $[a, b)$ from cause j, denoted by $Q_j(a, b)$, is the probability of failure in $[a, b)$ from risk j in the presence of all other risks, conditioned on survival of all risks to time a. So

$$Q_j(a, b) = P[a \le X_j < b, X_j < X_i \text{ for all } i \ne j \mid T \ge a]$$

$$= \int_a^b h_{X_j}(x) e^{-\int_a^x h_T(t)\,dt}\,dx$$

for $j = 1, 2, \ldots, k$. Rather than isolate individual risks, as in the case of net lifetimes, this quantity considers risk j as it works in the presence of the other $k - 1$ risks. The *probability of failure due to risk j*, π_j, is defined by $\pi_j = P[X_j = T]$, for $j = 1, 2, \ldots, k$. Since failure will occur from one of the causes,

$$\sum_{j=1}^{k} \pi_j = 1.$$

A simple example to illustrate some of the concepts in competing risks is given next before the general theory is developed.

Example 5.1

Consider an item subjected to $k = 2$ causes of failure. Let the random variables X_1 and X_2 be the net lives for causes C_1 and C_2. If the item under consideration is a calculator, for example, cause 1 might be dropping the calculator and cause 2 might be all other causes (for example, keyboard or display problems). In this case, X_1 is the life of the calculator if the only way it can fail is by being dropped. The second net life, X_2, is the lifetime of the calculator if it is bolted to a desk and cannot be dropped. The first crude life, Y_1, is the failure time of a calculator that failed due to being dropped in the presence of the second cause of failure. Likewise, Y_2 is the lifetime of a calculator that did not fail by being dropped, but was not bolted to a desk to avoid its being dropped. Let the observed lifetime, T, be the minimum of X_1 and X_2. Also assume that X_1 and X_2 are independent and have exponential distributions with means 1 and $1/2$, respectively. Thus,

$$S_{X_1}(t) = e^{-t} \qquad f_{X_1}(t) = e^{-t} \qquad h_{X_1}(t) = 1$$

$$S_{X_2}(t) = e^{-2t} \qquad f_{X_2}(t) = 2e^{-2t} \qquad h_{X_2}(t) = 2$$

for $t \ge 0$. The net probabilities of failure in the interval $[a, b)$ are

$$q_1(a, b) = 1 - e^{-\int_a^b 1\,dt} = 1 - e^{-(b-a)}$$

and

$$q_2(a, b) = 1 - e^{-\int_a^b 2\,dt} = 1 - e^{-2(b-a)}$$

for $a < b$. The crude probability of failure due to the first risk in the interval $[a, b)$, $Q_1(a, b)$, is the integral of the joint density of X_1 and X_2 over the shaded area in Figure 5.2 (illustrated for $a = 0.5$ and $b = 1.2$), divided by the integral of the joint density over the upper-right quadrant with respect to the point (a, a). Thus,

$$Q_1(a, b) = P[a \le X_1 < b \text{ and } X_1 < X_2 \mid T \ge a]$$

$$= \frac{P[a \le X_1 < b \text{ and } X_1 < X_2]}{P[X_1 \ge a, X_2 \ge a]}$$

$$= \frac{\displaystyle\int_a^b \int_{x_1}^\infty e^{-x_1} 2e^{-2x_2} dx_2 dx_1}{\displaystyle\int_a^\infty \int_a^\infty e^{-x_1} 2e^{-2x_2} dx_2 dx_1}$$

$$= \frac{1}{3}\left[1 - e^{-3(b-a)}\right]$$

for $a < b$. Similarly,

$$Q_2(a, b) = \frac{2}{3}\left[1 - e^{-3(b-a)}\right]$$

for $a < b$. Instead of using the definition of the $Q_i(a, b)$, the formula given earlier,

$$Q_j(a, b) = \int_a^b h_{X_j}(x) e^{-\int_a^x h_T(t)\, dt}\, dx$$

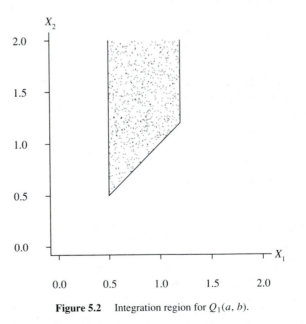

Figure 5.2   Integration region for $Q_1(a, b)$.

can be used to determine these quantities. For this particular example,

$$Q_1(a, b) = \int_a^b e^{-\int_a^x 3\,dt}\,dx = \frac{1}{3}\left[1 - e^{-3(b-a)}\right]$$

and

$$Q_2(a, b) = \int_a^b 2e^{-\int_a^x 3\,dt}\,dx = \frac{2}{3}\left[1 - e^{-3(b-a)}\right]$$

for $a < b$. The probability of failure due to risk 1, π_1, can be found by integrating the joint density of the net lives $f(x_1, x_2)$ over the area $X_1 < X_2$ or, equivalently, using $a = 0$ and $b = \infty$ as arguments in $Q_1(a, b)$, yielding $\pi_1 = 1/3$. Similarly, $\pi_2 = 2/3$.

The focus now shifts to the crude lives, Y_1 and Y_2. What is the survivor function for items that fail from one risk in the presence of the other risk? This survivor function is important because data collected in competing risks models often come in pairs: the cause of failure and the time of failure. The survivor function for the first crude lifetime, $S_{Y_1}(y_1)$, corresponds to a calculator that fails by being dropped in the presence of risk C_2. If an analyst had a large data set of calculator failure times for those calculators that failed by being dropped, an empirical survivor function should converge to $S_{Y_1}(y_1)$. The survivor function for Y_1 is

$$S_{Y_1}(y_1) = P[T \geq y_1 \mid X_1 = T]$$
$$= \frac{P[T \geq y_1, X_1 = T]}{\pi_1}$$
$$= \frac{\displaystyle\int_{y_1}^{\infty}\int_{x_1}^{\infty} e^{-x_1} 2e^{-2x_2}\,dx_2\,dx_1}{1/3}$$
$$= e^{-3y_1} \qquad y_1 \geq 0.$$

Similarly,

$$S_{Y_2}(y_2) = e^{-3y_2} \qquad y_2 \geq 0.$$

This surprising result, that both Y_1 and Y_2 have the same exponential distribution with a mean of 1/3, can be attributed to the definition of a crude lifetime. Since the two crude lifetimes are the minimum of two exponential random variables (the exponential net lifetimes), each will have an exponential distribution with a parameter being the sum of the rates. The crude lifetime Y_1, for example, consists of only those exponential(1) random variables that are smaller than another independent exponential(2) random variable.

As a result, there are two valid ways to generate a lifetime, T, that can be used in Monte Carlo simulation. First, taking the net lifetime perspective, generate an exponential(1) and an exponential(2) and choose the minimum. Second, taking the crude lifetime perspective, generate an exponential(3) and indicate this is failure from risk 1 with probability 1/3 and failure from risk 2 with probability 2/3.

At this point, a general theory for competing risks is developed based on the definitions for net and crude lifetimes given previously. Let $X_1, \ldots, X_k$ be the k continuous net lives and $T = \min\{X_1, \ldots, X_k\}$ be the observed failure time of the item. The X_j's are not necessarily independent as they were in Example 5.1. Letting the net lives have joint density $f(x_1, \ldots, x_k)$, the joint survivor function is

$$S(x_1, \ldots, x_k) = P[X_1 \geq x_1, \ldots, X_k \geq x_k]$$

$$= \int_{x_k}^{\infty} \cdots \int_{x_1}^{\infty} f(t_1, \ldots, t_k)\, dt_1 \cdots dt_k$$

and the marginal net survival function is

$$S_{X_j}(x_j) = P[X_j \geq x_j] = S(0, \ldots, x_j, \ldots, 0)$$

for $j = 1, 2, \ldots, k$. The survivor function for the observed lifetime T is

$$S_T(t) = P[T \geq t] = S(t, \ldots, t).$$

The probability of failure from risk j can be determined from the joint survivor function since

$$-\frac{\partial}{\partial x_j} S(x_1, \ldots, x_j, \ldots, x_k) = \lim_{\Delta x \to 0} \frac{[S(x_1, \ldots, x_j, \ldots, x_k) - S(x_1, \ldots, x_j + \Delta x, \ldots, x_k)]}{\Delta x}$$

so that

$$\pi_j = \int_0^{\infty} -\left[\frac{\partial}{\partial x_j} S(x_1, \ldots, x_j, \ldots, x_k)\right]_{x_1 = \cdots = x_k = x} dx$$

for $j = 1, 2, \ldots, k$.

To derive a survivor function for the crude lifetimes, let the random variable J be the index of the cause of failure so that

$$P[T \geq t, J = j] = P[X_j \geq t, X_j < X_i \text{ for all } i \neq j]$$

$$= \int_t^{\infty} \left[\int_{x_j}^{\infty} \cdots \int_{x_j}^{\infty} f(x_1, \ldots, x_k) \prod_{i \neq j} dx_i \right] dx_j,$$

$j = 1, 2, \ldots, k$, where the survivor function for T is obtained by conditioning

$$S_T(t) = P[T \geq t]$$

$$= \sum_{j=1}^{k} P[T \geq t, J = j].$$

When $t = 0$, each term in this summation is one of the π_j's since

$$\pi_j = P[J = j] = P[T \geq 0, J = j],$$

$j = 1, 2, \ldots, k$. Thus, the distribution of the crude life, Y_j, is the distribution of T conditioned on $J = j$:

$$S_{Y_j}(y_j) = P[T \geq y_j \mid J = j] = \frac{P[T \geq y_j, J = j]}{P[J = j]},$$

$j = 1, 2, \ldots, k$.

Example 5.2

Example 5.1, which considered two independent, exponentially distributed risks, is used to illustrate the use of the formulas developed thus far. As before, let the net lives have marginal survivor functions

$$S_{X_1}(t) = e^{-t} \qquad S_{X_2}(t) = e^{-2t}$$

for $t \geq 0$. Since the risks are independent, the joint survivor function is

$$S(x_1, x_2) = e^{-x_1 - 2x_2}$$

for $x_1 \geq 0$ and $x_2 \geq 0$. The probability of failure from the first risk is

$$\pi_1 = \int_0^\infty -[\frac{\partial}{\partial x_1} S(x_1, x_2)]_{x_1 = x_2 = x} dx$$

$$= \int_0^\infty -[-e^{-x_1 - 2x_2}]_{x_1 = x_2 = x} dx$$

$$= \int_0^\infty e^{-3x} dx$$

$$= 1/3.$$

Since $\pi_2 = 1 - \pi_1$,

$$\pi_2 = 2/3.$$

To find the survival probability conditioned on risk 1 being the cause of failure,

$$P[T \geq t, J = 1] = P[X_1 \geq t, X_1 < X_2]$$

$$= \int_t^\infty \left[\int_{x_1}^\infty f(x_1, x_2) dx_2 \right] dx_1$$

$$= \int\limits_{t}^{\infty} \int\limits_{x_1}^{\infty} 2 e^{-x_1 - 2x_2} dx_2 \, dx_1$$

$$= \int\limits_{t}^{\infty} e^{-3x_1} \, dx_1$$

$$= \frac{1}{3} e^{-3t} \qquad t \ge 0.$$

Similarly,

$$P[T \ge t, J = 2] = \frac{2}{3} e^{-3t} \qquad t \ge 0.$$

Thus, the survival function for the first crude lifetime is

$$S_{Y_1}(y_1) = \frac{P[T \ge y_1, J = 1]}{P[J = 1]} = e^{-3t} \qquad t \ge 0$$

and the survival function for the second crude lifetime is

$$S_{Y_2}(y_2) = \frac{P[T \ge y_2, J = 2]}{P[J = 2]} = e^{-3t} \qquad t \ge 0.$$

To this point, it has been shown how the distribution of the net lives $X_1, \ldots, X_k$ determines the distribution of the crude lives $Y_1, \ldots, Y_k$. Net lives can be interpreted as *potential lifetimes,* while crude lives are the *observed lifetimes.* When lifetime data for the known cause of failure are collected, the observed values are Y_j's. An important question is whether the distribution of each Y_j contains enough information to determine the distribution of the X_j's. In general, the answer is no, but under the assumption of independence of the net lives, the answer is yes. The following discussion considers results under the assumption of independent net lives. This independence can often be attained by grouping the k risks so that dependencies occur within, but not among, risks.

Since the observed data in a competing risks problem are the crude lives, the objective is to find the distribution of the net lives $X_1, \ldots, X_k$, assuming that $\pi_j = P[J = j]$ and $S_{Y_j}(t)$ are known, for $j = 1, 2, \ldots, k$ (for example, when estimated from a large sample). When the risks are independent, the distribution of the net lives may be determined from the distribution of the crude lives using

$$h_{X_j}(t) = \frac{\pi_j \, f_{Y_j}(t)}{\sum\limits_{i=1}^{k} \pi_i \, S_{Y_i}(t)} \qquad t \ge 0$$

for $j = 1, 2, \ldots, k$. This result is proved in Appendix C and is useful for determining the effect of removing one or more risks when the distributions of the crude lives are known from a data set.

Example 5.3

Consider Example 5.2 in which the $k = 2$ risks were assumed to be independent. If a large number of samples are collected, and the cause of failure is *identifiable* (that is, both the failure time and the index of the risk that caused failure are known), it may be possible to determine the distribution of the two crude lifetimes. If both are fitted with an exponential distribution with a failure rate $\lambda = 3$, and approximately one-third of the failures are from cause 1, then

$$\pi_1 = P[J = 1] = \frac{1}{3} \qquad \pi_2 = P[J = 2] = \frac{2}{3}$$

and

$$S_{Y_1}(t) = e^{-3t} \qquad S_{Y_2}(t) = e^{-3t}$$

for $t \geq 0$. Therefore, the hazard functions for the net lives are

$$h_{X_1}(t) = \frac{\frac{1}{3} 3e^{-3t}}{\frac{1}{3} e^{-3t} + \frac{2}{3} e^{-3t}} = 1 \qquad t \geq 0,$$

$$h_{X_2}(t) = \frac{\frac{2}{3} 3e^{-3t}}{\frac{1}{3} e^{-3t} + \frac{2}{3} e^{-3t}} = 2 \qquad t \geq 0.$$

This result is consistent with the previous two examples.

To summarize this section, competing risks models are appropriate when there are k causes of failure and the occurrence of failure due to any risk causes the item to fail. The net lifetimes occur if only one risk is evident at a time in the population. The crude lifetimes occur in the presence of all other risks. If the net lives are independent, once the distributions of $Y_1, \ldots, Y_k$ and $\pi_1, \ldots, \pi_k$ are determined, the distribution of the net lives $X_1, \ldots, X_k$ can be determined.

5.2   MIXTURES

In some situations, items may come from one of m populations, each with a distinct lifetime distribution. A reliability engineer, for instance, might have a component that was manufactured in one of two facilities, but is not certain which one the item came from. In *finite mixture* models, an item is assumed to be from one of m populations. As in the case of competing risks, the distribution of the time to failure can be expressed in terms of the distribution of each of the population's time to failure. Also, finite mixture models can be used to combine component distributions to form more complicated models, as was the case in competing risks. When there is a single population that is mixed by a continuous parameter (for example, the temperature of solder applied to a circuit board), a *stochastic parameter* model, or *continuous mixture* model, is appropriate.

The densities of *mixture distributions*, also called *compound distributions*, can be expressed as weighted sums of the distributions of component distributions. Assume that there is only one cause of failure and the failure time is T. A *mixture* model can be expressed by

$$f(t) = \int_{\text{all }\theta} f(t|\theta)\, p(\theta) d\theta,$$

where θ is called the *mix parameter* and $p(\theta)$ indicates the distribution of the mix parameter. If $p(\theta)$ is a probability mass function (that is, the mix parameter is discrete), this is a finite mixture model, and the integral can be replaced by a summation. If $p(\theta)$ is a probability density function (the mix parameter is continuous), this is a continuous mixture model.

A *finite mixture* applies when items can be divided into m populations by a characteristic of the item (for example, manufacturing facility or type of component used),

$$f(t) = \sum_{l=1}^{m} p_l\, f_l(t\,|\,\boldsymbol{\theta}_l),$$

where the $f_l(t\,|\,\boldsymbol{\theta}_l)$ are the population probability density functions, $\boldsymbol{\theta}_l$ is a vector of parameters for the distribution of population l, and the p_l are the *mix parameters,* where

$$\sum_{l=1}^{m} p_l = 1 \qquad p_l \geq 0 \quad \text{for} \quad l = 1, 2, \ldots, m$$

For example, assume factory 1 produces items with lifetime distribution $f_1(t)$, factory 2 produces items with lifetime distribution $f_2(t)$, ..., and factory m produces items with lifetime distribution $f_m(t)$. If $p_1, p_2, \ldots, p_m$ are the probabilities of selecting an item manufactured at each factory, the time to failure of an item has a finite mixture distribution. Alternatively, if *one* factory produces parts with quality defects (and thus they will fail soon after being placed into service) or without quality defects (and thus will undergo systematic failures), a finite mixture model with $m = 2$ would be appropriate. Any of the general parametric models introduced in Chapter 4 may be used to model the $f_l(t)$'s.

Example 5.4

If $m = 2$ facilities produce items with exponential(1) and exponential(2) lifetimes, respectively, and one-third of the items come from facility 1 and two-thirds come from facility 2, the probability density function of the time to failure of an item whose manufacturing site is unknown is

$$f(t) = p_1\, f_1(t\,|\,\lambda_1) + p_2\, f_2(t\,|\,\lambda_2)$$

$$= \frac{1}{3} e^{-t} + \frac{4}{3} e^{-2t} \qquad t \geq 0,$$

which is a finite mixture of the two populations. This model is a special case of the *hyper-exponential* distribution, which is the finite mixture of *m* exponential populations.

An identifiability problem exists in finite mixtures. Often it is impossible to determine the component distributions from the distribution of the population. The following is an example with $m = 2$.

Example 5.5

Consider the random variables T_1 and T_2, both defined as finite mixtures:

$$f_{T_1}(t) = \frac{2}{3} f_{U_1}(t) + \frac{1}{3} f_{U_2}(t) \qquad 0 \le t \le 1$$

and

$$f_{T_2}(t) = \frac{1}{2} f_{U_3}(t) + \frac{1}{2} f_{U_4}(t) \qquad 0 \le t \le 1,$$

where U_1 is U(0, 1), U_2 is U(1/4 , 3/4), U_3 is U(0, 3/4), and U_4 is U(1/4, 1). The random variables T_1 and T_2 have the same distribution. Their probability density functions are

$$f_{T_1}(t) = f_{T_2}(t) = \begin{cases} 2/3 & 0 \le t \le 1/4 \\ 4/3 & 1/4 < t \le 3/4 \\ 2/3 & 3/4 < t \le 1. \end{cases}$$

Thus, the two cannot be differentiated on the basis of sample data from the mixture distribution. This *identifiability* problem is important if the goal is to find the component distributions.

The identifiability problem exists in both competing risks and finite mixtures models. In competing risks, the problem is to identify which risk caused failure, whereas in finite mixtures it is to identify the component population distribution.

Combining competing risks and finite mixtures theory allows a rather complicated form of the density function:

$$f(t) = \sum_{l=1}^{m} p_l \left[\sum_{j=1}^{k_l} h_{lj}(t)\, e^{-\int_0^t \sum_{j=1}^{k_l} h_{lj}(\tau)d\tau} \right],$$

where *m* is the number of populations, $\sum_{l=1}^{m} p_l = 1$, k_l is the number of risks acting within the *l*th population, and $h_{lj}(t)$ is the hazard function for the *j*th risk within the *l*th population. Such a model would be appropriate when an item comes from one of *m* populations and may fail from one of several causes within each population. In a casualty insurance application, for example, there may be $m = 3$ populations of dwellings: single-family dwellings, condominiums, and apartments, each subjected to and insured for $k_1 = k_2 = k_3 = 5$ risks: fire, flood, tornado, earthquake, and burglary.

If the mix parameters in a finite mixture are allowed to be random variables, rather than constants, a wide variety of distributions follows. They are known as *continuous mixture models, stochastic parameter models*, or *Bayesian models*. Using Bayesian terminology, the *prior distribution* of the parameter considered random determines the unconditional distribution of the lifetime. Assuming that the random parameter has a continuous distribution,

$$f_T(t) = \int_{-\infty}^{\infty} f_{T|\theta}(t|\theta) f_\theta(\theta) \, d\theta,$$

where θ is the random parameter, $f_\theta(\theta)$ is the distribution of the random parameter, and $f_{T|\theta}(t|\theta)$ is the conditional distribution of the time to failure given the value of θ. Example 5.6 considers a positive random variable with a continuous random parameter.

Example 5.6

Let the random lifetime T have the exponential distribution with positive parameter λ_1:

$$f_{T|\lambda_1}(t|\lambda_1) = \lambda_1 e^{-\lambda_1 t} \qquad t \geq 0.$$

Now suppose that λ_1 is an exponential random variable with positive parameter λ_2:

$$f_{\lambda_1}(\lambda_1) = \lambda_2 e^{-\lambda_2 \lambda_1} \qquad \lambda_1 > 0.$$

That is, the time to failure has an exponential distribution whose failure rate is exponentially distributed. In this case, the unconditional distribution of T is found using integration by parts:

$$f_T(t) = \int_0^{\infty} \lambda_1 e^{-\lambda_1 t} \lambda_2 e^{-\lambda_2 \lambda_1} \, d\lambda_1$$

$$= \lambda_2 \int_0^{\infty} \lambda_1 e^{-\lambda_1 (t + \lambda_2)} d\lambda_1$$

$$= \left[\frac{-\lambda_2 \lambda_1 e^{-\lambda_1(t+\lambda_2)}}{t + \lambda_2} + \frac{\lambda_2}{t + \lambda_2} \int e^{-\lambda_1(t+\lambda_2)} d\lambda_1 \right]_0^{\infty}$$

$$= \left[\frac{-\lambda_1 \lambda_2 e^{-\lambda_1(t + \lambda_2)}}{t + \lambda_2} - \frac{\lambda_2}{(t + \lambda_2)^2} e^{-\lambda_1(t + \lambda_2)} \right]_0^{\infty}$$

$$= \frac{\lambda_2}{(t + \lambda_2)^2} \qquad t \geq 0,$$

which is recognized as a special case of the log logistic distribution.

As opposed to the list of models surveyed in the previous section, developed one by one, the number of models of this type grows rapidly as the number of conditional and prior distributions considered increases. In addition to continuous models having random parameters, discrete lifetime distributions may also have random parameters, as in Example 5.7.

Example 5.7

Let T have the Poisson distribution with random parameter λ:

$$f_{T \mid \lambda}(t \mid \lambda) = \frac{\lambda^t e^{-\lambda}}{t!} \qquad t = 0, 1, 2, \ldots,$$

where $\lambda > 0$. Now suppose that λ is a random variable having the gamma distribution with shape parameter κ and scale parameter δ:

$$f_\lambda(\lambda) = \frac{\delta(\delta\lambda)^{\kappa-1} e^{-\delta\lambda}}{\Gamma(\kappa)} \qquad \lambda > 0,$$

where $\kappa > 0$ and $\delta > 0$; that is, the time to failure has a Poisson distribution with a stochastic parameter having the gamma distribution. The unconditional distribution of the lifetime T is

$$f_T(t) = \int_0^\infty \frac{\lambda^t e^{-\lambda}}{t!} \frac{\delta(\delta\lambda)^{\kappa-1} e^{-\delta\lambda}}{\Gamma(\kappa)} \, d\lambda$$

$$= \frac{\delta^\kappa}{\Gamma(\kappa) t!} \int_0^\infty \lambda^{t+\kappa-1} e^{-(1+\delta)\lambda} \, d\lambda.$$

Making the substitution $u = (1 + \delta)\lambda$,

$$f_T(t) = \frac{\delta^\kappa}{\Gamma(\kappa) t!} \int_0^\infty \left(\frac{u}{1+\delta}\right)^{t+\kappa-1} e^{-u} \frac{1}{1+\delta} \, du$$

$$= \frac{\delta^\kappa (1+\delta)^{-(t+\kappa)}}{\Gamma(\kappa) t!} \int_0^\infty u^{t+\kappa-1} e^{-u} \, du$$

$$= \frac{\Gamma(t+\kappa) \, \delta^\kappa (1+\delta)^{-(t+\kappa)}}{\Gamma(\kappa) t!} \qquad t = 0, 1, 2, \ldots,$$

which is often called the gamma–Poisson distribution, since the gamma distribution indicates the mixture variable and the Poisson distribution indicates the lifetime distribution.

5.3   ACCELERATED LIFE

The *accelerated life* and *proportional hazards* models are appropriate for including a vector of covariates (for example, turning speed and feed rate for a drill bit) in a lifetime model. A *covariate,* often called an *explanatory variable,* is a variable that influences the survival time of the item under consideration. Covariates may account for the fact that the population is not truly homogeneous, or they may account for treatments imposed on the population.

The $q \times 1$ vector $\mathbf{z}$ contains q covariates associated with a particular item. These covariates may be treatments/stresses, intrinsic properties of items, or exogenous (environmental) variables. The simplest case is the two-population situation modeled by a single ($q = 1$) binary covariate z, where $z = 0$ corresponds to the control group and $z = 1$ corresponds to the treatment group. A second, slightly more complicated example is when a single covariate assumes a continuous value (for example, dosage in a medical setting or turning speed in a manufacturing setting). The objective in an analysis of this type might be to find the dosage or turning speed that minimizes risks or costs, respectively. Other possibilities for the elements of $\mathbf{z}$ include cumulative load applied, time-varying stresses, and environmental factors.

The covariates affect the rate at which the item ages in the accelerated life model and increase or decrease the hazard function in the proportional hazards model. These models were originally developed for medical settings, where covariates are usually patient characteristics such as age, gender, cholesterol level, or blood pressure. The models are often used to determine which covariate has the most significant impact on survival or to compare the survival patterns for different treatments (for example, chemotherapy versus surgery for cancer) by factoring out the impact of the covariates.

One issue of immediate interest is how to link the covariates to a lifetime distribution. One approach is to define one lifetime model when $\mathbf{z} = \mathbf{0}$ (often called the *baseline* model) and other models when $\mathbf{z} \neq \mathbf{0}$. One problem with this approach is that there may be too many models to define when $\mathbf{z} \neq \mathbf{0}$, so a single model appropriate for all values of $\mathbf{z}$ simplifies modeling.

The survivor function for T in the *accelerated life* model is

$$S(t) = S_0(t\,\psi(\mathbf{z})) \qquad t \geq 0,$$

where S_0 is a baseline survivor function and $\psi(\mathbf{z})$ is a *link function*. The baseline distribution corresponds to having all the covariates equal to zero. In a reliability setting, this is typically the normal operating conditions for the item. Other covariate vectors are often used for accelerated environmental conditions. In a biomedical setting, the baseline is typically the control group that receives either no treatment or the standard treatment. The covariates are linked to the lifetime by $\psi(\mathbf{z})$, which typically satisfies $\psi(\mathbf{0}) = 1$ and $\psi(\mathbf{z}) > 0$ for all $\mathbf{z}$. When a link function satisfies these conditions, then $\mathbf{z} = \mathbf{0}$ implies $S_0(t) \equiv S(t)$. The most general case is to let $\psi(\mathbf{z})$ be any function of the covariates. A popular choice is the log-linear link function $\psi(\mathbf{z}) = e^{\boldsymbol{\beta}'\mathbf{z}}$, where $\boldsymbol{\beta}$ is a $q \times 1$ vector of regression coefficients corresponding to the q covariates. In this model, the covariates accelerate [$\psi(\mathbf{z}) > 1$] or decelerate [$\psi(\mathbf{z}) < 1$] the rate at which the item moves through time with respect to the baseline case. Other, less popular choices for the link function are $\psi(\mathbf{z}) = \boldsymbol{\beta}'\mathbf{z}$ and $\psi(\mathbf{z}) = (\boldsymbol{\beta}'\mathbf{z})^{-1}$. Both choices suffer from the limitation that $\psi(\mathbf{z}) < 0$ for some values of $\boldsymbol{\beta}$, resulting in a constrained optimization problem when the models are fitted to data. The left-hand side of this model is often written as $S(t; \mathbf{z})$ since survival is now a function of both time and the covariate vector $\mathbf{z}$.

Another way of viewing the accelerated life model is to denote a lifetime as

$$T = T_0 / \psi(\mathbf{z}),$$

where T is the lifetime with covariates $\mathbf{z}$ and T_0 is the lifetime under baseline conditions ($\mathbf{z} = \mathbf{0}$). If a particular item, for example, has $\psi(\mathbf{z}) = 2$, then this item moves through time at twice the rate of an item under the baseline conditions. As the preceding equation indicates, this item's lifetime T is half of the lifetime of an item under baseline conditions T_0. If the log-linear link function is used, then this equation can be rewritten as

$$T_0 / T = e^{\beta' \mathbf{z}},$$

and taking logarithms gives

$$\log T_0 - \log T = \beta_1 z_1 + \beta_2 z_2 + \cdots + \beta_q z_q.$$

These models are often called *regression models* since the exponent of the link function, $\beta' \mathbf{z}$, parallels a multiple regression model from classical regression analysis. Regression modeling tools such as indicator variables, modeling of interaction terms, modeling of nonlinear relationships between variables, and stepwise selection of significant covariates can all be used here. Estimation of the regression coefficients $\beta_1, \ldots, \beta_q$ and the baseline distribution parameters is considered in Chapter 9.

The other lifetime distribution representations can be determined for accelerated life models. For example,

$$H(t) = - \log S(t)$$

$$= - \log(S_0(t\, \psi(\mathbf{z})))$$

$$= H_0(t\psi(\mathbf{z})) \qquad t \geq 0.$$

Similarly,

$$h(t) = H'(t)$$

$$= \frac{d}{dt} H_0(t\psi(\mathbf{z}))$$

$$= \psi(\mathbf{z})\, h_0(t\psi(\mathbf{z})) \qquad t \geq 0.$$

Finally,

$$f(t) = S(t)\, h(t)$$

$$= S_0(t\psi(\mathbf{z}))\, \psi(\mathbf{z})\, h_0(t\psi(\mathbf{z}))$$

$$= \psi(\mathbf{z})\, f_0(t\psi(\mathbf{z})) \qquad t \geq 0.$$

Example 5.8

Consider the case of a Weibull baseline function in an accelerated life model. Assume that the link function is given by $\psi(\mathbf{z}) = e^{\beta'\mathbf{z}}$. Find the survivor function and the probability that an item with covariates $\mathbf{z}$ fails by time 1000.

The baseline survivor function has a Weibull distribution with scale parameter λ and shape parameter κ:

$$S_0(t) = e^{-(\lambda t)^\kappa} \qquad t \geq 0.$$

The survivor function for an item with covariates $\mathbf{z}$ is

$$S(t) = S_0(\psi(\mathbf{z})\,t) = e^{-(\lambda\,\psi(\mathbf{z})\,t)^\kappa} = e^{-(\lambda\,e^{\beta'\mathbf{z}}\,t)^\kappa} \qquad t \geq 0.$$

The random lifetime has the Weibull distribution with scale parameter $\lambda\,e^{\beta'\mathbf{z}}$ and shape parameter κ. When the interest is in the probability of failure by time 1000, the complement of the survivor function should be used:

$$P[T \leq 1000] = 1 - S(1000) = 1 - e^{-(1000\lambda\,e^{\beta'\mathbf{z}})^\kappa}.$$

When all the parameters are defined (λ, κ, and $\boldsymbol{\beta}$), a specific value for this probability can be calculated for any covariate vector $\mathbf{z}$.

Example 5.9

The log logistic distribution has a tractable survivor function that can be used as a baseline in the accelerated life model. The baseline survivor function is

$$S_0(t) = \frac{1}{1 + (\lambda t)^\kappa} \qquad t \geq 0.$$

Assuming the log-linear form for the link function, the survivor function for an item with covariates $\mathbf{z}$ is

$$S(t) = S_0(\psi(\mathbf{z})\,t) = \frac{1}{1 + (\lambda\,\psi(\mathbf{z})\,t)^\kappa} = \frac{1}{1 + (\lambda\,e^{\beta'\mathbf{z}}t)^\kappa} \qquad t \geq 0.$$

The accelerated life model is useful in situations when testing items at their operating environments is too time consuming. It is often wiser to run a test in a more stressful environment, usually with respect to temperature, humidity, or vibration, which induces more failures. The results from the burn-in test can then be extrapolated back to the environment that the item will be used in.

The proportional hazards model, presented in Section 5.4, is another model for incorporating covariates in a survival model. The proportional hazards model has a unique feature that allows estimation of the regression parameters (the $\boldsymbol{\beta}$ vector) without knowledge of the baseline distribution.

5.4   PROPORTIONAL HAZARDS

One common feature of the accelerated life and proportional hazards lifetime models is that they are both used to account for the effects of covariates on a random lifetime. All the notation developed in Section 5.3 applies to proportional hazards models as well as accelerated life models. Whereas accelerated life models modify the rate that the item moves through time based on the values of the covariates, proportional hazards models modify the hazard function by the factor $\psi(\mathbf{z})$.

The *proportional hazards* model can be defined by

$$h(t) = \psi(\mathbf{z})\, h_0(t) \qquad t \geq 0.$$

The covariates increase the hazard function when $\psi(\mathbf{z}) > 1$ or decrease the hazard function when $\psi(\mathbf{z}) < 1$. As before, a popular choice for the link function is the log-linear form $\psi(\mathbf{z}) = e^{\boldsymbol{\beta}'\mathbf{z}}$, where $\boldsymbol{\beta}$ is a $q \times 1$ vector of regression coefficients corresponding to the q covariates.

The other lifetime distribution representations can be determined from this definition. For example,

$$H(t) = \int_0^t h(\tau)\, d\tau$$

$$= \int_0^t \psi(\mathbf{z})\, h_0(\tau)\, d\tau$$

$$= \psi(\mathbf{z})\, H_0(t) \qquad t \geq 0.$$

Table 5.1 gives a comparison of the various lifetime distribution representations for the accelerated life and proportional hazards models. This table allows a modeler to determine any of the first four lifetime distribution representations for either model once the baseline distribution and link function are specified, as illustrated in Example 5.10.

Example 5.10

Consider the case of a Weibull baseline function in a proportional hazards model. Find the hazard and survivor functions.

The baseline hazard function has a Weibull distribution with parameters λ and κ:

$$h_0(t) = \kappa \lambda^\kappa t^{\kappa - 1} \qquad t \geq 0 .$$

So the hazard function for an item with covariates $\mathbf{z}$ is

$$h(t) = \psi(\mathbf{z}) h_0(t) = \psi(\mathbf{z}) \kappa \lambda^\kappa t^{\kappa - 1} \qquad t \geq 0.$$

Using Table 5.1, the appropriate formula for determining the survivor function is

TABLE 5.1   LIFETIME DISTRIBUTION REPRESENTA-
TIONS FOR REGRESSION MODELS

	Accelerated Life	Proportional Hazards
$S(t)$	$S_0(t\psi(\mathbf{z}))$	$[S_0(t)]^{\psi(\mathbf{z})}$
$f(t)$	$\psi(\mathbf{z})f_0(t\psi(\mathbf{z}))$	$f_0(t)\psi(\mathbf{z})[S_0(t)]^{\psi(\mathbf{z})-1}$
$h(t)$	$\psi(\mathbf{z})h_0(t\psi(\mathbf{z}))$	$\psi(\mathbf{z})h_0(t)$
$H(t)$	$H_0(t\psi(\mathbf{z}))$	$\psi(\mathbf{z})\,H_0(t)$

$$S(t) = [S_0(t)]^{\psi(\mathbf{z})} \qquad t \geq 0.$$

Using the usual baseline for the Weibull distribution,

$$S(t) = [e^{-(\lambda t)^\kappa}]^{\psi(\mathbf{z})} = e^{-(\lambda t)^\kappa \psi(\mathbf{z})} \qquad t \geq 0.$$

This can be recognized as a Weibull lifetime with scale parameter $\lambda\psi(\mathbf{z})^{1/\kappa}$ and shape parameter κ. Example 5.8 showed that a Weibull baseline model under the accelerated life assumption also produced a Weibull time to failure. Thus, if a modeler specifies a Weibull baseline distribution in either model, the time to failure distribution will also have the Weibull distribution. The Weibull distribution is the only baseline distribution in which the accelerated life and the proportional hazards models coincide in this fashion. The values of the regression coefficients $\boldsymbol{\beta}$ will differ, however, since the functional form of $S(t)$ is not identical for the proportional hazards and accelerated life models.

Example 5.11

To illustrate the difference between the accelerated life and proportional hazards models graphically, consider the baseline hazard function

$$h_0(t) = \begin{cases} 1 & 0 \leq t < 1 \\ t & t \geq 1 \end{cases}$$

and a single binary covariate z. Assume that when $z = 0$ (the control case) the link function is $\psi(z) = 1$, and when $z = 1$ (the treatment case) the link function is $\psi(z) = 2$ for both models. The hazard functions for these cases are given in Figure 5.3. The baseline hazard function is given by the solid line and applies to both the accelerated life (AL) and proportional hazards (PH) models in the control case. The dashed line is the hazard function for the proportional hazards (PH) model in the treatment case. The hazard function is always twice the baseline case because

$$h_{\mathrm{PH}}(t) = \psi(z)\,h_0(t) \qquad t \geq 0.$$

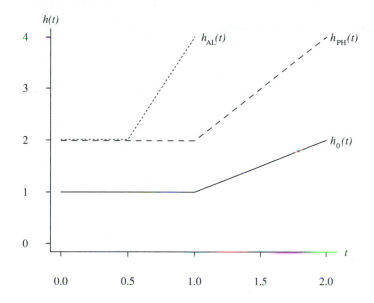

Figure 5.3 Hazard functions for a piecewise-continuous baseline hazard function. (*Source*: D. R. Cox and D. Oakes, *Analysis of Survival Data*, 1984. Adapted and reprinted by permission of Chapman and Hall, New York.)

The dotted line is the hazard function for the accelerated life model in the treatment case, where

$$h_{AL}(t) = \psi(z)h_0(t\psi(z)) \qquad t \geq 0.$$

So, in addition to doubling the risk that the item is subject to, the item also moves through time at twice the rate of an item in the control case.

A second example is given next to further illustrate the geometry associated with the accelerated life and proportional hazards models. This example focuses on the cumulative hazard functions for these two models.

Example 5.12

As in Example 5.11, consider a single binary covariate z, and assume that $\psi(0) = 1$ and $\psi(1) = 2$. Table 5.1 gives the cumulative hazard function for the accelerated life (AL) and proportional hazards (PH) models as

$$H_{AL}(t) = H_0(t\psi(z)) \qquad H_{PH}(t) = \psi(z)\,H_0(t)$$

for $t \geq 0$. The multiplicative influence of $\psi(z)$ on time in the accelerated life model and the multiplicative influence of $\psi(z)$ on the cumulative hazard function in the proportional hazards model are illustrated in Figure 5.4. The baseline cumulative hazard function is $H_0(t) = 0.1t^2$ and is plotted as a solid line. This is a special case of the Weibull distribution. For any vertical line, such as the one at $t = 1.9$,

$$H_{PH}(t) = 2H_0(t) \qquad t \geq 0.$$

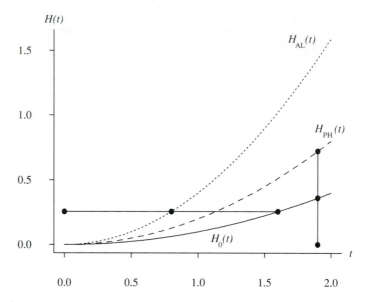

Figure 5.4   Cumulative hazard functions for the accelerated life and proportional hazards models.

For any horizontal line, such as the one at $H(t) = 0.256$,

$$H_{AL}(t) = H_0(2t) \qquad t \geq 0.$$

5.5   FURTHER READING

Further information on competing risks models is contained in David and Moeschberger (1978) and Birnbaum (1979), as well as in sections on the models in Crowder et al. (1991), Kalbfleisch and Prentice (1980), and Lawless (1982).

Mixture models are considered in Everitt and Hand (1981) and Lee (1993). Martz and Waller (1982) and Sander and Badoux (1991) consider Bayesian models in reliability, a generalization of what has been presented here.

The regression models, along with statistical methods for estimating the regression coefficients, are given in Cox and Oakes (1984), Crowder et al. (1991), Gertsbakh (1989), Kalbfleisch and Prentice (1980), and Lawless (1982). Nelson (1990) includes models associated with accelerated testing, many of which are related to the accelerated life model. As he indicates in his text, it is often the case that it is not possible to test at the operational stress due to time limitations. Consequently, it is necessary to assume that the accelerated life model applies beyond the experimental values of the covariates. It is usually best to use a range as wide as possible for the experimental levels of the covariate vector $\mathbf{z}$. The alternative forms for $\psi(\mathbf{z})$ are given in Kalbfleisch and Prentice (1980, p. 31) and Lawless (1982, p. 283).

Kalbfleisch and Prentice (1980, p. 33) give two generalizations of the accelerated life and proportional hazards models that do not significantly complicate estimation procedures. The first is to let $h_0(t)$ vary over r strata of the population. For the proportional hazards model, this is

$$h_j(t) = h_{0j}(t)\psi(\mathbf{z}) \qquad j = 1, 2, \ldots, r,$$

which is useful if one or possibly two of the explanatory variables do not have a multiplicative relationship with $h_0(t)$. The second involves time-dependent covariates $\mathbf{z}(t)$. Examples include varying drug dosage in a medical setting or varying the turning speed of a machine tool in an industrial setting. Example 5.11 is similar to an illustration from Cox and Oakes (1984, pp. 71–72). Example 5.12 is from Shih (1991).

5.6   EXERCISES

5.1.   Three independent risks act on a population. The net lives, X_j, are exponential(λ_j), for $j = 1, 2, 3$. Find
(a) $q_j(a, b)$ (b) $Q_{Y_j}(a, b)$ (c) π_j
for $j = 1, 2, 3$.

5.2.   A component can fail from one of two identifiable causes. You have collected a large number of failures of both types and determined that

$$\pi_1 = 0.73 \qquad \pi_2 = 0.27$$

and the crude lives have probability density functions

$$f_{Y_1}(t) = 1 \qquad 0 \le t \le 1$$

and

$$f_{Y_2}(t) = \theta t^{\theta - 1} \qquad 0 \le t \le 1; \theta > 0.$$

Find the distributions of the net lives, X_1 and X_2, assuming that the risks are independent.

5.3.   In a competing risks model, the distributions of the k crude lifetimes are exponential with identical parameter λ. In addition, the probabilities of failure from each of the risks (the π_j's) are known. Assuming that the net lives are independent, find
(a) the mean lifetime of the item.
(b) the mean lifetime of the item if risk j is eliminated, $j = 1, 2, \ldots, k$.

5.4.   Assume that the following are known in a competing risks model:

$$\pi_1 = \frac{1}{4} \qquad \pi_2 = \frac{3}{4} \qquad S_{Y_1}(t) = e^{-\alpha t} \qquad S_{Y_2}(t) = e^{-(\lambda t)^\kappa}$$

for $t \ge 0$. Assuming that the risks are independent, find
(a) the hazard function for the first net lifetime.
(b) an expression for $E[T]$.

(c) an expression for the expected time to failure if risk 2 is removed.

The solution to this problem may not be closed form.

5.5. If $X_1, X_2, \ldots, X_k$ are independent net lives and $X_j \sim$ exponential(λ_j) for $j = 1, 2, \ldots, k$, find $\pi_j = P[X_j = \min\{X_1, X_2, \ldots, X_k\}]$ for $j = 1, 2, \ldots, k$.

5.6. If X_1 and X_2 are independent net lives and $X_j \sim$ Weibull(λ_j, κ) for $j = 1, 2$, find $\pi_1 = P[X_1 = \min\{X_1, X_2\}]$.

5.7. Consider two independent, competing risks C_1 and C_2. The net lifetime for risk 1 has a log logistic distribution with λ_1 and κ_1. The net lifetime for risk 2 has a log logistic distribution with λ_2 and κ_2. Write an expression for π_1 and π_2.

5.8. Let T be the lifetime of an item subjected to three competing risks, for which the hazard functions for the crude lives are

$$h_{Y_1}(t) = \frac{a}{t + \alpha} \qquad t \geq 0,$$

$$h_{Y_2}(t) = bt \qquad t \geq 0,$$

and

$$h_{Y_3}(t) = \lambda \qquad t \geq 0.$$

Given the values of π_1, π_2, and π_3, give an expression for the hazard function for the first net lifetime.

5.9. Compare the expected times to failure in each of these two situations:

(a) A component is selected from a mixture distribution of two different exponential populations with failure rates λ_1 and λ_2 and mixture parameters p_1 and p_2.

(b) A component is selected from an exponential population with failure rate $p_1\lambda_1 + p_2\lambda_2$.

5.10. (Cox and Oakes, 1984, p. 20) Assume that the distribution of a lifetime is exponential with a random parameter that has the gamma distribution; that is,

$$S(t \mid \alpha) = e^{-\alpha t} \qquad t \geq 0; \alpha > 0$$

and

$$f_\alpha(\alpha) = \frac{\lambda(\lambda\alpha)^{\kappa-1} e^{-\lambda\alpha}}{\Gamma(\kappa)} \qquad \alpha > 0; \lambda > 0; \kappa > 0.$$

Find the unconditional probability density function of T. Is this distribution related to one encountered earlier? If so, which one, and what is the relationship. Also, show that T approaches an exponential distribution as κ approaches infinity.

5.11. Consider a continuous mixture model for which

$$f(t \mid \lambda) = \lambda e^{-\lambda t} \qquad t \geq 0$$

and λ has probability density function

$$f_\lambda(\lambda) = \frac{1}{\lambda \log 2} \qquad 1 < \lambda < 2.$$

(a) Show that $f_\lambda(\lambda)$ is a probability density function.

(b) Find the probability density function for the time to failure.

5.12. Consider a mixture model containing two populations with mixing parameters p_1 and p_2, means μ_1 and μ_2, and variances σ_1^2 and σ_2^2. Find the mean and variance of the model in terms of p_1, p_2, μ_1, μ_2, σ_1^2, and σ_2^2.

5.13. Find the mode of the log logistic distribution. If the mode of the log logistic distribution is t^*, what is the mode of the accelerated life model having log logistic baseline distribution with covariates $\mathbf{z}$ and link function $\psi(\mathbf{z})$?

5.14. A lifetime distribution is modeled with the accelerated life model with $q = 2$ covariates and Weibull baseline with parameters $\lambda = 0.003$ and $\kappa = 1.5$. If the regression vector is $\boldsymbol{\beta} = (-0.18 \quad 3.6)'$ and the log-linear form of the link function is used, find the probability that an item with covariates $z_1 = 5$ and $z_2 = 0.5$ will survive 12 time units.

5.15. Consider the baseline hazard function

$$h_0(t) = \begin{cases} 1 & 0 \le t < 1 \\ t & t \ge 1. \end{cases}$$

In a proportional hazards model, find the probability that an item with covariates $\mathbf{z}$ and link function $\psi(\mathbf{z})$ will survive to time t.

5.16. A proportional hazards model is applied to a lifetime that has a single binary covariate z with regression coefficient β, link function $\psi(z) = e^{\beta z}$, and Weibull baseline hazard function. Find

(a) the survivor function for the time to failure.

(b) the mean time to failure when $z = 0$.

(c) the mean time to failure when $z = 1$.

5.17. (Leemis, 1987) The following table gives formulas for generating event times from a renewal process and a nonhomogeneous Poisson process (NHPP), where the last event is assumed to have occurred at time a.

	Renewal	NHPP
Accelerated life	$t = a + \dfrac{H_0^{-1}(-\log(1-u))}{\psi(\mathbf{z})}$	$t = \dfrac{H_0^{-1}(H_0(a\psi(\mathbf{z})) - \log(1-u))}{\psi(\mathbf{z})}$
Proportional hazards	$t = a + H_0^{-1}\left(\dfrac{-\log(1-u)}{\psi(\mathbf{z})}\right)$	$t = H_0^{-1}\left(H_0(a) - \dfrac{\log(1-u)}{\psi(\mathbf{z})}\right)$

The renewal and NHPP algorithms are equivalent when $a = 0$ (since a renewal process is equivalent to a NHPP restarted at zero after each event); the accelerated life and proportional hazards models are equivalent when $\psi(\mathbf{z}) = 1$; and all four cases shown in the table are equivalent when $H_0(t) = \lambda t$ (the exponential case) because of the memoryless property. Write an algebraic statement that will generate a single lifetime variate (for example, either the renewal or NHPP situations with $a = 0$) from the exponential power baseline distribution with parameters λ and κ, assuming that $\psi(\mathbf{z}) = e^{\beta' \mathbf{z}}$. Assume that the survivor function for the exponential power distribution is

$$S(t) = e^{1 - e^{\lambda t^\kappa}} \qquad t \geq 0.$$

5.18. Consider an electrical component whose lifetime is being modeled by the proportional hazards model with $q = 2$ covariates: temperature z_1 (measured in degrees Celsius) and operating environment z_2. Assume that the Weibull baseline distribution and a log linear link function are used.

(a) What would you expect the sign (positive or negative) of $\hat{\beta}_1$ to be if a large sample of failure times and associated covariates was collected? Explain your reasoning.

(b) Find the probability that such a component survives to time t for any covariate vector $\mathbf{z}$ and regression coefficients $\boldsymbol{\beta}$.

6

Repairable Systems

So far, only nonrepairable systems of components have been considered. These components operate for a period of time, fail, and are discarded. These types of models are appropriate for items such as light bulbs and fuses, but are inappropriate for items such as automobiles or aircraft. *Repairable systems* are considered here, where a system makes the transition from the operating to the failed state and may then return to the operating state.

Three different types of models are presented in this chapter:

1. *Replacement models*: a new item replaces a failed item upon failure
2. *Maintenance models*: preventive maintenance is used to avoid or delay failure
3. *Repair models*: an item is repaired before returning to service

The appropriate model for a situation depends on the way failures are handled.

When the replacement time (for replacement models) or the down time (for maintenance or repair models) is negligible, *point process models* are appropriate. The three point process models considered here are Poisson processes, renewal processes, and non-homogeneous Poisson processes.

When the replacement, maintenance, or repair time is not negligible, the appropriate model may be an *alternating renewal process* or a *birth–death process*. These models consider the distribution of the down time separately from the time to failure and include performance measures such as availability. There is a well-developed literature in *stochastic processes* that includes models discussed in this chapter.

6.1 INTRODUCTION

A *repairable item* may be returned to an operating condition after failure to perform a required function by any method other than replacement of the entire item. This definition has been kept general in order to allow for replacement of a component to be considered a repair (for example, replacing a battery in a flashlight or a board in a computer terminal). Repairable items are of great interest since there are many more repairable items than nonrepairable items produced in industry. Note that the word *item* is used to refer generically to components or systems, since these models can be applied equally well to either.

There are three different types of situations to which the techniques described in this chapter can be applied:

1. *Replacement models*: spares are used when an item fails
2. *Maintenance models*: preventive maintenance is applied to circumvent catastrophic failure
3. *Repair models*: an item is repaired upon failure.

Each of these models is described in the following paragraphs.

Replacement models are used when a nonrepairable item is replaced with another item upon failure. Examples of situations for which a model of this type is appropriate are the "socket models": a bulb is placed in a socket and a new bulb (with either the same or a different lifetime distribution) immediately replaces the failed bulb. This is repeated either indefinitely (unlimited spares) or until all the spare bulbs are consumed. One popular question in a replacement model concerns the optimal number of spares that should be kept on hand in order to minimize both the cost of spares and the probability of exhausting the spares. This problem is often referred to as the *redundancy allocation problem*.

Another popular question concerns choosing the policy that should dictate when the replacement should be performed. Three common replacement policies are the failure, age, and block replacement policies. Under a *failure replacement policy,* items are replaced only when they fail. This is an appropriate policy if failure is not catastrophic and the replacement cost is small. The ×'s on the axis in Figure 6.1 denote one possible sequence of failures and replacements over time. The detection and replacement times are considered negligible here, so each × corresponds to a failure and associated replacement that occur at the same time. Under an *age replacement policy,* items are replaced upon failure or at a predetermined age c, whichever comes first. This leads to a failure–replacement sequence similar to the one shown on the time axis in Figure 6.2, where the time to replace an item is negligible. The ×'s on the axis denote replacement of failed items and the dots denote replacement of operating items. Under a *block replacement policy,* items are replaced upon failure and at times $c, 2c, 3c, \ldots$, where c is a predetermined time (for example, one year) when it is convenient to replace all operating items. Although the block replacement policy may be easy to administer, it may result in the replacement of an item that has only been in service a short period of time, as shown on the time axis in Figure 6.3.

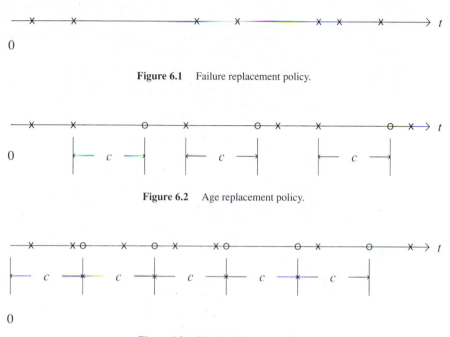

Figure 6.1   Failure replacement policy.

Figure 6.2   Age replacement policy.

Figure 6.3   Block replacement policy.

   The choice between these three replacement policies depends on the lifetime distribution of the item, the cost of failure, and administrative costs. Both age and block replacement policies collapse to a failure replacement policy as $c \to \infty$. Also, if $n_f(t)$ is the expected number of items consumed by time t under a failure replacement policy, $n_a(t)$ is the expected number of items consumed by time t under an age replacement policy, and $n_b(t)$ is the expected number of items consumed by time t under a block replacement policy, then

$$n_f(t) \le n_a(t) \le n_b(t) \qquad t > 0$$

for any positive constant c.

   Maintenance models are used when both preventive and corrective maintenance are applied to a system. Preventive maintenance is action taken on a system before it fails. Examples of preventive maintenance include changing the oil in an automobile, overhauling a jet engine, and lubricating a bearing. Corrective maintenance is action taken on a system upon failure. Examples of corrective maintenance include charging a dead battery in an automobile and repairing a failed printed circuit board in a disc drive. Both preventive and corrective maintenance typically involve taking a system out of normal operating conditions for a period of time to perform the maintenance. One popular question concerning a maintenance model is the optimal time for preventive maintenance to be performed. Automobile manufacturers, for example, typically recommend preventive maintenance times based on environmental conditions (for example, an oil change every 3000 miles in a dusty environment or every 6000 miles otherwise).

Finally, *repair models* are appropriate when action to repair an item is taken only when it fails. There may be certain situations for which preventive maintenance is impractical (for example, a satellite) or too costly. This leads to a series of failures that tend to be closer together as time passes if the item is deteriorating (an automobile) or farther apart as time passes if the item is improving (software).

Several probabilistic models will be presented in the subsequent sections. The appropriate model to choose depends on factors associated with the repairable item, such as the percentage of down time. If the total time an item is unavailable due to preventive maintenance or repair is negligible, then the point process models in Section 6.2 are appropriate. On the other hand, if the time an item is unavailable is not negligible, then alternating renewal models, presented in Section 6.3, or birth–death models, presented in Section 6.4, may be more appropriate.

6.2   POINT PROCESSES

When the time to repair or replace an item is negligible, point processes are appropriate for modeling the failure times. This would be the case for an automobile that works without failure for months, and then is in the shop for 1 hour for an oil change and lubrication where no mileage is accrued while the maintenance is being performed. These models would not be appropriate, for example, for an aircraft that spends several months having its engine overhauled before being placed back into service if availability is of interest.

Point process models can be applied to more than just repairable systems. Point processes have been used to describe arrivals to queues, earthquake times, and other physical phenomena. They have also been used to describe the occurrence times of sociological events such as crimes, strikes, bankruptcies, births, and wars.

A small but important bit of terminology is used to differentiate between types of nonrepairable items, which were considered in the previous chapters, and repairable items, which are considered here. A nonrepairable item, such as a light bulb, has *one* failure, and the term *burn-in* is used if its hazard function is decreasing and the term *wear-out* is used if its hazard function is increasing. Figure 6.4 shows sample hazard functions for an item that undergoes burn-in and another that wears out. The × on the time axis denotes one possible failure time. The lifetimes of nonrepairable items are described by the distribution of a *single* nonnegative random variable. On the contrary, a repairable item, such as an automobile, has *several* points in time where it may fail. In many situations, the intensity function, $\lambda(t)$, of a nonhomogeneous Poisson process may be the appropriate probabilistic mechanism for modeling the failure history of the item. The intensity function is analogous to the hazard function in the respect that higher levels of $\lambda(t)$ indicate an increased probability of failure. The term *improvement* is used if the intensity function is decreasing, and the term *deterioration* is used if the intensity function is increasing. Figure 6.5 shows sample intensity functions for an item that

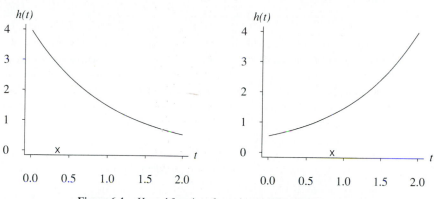

Figure 6.4   Hazard functions for an item with a DFR distribution (burn-in) and an item with an IFR distribution (wear-out).

improves and another that deteriorates. The ×'s on the time axis denote one realization of failure times. The deteriorating item has failures that tend to be more frequent as time passes, and the improving item has failures that tend to be less frequent as time passes. The failure times of repairable items are described by the probability mechanism underlying a *sequence* of random variables. These terms are summarized in Table 6.1.

Three point process models will be introduced in this section: Poisson processes, renewal processes, and nonhomogeneous Poisson processes. The notation for all the models given in this section is presented next.

In the point processes discussed in this section, failures occur at times $T_1, T_2, \ldots$, and the time to replace or repair an item is assumed to be negligible. The origin is defined to be $T_0 = 0$. The times between the failures are $X_1, X_2, \ldots$, so $T_k = X_1 + X_2 + \cdots + X_k$, for $k = 1, 2, \ldots$. The counting function $N(t)$ is the number of failures that occur in $(0, t]$. In other words,

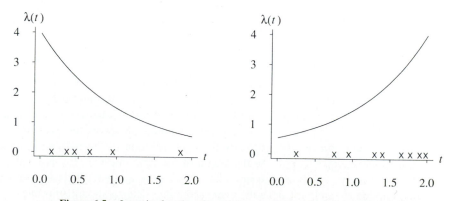

Figure 6.5   Intensity functions for an improving item and a deteriorating item.

TABLE 6.1   TERMINOLOGY FOR NONREPAIRABLE AND REPAIRABLE ITEMS

	Nonrepairable	Repairable
Item gets better as time passes	Burn-in, $h'(t) \leq 0$	Improving, $\lambda'(t) \leq 0$
Item gets worse as time passes	Wear-out, $h'(t) \geq 0$	Deteriorating, $\lambda'(t) \geq 0$

$$N(t) = \max \{ k \mid T_k \leq t \}$$

for $t > 0$. The nondecreasing, integer-valued process described by $\{N(t), t > 0\}$ is often called a *counting process* and satisfies these two properties:

1. If $t_1 < t_2$, then $N(t_1) \leq N(t_2)$.
2. If $t_1 < t_2$, then $N(t_2) - N(t_1)$ is the number of failures in the interval $(t_1, t_2]$.

Let $\Lambda(t) = E[N(t)]$ be the expected number of failures that occur in the interval $(0, t]$. The derivative of $\Lambda(t)$, which is $\lambda(t) = \Lambda'(t)$, is the rate of occurrence of failures. Figure 6.6 shows one realization of a point process, where $N(t)$ is shown as a step function and the ×'s denote the failure times on the horizontal axis. The curve for the expected number of events by time t, $\Lambda(t)$, is also on the same axis as $N(t)$. It should be kept in mind that $N(t)$ on this axis is a realization that will change from sample to sample, but $\Lambda(t)$ is the underlying probabilistic mechanism describing the sequence of events and does not change from sample to sample.

The behavior of the interevent times X_1, X_2, ... is always of interest in analyzing a repairable system. If the interevent times tend to decrease with time, the system is deteriorating; if the interevent times tend to increase with time, the system is improving. Other variables, such as a new untrained operator or repairman, must be considered when analyzing the failure times of a repairable system. These variables are ignored in the presentation of the probabilistic models, but can result in false conclusions if not considered along with the observed times between failures.

There are two properties that are important to discuss before introducing specific point processes. The first property is called *independent increments*. A point process has independent increments if the number of failures in mutually exclusive intervals is independent. As shown in Figure 6.7, this means that the number of failures between times t_1 and t_2 are independent of the number of failures between times t_3 and t_4, since the intervals $(t_1, t_2]$ and $(t_3, t_4]$ are nonoverlapping. A second property is called *stationarity*. A point process is stationary if the distribution of the number of failures in any time interval depends only on the length of the time interval. Equivalently, failures are no more or less likely at one time than another for an item. This is a rather restrictive assumption for an item, since the item can neither deteriorate nor improve.

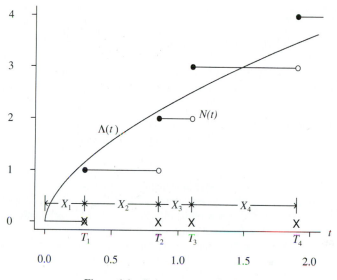

Figure 6.6   Point process realization.

Poisson Processes

The well-known Poisson process is a popular model due to its tractability, although it applies only to limited situations. These limited situations include replacement models with exponential standby items and repairable items with exponential times to failure and negligible repair times.

Definition 6.1   A counting process is a Poisson process with parameter $\lambda > 0$ if

- $N(0) = 0$,

- the process has independent increments, and

- the number of failures in any interval of length t has the Poisson distribution with parameter λt.

There are several implications to this definition of a Poisson process. First, by the last condition for a Poisson process, the distribution of the number of events in $(t_1, t_2]$ has

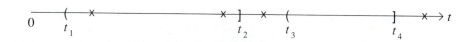

Figure 6.7   Independent increments illustration.

the Poisson distribution with parameter $\lambda(t_2 - t_1)$. Therefore, the probability mass function is

$$P[N(t_2) - N(t_1) = x] = \frac{[\lambda(t_2 - t_1)]^x e^{-\lambda(t_2 - t_1)}}{x!} \qquad x = 0, 1, 2, \ldots .$$

Second, the number of failures by time t, $N(t)$, has the Poisson distribution with mean $\Lambda(t) = E[N(t)] = \lambda t$, where λ is often called the rate of occurrence of failures. The intensity function is therefore $\lambda(t) = \Lambda'(t) = \lambda$. Third, as indicated in Property 4.10 of the exponential distribution, if $X_1, X_2, \ldots$ are independent and identically distributed exponential random variables, then $N(t)$ corresponds to a Poisson process.

Example 6.1

Consider a socket model in which an infinite supply of light bulbs is used in a single-component standby system composed of a single socket. As each bulb fails, it is immediately replaced by a new bulb, and each bulb has an exponential(λ) time to failure. Find the probability that there are n or fewer failures by time t.

Since the light bulb failure time distributions are each exponential, and the replacement time is negligible, a Poisson process is the appropriate model here. The probability that there are n or fewer failures by time t is therefore

$$P[N(t) \leq n] = \sum_{k=0}^{n} \frac{(\lambda t)^k e^{-\lambda t}}{k!} \qquad n = 0, 1, \ldots .$$

When $n = 0$, this solution reduces to the survivor function for an exponential distribution (the nonrepairable case). It is easily recognized here that the time of the nth failure has the Erlang distribution with scale parameter λ and shape parameter n, since $T_n = X_1 + X_2 + \cdots + X_n$.

This model is sometimes also called a *homogeneous Poisson process* indicating that the failure rate λ does not change with time (that is, the model is stationary). The next two models are generalizations of homogeneous Poisson processes. In a renewal process, the exponential assumption concerning the times between events is relaxed, and in a nonhomogeneous Poisson process, the stationarity assumption is relaxed.

Renewal Processes

A renewal process is a natural extension of a Poisson process in which the times between failure are assumed to have any lifetime distribution, rather than just the exponential distribution.

Definition 6.2   A point process is a *renewal process* if the times between failures $X_1, X_2, \ldots$ are independent and identically distributed nonnegative random variables.

The term *renewal* is appropriate for these models since an item is assumed to be renewed to its original state after it fails. This is typically not the case for a repairable system consisting of many components, since only a few of the components are replaced upon failure. The remaining components that did not fail will only be as good as new if they have exponential lifetimes. Renewal processes are often used, for example, to determine the number of spare components to take on a mission or to determine the timing of a sequence of repairs.

One classification of renewal processes that is useful in the study of socket models concerns the coefficient of variation γ of the distribution of the times between failures. This classification divides renewal processes into underdispersed and overdispersed processes.

Definition 6.3   A renewal process is *underdispersed (overdispersed)* if the coefficient of variation of the distribution of the times between failures is less than (greater than) 1.

Figure 6.8 shows three realizations of a renewal process. The first process is underdispersed since the coefficient of variation is less than 1. An extreme case of an underdispersed process is when the coefficient of variation is 0 (that is, a deterministic failure time for each item), which would yield a deterministic renewal process. The underdispersed process is much more regular in its failure times; hence, it is easier to determine when it is appropriate to replace an item if failure is catastrophic or expensive. A design engineer's goal might be to reduce the variability of the lifetime of an item, which in turn decreases the coefficient of variation. Reduced variation with increased mean is desirable for most items. The second axis in Figure 6.1 corresponds to a realization of a homogeneous Poisson process that has a coefficient of variation equal to 1 (since the mean and the standard deviation of the exponential distribution are equal). There is more clumping of failures than in the underdispersed case, and a replacement policy is ineffective here because of the memoryless property of the exponential distribution. The third axis corresponds to a realization of an overdispersed distribution. There is extreme clumping of failures together here, and many failures occur soon after an item

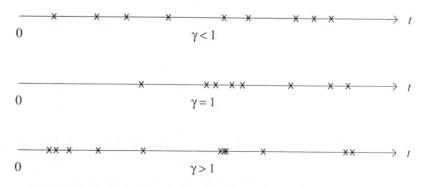

Figure 6.8   Classifying renewal processes based on the coefficient of variation.

is placed into service. Fortunately, the overdispersed case occurs less often in practice than the underdispersed case.

Two measures of interest that often arise when studying renewal processes are the distribution of T_n, the time of the nth failure, and the distribution of the number of failures by time t. In terms of the distribution of T_n, there are simple results for the expected value and variance of T_n, but the tractability of the distribution of T_n depends on the tractability of the distributions of the times between failure. Since $T_n = X_1 + X_2 + \cdots + X_n$, and the X_i's are independent and identically distributed, the expected value and variance of T_n are

$$E[T_n] = nE[X] \qquad V[T_n] = nV[X],$$

where $E[X]$ and $V[X]$ are the expected value and variance of the time between failures. The survivor function for the time of the nth failure, $S_{T_n}(t) = P[T_n \geq t]$, can be found as a function of the distribution of the X_i's and is tractable only for simple time between failure distributions.

The distribution of the number of failures by time t can be described by finding the values of the mass function $P[N(t) = n]$ for all n values. Since exactly n failures occurring by time t is equivalent to T_n being less than or equal to t and T_{n+1} being greater than t,

$$P[N(t) = n] = P[T_n \leq t < T_{n+1}]$$
$$= P[T_{n+1} \geq t] - P[T_n > t]$$
$$= S_{T_{n+1}}(t) - S_{T_n}(t)$$

for $n = 0, 1, \ldots, t > 0$ and continuous interevent time distribution. Although using the exponential distribution as the time to failure for each item reduces a renewal process to a Poisson process, it will be used in the next example because it is one of the only distributions for which these measures can easily be calculated.

Example 6.2

Consider a socket model for which the time to failure of each light bulb inserted in the socket has an exponential distribution with a failure rate of λ. Find the expected value and the variance of the time of failure n, the survivor function for failure n, and the probability mass function of the number of failures by time t.

First, since each item has a mean time to failure of $1/\lambda$, the expected value and the variance of the time of failure n are

$$E[T_n] = nE[X] = \frac{n}{\lambda} \qquad V[T_n] = nV[X] = \frac{n}{\lambda^2}$$

for $n = 0, 1, \ldots$. Since T_n is the sum of independent and identically distributed exponential random variables, it has the Erlang distribution with survivor function

$$S_{T_n}(t) = \sum_{k=0}^{n-1} \frac{(\lambda t)^k}{k!} e^{-\lambda t} \qquad t > 0.$$

To find the probability mass function for the number of failures by time t,

$$P[N(t) = n] = S_{T_{n+1}}(t) - S_{T_n}(t)$$

$$= \sum_{k=0}^{n} \frac{(\lambda t)^k}{k!} e^{-\lambda t} - \sum_{k=0}^{n-1} \frac{(\lambda t)^k}{k!} e^{-\lambda t}$$

$$= \frac{(\lambda t)^n}{n!} e^{-\lambda t}$$

for $n = 0, 1, 2, \ldots$ and $t > 0$.

A more complicated situation occurs when the gamma distribution is used to model the time between failures.

Example 6.3

Consider a socket model for which the lifetime of each light bulb to be placed in the socket has the gamma distribution with scale parameter $\lambda = 0.001$ and shape parameter $\kappa = 5.2$, where time is measured in hours. Find the probability that three light bulbs are sufficient to light the system for 8760 hours (1 year).

Since the mean of the gamma distribution is κ/λ, each light bulb has a mean time to failure of $\mu = 5.2/0.001 = 5200$ hours. This means that the expected time of failure number $n = 3$ is $nE[X] = 3(5200) = 15{,}600$ hours, or almost 2 years. This preliminary analysis indicates that the probability that three bulbs will be sufficient for 1 year of operation should be fairly high.

A result that can be used to determine the exact probability is that the sum of n independent and identically distributed gamma random variables also has a gamma distribution. This result is most easily seen by using the moment generating function approach to determine the distribution of the sum of random variables. Let the random variable X have a gamma distribution with parameters λ and κ. The moment generating function for X is

$$M_X(s) = E[e^{sX}]$$

$$= \int_0^\infty e^{sx} \frac{\lambda}{\Gamma(\kappa)} (\lambda x)^{\kappa-1} e^{-\lambda x} dx$$

$$= \frac{\lambda^\kappa}{\Gamma(\kappa)} \int_0^\infty x^{\kappa-1} e^{-x(\lambda-s)} dx$$

$$= \frac{\lambda^\kappa}{\Gamma(\kappa)} \int_0^\infty \left(\frac{u}{\lambda-s}\right)^{\kappa-1} e^{-u} \frac{1}{\lambda-s} du$$

$$= \left(\frac{\lambda}{\lambda-s}\right)^\kappa \frac{1}{\Gamma(\kappa)} \int_0^\infty u^{\kappa-1} e^{-u} du$$

$$= \left(\frac{\lambda}{\lambda-s}\right)^\kappa$$

for all $s < \lambda$. Since $X_1, X_2, \ldots, X_n$ are independent and identically distributed gamma random variables, the moment generating function for $T_n = X_1 + X_2 + \cdots + X_n$ is the product of n of these moment generating functions:

$$M_{T_n}(s) = \prod_{i=1}^{n} M_{X_i}(s) = \left(\frac{\lambda}{\lambda - s}\right)^{n\kappa}.$$

Thus, if the X_i's are independent and indentically distributed gamma random variables with parameters λ and κ, then the distribution of their sum has the gamma distribution with parameters λ and $n\kappa$.

For the problem at hand, this means that the time to the third failure, T_3, has a gamma distribution with scale parameter $\lambda = 0.001$ and shape parameter $n\kappa = 3(5.2) = 15.6$. To find the probability that T_3 exceeds 8760,

$$P[T_3 \geq 8760] = S_{T_3}(8760) = 1 - I(15.6, 8.76) = 0.977,$$

where I is the incomplete gamma function.

One final result concerning renewal processes involves $\Lambda(t) = E[N(t)]$. Although the derivation is not given here, $\Lambda(t)$ satisfies the *renewal equation*

$$\Lambda(t) = F(t) + \int_0^t F(t-s)d\Lambda(s),$$

where $F(t)$ is the cumulative distribution function of the X_i's. Equivalently, by taking the derivative of both sides with respect to t,

$$\lambda(t) = f(t) + \int_0^t f(t-s)\lambda(s)ds,$$

where $f(t)$ is the probability density function of the X_i's. This results in an integral equation, which can be solved by a Laplace transformation.

Nonhomogeneous Poisson Processes

The third and final point process introduced here is the nonhomogeneous Poisson process (NHPP). There are at least four reasons that an NHPP should be considered for modeling the failure sequence of a repairable item:

1. The homogeneous Poisson process is a special case of an NHPP.
2. The probabilistic model for an NHPP is mathematically tractable.
3. The statistical methods for an NHPP are also mathematically tractable.
4. Unlike a homogeneous Poisson process or a renewal process, the NHPP is capable of modeling improving and deteriorating systems.

One disadvantage with both Poisson processes and renewal processes is that they assume that the distribution of the time to failure for each item in a socket model is identical. This means that it is not possible for the item to improve or deteriorate. An NHPP is another generalization of the homogeneous Poisson process for which the stationarity assumption is relaxed. Instead of a constant rate of occurrence of failures λ, as in a homogeneous Poisson process, this rate varies over time according to $\lambda(t)$, which is often called the *intensity function*. The *cumulative intensity function* is defined by

$$\Lambda(t) = \int_0^t \lambda(\tau) d\tau$$

and is interpreted as the expected number of failures by time t. The cumulative intensity function is analogous to the renewal function from renewal theory. These two functions are generally used to describe the probabilistic mechanism for the failure times of the item, as opposed to the five distribution representations for nonrepairable items.

Definition 6.4   A counting process is a nonhomogeneous Poisson process with intensity function $\lambda(t) \geq 0$ if

- $N(0) = 0$,

- the process has independent increments, and

- the probability of exactly n events occurring in the interval $(a, b]$ is given by

$$P[N(b) - N(a) = n] = \frac{\left[\int_a^b \lambda(t) dt\right]^n e^{-\int_a^b \lambda(t) dt}}{n!}$$

for $n = 0, 1, \ldots$.

Thus, if the intensity function is decreasing, the item is improving, and if the intensity function is increasing, the item is deteriorating. For NHPPs, the times between failures are neither independent nor identically distributed. The time to the first failure in an NHPP has the same distribution as the time to failure of a single nonrepairable item with hazard function $\lambda(t)$. Subsequent failures follow a conditional version of the intensity function that does not depend on previous values of $\lambda(t)$. The times between these subsequent failures do not necessarily follow any of the distributions (for example, Weibull) considered earlier.

Since the independent increments property has been retained from the definition of a homogeneous Poisson process, this model assumes that previous repairs do not affect the future performance of the item. Although this may not be exactly true in practice, the NHPP model is still valuable because it is tractable and allows for improving and deteriorating systems. In addition, parameter estimation for the NHPP is simple, which is another attractive feature.

Example 6.4

Consider an NHPP with intensity function

$$\lambda(t) = \kappa\lambda^{\kappa}t^{\kappa-1} \qquad t > 0.$$

This can be recognized as the same functional form as the hazard function for a Weibull random variable with scale parameter λ and shape parameter κ and is often referred to as a power law process. For this intensity function, if $\kappa < 1$, the item is improving since the intensity function is decreasing, if $\kappa > 1$, the item is deteriorating since the intensity function is increasing; and if $\kappa = 1$, it reduces to a homogeneous Poisson process. Find the probability that there will be exactly n failures by time t. Also, if failure n occurs at time t_n, find the survivor function for the time to the next failure.

The number of failures by time t, $N(t)$, has probability mass function

$$P[N(t) = n] = \frac{\left[\int_0^t \lambda(\tau)d\tau \right]^n e^{-\int_0^t \lambda(\tau)d\tau}}{n!} \qquad n = 0, 1, \ldots$$

for $t > 0$. Using the fact that $\Lambda(t) = \int_0^t \kappa\lambda^{\kappa}\tau^{\kappa-1}d\tau = (\lambda t)^{\kappa}$, for $t > 0$

$$P[N(t) = n] = \frac{(\lambda t)^{\kappa n} e^{-(\lambda t)^{\kappa}}}{n!} \qquad n = 0, 1, \ldots$$

for $t > 0$. Finding the survivor function for the time to the next event involves conditioning. Using independent increments, the fact that $S(t) = e^{-H(t)}$ and conditioning, the conditional survivor function is

$$S_{T|T>t_n}(t) = e^{-(\Lambda(t) - \Lambda(t_n))} = e^{-((\lambda t)^{\kappa} - (\lambda t_n)^{\kappa})} = e^{-\lambda^{\kappa}(t^{\kappa} - t_n^{\kappa})} \qquad t > t_n.$$

One final topic, *superpositioning,* can be applied to any of the three point processes considered thus far. Poisson, renewal, and nonhomogeneous Poisson processes are useful for modeling the failure pattern of a *single* repairable item. In some situations it is important to model the failure pattern of several items simultaneously. Examples include a job shop with k machines, a military mission with k weapons, and phone calls arriving to an operator from k sources. Figure 6.9 shows a superposition of the failure times of the $k = 3$ items. The superposition of several point processes is the ordered sequence of all failures that occur in any of the individual point processes. An important result that applies to superpositions of NHPPs is that, if $\lambda_1(t), \lambda_2(t), \ldots, \lambda_k(t)$ are the intensity functions for k independent items, the intensity function for the superposition

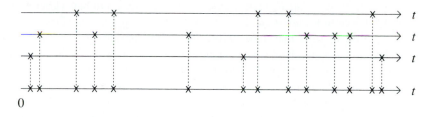

Figure 6.9   Superposition of three point processes.

is $\lambda(t) = \sum_{i=1}^{k} \lambda_i(t)$. This result is similar to the result concerning the hazard functions for net lives in competing risks.

This ends the presentation of the three point process models: Poisson processes, renewal processes, and nonhomogeneous Poisson processes. The first two models are only capable of modeling socket models for which the time between failures has a common distribution, whereas NHPPs are capable of modeling improving and deteriorating systems, which are more common in practice. These models are appropriate when there is a negligible down time (that is, failure and return to service occur at essentially the same point in time). The next two sections present models in which down time is modeled explicitly.

6.3   AVAILABILITY

An assumption in point process models is that the amount of time that an item spends out of service is negligible, which may not always be appropriate. There may be situations for which modeling the repair times separately from the failure times is appropriate. This section considers *availability* and a simple maintainability model known as an *alternating renewal process*.

As in the previous section, X_i denotes the ith time to failure and R_i is defined to be the ith time to repair, for $i = 1, 2, \ldots$. Figure 6.10 shows a typical realization of a process that alternates between the functioning and failed states as time passes. The $\times$'s denote the failure times and the dots denote the time when the item is returned to service. In most situations, the expected value of X_i is significantly larger than the expected value of R_i, which means that the item spends significantly more time available for use than being repaired.

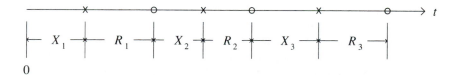

Figure 6.10   Failure and repair process realization.

The fact that R_i is being modeled as a single random variable can be misleading. As shown in Figure 6.11, R_i may have several components. First, when a failure occurs, a period of time may pass before the failure is detected. Second, once the failure is detected, it may take time to diagnose the problem and determine what action should be taken in order to bring the item back into working condition. Third, in some situations there is a delay in order to obtain parts and labor. Fourth, a time delay exists for the actual repair itself, and, finally, there may be some testing at the repair facility prior to returning the item to service. In the models presented here, all five of these components of the repair time of an item are collapsed into a single random variable, R_i, called the *repair time*.

The state of a binary repairable item at time t indicates the status of the item, either operating or failed.

Definition 6.5   The state of a repairable item at time t is

$$X(t) = \begin{cases} 0 & \text{the item is failed at time } t \\ 1 & \text{the item is functioning at time } t. \end{cases}$$

In Chapters 2 and 3, $X(t)$ was simply a random variable that went from state 1 to state 0 at time T in accordance with a probability mechanism defined by the survivor function $S(t)$. As indicated by the realization presented in Figure 6.12, this is now a function that alternates between 0 and 1 as time passes. One measure of performance associated with a repairable system is the fraction of time the system spends in state 1, which is often called its *availability*. If we were to track the cumulative fraction of time that the system spends operating in the previous realization, a graph such as the one shown in Figure 6.13 would result. An important characteristic of a graph of this type is that, if the distributions of the X_i's and R_i's do not change with time, then the fraction of time that the system spends in the up state approaches a constant value as time increases. This is not the case, however, for most repairable systems, since they either improve or degrade.

There are four different definitions for availability.

Definition 6.6   The *availability* of an item is the probability that it is functioning. Four types of availability measures are

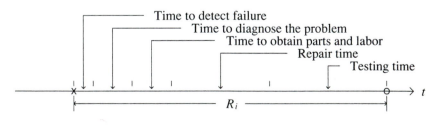

Figure 6.11   Partitioning the repair time.

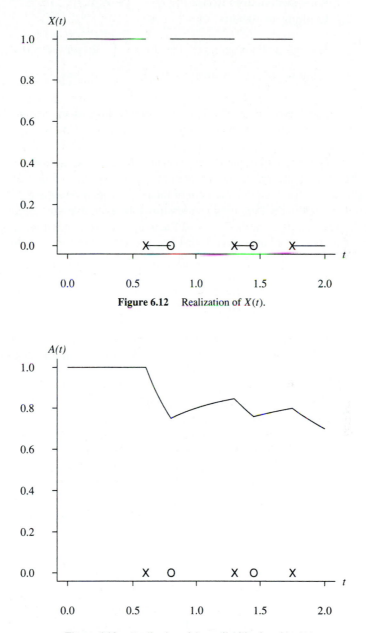

Figure 6.12   Realization of $X(t)$.

Figure 6.13   Realization of the availability function $A(t)$.

1. Point availability: $A(t) = P[X(t) = 1] = E[X(t)], \quad t > 0$
2. Limiting availability: $A = \lim_{t \to \infty} A(t)$
3. Average availability on $(0, c]$: $A_c = \dfrac{1}{c} \int_0^c A(t)dt, \quad c > 0$
4. Limiting average availability on $(0, c]$: $A_\infty = \lim_{c \to \infty} A_c$

The first type of availability, *point availability,* is the probability that the item is operating at time t. If repair is not possible, then $A(t)$ simplifies to a survivor function. If the item has stationary times to failure X_i and stationary times to repair R_i, then the point availability will approach a constant value as time increases. This value is known as the *limiting availability* and represents the long-term fraction of time that an item is available. If, for example, the item of interest is a jet aircraft and $A = 0.96$, then the conclusion is that in the long run the aircraft will be available 96% of the time. The *average availability* on $(0, c]$ is the expected fraction of the time the item is operating in the first c time units it is put into service, that is,

$$A_c = \frac{1}{c} E\left[\int_0^c X(t)dt \right] = \frac{1}{c} \int_0^c E[X(t)]dt = \frac{1}{c} \int_0^c A(t)dt.$$

Finally, the *limiting average availability* is the expected fraction of the time that the item is operating. If the limiting availability exists, then the limiting availability and the limiting average availability are equal.

The simplest case to consider when time is modeled as a continuous random variable is when X_i and R_i are exponential random variables. More complicated situations, such as nonstationarity or nonexponential failure and repair times, are often evaluated by Monte Carlo simulation rather than using an analytic approach. Let $X_1, X_2, \ldots$ be independent and identically distributed exponential random variables with failure rate λ_0, and let $R_1, R_2, \ldots$ be independent and identically distributed exponential random variables with repair rate λ_1. (Some authors use μ, rather than λ_1, for the repair rate. The notation λ_1 is used here to avoid possible confusion with the expected value of a random variable.) The transition diagram is shown in Figure 6.14. The infinitesimal generator for the model is straightforward since the item simply alternates between states 0 and 1. It is

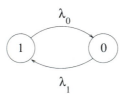

Figure 6.14   Transition diagram for an alternating renewal process.

$$\begin{bmatrix} -\lambda_0 & \lambda_0 \\ \lambda_1 & -\lambda_1 \end{bmatrix}.$$

This model is a special case of an *alternating renewal process* in which the time to every other renewal has the same distribution.

There are numerous ways to find $A(t)$, the probability that the item will be available at time t. Perhaps the simplest is to use conditioning. For a small time increment Δt,

$P[\text{item available at } t + \Delta t] = P[\text{item does not fail in } (t, t + \Delta t]] \, P[\text{item available at } t]$

$+ \, P[\text{item repaired in } (t, t + \Delta t]] \, P[\text{item not available at } t].$

In terms of $A(t)$, λ_0, and λ_1, this is

$$A(t + \Delta t) = (1 - \lambda_0 \Delta t) \, A(t) + \lambda_1 \Delta t (1 - A(t)).$$

Rearranging terms,

$$\frac{A(t + \Delta t) - A(t)}{\Delta t} = -(\lambda_0 + \lambda_1) \, A(t) + \lambda_1.$$

Taking the limit of both sides as Δt approaches 0 yields

$$A'(t) = -(\lambda_0 + \lambda_1) \, A(t) + \lambda_1,$$

for $t > 0$. This is an exact ordinary differential equation that can be solved with the aid of an integrating factor. Using the initial condition $A(0) = 1$, which means that the item is operating initially, the solution is

$$A(t) = \frac{\lambda_1}{\lambda_0 + \lambda_1} + \frac{\lambda_0}{\lambda_0 + \lambda_1} \, e^{-(\lambda_0 + \lambda_1)t} \qquad t > 0.$$

A graph of this curve with $\lambda_0 = 1$ and $\lambda_1 = 2$ is shown in Figure 6.15. Several features of this point availability function make it particularly easy to analyze. First, note that the limiting availability is $A = \lim_{t \to \infty} A(t) = \lambda_1 / (\lambda_0 + \lambda_1)$. Equivalently, since the mean time to failure (MTTF) is $1/\lambda_0$ and the mean time to repair (MTTR) is $1/\lambda_1$, $A = \text{MTTF}/(\text{MTTF} + \text{MTTR})$. Second, the average availability measures on $(0, c]$ can easily be determined. For example,

$$A_c = \frac{1}{c} \int_0^c A(t) \, dt$$

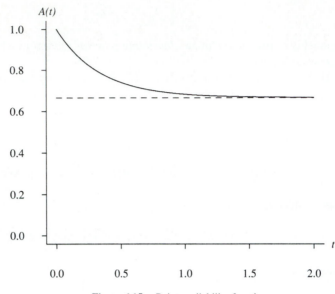

Figure 6.15   Point availability function.

$$= \frac{1}{c} \left[\int_0^c \frac{\lambda_1}{\lambda_0 + \lambda_1} + \frac{\lambda_0}{\lambda_0 + \lambda_1} e^{-(\lambda_0 + \lambda_1)t} dt \right]$$

$$= \frac{1}{c} \left[\frac{\lambda_1 c}{\lambda_0 + \lambda_1} - \frac{\lambda_0}{(\lambda_0 + \lambda_1)^2} e^{-(\lambda_0 + \lambda_1)c} + \frac{\lambda_0}{(\lambda_0 + \lambda_1)^2} \right].$$

When the limit is taken as $c \to \infty$, the limiting average availability on $(0, c]$ is

$$A_\infty = \lim_{c \to \infty} A_c = \frac{\lambda_1}{\lambda_0 + \lambda_1},$$

which is equal to the limiting availability.

Example 6.5

Consider a system whose failure and repair sequence is modeled by an alternating renewal process with the time to failure being exponentially distributed with a mean of 1000 hours and the repair time being exponentially distributed with a mean of 10 hours. Find

- the probability that the item is available at time 10 if it is initially operating,

- the limiting availability, and

- the average availability on $(0, 10]$.

In this case, $\lambda_0 = 0.001$ and $\lambda_1 = 0.1$. Assuming that $A(0) = 1$, the availability at time 10 is

$$A(10) = \frac{0.1}{0.001 + 0.1} + \frac{0.001}{0.001 + 0.1} e^{-(0.001 + 0.1)10} = 0.9937.$$

Second, the limiting availability is

$$A = \frac{0.1}{0.001 + 0.1} = 0.9901.$$

It is clear in this particular system, which has a high availability, that the point availability quickly approaches the limiting availability. Third, the average availability on $(0, 10]$ is

$$A_{10} = \frac{1}{10} \left[\frac{(0.1)(10)}{0.001 + 0.1} + \frac{0.001}{(0.001 + 0.1)^2} (1 - e^{-(0.001 + 0.1)10}) \right] = 0.9963.$$

The unavailability (1 minus the availability) is often of interest, as illustrated in the next example.

Example 6.6

A program is initiated to double the mean time to failure and halve the mean time to repair for a system. What effect will this have on the limiting unavailability of the system? Assume that the time to failure and time to repair are exponential.

Let A_1 be the limiting availability before any improvements are made to the system. The limiting unavailability of the system before any improvements are made is

$$1 - A_1 = 1 - \frac{\lambda_1}{\lambda_0 + \lambda_1} = \frac{\lambda_0}{\lambda_0 + \lambda_1}.$$

Doubling the mean time to failure, $1/\lambda_0$, is equivalent to halving the failure rate λ_0. Alternatively, halving the mean time to repair, $1/\lambda_1$, is equivalent to doubling the repair rate λ_1. Thus the limiting unavailability after the changes are made, $1 - A_2$, is

$$1 - A_2 = \frac{\lambda_0 / 2}{\lambda_0 / 2 + 2\lambda_1}.$$

This gives the general effect on the limiting unavailability for these system improvements for any λ_0 and λ_1. If the repair rate is significantly larger than the failure rate, which is often the case, then the first term in the denominator of both limiting unavailability expressions can be effectively ignored. This means that the two unavailabilities are approximately

$$1 - A_1 \approx \frac{\lambda_0}{\lambda_1} \quad \text{and} \quad 1 - A_2 \approx \frac{\lambda_0}{4\lambda_1},$$

which means that the unavailability is reduced by 75%. An unavailability of 0.04, for example, is reduced to approximately 0.01 if the mean time to failure is doubled and the mean time to repair is halved. If this particular alternating renewal process is an appropriate model, then doubling the mean time to failure for the system and halving the mean time to repair significantly affect the percentage of down time.

6.4 BIRTH–DEATH MODELS

A number of generalizations of the simple availability model were presented in the previous section. Models for which the times between transitions from one state to another are assumed to be exponential are called Markov models, and a special case called *birth–death* models is considered here. Birth–death models are appropriate in situations in which a counting variable can increase or decrease by one unit at a time. More specifically, if the counting variable increases by one unit, it is considered a "birth" and if the counting variable decreases by one unit, it is considered a "death." This continuous-time Markov process allows more than just the states 0 and 1 and is convenient for modeling more complicated availability problems.

Let λ_{ij} be the transition rate from state i to state j. When the subscript i is one less than j, this corresponds to a birth, and when the subscript i is one greater than j, this corresponds to a death. Thus j may only assume the values $i \pm 1$. The infinitesimal generator for a birth–death model is a tridiagonal matrix with negative diagonal elements, nonnegative off-diagonal elements and zeros elsewhere:

$$
\begin{bmatrix}
-\lambda_{01} & \lambda_{01} & 0 & 0 & . & . & . \\
\lambda_{10} & -(\lambda_{10} + \lambda_{12}) & \lambda_{12} & 0 & . & . & . \\
0 & \lambda_{21} & -(\lambda_{21} + \lambda_{23}) & \lambda_{23} & . & . & . \\
0 & 0 & \lambda_{32} & -(\lambda_{32} + \lambda_{34}) & & & \\
. & . & . & . & & & \\
. & . & . & . & & & \\
. & . & . & . & & &
\end{bmatrix}.
$$

The transition diagram for a birth–death process is shown in Figure 6.16. In most maintainability problems, there will be a finite number of states that the system can assume.

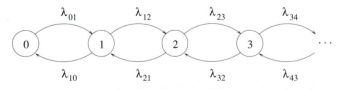

Figure 6.16   Birth–death transition diagram.

There are numerous results associated with birth–death processes, but only one will be illustrated here. Consider the transition time from state zero to state n. The expected value of this transition time is

$$\sum_{k=0}^{n-1} \frac{\sum_{i=0}^{k} \theta_i}{\theta_k \lambda_{k,k+1}},$$

where $\theta_0 = 1$ and $\theta_k = \dfrac{\lambda_{01}\lambda_{12}\cdots\lambda_{k-1,k}}{\lambda_{10}\lambda_{21}\cdots\lambda_{k,k-1}}$ for $k = 1, 2, \ldots$. A simple example illustrates the use of this formula.

Example 6.7

Consider the three-component series system with four cold standby spares shown in Figure 6.17. All components are identical with failure rates 0.005 failure per hour. In this particular system, the detection and switching times are negligible. There is a repair facility with two repairmen. The repair rate is 0.01 repair per hour, and only one repairman can work on an item at a time. Find the expected time to system failure (that is, when there are fewer than three operating components).

The counting variable in this problem is the number of failed components, which can assume the values 0, 1, 2, 3, 4, and 5, since when there are five failed units the system has failed. The transition diagram for this problem is shown in Figure 6.18. The upward transition rates are all equal to $(3)(0.005) = 0.015$, since this is a three-component competing risks situation. The upward transitions are the minimum of three independent exponential(0.005) random variables. The downward transition rates depend on the number of repairmen who are active. The infinitesimal generator for this problem is the 6×6 matrix

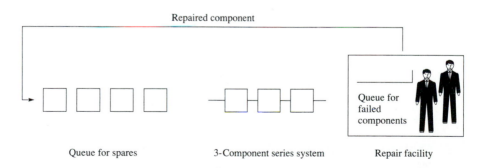

Repaired component

Queue for spares   3-Component series system   Queue for failed components   Repair facility

Figure 6.17   Three-component series system with repairable components. (*Source*: I. B. Gertsbakh, *Statistical Reliability Theory*, 1989. Adapted and reprinted by permission of Marcel Dekker, Inc., New York.)

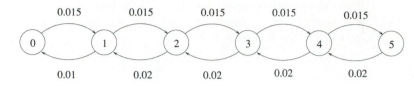

Figure 6.18   Transition diagram for the three-component series system.

$$\begin{bmatrix} -0.015 & 0.015 & 0 & 0 & 0 & 0 \\ 0.01 & -0.025 & 0.015 & 0 & 0 & 0 \\ 0 & 0.02 & -0.035 & 0.015 & 0 & 0 \\ 0 & 0 & 0.02 & -0.035 & 0.015 & 0 \\ 0 & 0 & 0 & 0.02 & -0.035 & 0.015 \\ 0 & 0 & 0 & 0 & 0.02 & -0.02 \end{bmatrix}.$$

The time for the system to make a transition from state 0 to state 5 denotes the time until system failure, ignoring the negligible replacement times. The θ_k parameters are

$$\theta_0 = 1 \qquad \theta_1 = \frac{0.015}{0.01} = 1.5 \qquad \theta_2 = \frac{(0.015)(0.015)}{(0.01)(0.02)} = 1.125$$

$$\theta_3 = \frac{(0.015)(0.015)(0.015)}{(0.01)(0.02)(0.02)} = 0.8438$$

$$\theta_4 = \frac{(0.015)(0.015)(0.015)(0.015)}{(0.01)(0.02)(0.02)(0.02)} = 0.6328$$

With these constants determined, the expected time to system failure is

$$\sum_{k=0}^{4} \frac{\sum_{i=0}^{k} \theta_i}{\theta_k \lambda_{k,k+1}} = \frac{1}{(1)(0.015)} + \frac{1+1.5}{(1.5)(0.015)} + \frac{1+1.5+1.125}{(1.125)(0.015)} + \cdots$$

$$+ \frac{1+1.5+1.125+\cdots+0.6328}{(0.6328)(0.015)} = 1283 \text{ hours.}$$

An analysis of this type allows the modeler to explore the impact of improving the reliability of the items, hiring a third repairman, or increasing the repair rate.

6.5   FURTHER READING

This chapter on repairable systems is rather introductory in nature, and there are a number of good references for further information on the models presented here. Social science applications of point processes (for example, criminology, politics, demography) are given in a monograph by Allison (1984). One of the first textbooks completely

devoted to repairable systems is Ascher and Feingold (1984). Others that consider
repairable systems include Crowder et al. (1991), Gertsbakh (1989), Grosh (1989), and
Wilson (1993). Martz and Waller (1982, pp. 83–86) list terminology associated with
repairable systems. Determining optimal block replacement policies is considered by
Crowell and Sen (1993). Repairability and maintainability issues need to be considered
along with reliability issues in the design phase of a system.

A good introductory text for Poisson processes is Ross (1993), and an advanced
text is Cinlar (1975). Renewal processes are considered in both Syski (1979) and Cinlar
(1975). Cox and Isham (1980) introduce underdispersed and overdispersed renewal
processes. Nonhomogeneous Poisson processes are introduced in Cinlar (1975). References to parameter estimation techniques for NHPPs are given in Section 8.4. Thompson (1988) considers point process applications in safety and reliability.

The four definitions for availability are from Barlow and Proschan (1981, p. 191).
The average availability on $(0, c]$ is a *time persistent statistic* and other related quantities
associated with availability (for example, its variance) can be calculated using formulas
in Law and Kelton (1991, p. 15). Example 6.6, which considered the impact of doubling
the mean time to failure and halving the mean time to repair, is motivated by a program
initiated by the United States Air Force called "Reliability and Maintainability 2000."

Availability models are considered in most reliability textbooks, and the
birth–death models and the example given here are introduced in Gertsbakh (1989,
p. 284). Markov models are emphasized in Trivedi (1982).

Dozens of papers have been written on reliability growth, and two of the most popular mathematical models for describing this phenomena are the Duane (Duane, 1964)
and Crow (Crow, 1982) models. Reliability growth can be applied to both nonrepairable
and repairable items.

6.6   EXERCISES

6.1. Consider the following data set of $n = 5$ observations:

$$16 \quad 29 \quad 34 \quad 71 \quad 135.$$

Write a paragraph indicating your approach to the analysis of this data set if the five values
are
(a) a set of failure times for five nonrepairable items placed on test simultaneously.
(b) a set of failure times for five nonrepairable items in a replacement model with negligible
    down time.
(c) a set of failure times for one repairable item with negligible replacement time.

6.2. A repairable system with negligible repair time fails according to a Poisson process with
rate $\lambda = 0.001$ failure per hour. Find the probability of two or fewer failures between 3000
and 6000 hours.

6.3. A repairable system with negligible repair time fails according to a renewal process with
interfailure time having the gamma distribution with parameters λ and κ. Find the probability of n or fewer failures between times 0 and c.

6.4. Perform the calculations to verify the numerical result at the end of Example 6.3.

6.5. Verify that the derivative of the renewal equation is satisfied when the items in a socket model have an exponential distribution.

6.6. Consider a renewal process for which the times between failures have the Weibull distribution with scale parameter λ and shape parameter κ. Find the expected value and variance of the time of failure n for $n = 1, 2, \ldots$.

6.7. A repairable system with negligible repair time fails according to a nonhomogeneous Poisson process with rate $\lambda(t) = 0.001 + 0.000001t$ failures per hour. Find the probability of two or fewer failures between times 3000 and 6000.

6.8. For a nonhomogeneous Poisson process with power law intensity function

$$\lambda(t) = \lambda\kappa(\lambda t)^{\kappa - 1} \qquad t > 0,$$

find the probability mass function for the number of events between times a and b.

6.9. Consider an age replacement policy situation for which items are replaced at failure or at time c, whichever comes first. Assuming that the time to failure has the Pareto distribution with parameters λ and κ, find the expected number of failures by time b. Assume that $\lambda << c << b$.

6.10. Two different maintenance procedures are to be compared for a repairable item: age replacement and block replacement. Assume that the item has a lifetime that is a mixture of three distributions: a Weibull distribution with $\lambda = 0.01$ and $\kappa = 0.6$ (with $p_1 = 0.05$), an exponential distribution with $\lambda = 0.002$ (with $p_2 = 0.45$), and a Weibull distribution with $\lambda = 0.001$ and $\kappa = 3.0$ (with $p_3 = 0.50$). Assume that time is measured in hours.
(a) Calculate the theoretical mean lifetime of the item.
(b) Use Monte Carlo simulation to compare the age replacement and block replacement maintenance strategies for the item with $c = 1000$ hours.

6.11. Eric drives a car whose failure times follow an NHPP with power law cumulative intensity function

$$\Lambda(t) = (\lambda t)^{\kappa} \qquad t \geq 0,$$

where t is measured in miles. If the car has 100,000 miles on the odometer, find the probability that Eric can make a 1000-mile trip without a failure.

6.12. Consider a repairable system that is being modeled as an alternating renewal process. The time to failure has a Weibull distribution with parameters λ_W and κ_W. The time to repair has a gamma distribution with parameters λ_G and κ_G. Find the mean and variance of the length of each renewal cycle.

6.13. A repairable component has an exponential time to failure with a mean of 1000 hours and a exponential repair time with a mean of 75 hours. If the component is operating at time 38, what is the probability that it will be operating at time 112?

6.14. Consider two components that are arranged in series. The first component is nonrepairable and fails according to an exponential distribution with rate λ_N. The second component is repairable and fails according to an exponential distribution with rate λ_F, and it can be repaired in an exponentially distributed time period with rate λ_R. Find the reliability at time t.

6.15. Find the expected time to system failure in Example 6.7 if the original system is modified so that it
(a) has one unit in cold standby (rather than four).
(b) has one repairman (rather than two).

7

Lifetime Data Analysis

The text takes an important turn at this point since we now consider estimating the parameters (for example, component reliabilities and distribution parameter values) that have been assumed to be known thus far. These parameters are usually estimated from data, although lists of estimates of parameter values are compiled for a preliminary reliability estimate in the design phase. For example, MIL-HDBK-217 (1992) contains failure rates for electronic components (for example, capacitors and diodes) when operating in a prescribed environment. Other standards and handbooks exist for mechanical components, such as motors or springs, as well as testing procedures.

In the remainder of the text, we will consider techniques for estimating parameters from data. There are always merits in obtaining raw data (that is, exact individual failure times), as opposed to grouped data (counts of the number of failures over prescribed time intervals), so this is the case we consider. The first section in this chapter reviews some properties of *point estimators*. Since point estimators for parameters are seldom exact, interval estimators of parameters are often used to indicate the accuracy of the point estimator. Interval estimators, commonly known as *confidence intervals,* are reviewed in the second section. The third section considers the *likelihood function* and its properties. The likelihood function is important for determining maximum likelihood estimators and estimating their variability. Asymptotic properties of the likelihood function are reviewed in the fourth section. The matrix of the expected values of the second partial derivatives of the log likelihood function is known as the *information matrix* and is useful for determining confidence intervals for parameter estimators. *Censoring* is a problem that occurs in lifetime data sets when only an upper or lower bound on the lifetime is known. Probabilistic methods for parameter estimation from censored data sets are outlined in the last section.

7.1   POINT ESTIMATION

A brief review of some properties of point estimators for parameters from a random sample is given in this section. A *point estimator* is a statistic used to estimate a population parameter. A familiar example is the use of the sample mean to estimate the population mean μ. Many argue that a point estimator by itself is of little use since it does not contain any information about the accuracy of the estimator, so *interval estimation* is considered in the next section. Interval estimators incorporate the variability of the point estimator to indicate the accuracy of the point estimator. Since the data in reliability studies generally consist of lifetimes, a data set is denoted by $t_1, t_2, \ldots, t_n$, where n is the sample size. The ordered observations (or order statistics) are denoted by $t_{(1)}, t_{(2)}, \ldots, t_{(n)}$. The distribution of a statistic is referred to as a *sampling distribution*. The properties of point estimators considered here are unbiasedness, variance, efficiency, and consistency.

In practically all statistical problems, there is no point estimator that will yield the exact value of the particular population parameter of interest. Since no point estimator is perfect, a desirable property is that the expected value of the sampling distribution of the point estimator be equal to the parameter.

Definition 7.1   The point estimator $\hat{\theta}$ is an *unbiased estimator* of θ if and only if $E[\hat{\theta}] = \theta$.

There may be several unbiased estimators for a particular population parameter, such as the sample mean and median for the population mean of a symmetric distribution.

Example 7.1

Show that the sample mean $\hat{\theta} = (1/n) \sum_{i=1}^{n} t_i$ is an unbiased estimator of θ for a random sample drawn from an exponential population with probability density function

$$f(t) = \frac{1}{\theta} e^{-t/\theta} \qquad t \geq 0,$$

that is, an exponential population with mean θ. Also, compute the variance of $\hat{\theta}$. The usual parameterization for the exponential distribution using the failure rate λ is replaced with $1/\theta$ throughout this chapter since many of the calculations are easier using θ.

To show that $\hat{\theta}$ is an unbiased estimator of θ, it is sufficient to show that $E[\hat{\theta}] = \theta$.

$$E[\hat{\theta}] = E\left[\frac{1}{n} \sum_{i=1}^{n} t_i \right]$$

$$= \frac{1}{n} \sum_{i=1}^{n} E[t_i]$$

$$= \frac{1}{n} (n\theta)$$

$$= \theta,$$

so $\hat{\theta}$ is an unbiased estimator of θ. To compute the variance of the estimator,

$$V[\hat{\theta}] = V\left[\frac{1}{n} \sum_{i=1}^{n} t_i \right]$$

$$= \frac{1}{n^2} \sum_{i=1}^{n} V[t_i]$$

$$= \frac{1}{n^2} (n\theta^2)$$

$$= \frac{\theta^2}{n},$$

which indicates that the variance of $\hat{\theta}$ decreases as n increases, $i = 1, 2, \ldots, n$. Given the choice among several unbiased estimators, it is wisest to choose the estimator with the smallest variance since it will be closest to the parameter θ on the average.

For this particular population distribution, it is possible to determine the sampling distribution of the statistic $\hat{\theta}$ using results from Chapter 4 concerning sums of independent and identically distributed exponential random variables. Since $\sum_{i=1}^{n} t_i$ is an Erlang random variable (a special case of the gamma distribution discussed in Section 4.4) with parameters $1/\theta$ and n, it follows that $\hat{\theta}$ is also an Erlang random variable with parameters n/θ and n, which agrees with the mean and variance of $\hat{\theta}$ determined earlier.

If there are two unbiased estimators for a parameter θ, a comparison between the two can be made with respect to the variance of the estimators.

Definition 7.2   Let $\hat{\theta}_1$ and $\hat{\theta}_2$ be two unbiased point estimators of the parameter θ. Then

$$\frac{V(\hat{\theta}_1)}{V(\hat{\theta}_2)}$$

is the *efficiency* of $\hat{\theta}_1$ relative to $\hat{\theta}_2$.

If the efficiency is less than 1, then $\hat{\theta}_1$ is the better unbiased estimator since its variability is smaller than the variability of $\hat{\theta}_2$. Similarly, if the efficiency is greater than 1, $\hat{\theta}_2$ is the better estimator.

Example 7.2

Consider the data points t_1, t_2, and t_3 sampled randomly from an exponential population with mean θ, and the two estimators $\hat{\theta}_1 = (t_1 + t_2 + t_3)/3$ (the sample mean) and $\hat{\theta}_2 = (t_1 + 4t_2 + t_3)/6$. Calculate the efficiency of $\hat{\theta}_1$ relative to $\hat{\theta}_2$.

First, to show that both estimators are unbiased

$$E[\hat{\theta}_1] = E\left[\frac{t_1 + t_2 + t_3}{3}\right] = \frac{1}{3}\left[E[t_1] + E[t_2] + E[t_3]\right] = \theta$$

and

$$E[\hat{\theta}_2] = E\left[\frac{t_1 + 4t_2 + t_3}{6}\right] = \frac{1}{6} E[t_1] + \frac{2}{3} E[t_2] + \frac{1}{6} E[t_3] = \theta.$$

Next, the variances are

$$V[\hat{\theta}_1] = V\left[\frac{t_1 + t_2 + t_3}{3}\right] = \frac{1}{9}\left[V(t_1) + V(t_2) + V(t_3)\right] = \frac{\theta^2}{3}$$

and

$$V[\hat{\theta}_2] = V\left[\frac{t_1 + 4t_2 + t_3}{6}\right] = \frac{1}{36}\left[V(t_1) + 16\,V(t_2) + V(t_3)\right] = \frac{\theta^2}{2},$$

yielding an efficiency of

$$\frac{V(\hat{\theta}_1)}{V(\hat{\theta}_2)} = \frac{2}{3}.$$

The sample mean $\hat{\theta}_1$ is clearly the preferred unbiased estimator since it has a variance that is two-thirds the variance of $\hat{\theta}_2$.

A lower bound on the variance of $\hat{\theta}$ is given by the Cramer–Rao inequality:

$$V[\hat{\theta}] \geq \frac{1}{nE\left[\left(\dfrac{\partial \log f(T)}{\partial \theta}\right)^2\right]},$$

where $f(t)$ is the probability density function of the population lifetime distribution and $\hat{\theta}$ is an unbiased estimator of θ. When the variance of $\hat{\theta}$ is equal to the right-hand side of the inequality, the estimator is known as a *minimum-variance unbiased estimator*. The inequality applies when $f(t)$ has continuous first-order partial derivatives and the domain of definition for T does not depend on any of the unknown parameters.

Example 7.3

Show that $\hat{\theta} = (1/n) \sum_{i=1}^{n} t_i$ is a minimum-variance unbiased estimator of θ for a random sample of size n from an exponential population with mean θ.
The probability density function is

$$f(t) = \frac{1}{\theta} e^{-t/\theta} \qquad t \geq 0,$$

so

$$\frac{\partial \log f(t)}{\partial \theta} = -\frac{1}{\theta} + \frac{t}{\theta^2}.$$

Since $E[T] = \theta$ and $E[T^2] = V[T] + (E[T])^2 = \theta^2 + \theta^2 = 2\theta^2$ for an exponential random variable,

$$E\left[\left(\frac{\partial \log f(T)}{\partial \theta}\right)^2\right] = E\left[\left(-\frac{1}{\theta} + \frac{T}{\theta^2}\right)^2\right]$$

$$= E\left[\frac{1}{\theta^2} - \frac{2T}{\theta^3} + \frac{T^2}{\theta^4}\right]$$

$$= \frac{1}{\theta^2} - \frac{2}{\theta^2} + \frac{2}{\theta^2}$$

$$= \frac{1}{\theta^2}.$$

The right-hand side of the Cramer–Rao inequality becomes

$$\frac{1}{nE\left[\left(\dfrac{\partial \log f(T)}{\partial \theta}\right)^2\right]} = \frac{1}{n/\theta^2} = \frac{\theta^2}{n},$$

which is the variance of $\hat{\theta}$ by Example 7.1. Therefore, $\hat{\theta} = (1/n) \sum_{i=1}^{n} t_i$ is a minimum-variance unbiased estimator of θ.

To this point, two properties have been considered with respect to point estimation: bias and variability. Since the objective of a good estimator is to minimize both bias and variation, trade-offs often need to be made. Figure 7.1 shows the sampling probability density functions of two point estimators $\hat{\theta}_1$ and $\hat{\theta}_2$, where θ_0 is the true value of the unknown parameter θ. Estimator $\hat{\theta}_1$ has a smaller variance, but is a biased estimator. Estimator $\hat{\theta}_2$ has a larger variance, but is an unbiased estimator. The choice between the two estimators concerns a trade-off between bias and variability. The mean squared error (MSE) for an estimator is a measure that incorporates bias and variability.

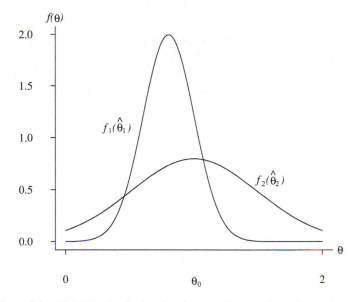

Figure 7.1   Probability density functions for two estimators of an unknown parameter θ.

Definition 7.3   If $\hat{\theta}$ is an estimator of θ, then the *mean squared error* is $E[(\hat{\theta} - \theta)^2]$.

The mean squared error can be broken into the variability and bias components as follows:

$$
\begin{aligned}
E[(\hat{\theta} - \theta)^2] &= E[\hat{\theta}^2 - 2\hat{\theta}\theta + \theta^2] \\
&= E[\hat{\theta}^2] - E[2\hat{\theta}\theta] + E[\theta^2] \\
&= E[\hat{\theta}^2] - 2\theta E[\hat{\theta}] + \theta^2 \\
&= E[\hat{\theta}^2] - E[\hat{\theta}]^2 + E[\hat{\theta}]^2 - 2\theta E[\hat{\theta}] + \theta^2 \\
&= V[\hat{\theta}] + (E[\hat{\theta}] - \theta)^2,
\end{aligned}
$$

where the first term is the variability of the estimator and the second term is the squared bias. Therefore, an unbiased estimator has a mean squared error equal to its variance.

Another important property of estimators is consistency. A consistent estimator is one that approaches the true parameter value as n increases.

Definition 7.4   The point estimator $\hat{\theta}$ is a *consistent estimator* of θ if and only if, for any positive constant ε,

$$\lim_{n \to \infty} P(|\hat{\theta} - \theta| < \varepsilon) = 1.$$

This definition emphasizes that the estimator is arbitrarily close (within ε) of the parameter θ as the sample size increases. Instead of using this definition to show that an estimator is consistent, it is often easier to show that the estimator is unbiased and that $\lim_{n \to \infty} V[\hat{\theta}] = 0$. Proving these two conditions is sufficient for showing consistency.

Example 7.4

Show that $\hat{\theta} = (1/n) \sum_{i=1}^{n} t_i$ is a consistent estimator of θ for $t_1, t_2, \ldots, t_n$ sampled randomly from an exponential population with mean θ.

There are two approaches to solving this problem. The first is to use the definition of a consistent estimator and compute $\lim_{n \to \infty} P(|\hat{\theta} - \theta| < \varepsilon)$ and show that this quantity is equal to 1. This can be done for this problem since $\hat{\theta}$ is an Erlang random variable with parameters n/θ and n. The second approach to showing that $\hat{\theta}$ is a consistent estimator for θ is to show that $\hat{\theta}$ is an unbiased estimator of θ and that the variance of $\hat{\theta}$ approaches zero as $n \to \infty$. Recall from Example 7.1 that

$$E[\hat{\theta}] = \theta \quad \text{and} \quad V[\hat{\theta}] = \frac{\theta^2}{n},$$

which indicates that $\hat{\theta}$ is unbiased for any sample size and $\lim_{n \to \infty} V[\hat{\theta}] = 0$. These two facts are sufficient to conclude that $\hat{\theta}$ is arbitrarily close to θ as n approaches infinity, and hence $\hat{\theta}$ is a consistent estimator of θ.

7.2   INTERVAL ESTIMATION

Confidence intervals give bounds calculated from data that contain a population parameter with a prescribed probability. A confidence interval contains more information than a point estimator for a parameter θ because it provides information about the accuracy of the point estimator. A confidence interval for a population parameter θ is given by

$$L < \theta < U,$$

where L and U are functions of the sample size n, the lifetimes $t_1, \ldots, t_n$, and the nominal (or stated) coverage of the interval $1 - \alpha$. The true value of the parameter θ is denoted by θ_0. The nominal coverage $1 - \alpha$ is determined by the modeler, and higher coverages result in wider confidence intervals. Popular choices for α are 0.10 and 0.05, commonly referred to as 90% and 95% confidence intervals.

A diagram for presenting the concept of a confidence interval is shown in Figure 7.2, where 90% confidence intervals computed from 10 different samples of size $n = 25$ drawn from an exponential population with $\theta_0 = 1$ are plotted on axes with the same units as θ. The point estimate is indicated by a point on each axis, and L and U are

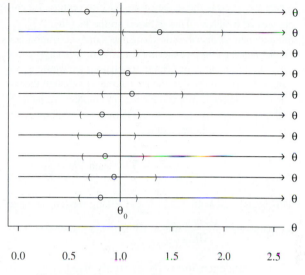

Figure 7.2   Ten 90% confidence intervals for θ.

indicated by left and right parentheses. The first and second confidence intervals in the figure do not contain the true parameter value θ_0. The first interval misses θ_0 low and the second interval misses θ_0 high. If a large number of these confidence intervals were computed, about 90% would contain the true parameter value, about 5% would fall above the parameter value ("missing high"), and about 5% would fall below the parameter value ("missing low"). It is also apparent that there is substantial variability in the widths of these confidence intervals. The nonsymmetry of the confidence intervals about the point estimate is due to the nonsymmetry of the chi-square distribution, as detailed in Example 7.5.

A confidence interval is *exact* if the probability that the interval covers the true parameter θ_0 is the stated coverage; that is, $P[L < \theta_0 < U] = 1 - \alpha$. In other words, a confidence interval is exact if the percentage of these intervals that contain θ_0 converges to $1 - \alpha$ when a large number of confidence intervals are computed for some fixed sample size n. There are relatively few exact confidence intervals in lifetime data analysis since the sampling distribution of parameters often tends to be complicated.

Example 7.5

Find an exact confidence interval for a data set of n independent exponential lifetimes. Discuss properties of the lower and upper limits.

A simple example of an exact $100(1 - \alpha)\%$ confidence interval for the population parameter θ when $t_1, t_2, \ldots, t_n$ are independent and identically distributed exponential random lifetimes with mean θ is

$$L = \frac{2 \sum_{i=1}^{n} t_i}{\chi^2_{2n,\,\alpha/2}} \quad \text{and} \quad U = \frac{2 \sum_{i=1}^{n} t_i}{\chi^2_{2n,\,1-\alpha/2}},$$

where $\chi^2_{2n,\,1-\alpha/2}$ is the value of the $\alpha/2$ percentile of a chi-square random variable with $2n$ degrees of freedom. This is based on the fact that $2\sum_{i=1}^{n} t_i/\theta \sim \chi^2(2n)$ by Property 4.7 of the exponential distribution using the parameterization considered here. The fact that this confidence interval is exact indicates that, if a large number of confidence intervals were calculated from an exponential population, we would expect a percentage equal to approximately $1 - \alpha$ of these confidence intervals to contain the true mean of the population.

As indicated in Example 7.1, the random variable $\sum_{i=1}^{n} t_i$ has an Erlang distribution with parameters $1/\theta$ and n; then the random variables L and U are each a constant times an Erlang random variable; that is,

$$L = \frac{2}{\chi^2_{2n,\,\alpha/2}} \sum_{i=1}^{n} t_i \quad \text{and} \quad U = \frac{2}{\chi^2_{2n,\,1-\alpha/2}} \sum_{i=1}^{n} t_i .$$

This means that both L and U are Erlang random variables with a correlation of 1, and L has parameters $\dfrac{\chi^2_{2n,\,\alpha/2}}{2\theta}$ and n, while U has parameters $\dfrac{\chi^2_{2n,\,1-\alpha/2}}{2\theta}$ and n.

Many confidence intervals currently used are *approximate,* rather than exact. A confidence interval is approximate if the probability of covering the true parameter value θ_0 is not the stated coverage for all sample sizes n; that is, $P[L < \theta_0 < U] \neq 1 - \alpha$. Equivalently, a confidence interval is approximate if the fraction of a large number of confidence intervals that cover the parameter is not $1 - \alpha$:

$$\lim_{m \to \infty} \sum_{i=1}^{m} \frac{I(L_i, U_i)}{m} \neq 1 - \alpha$$

for any sample size n, where L_i and U_i are the lower and upper confidence limits from data set i, and $I(L_i, U_i)$ is an indicator function that assumes the value 1 if $L_i < \theta_0 < U_i$ and 0 otherwise, for $i = 1, 2, \ldots, m$. Many confidence intervals are based on large-sample methods, and their coverage converges to the nominal coverage as $n \to \infty$; that is, they are asymptotically exact.

The random variables L and U have a joint distribution. As shown in Figure 7.3, level curves (contours) of the joint density of L and U for a confidence interval are typically concentric curves when L and U are continuous. All confidence intervals must lie above the line $L = U$, since the upper limit is always greater than or equal to the lower limit. The value of the true population parameter is $\theta_0 = 1$, and any confidence interval that lies to the northwest of the point (θ_0, θ_0) contains the true parameter θ_0 since $L < \theta_0 < U$. Thus the probability of covering θ_0 is

$$P[L < \theta_0 < U] = \int_{-\infty}^{\theta_0} \int_{\theta_0}^{\infty} f(l, u) \, du \, dl,$$

where $f(l, u)$ is the joint probability density function of l and u, and a confidence interval procedure is exact if this probability is equal to the stated coverage $1 - \alpha$ for all n.

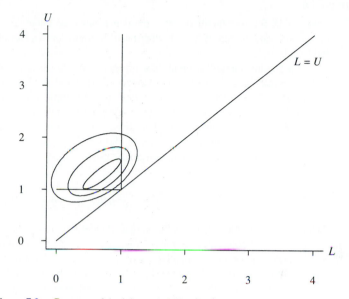

Figure 7.3   Contours of the joint probability density function of L and U with $\theta_0 = 1$.

If the actual coverage of a confidence interval is close to the stated coverage, other factors should be considered in selecting a confidence interval. Two of these factors are the expected interval width and the variance of the interval width, where the interval width is $W = U - L$. Assuming two confidence interval procedures have the same coverage, the one with the smaller expected width or width variance should be chosen. The mean interval width is

$$E[W] = \int_{-\infty}^{\infty} \int_{l}^{\infty} (u-l)\, f(l,u)\, du\, dl,$$

and the variance of the interval width is

$$V[W] = \int_{-\infty}^{\infty} \int_{l}^{\infty} [(u-l) - E[W]]^2\, f(l,u)\, du\, dl.$$

A confidence interval scatterplot (CIS) is a plot of many confidence intervals, (l, u). It indicates the shape of the joint distribution of L and U and can be used for evaluating the effectiveness of a particular confidence interval procedure. Points falling to the right of $l = \theta_0$ are confidence intervals when l is larger than θ_0 ("missing high"), and points falling below $u = \theta_0$ are confidence intervals when u is smaller than θ_0 ("missing low").

Example 7.6

Make a CIS for five hundred 90% confidence intervals generated from data sets of size $n = 10$ independent and identically distributed lifetimes drawn from an exponential population with $\theta_0 = 1$.

Each point plotted in Figure 7.4 represents the lower and upper bounds of a single confidence interval computed from 10 independent exponential random variables, each with a mean of 1. The exact confidence interval from Example 7.5 is used here, and 60 of the 500 confidence intervals do not contain the true parameter value θ_0. As alluded to earlier, all the confidence intervals lie on a line through the origin. Instead of using the exact formula for a confidence interval for exponential data, the confidence interval typically used for sampling from a normal population can be used:

$$\bar{x} \pm t_{9,0.05}\,\frac{s}{\sqrt{10}},$$

where $\bar{x}$ is the sample mean, s is the sample standard deviation, and $t_{9,0.05}$ is the 0.95 quantile of a t distribution with 9 degrees of freedom. As a result of using the wrong confidence interval formula for an exponential population, Figure 7.5 shows that 65 of the intervals now do not contain θ_0, and a vastly different joint distribution for L and U emerges. Using this "classical" confidence interval based on normal sampling theory results in an approximate confidence interval, and the fraction of confidence intervals that contain $\theta_0 = 1$ does not converge to $1 - \alpha = 0.90$.

A variation of this CIS follows using the same 500 confidence intervals. Figure 7.6 is the previous figure rotated 45° clockwise, yielding a graph with the midpoint of the inter-

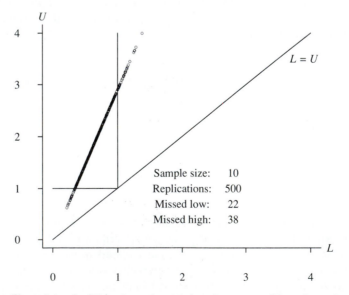

Figure 7.4   Confidence interval scatterplot using exact confidence intervals.

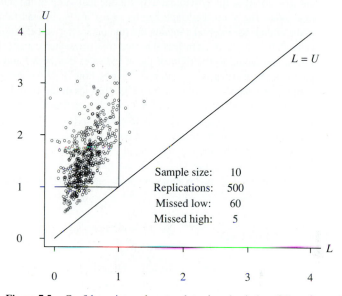

Figure 7.5   Confidence interval scatterplot using classical confidence intervals.

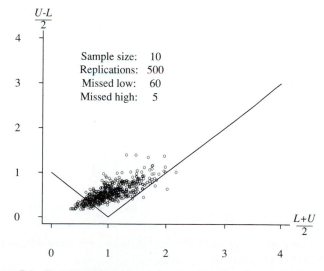

Figure 7.6   Rotated confidence interval scatterplot using classical confidence intervals.

val $[(l + u)/2])$ as the horizontal axis and the halfwidth of the interval $[(u - l)/2]$ as the vertical axis. The V on the graph has its vertex at $(\theta_0, 0)$, and falling within the V indicates that a confidence interval contains the true parameter value; falling to the left of the V indicates that both l and u are less than the true parameter value (that is, the interval "missed low"), and falling to the right of the V indicates that both l and u are greater than the true parameter value (that is, the interval "missed high"). If the upper and lower limits of many confidence intervals are plotted on a CIS, the bias of the confidence interval procedure (that is, the shift to the left or right of θ_0) can be seen since the midpoint may not be centered around the true parameter value. The actual coverage of the confidence interval procedure can be estimated by finding the fraction of points falling in the V. The expected halfwidth can be estimated by the average height of the points on the graph, and the variance of the halfwidth can be estimated by the dispersion of the heights of the plotted values. Changing α for the plot in Figure 7.6 shifts the points up (down) for decreased (increased) α.

7.3   LIKELIHOOD THEORY

Let $t_1, t_2, \ldots, t_n$ be lifetimes sampled randomly from a population of items with a lifetime distribution having a probability density function $f(t)$. This distribution has a vector $\boldsymbol{\theta} = (\theta_1, \theta_2, \ldots, \theta_p)'$ of unknown parameters associated with it, where p is the number of unknown parameters. Since the lifetimes are independent, the likelihood function, $L(\mathbf{t}, \boldsymbol{\theta})$, is the product of the probability density function evaluated at each sample point:

$$L(\mathbf{t}, \boldsymbol{\theta}) = \prod_{i=1}^{n} f(t_i, \boldsymbol{\theta}),$$

where $\mathbf{t} = (t_1, t_2, \ldots, t_n)$. The maximum likelihood estimator $\hat{\boldsymbol{\theta}}$ is found by maximizing $L(\mathbf{t}, \boldsymbol{\theta})$ with respect to $\boldsymbol{\theta}$. Thus $\hat{\boldsymbol{\theta}}$ corresponds to the distribution that is most likely to have produced the data $t_1, t_2, \ldots, t_n$.

Figure 7.7 illustrates the maximum likelihood estimator for θ for an exponential population and a sample size of $n = 4$. Consider all the allowable θ values for an exponential distribution (that is, $\theta > 0$). The θ value depicted in Figure 7.7 (shown as the probability density function with $\hat{\theta} = 1$) is that which maximizes the product of the density values at the data points.

In practice, it is often easier to maximize the log likelihood function $\log L(\mathbf{t}, \boldsymbol{\theta})$ to find the vector of maximum likelihood estimators, which is valid because the logarithm function is monotonic. The log likelihood function is

$$\log L(\mathbf{t}, \boldsymbol{\theta}) = \sum_{i=1}^{n} \log f(t_i, \boldsymbol{\theta})$$

and is asymptotically normally distributed by the central limit theorem, since it consists of the sum of n independent terms.

Since $L(\mathbf{t}, \boldsymbol{\theta})$ is a joint probability density function for $t_1, t_2, \ldots, t_n$, it must integrate to 1:

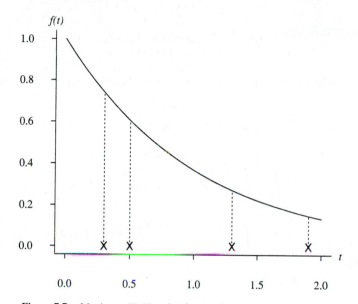

Figure 7.7 Maximum likelihood estimation for the exponential distribution.

$$\int_0^\infty \int_0^\infty \cdots \int_0^\infty L(\mathbf{t}, \boldsymbol{\theta})\, d\mathbf{t} = 1. \tag{7.1}$$

Assuming that the likelihood function is continuous (and hence differentiation and integration can be interchanged), the partial derivative of the left-hand side with respect to one of the parameters, θ_i, yields

$$\frac{\partial}{\partial \theta_i} \int_0^\infty \int_0^\infty \cdots \int_0^\infty L(\mathbf{t}, \boldsymbol{\theta})\, d\mathbf{t} = \int_0^\infty \int_0^\infty \cdots \int_0^\infty \frac{\partial}{\partial \theta_i} L(\mathbf{t}, \boldsymbol{\theta})\, d\mathbf{t}$$

$$= \int_0^\infty \int_0^\infty \cdots \int_0^\infty \frac{\partial \log L(\mathbf{t}, \boldsymbol{\theta})}{\partial \theta_i} L(\mathbf{t}, \boldsymbol{\theta})\, d\mathbf{t} \tag{7.2}$$

$$= E\left[\frac{\partial \log L(\mathbf{t}, \boldsymbol{\theta})}{\partial \theta_i}\right]$$

$$= E[U_i(\boldsymbol{\theta})] \qquad i = 1, 2, \ldots, p,$$

where $\mathbf{U}(\boldsymbol{\theta}) = (U_1(\boldsymbol{\theta}), U_2(\boldsymbol{\theta}), \ldots, U_p(\boldsymbol{\theta}))'$ is often called the *score vector*. The $\mathbf{t}$ argument has been dropped for compactness. Differentiating the right-hand side of (7.1) with respect to θ_i yields the result

$$E[U_i(\boldsymbol{\theta})] = 0 \qquad i = 1, 2, \ldots, p,$$

or, in vector form,

$$E[\mathbf{U}(\boldsymbol{\theta})] = \mathbf{0}. \tag{7.3}$$

Differentiating (7.2) with respect to θ_j yields (using the chain rule)

$$\frac{\partial}{\partial \theta_j} \int_0^\infty \int_0^\infty \cdots \int_0^\infty \frac{\partial \log L(\mathbf{t}, \boldsymbol{\theta})}{\partial \theta_i} L(\mathbf{t}, \boldsymbol{\theta}) \, dt$$

$$= \int_0^\infty \int_0^\infty \cdots \int_0^\infty \left(\frac{\partial \log L(\mathbf{t}, \boldsymbol{\theta})}{\partial \theta_i} \frac{\partial L(\mathbf{t}, \boldsymbol{\theta})}{\partial \theta_j} + \frac{\partial^2 \log L(\mathbf{t}, \boldsymbol{\theta})}{\partial \theta_i \partial \theta_j} L(\mathbf{t}, \boldsymbol{\theta}) \right) dt$$

$$= \int_0^\infty \int_0^\infty \cdots \int_0^\infty \left(\frac{\partial \log L(\mathbf{t}, \boldsymbol{\theta})}{\partial \theta_i} \frac{\partial \log L(\mathbf{t}, \boldsymbol{\theta})}{\partial \theta_j} L(\mathbf{t}, \boldsymbol{\theta}) + \frac{\partial^2 \log L(\mathbf{t}, \boldsymbol{\theta})}{\partial \theta_i \partial \theta_j} L(\mathbf{t}, \boldsymbol{\theta}) \right) dt$$

$$= E\left[U_i(\boldsymbol{\theta}) U_j(\boldsymbol{\theta}) \right] + E\left[\frac{\partial^2 \log L(\mathbf{t}, \boldsymbol{\theta})}{\partial \theta_i \partial \theta_j} \right] \qquad i = 1, 2, \ldots, p,$$

Since this expression is the second derivative of the left-hand side of (7.1), and the second derivative of the right-hand side of (7.1) is zero,

$$E\left[\frac{-\partial^2 \log L(\mathbf{t}, \boldsymbol{\theta})}{\partial \theta_i \partial \theta_j} \right] = E\left[U_i(\boldsymbol{\theta}) U_j(\boldsymbol{\theta}) \right] \qquad \begin{matrix} i = 1, 2, \ldots, p, \\ j = 1, 2, \ldots, p. \end{matrix}$$

By equation (7.3), it is known that $E[U_i(\boldsymbol{\theta})] = E[U_j(\boldsymbol{\theta})] = 0$ for $i = 1, 2, \ldots, p$ and $j = 1, 2, \ldots, p$, and hence

$$E\left[\frac{-\partial^2 \log L(\mathbf{t}, \boldsymbol{\theta})}{\partial \theta_i \partial \theta_j} \right] = \text{Cov}(U_i(\boldsymbol{\theta}), U_j(\boldsymbol{\theta})) \qquad \begin{matrix} i = 1, 2, \ldots, p, \\ j = 1, 2, \ldots, p. \end{matrix}$$

These elements form a $p \times p$ *Fisher information matrix, $I(\boldsymbol{\theta})$,* whose diagonal elements are the variances of the elements of the score vector, and the off-diagonal elements are covariances.

To review the results so far, the $p \times 1$ score vector $\mathbf{U}(\boldsymbol{\theta})$ has components

$$U_i(\boldsymbol{\theta}) = \frac{\partial \log L(\mathbf{t}, \boldsymbol{\theta})}{\partial \theta_i} \qquad i = 1, 2, \ldots, p,$$

which, when equated to zero and solved, yields the $p \times 1$ maximum likelihood estimate vector $\hat{\boldsymbol{\theta}}$. The expected value of the score vector has components

$$E[U_i(\boldsymbol{\theta})] = 0 \qquad i = 1, 2, \ldots, p,$$

and variance–covariance matrix

$$I(\boldsymbol{\theta}) = E[\mathbf{U}(\boldsymbol{\theta})\,\mathbf{U}'(\boldsymbol{\theta})].$$

This matrix has components

$$E\left[\frac{-\partial^2 \log L(\mathbf{t}, \boldsymbol{\theta})}{\partial\,\theta_i\,\partial\,\theta_j}\right] \qquad \begin{array}{l} i = 1, 2, \ldots, p, \\ j = 1, 2, \ldots, p, \end{array}$$

and is often called the Fisher information matrix.

Example 7.7

Let $t_1, t_2, \ldots, t_n$ be a random sample from an exponential population with $p = 1$ parameter θ, the population mean

$$f(t, \theta) = \frac{1}{\theta}\, e^{-t/\theta} \qquad t \geq 0.$$

Find the score vector and maximum likelihood estimator for θ. Also, show that the expected value of the score vector is zero and that the variance of the score vector is equal to the information matrix.

The likelihood function is

$$L(\mathbf{t}, \theta) = \prod_{i=1}^{n} f(t_i, \theta)$$

$$= \prod_{i=1}^{n} \frac{1}{\theta}\, e^{-t_i/\theta}$$

$$= \theta^{-n}\, e^{-\sum_{i=1}^{n} t_i/\theta}.$$

The log likelihood function is

$$\log L(\mathbf{t}, \theta) = -n \log \theta - \sum_{i=1}^{n} t_i / \theta.$$

The score vector has only one element since there is only one parameter:

$$U(\theta) = \frac{\partial \log L(\mathbf{t}, \theta)}{\partial\,\theta} = -\frac{n}{\theta} + \frac{\sum_{i=1}^{n} t_i}{\theta^2}.$$

Equating the score to zero and solving for θ yields the maximum likelihood estimator:

$$\hat{\theta} = \frac{1}{n} \sum_{i=1}^{n} t_i,$$

which is the sample mean. The derivative of the score vector is

$$\frac{\partial^2 \log L(\mathbf{t}, \theta)}{\partial \theta^2} = \frac{n}{\theta^2} - \frac{2 \sum_{i=1}^{n} t_i}{\theta^3}.$$

Next check two of the results associated with the score vector. The first result is that $E[U(\theta)] = 0$. Now

$$E[U(\theta)] = E\left[-\frac{n}{\theta} + \frac{1}{\theta^2} \sum_{i=1}^{n} t_i\right] = -\frac{n}{\theta} + \frac{1}{\theta^2} E\left[\sum_{i=1}^{n} t_i\right] = -\frac{n}{\theta} + \frac{1}{\theta^2} n \theta = 0$$

since $E[t_i] = \theta$ for $i = 1, 2, \ldots, n$. The second result is that the information matrix is equal to the variance–covariance matrix of the score vector. The information matrix, which only has a single element, is

$$I(\theta) = E\left[\frac{-\partial^2 \log L(\mathbf{t}, \theta)}{\partial \theta^2}\right]$$

$$= E\left[-\frac{n}{\theta^2} + \frac{2 \sum_{i=1}^{n} t_i}{\theta^3}\right]$$

$$= -\frac{n}{\theta^2} + \frac{2}{\theta^3} E\left[\sum_{i=1}^{n} t_i\right]$$

$$= \frac{n}{\theta^2}.$$

To see that this is the same as the variance of the score vector,

$$V\left[\frac{\partial \log L(\mathbf{t}, \theta)}{\partial \theta}\right] = V\left[-\frac{n}{\theta} + \frac{\sum_{i=1}^{n} t_i}{\theta^2}\right] = \frac{1}{\theta^4} V\left[\sum_{i=1}^{n} t_i\right] = \frac{n}{\theta^2}$$

since $V(t_i) = \theta^2$ for $i = 1, 2, \ldots, n$.

As with any inference technique, it is always desirable to draw identical conclusions regardless of the parameterization used on the survival distribution. If a one-to-one parameter transformation $\phi = g(\theta)$ is introduced, the score is divided by $g'(\theta)$, and the information is divided by $(g'(\theta))^2$.

Example 7.8

If the exponential distribution from the previous example is parameterized with failure rate $\lambda = g(\theta) = 1/\theta$, then, by the *invariance property* (functions of maximum likelihood estimators are maximum likelihood estimators),

$$\hat{\lambda} = \frac{n}{\displaystyle\sum_{i=1}^{n} t_i}.$$

Since $g'(\theta) = -\theta^{-2}$, the score is

$$U(\lambda) = \frac{\partial \log L(\mathbf{t}, \lambda)}{\partial \lambda} = \frac{-n\lambda + \lambda^2 \displaystyle\sum_{i=1}^{n} t_i}{-\lambda^2} = \frac{n}{\lambda} - \sum_{i=1}^{n} t_i$$

and the information matrix is

$$I(\lambda) = E\left[\frac{-\partial^2 \log L(\mathbf{t}, \lambda)}{\partial \lambda^2}\right] = \frac{n\lambda^2}{(-\lambda^2)^2} = \frac{n}{\lambda^2}.$$

The *observed information matrix, $O(\hat{\boldsymbol{\theta}})$,* is often used to estimate the information matrix $I(\boldsymbol{\theta})$. For many parametric distributions, it is a consistent estimator of the information matrix. Its elements are

$$\left[\frac{-\partial^2 \log L(\mathbf{t}, \boldsymbol{\theta})}{\partial \theta_i \, \partial \theta_j}\right]_{\boldsymbol{\theta} = \hat{\boldsymbol{\theta}}} \qquad \begin{array}{l} i = 1, 2, \ldots, p, \\ j = 1, 2, \ldots, p. \end{array}$$

Example 7.9

For the exponential distribution parameterized by its mean θ, the observed information matrix is

$$O(\hat{\theta}) = \left[\frac{-\partial^2 \log L(\mathbf{t}, \boldsymbol{\theta})}{\partial \theta^2}\right]_{\theta = \hat{\theta}}$$

$$= \left[-\frac{n}{\theta^2} + \frac{2 \displaystyle\sum_{i=1}^{n} t_i}{\theta^3}\right]_{\theta = \hat{\theta}}$$

$$= \frac{n}{\hat{\theta}^2},$$

which converges to the information matrix since $\hat{\theta} = (1/n) \sum_{i=1}^{n} t_i$ converges to θ for large n. Therefore, $O(\hat{\theta})$ is a consistent estimator of $I(\theta)$ when sampling from an exponential population.

Example 7.10 illustrates a two-parameter model.

Example 7.10

Let $t_1, t_2, \ldots, t_n$ be a random sample from an *inverse Gaussian* (Wald) population having positive parameters λ and μ, probability density function

$$f(t) = \sqrt{\frac{\lambda}{2\pi}}\, t^{-3/2}\, e^{-\frac{\lambda}{2\mu^2 t}(t-\mu)^2} \qquad t \geq 0,$$

and mean μ. The likelihood function is

$$L(\mathbf{t}, \lambda, \mu) = \prod_{i=1}^{n} \sqrt{\frac{\lambda}{2\pi}}\, t_i^{-3/2}\, e^{-\frac{\lambda}{2\mu^2 t_i}(t_i-\mu)^2}$$

$$= \lambda^{n/2}(2\pi)^{-n/2}\left(\prod_{i=1}^{n} t_i\right)^{-3/2} e^{-\frac{\lambda}{2\mu^2}\sum_{i=1}^{n}\frac{(t_i-\mu)^2}{t_i}}$$

for $t_i \geq 0$, $i = 1, 2, \ldots, n$. The log likelihood function is

$$\log L(\mathbf{t}, \lambda, \mu) = \frac{n}{2}\log\lambda - \frac{n}{2}\log(2\pi) - \frac{3}{2}\sum_{i=1}^{n}\log t_i - \frac{\lambda}{2\mu^2}\sum_{i=1}^{n}\frac{(t_i-\mu)^2}{t_i}.$$

The score vector, $\mathbf{U}(\lambda, \mu)$, has two components:

$$\frac{\partial \log L(\mathbf{t}, \lambda, \mu)}{\partial \lambda} = \frac{n}{2\lambda} - \frac{1}{2\mu^2}\sum_{i=1}^{n}\frac{(t_i-\mu)^2}{t_i}$$

and

$$\frac{\partial \log L(\mathbf{t}, \lambda, \mu)}{\partial \mu} = \frac{\lambda}{\mu^3}\left[\sum_{i=1}^{n} t_i - n\mu\right].$$

When the second equation is equated to zero, the maximum likelihood estimator $\hat{\mu}$ is determined. When $\hat{\mu}$ is used as an argument in the first equation and it is solved for $\hat{\lambda}$, the maximum likelihood estimators are

$$\hat{\mu} = \frac{1}{n}\sum_{i=1}^{n} t_i \qquad \hat{\lambda} = \left[\frac{1}{n}\sum_{i=1}^{n}\frac{1}{t_i} - \frac{n}{\sum_{i=1}^{n} t_i}\right]^{-1}.$$

The second derivatives of the log likelihood function are

$$\frac{\partial^2 \log L(\mathbf{t}, \lambda, \mu)}{\partial \lambda^2} = -\frac{n}{2\lambda^2},$$

$$\frac{\partial^2 \log L(\mathbf{t}, \lambda, \mu)}{\partial \lambda \partial \mu} = \frac{1}{\mu^3}\sum_{i=1}^{n} t_i - \frac{n}{\mu^2},$$

$$\frac{\partial^2 \log L(\mathbf{t}, \lambda, \mu)}{\partial \mu^2} = -\frac{3\lambda\sum_{i=1}^{n} t_i}{\mu^4} + \frac{2n\lambda}{\mu^3}.$$

Since $E[T] = \mu$ (a result cited at the end of the chapter), the Fisher information matrix consists of the expected values of the negatives of these derivatives:

$$I(\lambda, \mu) = \begin{pmatrix} E\left[\dfrac{-\partial^2 \log L(\mathbf{t}, \lambda, \mu)}{\partial \lambda^2}\right] & E\left[\dfrac{-\partial^2 \log L(\mathbf{t}, \lambda, \mu)}{\partial \lambda \partial \mu}\right] \\ E\left[\dfrac{-\partial^2 \log L(\mathbf{t}, \lambda, \mu)}{\partial \mu \partial \lambda}\right] & E\left[\dfrac{-\partial^2 \log L(\mathbf{t}, \lambda, \mu)}{\partial \mu^2}\right] \end{pmatrix}$$

$$= \begin{pmatrix} \dfrac{n}{2\lambda^2} & 0 \\ 0 & \dfrac{n\lambda}{\mu^3} \end{pmatrix},$$

where the off-diagonal elements being zero implies that the elements of the score vector are uncorrelated. Although this example has simple closed-form expressions for the Fisher information matrix, it is often the case that the elements of the Fisher information matrix are not closed form. The observed information matrix uses the maximum likelihood estimates

$$O(\hat{\lambda}, \hat{\mu}) = \begin{pmatrix} \dfrac{-\partial^2 \log L(\mathbf{t}, \lambda, \mu)}{\partial \lambda^2} & \dfrac{-\partial^2 \log L(\mathbf{t}, \lambda, \mu)}{\partial \lambda \partial \mu} \\ \dfrac{-\partial^2 \log L(\mathbf{t}, \lambda, \mu)}{\partial \mu \partial \lambda} & \dfrac{-\partial^2 \log L(\mathbf{t}, \lambda, \mu)}{\partial \mu^2} \end{pmatrix}_{\lambda = \hat{\lambda}, \mu = \hat{\mu}}$$

$$= \begin{pmatrix} \dfrac{n}{2\hat{\lambda}^2} & 0 \\ 0 & \dfrac{n\hat{\lambda}}{\hat{\mu}^3} \end{pmatrix}.$$

7.4   ASYMPTOTIC PROPERTIES

When the sample size n is large, there are some asymptotic results concerning the likelihood function that are useful for determining confidence intervals and performing hypothesis testing. As indicated in the last section, the $p \times 1$ score vector $\mathbf{U}(\boldsymbol{\theta})$ has components

$$U_i(\boldsymbol{\theta}) = \frac{\partial \log L(\mathbf{t}, \boldsymbol{\theta})}{\partial \theta_i} = \frac{\partial}{\partial \theta_i} \sum_{j=1}^{n} \log f(t_j, \boldsymbol{\theta})$$

for $i = 1, 2, \ldots, p$. Therefore, each element of the score vector is a sum of random variables, and, when n is large, the elements are asymptotically normally distributed by the central limit theorem. More specifically, the score vector $\mathbf{U}(\boldsymbol{\theta})$ is asymptotically normal with mean $\mathbf{0}$ and variance–covariance matrix $I(\boldsymbol{\theta})$. This means that when the true value for the parameter vector is $\boldsymbol{\theta}_0$ then

$$\mathbf{U}'(\boldsymbol{\theta}_0) \; I(\boldsymbol{\theta}_0)^{-1} \; \mathbf{U}(\boldsymbol{\theta}_0)$$

is asymptotically chi-square with p degrees of freedom. This can be used to determine confidence intervals and perform hypothesis tests with respect to $\boldsymbol{\theta}$.

The point estimate for the parameter vector $\hat{\boldsymbol{\theta}}$ can also be used for confidence intervals and hypothesis testing. As indicated in a result cited at the end of this chapter, $\hat{\boldsymbol{\theta}}$ is asymptotically normal with mean $\boldsymbol{\theta}$ and variance–covariance matrix $I^{-1}(\boldsymbol{\theta})$, so when $\boldsymbol{\theta} = \boldsymbol{\theta}_0$,

$$(\hat{\boldsymbol{\theta}} - \boldsymbol{\theta}_0)' \; I(\boldsymbol{\theta}_0) \; (\hat{\boldsymbol{\theta}} - \boldsymbol{\theta}_0)$$

is also asymptotically chi-square with p degrees of freedom. Two statistics that are asymptotically equivalent to this statistic and that can be used to estimate the value of the chi-square random variable are

$$(\hat{\boldsymbol{\theta}} - \boldsymbol{\theta}_0)' \; I(\hat{\boldsymbol{\theta}}) \; (\hat{\boldsymbol{\theta}} - \boldsymbol{\theta}_0)$$

and

$$(\hat{\boldsymbol{\theta}} - \boldsymbol{\theta}_0)' \; O(\hat{\boldsymbol{\theta}}) \; (\hat{\boldsymbol{\theta}} - \boldsymbol{\theta}_0).$$

A third asymptotic result involves the likelihood ratio statistic

$$2[\log L(\hat{\boldsymbol{\theta}}) - \log L(\boldsymbol{\theta})] = 2 \log \left[\frac{L(\hat{\boldsymbol{\theta}})}{L(\boldsymbol{\theta})} \right],$$

which is asymptotically chi-square with p degrees of freedom. More information on the conditions necessary for these asymptotic properties to apply are given at the end of the chapter.

Example 7.11

To illustrate the normality of the score vector $\mathbf{U}(\boldsymbol{\theta})$, consider a population of items with exponential times to failure. In this case, the score vector is

$$U(\theta) = -\frac{n}{\theta} + \frac{\sum_{i=1}^{n} t_i}{\theta^2} .$$

For simplicity, it is assumed that the mean of the exponential population is $\theta = 1$. The score vector reduces to

$$U(\theta) = \sum_{i=1}^{n} t_i - n.$$

Since each t_i is exponential, $\sum_{i=1}^{n} t_i$ has an Erlang distribution with parameters 1 and n. So $U(\theta)$ has a "shifted" (in the sense of a shift or guarantee parameter described in Section 4.1) Erlang distribution with probability density function

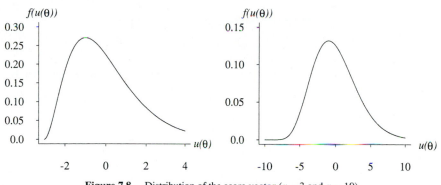

Figure 7.8   Distribution of the score vector ($n = 3$ and $n = 10$).

$$f(t) = \frac{1}{(n-1)!} (t+n)^{n-1} e^{-(t+n)} \qquad t \geq -n,$$

which has an expected value of zero. Figure 7.8 shows graphs of the distribution of $U(\theta)$ for $n = 3$ and $n = 10$. The distribution is skewed for $n = 3$ and is approaching a more symmetric, bell-shaped distribution at $n = 10$. The mean and variance of the score vector are

$$E[U(\theta)] = E[\sum_{i=1}^{n} t_i - n] = \sum_{i=1}^{n} E[t_i] - n = 0$$

and

$$V[U(\theta)] = V[\sum_{i=1}^{n} t_i - n] = V[\sum_{i=1}^{n} t_i] = \sum_{i=1}^{n} V[t_i] = n,$$

which confirms the previous statement that $\mathbf{U}(\theta)$ is asymptotically normal with a mean of $\mathbf{0}$ and variance–covariance matrix $I(\theta)$. [See Example 7.7 for the derivation of $I(\theta)$ for an exponential population.]

7.5   CENSORING

Censoring occurs frequently in lifetime data because it is often impossible or impractical to observe the lifetimes of all the items on test. A censored observation occurs when only a bound is known on the time of failure. A data set for which all failure times are known is called a *complete data set*. Figure 7.9 shows a complete data set of $n = 5$ items placed on test, where the $\times$'s denote failure times. If a data set contains one or more censored observations, it is called a *censored data set*.

It is always best to obtain exact failure times, rather than grouping the failure times into intervals, so with the exception of life tables (used by actuaries, in which a time interval is typically one year), exact failure times are assumed to be known for uncensored observations.

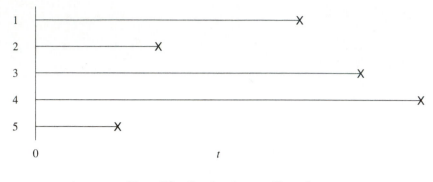

Figure 7.9   Complete data set with $n = 5$.

The most frequent type of censoring is known as *right censoring*. In a right-censored data set, there are one or more items for which only a lower bound is known on the lifetime. In an industrial life testing situation, for example, 10 machines are put into service on January 1, and 7 of them have failed by December 31. The data set consists of the seven failure times and three right-censored observations, since their failure times occur sometime after 365 days. In a medical study, patients can either still be alive at the end of the study or the researchers can lose contact with patients (for example, if they leave town), which constitutes a right-censored observation. The number of items placed on test is still denoted by n and the number of observed failures is denoted by r.

Three special cases of right censoring often occur in reliability and life testing situations. The first is Type II or *order statistic* censoring. As shown in Figure 7.10, this corresponds to terminating a study upon one of the ordered failures. The diagram corresponds to a set of $n = 5$ items placed on a test that is terminated when $r = 3$ failures are observed. In Type II censoring, the time to complete the test is random. The second special case is Type I or *time* censoring. As shown in Figure 7.11, this corresponds to terminating the study at a particular time. The diagram shows a set of $n = 5$ items placed on a test that is terminated at the time indicated by the vertical line. In Type I censoring, the number of failures is random.

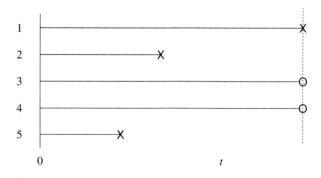

Figure 7.10   Type II right-censored data set with $n = 5$ and $r = 3$.

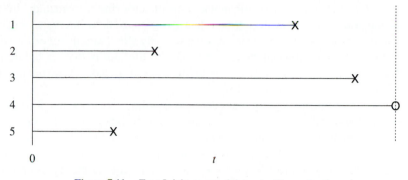

Figure 7.11   Type I right-censored data set with $n = 5$ and $r = 4$.

Finally, *random censoring* occurs when individual items are withdrawn from the test at any time during the study. It is usually assumed that the ith lifetime t_i and the ith censoring time c_i are independent random variables. In other words, in a randomly censored data set, items cannot be censored because they are at unusually high or low risk of failure. As shown in Figure 7.12 for a set of $n = 5$ items, this allows for different censoring times for each item.

Left censoring occurs less frequently than right censoring. Scientific applications for which the precision of the measuring equipment is finite (for example, in the earth sciences, when a gas cannot be measured below a threshold of six parts per million with a particular measuring device) may yield a data set containing left-censored observations.

The following example of a situation for which a data set may contain both left- and right-censored observations is referenced at the end of the chapter. A psychiatrist traveled to Africa to determine the age at which children have learned to perform a particular task. In this case, the lifetime was the time between the date of birth and the date the child is able to perform the task. Those children who already knew how to perform the task when he arrived to an African village were left-censored observations, and those that did not learn the task by the time he departed were right-censored observations.

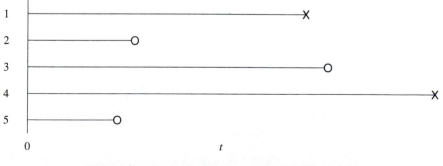

Figure 7.12   Randomly right-censored data set with $n = 5$ and $r = 2$.

Interval censoring is still another type of censoring for which the lifetime falls into an interval. This is the case when data are grouped into intervals. Interval censoring also occurs when an item is checked periodically (for example, once a week) for failure. In this case, the information known about the lifetime is that its failure time occurred during the interval prior to when failure was detected. A taxonomy for censoring schemes is shown in Figure 7.13.

Of the following three approaches to handling the problems of censoring, only one is both valid and practical. The first approach is to ignore all the censored values and to perform analysis only on those items that were observed to fail. Although this simplifies the mathematics involved, it is not a valid approach. If, for example, this approach is used on a right-censored data set, the analyst is discarding the right-censored values, and these are the items that have survived the longest. In this case, an overly pessimistic result concerning the lifetime distribution will be arrived at since the best items have been excluded from the analysis. A second approach is to wait for all the right-censored observations to fail. Although this approach is valid statistically, it is not practical. In an industrial setting, waiting for the last light bulb to burn out or the last machine to fail may take so long that the product being tested will not get to market in time. In a medical setting, waiting for the last patient to die from a particular disease may take decades. For these reasons, the proper approach is to handle censored observations probabilistically, including the censored values in the likelihood function.

The likelihood function for a censored data set can be written in several different equivalent forms. Let $t_1, t_2, \ldots, t_n$ be independent observations denoting lifetimes sampled randomly from a population. The corresponding right-censoring times are denoted by $c_1, c_2, \ldots, c_n$. In the case of Type I right censoring, $c_1 = c_2 = \cdots = c_n = c$. The set U contains the indexes of the items that are observed to fail during the test (the uncensored observations):

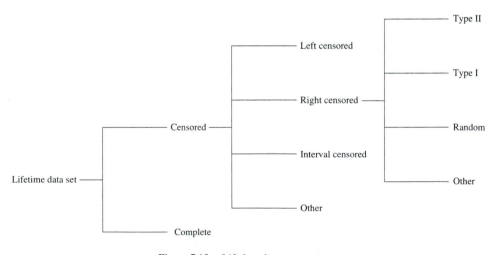

Figure 7.13   Lifetime data set taxonomy.

$$U = \{\, i \,|\, t_i \le c_i \}.$$

The set C contains the indexes of the items whose failure time exceeds the corresponding censoring time (they are right censored):

$$C = \{\, i \,|\, t_i > c_i \}.$$

Example 7.12

Consider the case of $n = 5$ items placed on test as indicated in Figure 7.14. In this particular case, the first, second, and fourth items were observed to fail, and the third and fifth were right-censored observations. The sets U and C are

$$U = \{1, 2, 4\} \quad \text{and} \quad C = \{3, 5\}.$$

The usual form for lifetime data is given by the pairs (x_i, δ_i), where $x_i = \min\{t_i, c_i\}$ and δ_i is a censoring indicator variable:

$$\delta_i = \begin{cases} 0 & t_i > c_i \\ 1 & t_i \le c_i \end{cases}$$

for $i = 1, 2, \ldots, n$. Hence δ_i is 1 if the failure of item i is observed and 0 if the failure of item i is right censored, and x_i is the failure time ($\delta_i = 1$) or the censoring time ($\delta_i = 0$). If the vector $\boldsymbol{\theta} = (\theta_1, \theta_2, \ldots, \theta_p)'$ is the vector of unknown parameters, then ignoring a constant factor, the likelihood function is

$$L(\mathbf{x}, \boldsymbol{\theta}) = \prod_{i \in U} f(t_i, \boldsymbol{\theta}) \prod_{i \in C} S(c_i, \boldsymbol{\theta})$$

where $S(c_i, \boldsymbol{\theta})$ is the survivor function with parameters $\boldsymbol{\theta}$ evaluated at censoring time i,

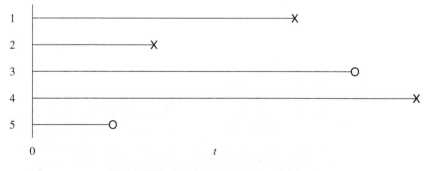

Figure 7.14   Randomly right-censored data set.

$i \in C$. The reason that the survivor function is the appropriate term in the likelihood function for a right-censored observation is that $S(c_i, \boldsymbol{\theta})$ is the probability that item i survives to c_i. The log likelihood function is

$$\log L(\mathbf{x}, \boldsymbol{\theta}) = \sum_{i \in U} \log f(t_i, \boldsymbol{\theta}) + \sum_{i \in C} \log S(c_i, \boldsymbol{\theta}),$$

or

$$\log L(\mathbf{x}, \boldsymbol{\theta}) = \sum_{i \in U} \log f(x_i, \boldsymbol{\theta}) + \sum_{i \in C} \log S(x_i, \boldsymbol{\theta}).$$

Since the density function is the product of the hazard function and the survivor function, the log likelihood function can be simplified to

$$\log L(\mathbf{x}, \boldsymbol{\theta}) = \sum_{i \in U} \log h(x_i, \boldsymbol{\theta}) + \sum_{i \in U} \log S(x_i, \boldsymbol{\theta}) + \sum_{i \in C} \log S(x_i, \boldsymbol{\theta})$$

or

$$\log L(\mathbf{x}, \boldsymbol{\theta}) = \sum_{i \in U} \log h(x_i, \boldsymbol{\theta}) + \sum_{i=1}^{n} \log S(x_i, \boldsymbol{\theta}).$$

Finally, to write the log likelihood in terms of the hazard and cumulative hazard functions only,

$$\log L(\mathbf{x}, \boldsymbol{\theta}) = \sum_{i \in U} \log h(x_i, \boldsymbol{\theta}) - \sum_{i=1}^{n} H(x_i, \boldsymbol{\theta}),$$

since $H(t) = -\log S(t)$. The choice of which of these three expressions for the log likelihood may be used for a particular distribution depends on the particular forms of $S(t)$, $f(t)$, $h(t)$, and $H(t)$.

7.6   FURTHER READING

Grosh (1989) reviews U.S. government documents related to reliability, including MIL-HDBK-217. The conditions associated with the Cramer–Rao inequality are given in Hogg and Craig (1995) and Larsen and Marx (1986, p. 248). A reference on order statistics is given by Galambos (1978).

   The work on the joint distribution of the lower and upper limits for a confidence interval is given in Kang and Schmeiser (1990).

   Figure 7.6 was suggested by Schmeiser (1984). Cox and Hinkley (1974, p. 109) and Kalbfleisch and Prentice (1980, p. 47) contain the result concerning one-to-one parameter transformations. They also contain excellent treatments of likelihood theory. The result concerning $E[T]$ for the inverse Gaussian distribution used in Example 7.10 is given in Johnson and Kotz (1970, p. 140).

Kalbfleisch and Prentice (1980, p. 51), Lawless (1982, pp. 522–527), and sections in Hinkley et al. (1991) consider the asymptotic properties presented here. Other books on lifetime data analysis include Cox and Oakes (1984), Crowder et al. (1991), Elandt-Johnson and Johnson (1980), Kapur and Lamberson (1977), Lee (1992), Nelson (1982), and Zacks (1992).

The example of the psychiatrist that traveled to Africa is from Miller (1981, p. 7) and Leiderman et al. (1973). Lawless (1982, p. 101) gives the joint probability density function of $t_{(1)}, t_{(2)}, \ldots, t_{(r)}$ in the case of Type II censoring as

$$\frac{n!}{(n-r)!} \prod_{i \in U} f(t_{(i)}, \boldsymbol{\theta}) \prod_{i \in C} S(t_{(r)}, \boldsymbol{\theta})$$

for $t_{(1)} < t_{(2)} < \cdots < t_{(r)}$. Data sets that are Type II or Type I censored are special cases of multiple or progressive Type II or Type I censored data sets. In progressive censoring, multiple items may be removed from test simultaneously at certain points in time as the test progresses. Lawless (1982, p. 33) considers progressive Type II censoring. Graphical methods for censored data are outlined in Gentleman and Crowley (1991).

7.7   EXERCISES

7.1. List five reasons why a lifetime data analysis might be performed. You may consider reliability, actuarial, and biostatistical applications.

7.2. Find the maximum likelihood estimator for θ if $t_1, t_2, \ldots, t_n$ are independent observations from a population with probability density function

$$f(t) = \frac{\theta}{t^{\theta+1}} \qquad t \geq 1; \theta > 0.$$

7.3. Given that $\sqrt{n}(\theta - \hat{\theta})$ has a t distribution with n degrees of freedom, find a $100(1 - \alpha)\%$ confidence interval for the parameter θ.

7.4. If $t_1, t_2, \ldots, t_n$ are n independent observations from a log normal distribution with probability density function

$$f(t) = \frac{1}{\sqrt{2\pi}\sigma t} e^{-\frac{1}{2}\left(\frac{\log t - \mu}{\sigma}\right)^2} \qquad t \geq 0; \sigma > 0, -\infty < \mu < \infty,$$

find the maximum likelihood estimators and $100(1 - \alpha)\%$ confidence intervals for the parameters μ and σ in terms of $t_1, t_2, \ldots, t_n$.

7.5. Verify the results from Example 7.8 by deriving the score vector and information matrix for an exponential population parameterized by the failure rate λ.

7.6. Let $t_1, t_2, \ldots, t_n$ be independent, exponentially distributed lifetimes with probability density function

$$f(t) = \frac{1}{\theta} e^{-t/\theta} \qquad t \geq 0; \theta > 0.$$

Assume that a life test without replacement of items having this probability density function is performed.

(a) If the test is terminated after r failures have occurred, find the mean, variance, and moment generating function of the time to complete the test.

(b) If the data set is censored at time c, find the distribution name, parameter values, mean, and variance of the number of failures that are observed.

7.7. If n items from an exponential population with parameter λ are placed on test and the test is terminated after r failures have occurred, show that

$$V\left[\sum_{i=1}^{n} x_i\right] = \frac{r}{\lambda^2}$$

where $x_i = \min\{t_i, c_i\}$, t_i is the time of the ith failure, and c_i is the censoring time for the ith item, $i = 1, 2, \ldots, n$.

7.8. If n items from an exponential population with parameter λ are placed on test, and the test is terminated after r failures have occurred, find the expected time to complete the test if
(a) failed items are not replaced.
(b) failed items are immediately replaced with new items.

7.9. Consider n items with independent exponential lifetimes with a failure rate λ that are placed on test. Find the joint probability density function of the first two lifetime order statistics, $t_{(1)}$ and $t_{(2)}$. Show that it is a legitimate probability density function.

7.10. How would you estimate λ in the exponential distribution if you place n items on test for c time units and there are no failures?

7.11. Find the score, maximum likelihood estimator, and Fisher information matrix for a Type II censored random sample from a population with

$$f(t) = \frac{\theta}{t^{\theta+1}} \qquad t \geq 1; \theta > 0.$$

8

Parametric Estimation for Models Without Covariates

This chapter investigates fitting two of the distributions presented in Chapter 4, the exponential and Weibull distributions, to a data set of failure times. Other distributions, such as the gamma distribution or the exponential power distribution, have analogous methods of parameter estimation. Four sample data sets are introduced in the first section and are used throughout this and subsequent chapters. Parametric estimation techniques for a complete or right-censored data set of failure times without covariates are considered here. Point and interval estimators for the parameters are determined. It is assumed that exact values for the lifetimes and censoring times are available. Grouped data are considered in Chapter 10.

8.1 SAMPLE DATA SETS

Some lifetime data sets are presented here that are used to illustrate inferential techniques in this and subsequent chapters. Only right censoring is considered. Left censoring can be handled in an analogous manner. The four types of lifetime data sets presented here are

1. a complete data set,
2. a Type II censored data set (order statistic right censoring),
3. a randomly censored data set with a single binary covariate, and
4. a Type I censored data set with a single covariate.

In all cases, n is the number of items placed on test and r is the number of observed failures.

A complete data set is typically the easiest to analyze since extensive work has already been performed to find point and interval estimators for parameters.

Example 8.1

A complete data set of $n = 23$ ball bearing failure times to test the endurance of deep-groove ball bearings has been extensively studied. The ordered set of failure times measured in 10^6 revolutions is

$$17.88 \quad 28.92 \quad 33.00 \quad 41.52 \quad 42.12 \quad 45.60 \quad 48.48 \quad 51.84 \quad 51.96$$
$$54.12 \quad 55.56 \quad 67.80 \quad 68.64 \quad 68.64 \quad 68.88 \quad 84.12 \quad 93.12 \quad 98.64$$
$$105.12 \quad 105.84 \quad 127.92 \quad 128.04 \quad 173.40.$$

Another type of data set is a Type II right-censored data set, illustrated by the following example.

Example 8.2

A Type II right-censored data set of $n = 15$ automotive a/c switches has been collected. The test was terminated when the fifth failure occurred. The $r = 5$ ordered observed failure times measured in number of cycles are

$$1410 \quad 1872 \quad 3138 \quad 4218 \quad 6971.$$

An example of a randomly right-censored data set is drawn from the biostatistical literature.

Example 8.3

An experiment is conducted to determine the effect of a drug named 6-mercaptopurine (6-MP) on leukemia remission times. A sample of $n = 21$ leukemia patients is treated with 6-MP, and the times of remission are recorded. There are $r = 9$ individuals for whom the remission time is observed, and the remission times for the remaining 12 individuals are randomly censored on the right. Letting an asterisk denote a censored observation, the remission times (in weeks) are

$$6 \quad 6 \quad 6 \quad 6^* \quad 7 \quad 9^* \quad 10 \quad 10^* \quad 11^* \quad 13 \quad 16$$
$$17^* \quad 19^* \quad 20^* \quad 22 \quad 23 \quad 25^* \quad 32^* \quad 32^* \quad 34^* \quad 35^*.$$

In addition, 21 other leukemia patients are not given the drug, and they serve as a control group. In this case there is no censoring and the remission times are

$$1 \quad 1 \quad 2 \quad 2 \quad 3 \quad 4 \quad 4 \quad 5 \quad 5 \quad 8 \quad 8$$
$$8 \quad 8 \quad 11 \quad 11 \quad 12 \quad 12 \quad 15 \quad 17 \quad 22 \quad 23.$$

This data set illustrates the simplest possible use of a covariate for modeling, a single binary covariate indicating the group each data value belongs to.

Finally, a data set containing a nonbinary covariate is given.

Example 8.4

Forty motorettes were placed on test at four different temperatures, 150°, 170°, 190°, and 220°C. This is an accelerated test and the modeler is trying to determine how well the motors will perform at the operating temperature of 130°C. Ten motorettes were placed on test at each temperature level, and Type I censoring occurs at each temperature level. The failure times (in hours) at 150°C are

8064*   8064*   8064*   8064*   8064*   8064*   8064*   8064*   8064*   8064*,

that is, there were no failures at 8064 hours. The data at 170°C are

1764   2772   3444   3542   3780   4860   5196   5448*   5448*   5448*.

The data at 190°C are

408   408   1344   1344   1440   1680*   1680*   1680*   1680*   1680*.

The data at 220°C are

408   408   504   504   504   528*   528*   528*   528*   528*.

The motorettes were periodically inspected for failure, and each failure time listed above is the midpoint of the period in which the failure occurred.

The purpose of this chapter is to present parametric techniques for analyzing complete and right-censored data sets with no covariates. The next section is devoted to the exponential distribution, and the subsequent section is devoted to the Weibull distribution. Chapter 9 presents parameter estimation techniques for models that explicitly account for covariates.

8.2 EXPONENTIAL DISTRIBUTION

The exponential distribution is popular due to its tractability for parameter estimation and inference. The general likelihood theory developed in Chapter 7 is used to estimate the $p = 1$ parameter. The exponential distribution can be parameterized by either its failure rate λ or its mean $\mu = 1/\lambda$. Using the failure rate to parameterize the distribution, the survivor, density, hazard, and cumulative hazard functions are

$$S(t, \lambda) = e^{-\lambda t} \qquad f(t, \lambda) = \lambda e^{-\lambda t} \qquad h(t, \lambda) = \lambda \qquad H(t, \lambda) = \lambda t$$

for all $t \geq 0$. Note that the unknown parameter λ has been added as an argument in these lifetime distribution representations since it is now also an argument in the likelihood function and is estimated from data.

All the analysis in this and subsequent sections assumes that a *random sample* of n items from a population has been placed on a test and subjected to typical field operating conditions. Equivalently, $t_1, t_2, \ldots, t_n$ are independent and identically distributed random lifetimes from a particular population distribution (exponential in this section). As with all statistical inference, care must be taken to ensure that a random sample of lifetimes is collected. Consequently, random numbers should be used to determine which n items to place on test. Laboratory conditions should adequately mimic field conditions. Only representative items should be placed on test because items manufactured using a previous design may have a different failure pattern than those with the current design.

Four classes of data sets (complete, Type II, Type I, and random right censoring) are considered separately, followed by subsections on comparing two exponential populations and life testing.

Complete Data Sets

A complete data set consists of failure times $t_1, t_2, \ldots, t_n$. Although lowercase letters are used to denote the failure times here to be consistent with the notation for censoring times, the failure times are nonnegative random variables. The likelihood function can be written as a product of the density functions evaluated at the failure times:

$$L(\lambda) = \prod_{i=1}^{n} f(t_i, \lambda).$$

Note that the argument **t** has been left out of the likelihood expression for compactness. Using the last expression for the log likelihood function from Section 7.5,

$$\log L(\lambda) = \sum_{i \in U} \log h(x_i, \lambda) - \sum_{i=1}^{n} H(x_i, \lambda) = \sum_{i=1}^{n} [\log h(t_i, \lambda) - H(t_i, \lambda)],$$

where $x_i = \min\{t_i, c_i\}$ for $i = 1, 2, \ldots, n$. For the exponential distribution, this is

$$\log L(\lambda) = \sum_{i=1}^{n} [\log \lambda - \lambda\, t_i] = n \log \lambda - \lambda \sum_{i=1}^{n} t_i.$$

To determine the maximum likelihood estimator for λ, the single element score vector

$$U(\lambda) = \frac{\partial \log L(\lambda)}{\partial \lambda} = \frac{n}{\lambda} - \sum_{i=1}^{n} t_i,$$

often called the *score statistic,* is equated to zero, yielding

$$\hat{\lambda} = \frac{n}{\displaystyle\sum_{i=1}^{n} t_i}.$$

Example 8.5

Consider fitting the exponential distribution to the 6-MP control group data with $n = 21$ observations. The total time on test is

$$\sum_{i=1}^{21} t_i = 182$$

weeks. The maximum likelihood estimator is

$$\hat{\lambda} = \frac{21}{\displaystyle\sum_{i=1}^{21} t_i} = \frac{21}{182} = 0.115$$

remission per week. Figure 8.1 shows the empirical survivor function, which takes a downward step of $1/n = 1/21$ at each data point, along with the survivor function for the fitted exponential distribution. Empirical and fitted distributions are traditionally compared by using the survivor function, since the probability density function and hazard function suffer from the drawback of requiring the data to be divided into cells to plot the empirical distribution. In spite of the discrete nature of the data, the excessive number of ties, and the fact that the sample size is rather small, the exponential distribution does a reasonable job of approximating the empirical survivor function.

To find the information matrices, the derivative of the score statistic is required:

$$\frac{\partial^2 \log L(\lambda)}{\partial \lambda^2} = -\frac{n}{\lambda^2}.$$

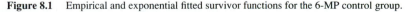

Figure 8.1   Empirical and exponential fitted survivor functions for the 6-MP control group.

Taking the expected value of the negative of this quantity yields the 1×1 Fisher information matrix:

$$I(\lambda) = E\left[\frac{-\partial^2 \log L(\lambda)}{\partial \lambda^2}\right] = E\left[\frac{n}{\lambda^2}\right] = \frac{n}{\lambda^2}.$$

If the maximum likelihood estimator $\hat{\lambda}$ is used as an argument in the second partial derivative of the log likelihood function, the 1×1 observed information matrix is obtained.

$$O(\hat{\lambda}) = \left[\frac{-\partial^2 \log L(\lambda)}{\partial \lambda^2}\right]_{\lambda = \hat{\lambda}} = \frac{n}{\hat{\lambda}^2} = \frac{\left(\sum\limits_{i=1}^{n} t_i\right)^2}{n}.$$

Asymptotic confidence intervals for λ based on the likelihood ratio statistic or the observed information matrix are unnecessary in this case since the sampling distribution of $\sum_{i=1}^{n} t_i$ is tractable. In particular, from Property 4.7 of the exponential distribution

$$2\lambda \sum_{i=1}^{n} t_i = \frac{2n\lambda}{\hat{\lambda}}$$

has the chi-square distribution with $2n$ degrees of freedom. Therefore, with probability $1 - \alpha$,

$$\chi^2_{2n, 1-\alpha/2} < \frac{2n\lambda}{\hat{\lambda}} < \chi^2_{2n, \alpha/2},$$

where $\chi^2_{2n, p}$ is the $(1-p)$th fractile of the chi-square distribution with $2n$ degrees of freedom. Solving for λ yields the $100(1 - \alpha)\%$ confidence interval:

$$\frac{\hat{\lambda} \, \chi^2_{2n, 1-\alpha/2}}{2n} < \lambda < \frac{\hat{\lambda}\chi^2_{2n, \alpha/2}}{2n}.$$

Example 8.6

Consider the complete data set of $n = 23$ ball bearing failure times. For this particular data set, the total time on test is $\sum_{i=1}^{n} t_i = 1661.16$, yielding a maximum likelihood estimator

$$\hat{\lambda} = \frac{n}{\sum\limits_{i=1}^{n} t_i} = \frac{23}{1661.16} = 0.0138$$

failure per 10^6 revolutions. The value of the log likelihood function at the maximum likelihood estimator is $\log L(\hat{\lambda}) = -121.435$, which is used later in this chapter when comparing the exponential and Weibull fits to this data set. The observed information matrix is

$$O(\hat{\lambda}) = \left[\frac{-\partial^2 \log L(\lambda)}{\partial \lambda^2} \right]_{\lambda = \hat{\lambda}} = \frac{\left(\sum\limits_{i=1}^{n} t_i \right)^2}{n} = \frac{(1661.16)^2}{23} = 119,976.$$

Since the data set is complete, an exact 95% confidence interval for the failure rate of the distribution can be determined. Since $\chi^2_{46,\,0.975} = 29.16$ and $\chi^2_{46,\,0.025} = 66.62$, the formula for the confidence interval

$$\frac{\hat{\lambda}\, \chi^2_{2n,\,1-\alpha/2}}{2n} < \lambda < \frac{\hat{\lambda}\, \chi^2_{2n,\,\alpha/2}}{2n}$$

becomes

$$\frac{(0.0138)(29.16)}{46} < \lambda < \frac{(0.0138)(66.62)}{46}$$

or

$$0.00878 < \lambda < 0.0201.$$

Note that, due to the use of the chi-square distribution for this confidence interval, the interval is not symmetric about the maximum likelihood estimator. For this and subsequent examples, care has been taken to perform intermediate calculations involving numeric quantities such as critical values or total time on test values to as much precision as possible; then final values are reported using only significant digits.

Figure 8.2 shows the empirical survivor function, which takes a downward step of $1/n = 1/23$ at each data point, along with the survivor function for the fitted exponential

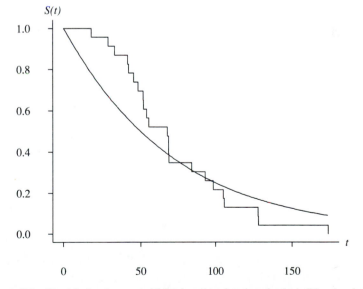

Figure 8.2   Empirical and exponential fitted survivor functions for the ball bearing data set.

distribution. Although more details are given later concerning goodness-of-fit tests, it is apparent from this figure that the exponential is a very poor fit. This particular data set was chosen for this example to illustrate one of the shortcomings of using the exponential distribution to model any data set without assessing the adequacy of the fit. Extreme caution must be exercised when using the exponential distribution since, as indicated in Figure 8.2, the exponential distribution is a poor fit for this data set. The distribution is probably in the IFR class, since the ball bearings are wearing out. As shown in the next section, the Weibull distribution is a much better approximation to this particular data set. Since the exponential distribution can be fitted to any data set that has at least one observed failure, the adequacy of the model must always be assessed. The point and interval estimators associated with the exponential distribution are legitimate only if the data set is a random sample from an exponential population.

The importance of model adequacy assessments, such as those indicated in the previous example, applies to all fitted distributions, not just the exponential distribution. Furthermore, if a modeler knows the failure physics (for example, fatigue crack growth) underlying a process, then an appropriate model consistent with the failure physics should be chosen.

It is possible to find point and interval estimators for measures other than λ by using the invariance property for maximum likelihood estimators and by rearranging the confidence interval formula. Define $L = \hat{\lambda}\chi^2_{2n,\,1-\alpha/2}/2n$ as the lower limit on the confidence interval for λ and $U = \hat{\lambda}\chi^2_{2n,\,\alpha/2}/2n$ as the upper limit on the confidence interval for λ. If the measure of interest is $\mu = 1/\lambda$, for example, then the point estimator is $\hat{\mu} = (1/n)\sum_{i=1}^{n} t_i$, which is the sample mean. Rearranging the previous confidence interval expression as

$$L < \lambda < U$$

yields

$$\frac{1}{U} < \mu < \frac{1}{L}.$$

As a second example, consider the probability of survival to a fixed time t, $S(t) = e^{-\lambda t}$. The maximum likelihood estimator for this quantity is

$$\hat{S}(t) = e^{-\hat{\lambda} t}.$$

An interval estimator, on the other hand, can be found by rearranging the interval estimator for λ:

$$L < \lambda < U$$

$$-U < -\lambda < -L$$

$$e^{-Ut} < e^{-\lambda t} < e^{-Lt}$$

$$e^{-Ut} < S(t) < e^{-Lt}.$$

Example 8.7

Assuming that the exponential distribution is an appropriate model for the ball bearing data set (which it clearly is not, as indicated earlier), find point estimators and 95% interval estimators for the mean and for the probability that a ball bearing is functioning at time 100 (that is, 100,000,000 cycles since the data are given in 10^6 cycles).
The point estimators in this case are

$$\hat{\mu} = \frac{1}{n} \sum_{i=1}^{n} t_i = \frac{1661.16}{23} = 72.2,$$

or 72,200,000 cycles and

$$\hat{S}(t) = e^{-\hat{\lambda}t},$$

which is $\hat{S}(100) = e^{-(0.0138)(100)} = 0.250$. The values of L and U for the 95% confidence interval from the previous example for λ are $L = 0.00878$ and $U = 0.0201$. Finding a confidence interval for the mean requires taking reciprocals of these limits:

$$\frac{1}{0.0201} < \mu < \frac{1}{0.00878}$$

$$49.9 < \mu < 113.9.$$

To determine a 95% confidence interval for $S(100)$ requires a different manipulation of the L and U values:

$$e^{-Ut} < S(t) < e^{-Lt}$$

$$e^{-(0.0201)(100)} < S(100) < e^{-(0.00878)(100)}$$

$$0.135 < S(100) < 0.416.$$

Although the manipulation of the confidence interval for λ is performed here in the case of a complete data set, these techniques may also be applied to any of the right-censoring mechanisms to be described in the next three subsections.

Type II Censored Data Sets

A life test of n items that is terminated when r failures have occurred produces a Type II censored data set. The previous subsection is a special case of Type II censoring when $r = n$. As before, assume that the failure times are $t_1, t_2, \ldots, t_n$, the test is terminated upon the rth ordered failure, the censoring times are $c_1 = c_2 = \cdots = c_n = t_{(r)}$ for all items, and $x_i = \min\{t_i, c_i\}$ for $i = 1, 2, \ldots, n$.

The log likelihood function is

$$\log L(\lambda) = \sum_{i \in U} \log h(x_i, \lambda) - \sum_{i=1}^{n} H(x_i, \lambda) = r \log \lambda - \lambda \sum_{i=1}^{n} x_i$$

since there are r observed failures. The expression

$$\sum_{i=1}^{n} x_i = \sum_{i \in U} t_i + \sum_{i \in C} c_i = \sum_{i=1}^{r} t_{(i)} + (n - r)\, t_{(r)},$$

where $t_{(1)} < t_{(2)} < \cdots < t_{(r)}$ are the order statistics of the observed failures, is often called the *total time on test*. It represents the total accumulated time that the n items accrue while on test.

To determine the maximum likelihood estimator, the log likelihood function is differentiated with respect to λ,

$$U(\lambda) = \frac{\partial \log L(\lambda)}{\partial \lambda} = \frac{r}{\lambda} - \sum_{i=1}^{n} x_i$$

and is equated to zero, yielding the maximum likelihood estimator

$$\hat{\lambda} = \frac{r}{\sum_{i=1}^{n} x_i}.$$

The second partial derivative of the log likelihood function is

$$\frac{\partial^2 \log L(\lambda)}{\partial \lambda^2} = -\frac{r}{\lambda^2}$$

so the information matrix is

$$I(\lambda) = E\left[\frac{-\partial^2 \log L(\lambda)}{\partial \lambda^2}\right] = \frac{r}{\lambda^2}$$

and the observed information matrix is

$$O(\hat{\lambda}) = \left[\frac{-\partial^2 \log L(\lambda)}{\partial \lambda^2}\right]_{\lambda = \hat{\lambda}} = \frac{r}{\hat{\lambda}^2} = \frac{\left(\sum_{i=1}^{n} x_i\right)^2}{r}.$$

Exact confidence intervals and hypothesis tests concerning λ can be derived by using the result

$$2\lambda \sum_{i=1}^{n} x_i = \frac{2r\lambda}{\hat{\lambda}} \sim \chi^2(2r),$$

where $\chi^2(2r)$ is the chi-square distribution with $2r$ degrees of freedom. This result can be proved in a similar fashion to Property 4.7 of the exponential distribution. Using this fact, it can be stated with probability $1 - \alpha$ that

$$\chi^2_{2r,\,1-\alpha/2} < \frac{2r\lambda}{\hat{\lambda}} < \chi^2_{2r,\,\alpha/2}.$$

Rearranging terms yields an exact $100(1 - \alpha)\%$ confidence interval for the failure rate λ:

$$\frac{\hat{\lambda}\,\chi^2_{2r,\,1-\alpha/2}}{2r} < \lambda < \frac{\hat{\lambda}\,\chi^2_{2r,\,\alpha/2}}{2r}.$$

Example 8.8

Consider the Type II right-censored data set of automotive switches, where $n = 15$ and there are $r = 5$ observed failures, which are

$$t_{(1)} = 1410, \quad t_{(2)} = 1872, \quad t_{(3)} = 3138, \quad t_{(4)} = 4218, \quad t_{(5)} = 6971.$$

For this particular data set, the total time on test is $\sum_{i=1}^{n} x_i = 87,319$ cycles, yielding a maximum likelihood estimator

$$\hat{\lambda} = \frac{r}{\displaystyle\sum_{i=1}^{n} x_i} = \frac{5}{87,319} = 0.00005726$$

failure per cycle. Equivalently, the maximum likelihood estimator for the mean of the distribution is

$$\hat{\mu} = \frac{\displaystyle\sum_{i=1}^{n} x_i}{r} = \frac{87,319}{5} = 17,464$$

cycles to failure. The observed information matrix based on using the failure rate as the unknown parameter is

$$O(\hat{\lambda}) = \left[\frac{-\partial^2 \log L(\lambda)}{\partial \lambda^2} \right]_{\lambda = \hat{\lambda}} = \frac{\left(\displaystyle\sum_{i=1}^{n} x_i \right)^2}{r} = \frac{(87,319)^2}{5} = 1,525,000,000.$$

Since the data set is Type II right censored, an exact 95% confidence interval for the failure rate of the distribution can be determined. Using the chi-square critical values, $\chi^2_{10,\,0.975} = 3.247$ and $\chi^2_{10,\,0.025} = 20.49$, the formula for the confidence interval

$$\frac{\hat{\lambda} \, \chi^2_{2r, \, 1 - \alpha/2}}{2r} < \lambda < \frac{\hat{\lambda} \, \chi^2_{2r, \, \alpha/2}}{2r}$$

becomes

$$\frac{(0.00005726)(3.247)}{10} < \lambda < \frac{(0.00005726)(20.49)}{10}$$

or

$$0.00001859 < \lambda < 0.0001173.$$

This is equivalent to a 95% confidence interval for the mean number of cycles to failure of

$$8525 < \mu < 53,785.$$

Not surprisingly, with only five observed failures, this is a rather wide confidence interval for μ, and hence there is not as much precision as in the ball bearing example, where there were 23 observed failures. Assessing the adequacy of the fit is more difficult in the case of censoring, since it is impossible to determine what the lifetime distribution looks like after the last observed failure time, which is 6971 in this case. Figure 8.3 shows the empirical survivor function and the associated fitted exponential survivor function. In this case, the exponential distribution appears to adequately model the lifetimes through time 6971.

Hypothesis testing, which is the rough equivalent of interval estimation, is also possible in the case of Type II censoring since the sampling distribution of $2\lambda \sum_{i=1}^{n} x_i$ is

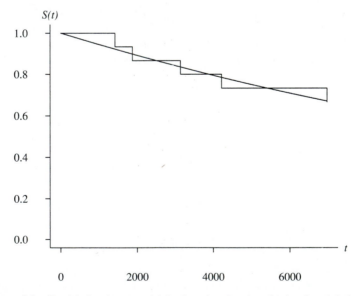

Figure 8.3   Empirical and exponential fitted survivor functions for the a/c switch data set.

tractable. To briefly review some of the basics of hypothesis testing, the *null hypothesis* H_0 is a statement of belief that is being tested. If enough statistical evidence is gathered to indicate that H_0 is probably not true, the investigator decides to *reject* H_0. If H_0 is not rejected, the investigator decides to *accept* H_0, although some state this decision as "fail to reject H_0" since there is not enough statistical evidence to reject the null hypothesis. The four conditional probabilities given next show some of the risks associated with a hypothesis test. The first part of each event in the probability statement concerns the *action* that the investigator takes, and the conditional part of each event concerns the true state of nature. First,

$$P[\text{reject } H_0 \mid H_0 \text{ is true}] = P[\text{Type I error}] = \alpha$$

is known as the *significance level* of the test. Second,

$$P[\text{accept } H_0 \mid H_0 \text{ is true}] = 1 - \alpha$$

is known as the *confidence level* of the test and is analogous to the stated coverage for a confidence interval. Third,

$$P[\text{accept } H_0 \mid H_0 \text{ is false}] = P[\text{Type II error}] = \beta$$

measures the risk associated with accepting the null hypothesis when H_0 is not true. Finally,

$$P[\text{reject } H_0 \mid H_0 \text{ is false}] = 1 - \beta$$

is known as the *power* of the test. Note that the last two of these probabilities are functions of how far away from H_0 the true state of nature is. The best situation for an investigator is to have a test with high power and low significance level. Some other aspects of hypothesis testing, such as the alternative hypothesis, one- and two-tailed tests, and *P*-values are illustrated in the next example. The example shows how a life test can be used to check a manufacturer's claimed mean time to failure.

Example 8.9

The producer of the automotive switches tested in the previous example claims that the mean time to failure of their switches is $\mu = 100,000$ cycles. Is there enough evidence in the data set of 15 switches placed on test to conclude that the mean time to failure is less than 100,000 cycles? Assume that the automotive switch lifetimes are exponentially distributed.

The producer's claim is certainly suspect, since the maximum likelihood estimator for the mean time to failure is $\hat{\mu} = 17,464$ from the previous example. In this case, the null and alternative hypotheses are

$$H_0: \mu = 100,000,$$

$$H_1: \mu < 100,000$$

or, equivalently,

$$H_0: \lambda = 0.00001,$$

$$H_1: \lambda > 0.00001$$

in terms of the failure rate. Since small values of $\sum_{i=1}^{n} x_i$ lead to rejecting H_0, the attained level of significance (P-value) is

$$p = P[\sum_{i=1}^{n} x_i < 87,319 \mid \lambda = 0.00001].$$

Since $2\lambda \sum_{i=1}^{n} x_i \sim \chi^2(2r)$, the P-value, when H_0 is true, is

$$p = P[(2)(0.00001) \sum_{i=1}^{n} x_i < (2)(0.00001)(87,319)]$$

$$= P[\chi^2(10) < 1.746]$$

$$= 0.002.$$

Although the data set is small, there is adequate evidence from this data set to conclude that the mean number of cycles to failure is less than 100,000 (for example, the null hypothesis can be rejected at $\alpha = 0.10, 0.05$, and 0.01).

The fact that the distribution of $2\lambda \sum_{i=1}^{n} x_i = 2r\lambda/\hat{\lambda}$ is independent of n means that $\hat{\lambda}$ has the same precision in a test of r items tested until all have failed as that for a test of n items tested until r items have failed. Thus the justification for obtaining a Type II censored data set over a complete data set is time savings. The additional costs associated with this time savings are the $n - r$ additional test stands and the additional $n - r$ items to place on test. As illustrated in the next example, Property 4.9 of the exponential distribution section can be used to determine the time savings associated with a Type II censored test.

Example 8.10

Cindy and David are testing items from a population having an exponential time to failure. Cindy places six items on test and waits until they all fail. David, on the other hand, places ten items on test and discontinues testing when the sixth failure occurs. As indicated earlier, their estimators for the failure rate have the same precision. What time savings can David expect by placing the four additional items on test?

By Property 4.9 of the exponential distribution, the expected time for Cindy to complete her test is

$$\frac{1}{\lambda} \left[\frac{1}{6} + \frac{1}{5} + \frac{1}{4} + \frac{1}{3} + \frac{1}{2} + 1 \right] = \frac{49}{20\lambda},$$

which also happens to be the expected time to failure for a parallel system of six exponential components. The expected time for David to complete his test is

$$\frac{1}{\lambda}\left[\frac{1}{10} + \frac{1}{9} + \frac{1}{8} + \frac{1}{7} + \frac{1}{6} + \frac{1}{5}\right] = \frac{2131}{2520\lambda},$$

which also happens to be the expected time to failure for a 5-out-of-10 system of exponential components. The ratio of David's expected test time to Cindy's expected test time is 0.345, so David can expect to finish his test about 65% sooner than Cindy. The price that David pays for this time savings is in the four additional test stands and the four additional items to place on test. The cost of failed items is identical for Cindy and David since six items fail in both tests, and the four that survive David's test are as good as new by the memoryless property.

If a limited number of test stands are available for testing, the only way to speed up the test is to perform a test with replacement in which failed items are immediately replaced with new items. This will significantly decrease the time to complete the test, which is terminated when r of the items fail. The sequence of failures in this case is a Poisson process with rate $n\lambda$.

Although the inference for Type II censoring is tractable, the unfortunate consequence is that the time to complete the test is a random variable. Constraints on the time to run an experiment may make a Type I censored data set more practical.

Type I Censored Data Sets

The analysis for Type I censored data sets is similar to that for the Type II case. The test is terminated at time c. The censoring times for each item on test are the same: $c_1 = c_2 = \cdots = c_n = c$. The number of observed failures, r, is a random variable. The total time on test in this case is

$$\sum_{i=1}^{n} x_i = \sum_{i \in U} t_i + \sum_{i \in C} c_i = \sum_{i=1}^{r} t_{(i)} + (n - r)c.$$

As before, the log likelihood function is

$$\log L(\lambda) = \sum_{i \in U} \log h(x_i, \lambda) - \sum_{i=1}^{n} H(x_i, \lambda) = r \log \lambda - \lambda \sum_{i=1}^{n} x_i,$$

and the score statistic is

$$U(\lambda) = \frac{r}{\lambda} - \sum_{i=1}^{n} x_i.$$

The maximum likelihood estimator for $r > 0$ is $\hat{\lambda} = r/\sum_{i=1}^{n} x_i$, the information matrix is $I(\lambda) = r/\lambda^2$, and the observed information matrix is $O(\hat{\lambda}) = r/\hat{\lambda}^2$. The functional form of the maximum likelihood estimator is identical to the Type II censoring case. Type I cen-

Figure 8.4   Approximation technique for confidence intervals in the case of Type I censoring.

soring has a larger total time on test $\sum_{i=1}^{n} x_i$ than the corresponding Type II censoring case, since a Type I test ends *between* failures r and $r + 1$. Thus the expected value of $\hat{\lambda}$ is smaller for Type I censoring than for Type II censoring. One problem that arises here is that the sampling distribution of $\sum_{i=1}^{n} x_i$ is no longer tractable, so an exact confidence interval for λ is unknown. Although many more complicated methods exist, one of the best approximation methods is to assume that $2\lambda \sum_{i=1}^{n} x_i$ has the chi-square distribution with $2r + 1$ degrees of freedom. This approximation, illustrated in Figure 8.4, is based on the fact that if $c = t_{(r)}$, then $2\lambda \sum_{i=1}^{n} x_i \sim \chi^2(2r)$, and if $c = t_{(r+1)}$, then $2\lambda \sum_{i=1}^{n} x_i \sim \chi^2(2r + 2)$, so, since c is between $t_{(r)}$ and $t_{(r+1)}$, $2\lambda \sum_{i=1}^{n} x_i$ will be approximately chi-square with $2r + 1$ degrees of freedom.

Example 8.11

A life test of $n = 100$ light bulbs is run for $c = 5000$ hours. Failed items are not replaced upon failure in this Type I censored data set. If the total time on test is $\sum_{i=1}^{n} x_i = 384,968$ hours, and $r = 32$ failures are observed, find a point and interval estimator for the failure rate.

It is impossible to check to see whether the exponential distribution is an appropriate model for the light bulb failure times from the problem statement, since the actual failure times are not given. Assuming that the model is appropriate, the maximum likelihood estimator for the failure rate is

$$\hat{\lambda} = \frac{r}{\sum\limits_{i=1}^{n} x_i} = \frac{32}{384,968} = 0.0000831$$

failure per hour, or, equivalently, the maximum likelihood estimator for the mean is its reciprocal, 12,030 hours. To obtain an approximate 95% confidence interval for the failure rate, the chi-square critical values for $2r + 1 = 65$ degrees of freedom must be determined. They are $\chi^2_{65,\,0.975} = 44.60$ and $\chi^2_{65,\,0.025} = 89.18$; the formula for the confidence interval

$$\frac{\hat{\lambda}\, \chi^2_{2r+1,\,1-\alpha/2}}{2r} < \lambda < \frac{\hat{\lambda}\, \chi^2_{2r+1,\,\alpha/2}}{2r}$$

becomes

$$\frac{(0.0000831)(44.60)}{64} < \lambda < \frac{(0.0000831)(89.18)}{64}$$

or

$$0.0000579 < \lambda < 0.000116.$$

This is equivalent to a 95% confidence interval for the mean number of cycles to failure of

$$8630 < \mu < 17,260.$$

Randomly Censored Data Sets

Most of the examples that have the random censoring mechanism for which the failure times t_i and the censoring times c_i are independent random variables are from biostatistics. Random censoring occurs frequently in biostatistics since it is not always possible to control the time patients enter and exit the study. The log likelihood function, score statistic, information matrix, and observed information matrix are the same as in the previous section. The total time on test is now simply

$$\sum_{i=1}^{n} x_i = \sum_{i \in U} t_i + \sum_{i \in C} c_i.$$

The sampling distribution of $\sum_{i=1}^{n} x_i$ is more complicated in this case, so asymptotic properties must be used in order to determine approximate confidence intervals for λ. In the example that follows, three different approximation procedures for determining a confidence interval for λ are illustrated.

The first technique is based on an approximation to a result from the Type II censoring case: $2\lambda \sum_{i=1}^{n} x_i \sim \chi^2(2r)$. The second is based on the likelihood ratio statistic, where $2[\log L(\hat{\lambda}) - \log L(\lambda)]$ is asymptotically chi-square with 1 degree of freedom. The third technique is based on the fact that the maximum likelihood estimator $\hat{\lambda}$ is asymptotically normal with a variance that is the inverse of the observed information matrix. Since this third technique results in a symmetric confidence interval, it should only be used with very large sample sizes.

Example 8.12

The treatment group in the leukemia study in Example 8.3 (those who receive the drug 6-MP) is considered here. For this data set, there are $n = 21$ individuals on test and $r = 9$ observed failures. The total time on test in this case is $\sum_{i=1}^{n} x_i = 359$ weeks.

The log likelihood function for this data set is

$$\log L(\lambda) = r \log \lambda - \lambda \sum_{i=1}^{n} x_i = 9 \log \lambda - 359\lambda.$$

As shown by the vertical dashed line in Figure 8.5, this function is maximized at

$$\hat{\lambda} = \frac{r}{\sum_{i=1}^{n} x_i} = \frac{9}{359} = 0.0251.$$

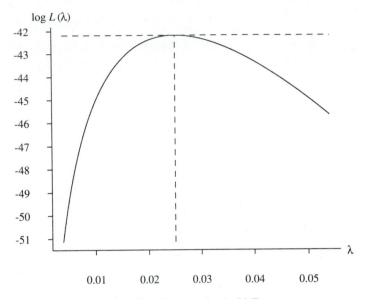

Figure 8.5   Log likelihood function for the 6-MP treatment group.

The maximum likelihood estimator of the expected remission time is $\hat{\mu} = 359/9 = 39.9$ weeks. The value of the log likelihood function at the maximum likelihood estimator is $\log L(\hat{\lambda}) = -42.17$, as indicated by the horizontal dashed line in Figure 8.5. The observed information matrix is

$$O(\hat{\lambda}) = \frac{\left(\sum\limits_{i=1}^{n} x_i \right)^2}{r} = \frac{(359)^2}{9} = 14,320 \, .$$

The three approximation techniques for determining an interval estimator for λ are outlined next.

Under the assumption that $2\lambda \sum_{i=1}^{n} x_i$ is approximately chi-square with $2r$ degrees of freedom (this is satisfied exactly in the Type II censoring case), an approximate $100(1 - \alpha)\%$ confidence interval for λ is

$$\frac{\hat{\lambda} \, \chi^2_{2r, 1-\alpha/2}}{2r} < \lambda < \frac{\hat{\lambda} \chi^2_{2r, \alpha/2}}{2r}$$

which is, in this example, with $\alpha = 0.05$,

$$\frac{(9)(8.23)}{(359)(18)} < \lambda < \frac{(9)(31.53)}{(359)(18)}$$

since $\chi^2_{18, 0.975} = 8.23$ and $\chi^2_{18, 0.025} = 31.53$, or

$$0.0115 < \lambda < 0.0439.$$

The second interval estimator for λ is based on the likelihood ratio statistic $2[\log L(\hat{\lambda}) - \log L(\lambda)]$, which is asymptotically chi-square with 1 degree of freedom. Thus, with probability $1 - \alpha$, the inequality

$$2[\log L(\hat{\lambda}) - \log L(\lambda)] < \chi^2_{1,\,\alpha}$$

is satisfied. For this particular example and $\alpha = 0.05$, this can be rearranged as

$$\log L(\lambda) > \log L(\hat{\lambda}) - \frac{3.84}{2}$$

since $\chi^2_{1,\,0.05} = 3.84$, or

$$\log L(\lambda) > -42.17 - \frac{3.84}{2}.$$

As shown by the horizontal dashed lines in Figure 8.6, this corresponds to all values of λ for which the log likelihood function is within $3.84/2 = 1.92$ units of its largest value. The inequality reduces to

$$9 \log \lambda - 359\,\lambda > -42.17 - 1.92,$$

which must be solved numerically to determine the end points. Most computer languages

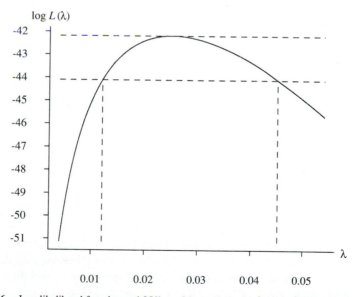

Figure 8.6   Log likelihood function and 95% confidence limits for λ using the likelihood ratio statistic. (*Source*: D. R. Cox and D. Oakes, *Analysis of Survival Data*, 1984. Adapted and reprinted by permission of Chapman and Hall, New York.)

have an equation solver that can determine the two λ values satisfying $9 \log \lambda - 359 \lambda = -42.17 - 1.92 = 44.09$. In this particular example, the confidence interval is

$$0.0120 < \lambda < 0.0452,$$

which is shifted slightly to the right of the previous interval estimator. The lower and upper bounds for this confidence interval are indicated by the vertical dashed lines in Figure 8.6.

The final interval estimator for λ is based on the fact that the sampling distribution of $\hat{\lambda}$ is asymptotically normal with mean λ and variance $I(\lambda)^{-1}$. Replacing $I(\lambda)$ by the observed information matrix $O(\hat{\lambda})$ with probability $1 - \alpha$,

$$-z_{\alpha/2} < \frac{\hat{\lambda} - \lambda}{O(\hat{\lambda})^{-1/2}} < z_{\alpha/2},$$

where $z_{\alpha/2}$ is the $1 - \alpha/2$ fractile of the standard normal distribution. This is equivalent to

$$\hat{\lambda} - z_{\alpha/2}\, O(\hat{\lambda})^{-1/2} < \lambda < \hat{\lambda} + z_{\alpha/2}\, O(\hat{\lambda})^{-1/2}.$$

For this particular example, a 95% confidence interval for λ is

$$\frac{9}{359} - (1.96)(14,320)^{-1/2} < \lambda < \frac{9}{359} + (1.96)(14,320)^{-1/2}$$

or

$$0.0087 < \lambda < 0.0415,$$

having lower bounds than the previous two interval estimators.

To summarize, the maximum likelihood estimator for the failure rate in the random censoring case is the same as in the complete, Type II and Type I censoring cases: $\hat{\lambda} = r / \sum_{i=1}^{n} x_i$. There are three approximation methods for interval estimation, two based on the chi-square distribution and one on the normal distribution. The interval based on the normal distribution is symmetric and is therefore recommended only in the case of extremely large sample sizes.

Comparing Two Exponential Populations

Situations often arise when it is appropriate to compare the failure rates of two exponential populations based on data collected from each of the two populations. Examples include comparing the survival of one brand of integrated circuit versus another, comparing the survival of a single item at two levels of an environmental variable, and, in biostatistics, comparing the survival of individuals receiving two different treatments for a disease. Let the failure rate in the first population be λ_1 and the failure rate in the second population be λ_2.

As in the previous subsections, x denotes the minimum of the lifetime t and the censoring time c. The two data sets are denoted by

$$x_{11}, x_{12}, \ldots, x_{1n_1},$$

the n_1 values from the first population, and

$$x_{21}, x_{22}, \ldots, x_{2n_2},$$

the n_2 values from the second population. Thus x_{ji} is observation i (failure or right-censoring time) from population j. Assume further that $r_1 > 0$ failures are observed in the first population and that $r_2 > 0$ failures are observed in the second population. For tractability, it is assumed that the tests performed on both populations use Type II censoring. This assumption allows exact confidence intervals for λ_1/λ_2 to be derived. Approximate methods exist when other types of censoring are used. In addition, these methods generalize to the case of comparing more than two populations.

Since $2\lambda_1 \sum_{i=1}^{n_1} x_{1i}$ has the chi-square distribution with $2r_1$ degrees of freedom and $2\lambda_2 \sum_{i=1}^{n_2} x_{2i}$ has the chi-square distribution with $2r_2$ degrees of freedom, the statistic

$$\frac{2\lambda_1 \sum_{i=1}^{n_1} x_{1i}/2r_1}{2\lambda_2 \sum_{i=1}^{n_2} x_{2i}/2r_2} = \frac{r_2\lambda_1 \sum_{i=1}^{n_1} x_{1i}}{r_1\lambda_2 \sum_{i=1}^{n_2} x_{2i}} = \frac{\lambda_1 \hat{\lambda}_2}{\lambda_2 \hat{\lambda}_1}$$

has the F distribution with $2r_1$ and $2r_2$ degrees of freedom. This is true because the ratio of two chi-square random variables divided by their respective degrees of freedom results in an F random variable. So with probability $1 - \alpha$

$$F_{2r_1, 2r_2, 1-\alpha/2} < \frac{\lambda_1 \hat{\lambda}_2}{\lambda_2 \hat{\lambda}_1} < F_{2r_1, 2r_2, \alpha/2}$$

or

$$\frac{\hat{\lambda}_1}{\hat{\lambda}_2} F_{2r_1, 2r_2, 1-\alpha/2} < \frac{\lambda_1}{\lambda_2} < \frac{\hat{\lambda}_1}{\hat{\lambda}_2} F_{2r_1, 2r_2, \alpha/2}.$$

Two points are important to keep in mind with respect to this confidence interval. First, it is typically of interest to see whether this confidence interval contains 1, which indicates that there is no statistical evidence to conclude that the failure rates of the two populations are different. Second, if the null hypothesis

$$H_0: \lambda_1 = \lambda_2$$

is to be tested directly, then there is cancellation in $\lambda_1 \hat{\lambda}_2/\lambda_2 \hat{\lambda}_1$ under H_0, so $\hat{\lambda}_2/\hat{\lambda}_1$ has the F distribution with $2r_1$ and $2r_2$ degrees of freedom.

Example 8.13

Consider the case of the automotive switches from Example 8.2. In the first population, $n_1 = 15$, $r_1 = 5$, $\sum_{i=1}^{15} x_{1i} = 87,319$, and $\hat{\lambda}_1 = 5/87,319$. If another brand of automotive switches is tested yielding $n_2 = 20$, $r_2 = 8$, $\sum_{i=1}^{20} x_{2i} = 148,364$, and $\hat{\lambda}_2 = 8/148,364$, find a 95% confidence interval for λ_1 / λ_2 and test the hypothesis

$$H_0: \lambda_1 = \lambda_2,$$

$$H_1: \lambda_1 > \lambda_2.$$

Utilizing the appropriate fractiles for the F distribution with 10 and 16 degrees of freedom yields

$$\frac{(5)(148,364)}{(8)(87,319)}(0.286) < \frac{\lambda_1}{\lambda_2} < \frac{(5)(148,364)}{(8)(87,319)}(2.986)$$

$$0.304 < \frac{\lambda_1}{\lambda_2} < 3.171.$$

To determine the P-value for this hypothesis test, note that small values of the test statistic $\hat{\lambda}_2 / \hat{\lambda}_1$ lead to rejecting H_0 since the alternative hypothesis is one-tailed. Thus, when H_0 is true,

$$p = P\left[\frac{\hat{\lambda}_2}{\hat{\lambda}_1} < \frac{(8)(87,319)}{(5)(148,364)}\right] = P[F(10, 16) < 0.942] = 0.477.$$

Using this P-value, it can be concluded that there is not enough evidence in the data to conclude that the failure rates are significantly different. This is consistent with the fact that the confidence interval for λ_1 / λ_2 contains 1.

Life Testing

One final topic before we leave the exponential distribution is how to determine the appropriate values for n and r for a life test. The number of items on test, n, and the observed number of failures, r, influence the time to complete the test and the confidence in the estimator of λ.

Consider the situation of a producer shipping a lot of items with exponential(λ) lifetimes to a consumer. A sample of n of these items is placed on test until r of the items have failed. Let the hypothesis test be

$$H_0: \lambda = \lambda_0,$$

$$H_1: \lambda > \lambda_0,$$

where λ_0 is either the failure rate of the items claimed by the producer or an acceptable failure rate determined by the consumer. The consumer is obviously concerned if H_0 is rejected, since this means that the failure rate is higher than λ_0.

As is the case with all hypothesis testing, two different types of errors can be made. The first type of error, which adversely affects the producer, corresponds to rejecting H_0 when H_0 is true (that is, not shipping a good lot of items). The probability that this type of error occurs is called the *producer's risk* and is defined to be

$$\alpha = P[\text{rejecting } H_0 \mid \lambda = \lambda_0].$$

The second type of error, which adversely affects the consumer, corresponds to not rejecting H_0 when H_1 is true (shipping a bad lot of items). In this case the consumer will be shipped an item of lower quality than claimed by the producer. The probability that this type of error will occur is called the *consumer's risk* and is defined to be

$$\beta = P[\text{not rejecting } H_0 \mid \lambda = \lambda_1].$$

The consumer must specify λ_1 greater than λ_0, where λ_1 is a failure rate that is unacceptably high.

When H_0 is true and there is Type II censoring,

$$2\lambda_0 \sum_{i=1}^{n} x_i \sim \chi^2(2r).$$

Note that smaller values of $\sum_{i=1}^{n} x_i$ indicate a higher failure rate and hence will lead to rejecting H_0. Therefore, the null hypothesis is rejected when

$$2\lambda_0 \sum_{i=1}^{n} x_i < \chi^2_{2r,\, 1-\alpha}.$$

A power function $P(\lambda)$, illustrated in Figure 8.7, gives the probability of rejecting H_0 for different values of the failure rate λ. Some analysts prefer to see the complement of the power function, known as the *operating characteristic curve,* which is the probability of accepting the lot for various values of λ. Note that when $\lambda = \lambda_0$ the probability of rejecting H_0 is α, the producer's risk. It is unusual to find an r value such that the curve will *exactly* pass through the points (λ_0, α) and $(\lambda_1, 1 - \beta)$. The problem is usually stated to find the smallest r such that $P(\lambda_0) = \alpha$ and $P(\lambda_1) \geq 1 - \beta$. In particular, when $\lambda = \lambda_1$, it is now the case that $2\lambda_1 \sum_{i=1}^{n} x_i \sim \chi^2(2r)$, so

$$P(\lambda_1) = P[2\lambda_0 \sum_{i=1}^{n} x_i < \chi^2_{2r,\, 1-\alpha} \mid \lambda = \lambda_1]$$

$$= P[2\lambda_1 \sum_{i=1}^{n} x_i < \frac{\lambda_1}{\lambda_0} \chi^2_{2r,\, 1-\alpha} \mid \lambda = \lambda_1]$$

$$= P[\chi^2(2r) < \frac{\lambda_1}{\lambda_0} \chi^2_{2r,\, 1-\alpha} \mid \lambda = \lambda_1]$$

$$\geq 1 - \beta.$$

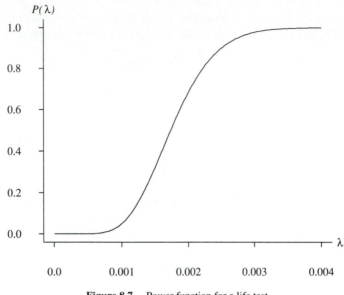

Figure 8.7   Power function for a life test.

Thus the constraints of the test are satisfied when

$$\chi^2_{2r,\,\beta} \le \frac{\lambda_1}{\lambda_0}\, \chi^2_{2r,\,1-\alpha}.$$

Once the producer's risk α, the consumer's risk β, and the failure rates λ_0 and λ_1 are defined, the smallest value of r satisfying the above inequality can be determined. If χ^2 tables are used, it typically requires trial and error to determine the appropriate value of r.

Example 8.14

A producer claims that his product has a mean time to failure of 1000 hours. The consumer wants the lot to be rejected with a probability of 0.90 when the true mean time to failure is 400. Assuming that the producer's risk is 0.05 and the lifetimes are exponentially distributed, what is the smallest number of observed failures r necessary to satisfy both the producer and the consumer.

Converting to failure rates, the hypothesis being tested here is (since $\lambda_0 = 0.001$)

$$H_0 : \lambda = 0.001$$

$$H_1 : \lambda > 0.001$$

and the other parameters are $\lambda_1 = 0.0025$, $\alpha = 0.05$, and $\beta = 0.10$. To find the smallest value of r that satisfies

$$\frac{\chi^2_{0.10, 2r}}{\chi^2_{0.95, 2r}} \le \frac{\lambda_1}{\lambda_0} = \frac{0.0025}{0.001} = 2.5$$

requires trial and error for different fractiles of the chi-square distribution. The smallest value of r satisfying the inequality is $r = 11$. Therefore, the test will be conducted until there are 11 failures, and H_0 will be rejected if

$$(2)(0.001) \sum_{i=1}^{n} x_i < 12.3,$$

since $\chi^2_{22, 0.95} = 12.3$. Figure 8.7 is the power function $P(\lambda) = P[(2)(0.001)\sum_{i=1}^{n} x_i < 12.3 | \lambda]$ for this particular test ($\lambda_0 = 0.001$, $\lambda_1 = 0.0025$, $\alpha = 0.05$, $\beta = 0.10$, and $r = 11$).

The choice of how many items to place on test n depends on whether there is a rush to complete the life test. Property 4.9 associated with the exponential distribution, which concerns the expected values of the order statistics, is useful here:

$$E[T_{(r)}] = \sum_{i=1}^{r} \frac{1}{(n - i + 1)\lambda}$$

for $r = 1, 2, \ldots, n$. This formula gives the expected time of the rth ordered failure (that is, the expected test duration), and large values of n significantly decrease the testing time.

Example 8.15

In the previous example with $r = 11$, the expected time to complete the test when H_0 is true is

$$E[T_{(11)}] = \frac{1}{\lambda_0} \sum_{i=1}^{11} \frac{1}{n - i + 1} = 1000 \left[\frac{1}{n} + \frac{1}{n-1} + \cdots + \frac{1}{n - 10} \right].$$

Table 8.1 gives the expected time to complete the test for various values of n. Determining the appropriate value for n depends on costs, such as the cost of testing n items simultaneously, the opportunity cost of having to wait for the results, and so on.

There are six ways to decrease the duration of a life test so that a conclusion can be reached sooner. First, as alluded to in the previous example, the number of items on test,

TABLE 8.1   EXPECTED TIME TO COMPLETE A LIFE TEST WHEN $r = 11$ AND $\lambda = 0.001$

n	11	12	13	15	20	100	1000
$E[T_{(11)}]$	3020	2103	1680	1234	769	116	11

n, can be increased. Second, it is not always necessary to wait until all r items fail to reach a conclusion. In the previous example, the null hypothesis is rejected if $(2)(0.001)\sum_{i=1}^{n} x_i < 12.3$ or, equivalently, if the total time on test $\sum_{i=1}^{n} x_i < 6150$. This means that if the total time on test reaches 6150 hours before the 11th failure occurs, then H_0 is not rejected. This is typically called a *truncated test* and is illustrated in Figure 8.8. The total time on test is plotted on the horizontal axis, and the number of observed failures is plotted on the vertical axis. A life test takes a stair-step path, starting at $(0, 0)$ through the rectangle as the test proceeds. If the path intersects the top of the rectangle, the null hypothesis is rejected, and if the path intersects the right-hand side of the rectangle, the null hypothesis is accepted. In this truncated test, both the expected number of failed items and the expected time to complete the test are lower than the corresponding values for a life test that terminates when all r items fail before reaching a conclusion.

The third technique for drawing a conclusion more quickly is to immediately replace each failed item with a new item. This is often referred to as a *life test with replacement*, and the sequence of failures is a Poisson process with rate $n\lambda$, due to the exponential distribution's memoryless property. The fourth technique involves sequential sampling, which further decreases the expected time to complete the test. A sequential life test typically eliminates part of the lower-right and upper-left portions of the decision region depicted in Figure 8.8. Conclusions are arrived at more quickly on lots containing particularly high- and low-reliability items.

Fifth, a *Bayesian reliability demonstration test* can be used if previous life tests on the item have been performed or if previous engineering experience is available on the item. In this case a *prior distribution* is fitted to the previous life test data and, if the

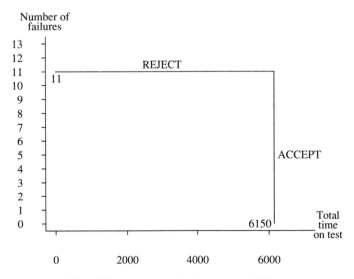

Figure 8.8   Decision region for a truncated life test.

estimated failure rates are low, the testing time is reduced. Finally, *accelerated life testing* may be used to induce more failures and hence decrease the test time. Accelerated testing has the drawback that failures may be induced at accelerated conditions that may not exist at operating conditions. References to all six of these methods are given at the end of this chapter.

8.3   WEIBULL DISTRIBUTION

As mentioned earlier, the Weibull distribution is typically more appropriate for modeling the lifetimes of items with increasing and decreasing failure rates, such as mechanical items. Rather than looking at each censoring mechanism (no censoring, Type II censoring, Type I censoring) individually, we shall proceed directly to the general case of random censoring.

As before, let $t_1, t_2, \ldots, t_n$ be the failure times, $c_1, c_2, \ldots, c_n$ be the censoring times, and $x_i = \min\{t_i, c_i\}$ for $i = 1, 2, \ldots, n$. The Weibull distribution has hazard and cumulative hazard functions

$$h(t, \lambda, \kappa) = \kappa\lambda(\lambda t)^{\kappa - 1} \qquad t \geq 0,$$

and

$$H(t, \lambda, \kappa) = (\lambda t)^{\kappa} \qquad t \geq 0.$$

When there are r observed failures, the log likelihood function is

$$\log L(\lambda, \kappa) = \sum_{i \in U} \log h(x_i, \lambda, \kappa) - \sum_{i=1}^{n} H(x_i, \lambda, \kappa)$$

$$= \sum_{i \in U} (\log \kappa + \kappa \log \lambda + (\kappa - 1) \log x_i) - \sum_{i=1}^{n} (\lambda x_i)^{\kappa}$$

$$= r \log \kappa + \kappa r \log \lambda + (\kappa - 1) \sum_{i \in U} \log x_i - \lambda^{\kappa} \sum_{i=1}^{n} x_i^{\kappa},$$

and the 2×1 score vector has elements

$$U_1(\lambda, \kappa) = \frac{\partial \log L(\lambda, \kappa)}{\partial \lambda} = \frac{\kappa r}{\lambda} - \kappa\lambda^{\kappa - 1} \sum_{i=1}^{n} x_i^{\kappa}$$

and

$$U_2(\lambda, \kappa) = \frac{\partial \log L(\lambda, \kappa)}{\partial \kappa} = \frac{r}{\kappa} + r \log \lambda + \sum_{i \in U} \log x_i - \sum_{i=1}^{n} (\lambda x_i)^{\kappa} \log (\lambda x_i).$$

When these equations are set equal to zero, the simultaneous equations have no closed-form solution for $\hat{\lambda}$ and $\hat{\kappa}$:

$$\frac{\kappa r}{\lambda} - \kappa \lambda^{\kappa-1} \sum_{i=1}^{n} x_i^{\kappa} = 0,$$

$$\frac{r}{\kappa} + r \log \lambda + \sum_{i \in U} \log x_i - \sum_{i=1}^{n} (\lambda x_i)^{\kappa} \log (\lambda x_i) = 0.$$

One piece of good fortune, however, to avoid solving a 2×2 set of nonlinear equations, is that this first equation can be solved for λ in terms of κ as follows:

$$\lambda = \left(\frac{r}{\sum_{i=1}^{n} x_i^{\kappa}} \right)^{1/\kappa}.$$

Notice that, when $\kappa = 1$, λ reduces to the maximum likelihood estimator for the exponential distribution. Using this expression for λ in terms of κ in the second element of the score vector yields a single, albeit more complicated, expression with κ as the only unknown. Applying some algebra, this equation reduces to

$$g(\kappa) = \frac{r}{\kappa} + \sum_{i \in U} \log x_i - \frac{r \sum_{i=1}^{n} x_i^{\kappa} \log x_i}{\sum_{i=1}^{n} x_i^{\kappa}} = 0,$$

which must be solved iteratively. One technique that can be used here is the Newton–Raphson procedure, which uses

$$\kappa_{i+1} = \kappa_i - \frac{g(\kappa_i)}{g'(\kappa_i)},$$

where κ_0 is an initial estimator. The iterative procedure can be repeated until the desired accuracy for κ is achieved; that is, $|\kappa_{i+1} - \kappa_i| < \varepsilon$. When the accuracy is achieved, the maximum likelihood estimator $\hat{\kappa}$ is used to calculate $\hat{\lambda} = (r / \sum_{i=1}^{n} x_i^{\hat{\kappa}})^{1/\hat{\kappa}}$. The derivative of $g(\kappa)$ reduces to

$$g'(\kappa) = -\frac{r}{\kappa^2} - \frac{r}{\left(\sum_{i=1}^{n} x_i^{\kappa} \right)^2} \left[\left(\sum_{i=1}^{n} x_i^{\kappa} \right) \left(\sum_{i=1}^{n} (\log x_i)^2 x_i^{\kappa} \right) - \left(\sum_{i=1}^{n} x_i^{\kappa} \log x_i \right)^2 \right].$$

Determining an initial estimator κ_0 is not trivial. A graphical technique that can be used to assess model adequacy and provide a least squares estimator for κ_0 is described in

Appendix D. When there are no censored observations, an initial estimator κ_0 is referenced at the end of this chapter. For numerical stability, many analysts prefer to work
with the logarithms of the lifetimes and fit the associated extreme value distribution.
The derivation for the procedure is outlined in Appendix E. A multivariate version of
the Newton–Raphson procedure, which can be used for solving more general systems of
equations, is given at the end of this chapter.

The 2×2 Fisher and observed information matrices are based on the following
partial derivatives:

$$\frac{-\partial^2 \log L(\lambda, \kappa)}{\partial \lambda^2} = \frac{\kappa r}{\lambda^2} + \kappa(\kappa - 1)\lambda^{\kappa - 2} \sum_{i=1}^{n} x_i^{\kappa},$$

$$\frac{-\partial^2 \log L(\lambda, \kappa)}{\partial \lambda \partial \kappa} = -\frac{r}{\lambda} + \left[\left(\kappa \lambda^{\kappa - 1} \right) \left(\sum_{i=1}^{n} x_i^{\kappa} \log x_i \right) + \left(\sum_{i=1}^{n} x_i^{\kappa} \right) \left(\kappa \lambda^{\kappa - 1} \log \lambda + \lambda^{\kappa - 1} \right) \right]$$

$$= -\frac{r}{\lambda} + \lambda^{\kappa - 1} \left[\kappa \sum_{i=1}^{n} x_i^{\kappa} \log x_i + (1 + \kappa \log \lambda) \sum_{i=1}^{n} x_i^{\kappa} \right],$$

$$\frac{-\partial^2 \log L(\lambda, \kappa)}{\partial \kappa^2} = \frac{r}{\kappa^2} + \sum_{i=1}^{n} (\lambda x_i)^{\kappa} (\log \lambda x_i)^2.$$

The expected values of these quantities are not tractable, so the Fisher information
matrix does not have closed-form elements. The observed information matrix, however,
can be determined by using $\hat{\lambda}$ and $\hat{\kappa}$ as arguments in these expressions.

Example 8.16

In the previous section, it was seen that the exponential distribution poorly approximated
the ball bearing data set. Using the same data set, the fitted Weibull distribution has maximum likelihood estimators $\hat{\lambda} = 0.0122$ and $\hat{\kappa} = 2.10$. These maximum likelihood estimators
were determined using a computer program that implemented the Newton-Raphson tech-
nique described previously. Figure 8.9 shows the empirical survival function along with the
exponential and Weibull fits to the data. It is clear that the Weibull distribution is superior
to the exponential in fitting the ball bearing failure times since it is capable of modeling
wear-out. The log likelihood function evaluated at the maximum likelihood estimators is
$\log L(\hat{\lambda}, \hat{\kappa}) = -113.691$. The log likelihood function is shown in Figure 8.10. The observed
information matrix is

$$O(\hat{\lambda}, \hat{\kappa}) = \begin{bmatrix} 681,000 & 875 \\ 875 & 10.4 \end{bmatrix},$$

revealing a positive correlation between the elements of the score vector. Using the fact that
the likelihood ratio statistic, $2[\log L(\hat{\lambda}, \hat{\kappa}) - \log L(\lambda, \kappa)]$, is asymptotically $\chi^2(2)$, a 95%
confidence region for the parameters is all λ and κ satisfying

$$2[-113.691 - \log L(\lambda, \kappa)] < 5.99,$$

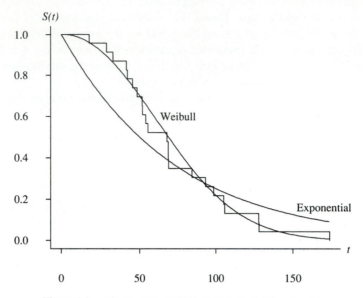

Figure 8.9   Exponential and Weibull fits to the ball bearing data.

since $\chi^2_{2,0.05} = 5.99$. The 95% confidence region is shown in Figure 8.11, and, not surprisingly, the line $\kappa = 1$ is not interior to the region. This indicates that the exponential distribution is not an appropriate model for this particular data set. Note that the boundary of this region is a level surface of the log likelihood function shown in Figure 8.10 that is cut $5.99/2$ units below the maximum of the log likelihood function.

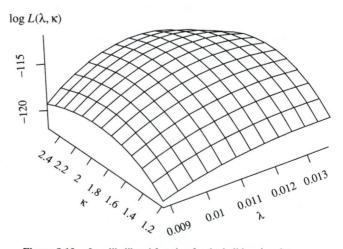

Figure 8.10   Log likelihood function for the ball bearing data.

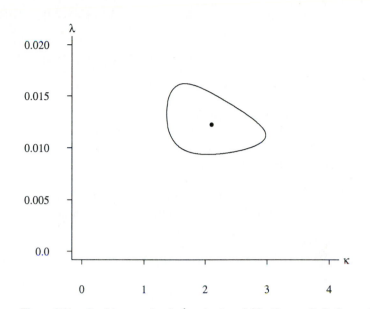

Figure 8.11   Confidence region for λ and κ ($\alpha = 0.05$). (*Source*: D. R. Cox and D. Oakes, *Analysis of Survival Data*, 1984. Adapted and reprinted by permission of Chapman and Hall.)

As further proof that the Weibull distribution is a significantly better model than the exponential, the likelihood ratio statistic can be used to determine whether κ is significant. Evaluating the log likelihood values at the maximum likelihood estimators in the Weibull and exponential fits, the likelihood ratio statistic is

$$2[\log L(\hat{\lambda}, \hat{\kappa}) - \log L(\hat{\lambda})] = 2[-113.691 + 121.435] = 15.488.$$

This value shows that κ is significant when compared with the critical value $\chi^2_{1, 0.05} = 3.84$.

If we are still uncertain as to whether κ is significantly different from 1, the standard errors of the distribution of the parameter estimators can be computed by using the inverse of the observed information matrix

$$O^{-1}(\hat{\lambda}, \hat{\kappa}) = \begin{bmatrix} 0.00000165 & -0.000139 \\ -0.000139 & 0.108 \end{bmatrix}.$$

This matrix is the variance–covariance matrix for the parameter estimators $\hat{\lambda}$ and $\hat{\kappa}$. The standard errors of the parameter estimators are the square roots of the diagonal elements

$$\hat{\sigma}_{\hat{\lambda}} = 0.00128 \qquad \hat{\sigma}_{\hat{\kappa}} = 0.329.$$

Thus an asymptotic 95% confidence interval for κ is

$$2.10 - (1.96)(0.329) < \kappa < 2.10 + (1.96)(0.329)$$

or

$$1.46 < \kappa < 2.74,$$

since $z_{0.025} = 1.96$. Since this confidence interval does not contain 1, κ is significant.

Lest the reader come to the conclusions that the exponential distribution can never be used and that the Weibull distribution is adequate for all distributions, one final (contrived) example follows. The Weibull distribution always provides a better fit than the exponential distribution since it is a generalization of the exponential distribution. There are situations, however, where the estimator for κ is so close to 1 that it does not warrant inclusion in the model. The following example also illustrates that the Weibull distribution does not always adequately model a lifetime data set.

Example 8.17

Consider the complete data set of $n = 10$ lifetimes:

$$1 \quad 5 \quad 6 \quad 10 \quad 54 \quad 82 \quad 85 \quad 86 \quad 90 \quad 91.$$

The total time on test is $\sum_{i=1}^{10} x_i = 510$, so the maximum likelihood estimator for the exponential distribution is

$$\hat{\lambda} = \frac{10}{510} = 0.0196.$$

The Weibull parameter estimators for this data set are

$$\hat{\lambda} = 0.0202 \qquad \hat{\kappa} = 0.927.$$

Since κ is so close to 1, using the extra parameter from the Weibull distribution to model these lifetimes is clearly not warranted. Figure 8.12 shows that both the exponential and Weibull distributions do an equally poor job of modeling the lifetimes. The Weibull distribution was "tricked" by early (1, 5, 6) and late (82, 85, 86, 90, 91) failures clustered together. A more appropriate model for this data set is one that can achieve a bathtub-shaped hazard function, such as the exponential power distribution.

8.4   FURTHER READING

The ball bearing data set is from Lieblein and Zelen (1956), the automotive a/c data set is from Kapur and Lamberson (1977, pp. 253–254), the 6-MP data set is from Gehan (1965), and the motorette data set is from Nelson and Hahn (1972).

Most textbooks on reliability consider the topic of estimating parameters for a parametric distribution based on failure data. The techniques used in Example 8.7 are

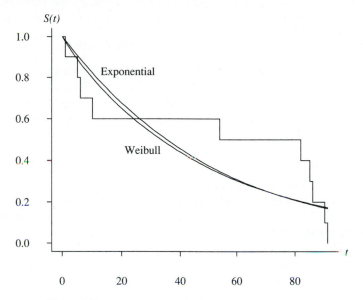

Figure 8.12   Exponential and Weibull fits to a lifetime data set.

presented in Lawless (1982, pp. 103–104). Martz and Waller (1982, p. 54) give an expression for the expected value and variance of $\hat{\lambda}$ for a complete data set,

$$E[\hat{\lambda}] = \frac{n}{n-1}\lambda \qquad V[\hat{\lambda}] = \frac{n^2}{(n-1)^2(n-2)}\lambda^2,$$

indicating that there is a slight positive bias since $E[\hat{\lambda}] > \lambda$ for all sample sizes n, although the estimate is asymptotically unbiased since $\lim_{n\to\infty} E[\hat{\lambda}] = \lambda$. Lawless (1982, pp. 107–111) lists and compares several interval estimators used on Type I censored data sets. Kapur and Lamberson (1977, pp. 285–287) suggest another approach for modifying the degrees of freedom for the chi-square critical values in the Type I censoring case. Example 8.12 and Figure 8.6 are given in Cox and Oakes (1984, pp. 39–40). Epstein and Sobel (1953) is one of the first papers concerning life testing. Grosh (1989, pp. 176–267), Kapur and Lamberson (1977, pp. 342–365), Lawless (1982, pp. 117–126), Martz and Waller (1982, pp. 129–137), Zacks (1992, pp. 177–198), and others contain separate sections on life testing. Moura (1991) contains information on how to determine the sample size for a life test.

Finding the maximum likelihood estimator for the shape parameter in the Weibull distribution involves a one-dimensional search using the Newton–Raphson technique. This single-dimensional search is possible because $\hat{\lambda}$ could be written in terms of $\hat{\kappa}$. An initial estimate for κ is given by Law and Kelton (1991, p. 334) and Menon (1963) for a complete data set. (See Appendix D.) It will not always be the case that a multidimensional search can be reduced to a one-dimensional search. Kalbfleisch and Prentice

(1980, pp. 55–58) give a multidimensional version of the Newton–Raphson technique that can be used iteratively to find the maximum likelihood estimator vector $\boldsymbol{\theta}$:

$$\boldsymbol{\theta}_{i+1} = \boldsymbol{\theta}_i + I(\boldsymbol{\theta}_i)^{-1}\mathbf{U}(\boldsymbol{\theta}_i)$$

for $i = 0, 1, \ldots$, given an initial estimate $\boldsymbol{\theta}_0$. The presentation of topics in this chapter generally follows Chapter 3 in Cox and Oakes (1984), and they give another test for exponentiality on pages 43–45. In addition, they use the likelihood ratio statistic to test for significance on page 101. Crowder et al. (1991, pp. 37–43) fit the Weibull and log normal distributions to the ball bearing data and conclude that the log normal distribution might provide a slightly better fit. Dodson (1995) considers the Weibull distribution exclusively.

Cohen and Whitten (1988) consider parameter estimation for several parametric distributions. Chhikara and Folks (1989) consider parameter estimation for the inverse Gaussian distribution and Bowman and Shenton (1988) consider parameter estimation for the gamma distribution. One important topic that has been completely ignored in this chapter is how to choose a parametric model among alternatives. Cox and Oakes (1984, pp. 24–28), Law and Kelton (1991, pp. 325–419), and Martz and Waller (1982, pp. 105–117) provide general guidelines. Estimation for point processes is not considered here, but examples of parametric and nonparametric techniques for estimating the cumulative intensity function for an NHPP and generating realizations for simulation models are given in Crow (1982), Rigdon and Basu (1989), Lee et al. (1991), Leemis (1991), and Chan and Rueda (1992). These authors consider the power law process and more general cases. Software for parameter estimation is reviewed in Nelson (1990, pp. 238–239).

8.5 EXERCISES

8.1. Show that when a sample is taken from an exponential(λ) population with Type II right censoring

$$\frac{2r\lambda}{\hat{\lambda}} \sim \chi^2(2r)$$

where $\chi^2(2r)$ is the chi-square distribution with $2r$ degrees of freedom.

8.2. Consider a Type II censored sample of size n from an exponential population with mean θ. Show that the maximum likelihood estimate $\hat{\theta}$ is unbiased.

8.3. (Leemis and Shih, 1989) Assume that the lifetime of a particular item has the exponential distribution with a mean of θ. A data set of n values contains three different types of observations. The first $l - 1$ failures are left censored at $t_{(l)}$, the order statistics $t_{(l)}, \ldots, t_{(r)}$ are observed, and the remaining failure times are right censored at $t_{(r)}$. Assume that all censoring is order statistic (Type II) censoring. Write an equation that, when solved, gives the maximum likelihood estimator $\hat{\theta}$. Solve for $\hat{\theta}$ for the data set ($n = 5$, $l = 2$, and $r = 3$)

$$4.0 \quad 6.8$$

to three decimal places.

8.4. For a left- and right-censored data set from an exponential population described in the previous question, Sarhan and Greenberg (1962, Chapter 11) give the best linear unbiased estimate as

$$\hat{\theta} = \frac{1}{K} \left\{ \left[\frac{\displaystyle\sum_{i=1}^{l} \frac{1}{n-i+1}}{\displaystyle\sum_{i=1}^{l} \frac{1}{(n-i+1)^2}} - (n-l+1) \right] t_{(l)} + (n-r)t_{(r)} + \sum_{i=l}^{r} t_{(i)} \right\}$$

where

$$K = \frac{\left[\displaystyle\sum_{i=1}^{l} 1/(n-i+1) \right]^2}{\displaystyle\sum_{i=1}^{l} 1/(n-i+1)^2} + (r-l).$$

Show that $\hat{\theta}$ is an unbiased estimate of θ.

8.5. (Epstein and Sobel, 1953) Compare the expected time to complete a life test of items with exponentially distributed times to failure without replacement for a complete data set with r observed failures with a Type II censored data set with r out of n observed failures.

8.6. Compare the expected time to complete a Type II censored life test with and without replacement.

8.7. Assume that a life test without replacement is conducted on n items from an exponential population with failure rate λ. The exact failure times are not known, but the test is terminated upon the rth ordered failure at time $t_{(r)}$. Estimate λ.

8.8. Write a computer program that computes point and 95% confidence interval estimates of the mean, variance, and certain percentiles of the exponential distribution for any complete or Type II censored data set with $r = 1, 2, \ldots, 25$ observed lifetimes. The input to the program is in three parts:
(a) Number of items on test, n
(b) Number of observed failures, r
(c) r observed failures
The output from the program is:
(a) Sample statistics such as n, r, the total time on test, $t_{(1)}$, $t_{(r)}$, and, if the data are complete, the sample mean, standard deviation, coefficient of variation, skewness, and kurtosis
(b) Point and interval estimates for the mean time to failure at $\alpha = 0.05$
(c) Point and interval estimates for σ^2 at $\alpha = 0.05$
(d) Point and interval estimates for $t_{0.01}$, $t_{0.50}$, and $t_{0.99}$ at $\alpha = 0.05$
Test your program using the ball bearing data, the Type II right-censored data set from pre-production burn-in with $n = 25$, $r = 5$: 3, 4, 7, 9, and 120 (in hours), from Jensen and Petersen (1982, p. 40), and the Type II right-censored automotive a/c switch failure data with $n = 15$, $r = 5$: 1410, 1872, 3138, 4218, 6971 (in cycles), from Kapur and Lamberson (1977, p. 254).

8.9. (Lawless, 1982, p. 107) Write a Monte Carlo simulation program that computes approximate confidence intervals for the mean time to failure θ in the exponential distribution when there is Type I censoring. The five different approximation schemes are outlined next. First, the random variable

$$\frac{\hat{\theta} - \theta}{I(\hat{\theta})^{-1/2}}$$

is asymptotically standard normal. Note that the potential censoring times must be known to compute this quantity. Second, the random variable

$$\frac{\hat{\theta} - \theta}{O(\hat{\theta})^{-1/2}}$$

is also asymptotically standard normal. Third, consider the distribution of $\hat{\phi} = \hat{\theta}^{-1/3}$. The random variable

$$\frac{\hat{\phi} - \phi}{(\hat{\phi}^2 / 9\hat{Q})^{1/2}}$$

is asymptotically standard normal, where $\hat{Q} = \sum_{i=1}^{n}(1 - e^{-c_i/\hat{\theta}})$. As with the first result, the potential censoring times must be known to use this result. Fourth, the random variable

$$\frac{\hat{\phi} - \phi}{(\hat{\phi}^2 / 9r)^{1/2}}$$

is asymptotically standard normal. Finally, the random variable

$$2r\hat{\theta}/\theta$$

is approximately chi-square with $2r + 1$ degrees of freedom. Generate variates from the unit exponential distribution. Assume that the censoring times are identical; that is, $c_1 = c_2 = \cdots = c_n = L$. Generate 2000 confidence intervals for each of the following conditions. Vary these parameters in your simulation:

(a) Expected fraction censored (10%, 30%)
(b) Nominal confidence interval coverage (0.90, 0.95)
(c) Sample size (10, 25)
(d) Five confidence interval procedures

For each experiment, calculate:

(a) Coverage
(b) Mean halfwidth of the confidence interval
(c) Variance of the halfwidth of the confidence interval

8.10　Consider an exponential population with failure rate λ. A life test with replacement is terminated when r failures occur or at time c, whichever occurs first. This is a combination of Type I and Type II censoring. Find the expected number of items that fail during the test as a function of λ.

8.11   An item may fail from one of $k = 2$ causes of failure. A life test of n items is terminated at time c (Type I right censoring). Assume that $r_1 > 0$ items fail from cause 1 at times $t_{11}, t_{12}, \ldots, t_{1r_1}$ and that $r_2 > 0$ items fail from cause 2 at times $t_{21}, t_{22}, \ldots, t_{2r_2}$, where $r_1 + r_2 = r$. If the net lifetimes of the first two failure modes are independent and the crude lifetimes have the exponential distribution, estimate the hazard function for the item if the first risk is removed. (*Hint:* Keep in mind that an item that fails from one of the risks is a right-censored observation for the other risk.)

8.12.   For a life test of n exponential items without replacement continued until all units fail, show that $E[\hat{\lambda}] = [n/(n-1)]\lambda$, where λ is the population failure rate and $\hat{\lambda}$ is the maximum likelihood estimator for λ. Thus an unbiasing constant for $\hat{\lambda}$ is $u_n = (n-1)/n$. Equivalently,

$$E\left[\frac{n-1}{n}\hat{\lambda}\right] = E[u_n \hat{\lambda}] = \lambda.$$

Find unbiasing constants for the case of Type II right censoring.

8.13.   Give a point and 95% interval estimator for the median lifetime of the 6-MP treatment group assuming that the data have been drawn from an exponential population.

8.14.   Consider a life test of n exponential components with failed components immediately replaced upon failure. If you observe that $r > 0$ items have failed by time c, but you do not know the actual failure times, what is the maximum likelihood estimator for λ?

8.15.   Report the P-value for the F test to determine whether the two populations (control and 6-MP) in the leukemia study have the same failure rate. Note that the statistic will approximately have the F distribution since the censoring mechanism for the group that received the drug is not Type II censoring.

8.16.   Consider the following Type II censored data set for the lifetime of a product ($n = 5$ and $r = 3$) drawn from an exponential population with failure rate λ:

$$3.6 \quad 3.9 \quad 8.5.$$

(a) Find the maximum likelihood estimator for the mean of the population.
(b) Find the maximum likelihood estimator for $S(5)$.
(c) Find an 80% confidence interval for $E[T^3]$.
(d) Find a 95% one-sided lower confidence interval for $S(5)$.
(e) Find the P-value for the test $H_0: \lambda = 0.04$ versus $H_1: \lambda > 0.04$.
(f) Find the value of the log likelihood function at the maximum likelihood value.
(g) Find the value of the observed information matrix.
(h) Assume the data values

$$3.8 \quad 4.6 \quad 6.0 \quad 9.6$$

constitute a complete data set for a different product. Find a 90% confidence interval for the ratio of the failure rates of the two products if both are assumed to come from exponential populations.

8.17.   Consider a life test procedure when the lifetimes have the exponential distribution. If $\lambda_0 = 0.01$ failures per hour, $\lambda_1 = 0.02$ failures per hour, $\alpha = 0.1$, and $\beta = 0.1$, how should n and r be chosen in a Type II censored data set so that the test will have an expected duration of 50 hours under H_0? Assume that the alternative hypothesis is $H_1: \lambda > \lambda_0$.

8.18. (Epstein and Sobel, 1955) Sequential life tests are often used to decrease the expected total time on test. Consider such a test based on the exponential distribution with a mean time to failure of θ. The null hypothesis is $\theta = \theta_0$ and the alternative is $\theta < \theta_0$. The producer's risk is α at $\theta = \theta_0$ and the consumer's risk is β at $\theta = \theta_1$. Let

$$W(t) = \left(\frac{\theta_0}{\theta_1}\right)^{r(t)} \exp\left[-\left(\frac{1}{\theta_1} - \frac{1}{\theta_0}\right) T(t)\right]$$

where $r(t)$ is the number of failures at time t and $T(t)$ is the total time on test by time t. As long as $B < W(t) < A$, testing continues. If, however, $W(t) \le B$, H_0 is rejected, and if $W(t) \ge A$, there is not enough evidence in the data to reject H_0. Approximate values for A and B are given by Lawless (1982, p. 125) as $A = (1 - \beta)/\alpha$ and $B = \beta/(1 - \alpha)$. Plot $W(t)$ between $t = 0$ and $t = 6971$ for the data set in Kapur and Lamberson (1977, p. 254) with $n = 15$ and $r = 5$: 1410, 1872, 3138, 4218, 6971. The parameters for the test are $\theta_0 = 30,000$ hours, $\theta_1 = 10,000$ hours, $\alpha = 0.05$, and $\beta = 0.10$.

8.19. Consider a life testing situation for which a manufacturer claims that his product has an exponential time to failure with a mean of 10,000 hours. A consumer questions this claim and will tolerate a consumer's risk of no more than $\beta = 0.10$ when the population mean is 3500 hours. Find the smallest number of failures to satisfy both the producer and consumer if the producer's risk is $\alpha = 0.025$. Assume that there is Type II censoring.

8.20. Jill fits the ball bearing data set to the Weibull distribution parameterized as

$$S(t) = e^{-(\lambda t)^\kappa} \qquad t \ge 0,$$

yielding maximum likelihood estimates $\hat{\lambda} = 0.0122$ and $\hat{\kappa} = 2.10$. Lindsey also wants to fit the same data set to the Weibull distribution, but she uses the parameterization

$$S(t) = e^{-\rho t^\beta} \qquad t \ge 0.$$

What will be the maximum likelihood estimates $\hat{\rho}$ and $\hat{\beta}$ that Lindsey obtains for the ball bearing data set?

8.21. Write a computer program for determining the regression and maximum likelihood estimates for the Weibull distribution parameters for complete and right-censored data sets. Also, print out the observed information matrix. Test your program on the ball bearing, automotive switch, and 6-MP treatment group lifetimes.

8.22. Find the elements of the score vector for the log logistic distribution for a randomly right-censored data set.

8.23. Find the elements of the score vector for the exponential power distribution for a randomly right-censored data set.

8.24. Write a computer program to determine the method of moments estimates for the parameters of the log normal distribution for a complete data set. Test the program on the ball bearing data.

8.25. An engineer places n items on test and observes r failures. Assuming that the population follows the log logistic distribution and censoring is random, set up an expression for the boundary of a 95% confidence region for the shape parameter κ and scale parameter λ of the log logistic distribution based on the likelihood ratio statistic. Assume that the survivor function for the log logistic distribution is

$$S(t) = \frac{1}{1 + (\lambda t)^\kappa} \qquad t \geq 0,$$

for $\lambda > 0$ and $\kappa > 0$. It is not necessary to solve for the maximum likelihood estimators.

8.26. Find the maximum likelihood estimators for the parameters in a NHPP with a power law intensity function

$$\lambda(t) = \lambda^\kappa \kappa t^{\kappa - 1} \qquad t \geq 0.$$

(*Hint*: Crowder et al. (1991, p. 166) give the likelihood function for NHPPs as

$$L(\lambda, \kappa) = \left\{ \prod_{i=1}^{n} \lambda(t_i) \right\} e^{-\int_0^c \lambda(t)\, dt}$$

where $t_1, t_2, \ldots, t_n$ are the observed failure times for a process observed on $(0, c]$.)

8.27. A life test of n items with identical gamma(λ, κ) distributions is conducted. Find the expected number of failures between times c_1 and c_2 (where $0 < c_1 < c_2$) if components are not replaced upon failure.

9

Parametric Estimation for Models with Covariates

Parameter estimation for the accelerated life and proportional hazards models, which were introduced in Chapter 5, is considered in this chapter. Since there is now a vector of covariates, in addition to just a failure or censoring time for each item on test, special notation must be added to accommodate the covariates. The accelerated life and proportional hazards models are considered separately, since they require different approaches for parameter estimation. The proportional hazards model has the unique feature that the baseline distribution need not be defined in order to estimate the regression coefficients associated with the covariates.

9.1   MODEL FORMULATION

The purpose of a model of dependence is to include a vector of covariates $\mathbf{z} = (z_1, z_2, \ldots, z_q)'$ in a survival distribution. The reason for including this vector may be to determine which covariates significantly affect survival, to determine the impact of changing one or more of the covariates, or to fit a more complicated distribution from a small data set, as opposed to fitting separate distributions for each level of the covariates. As indicated in Chapter 5, one way to define the accelerated life model is through the survivor function

$$S(t, \mathbf{z}) = S_0(t\,\psi(\mathbf{z})),$$

where S_0 is a baseline survivor function and $\psi(\mathbf{z})$ is a link function satisfying $\psi(\mathbf{0}) = 1$ and $\psi(\mathbf{z}) \geq 0$ for all $\mathbf{z}$. The covariate vector $\mathbf{z}$ has been added as an argument to the survivor function, since the probability of survival to time t is a function of both time and the covariate values. When $\psi(\mathbf{z}) > 1$, the covariates increase the rate at which the item moves through time. When $\psi(\mathbf{z}) < 1$, the covariates decrease the rate at which the item moves through time. The link function is assumed to have the log linear form $\psi(\mathbf{z}) = e^{\boldsymbol{\beta}'\mathbf{z}}$ throughout this chapter, where $\boldsymbol{\beta} = (\beta_1, \beta_2, \ldots, \beta_q)'$. The proportional hazards model can be defined by

$$h(t, \mathbf{z}) = \psi(\mathbf{z})\, h_0(t),$$

where $h_0(t)$ is a baseline hazard function. The covariates increase the hazard function when $\psi(\mathbf{z}) > 1$ or decrease the hazard function when $\psi(\mathbf{z}) < 1$. For both the accelerated life and proportional hazards models, the other lifetime distribution representations are given in Table 5.1. The purpose of this chapter is to estimate the $q \times 1$ vector of regression coefficients $\boldsymbol{\beta}$ from a data set consisting of n items on test and r observed failure times.

A data set in the case of a model of dependence is slightly more complicated due to the covariates. The failure time of the ith item on test, t_i, is either observed or right-censored at time c_i. As before, let $x_i = \min\{t_i, c_i\}$ and δ_i be a censoring indicator variable (1 for an observed failure and 0 for a censored value), for $i = 1, 2, \ldots, n$. In addition, a vector of covariates $\mathbf{z}_i = (z_{i1}, z_{i2}, \ldots, z_{iq})'$ is collected for each item on test, $i = 1, 2, \ldots, n$. Thus z_{ij} is the value of covariate j for item i, $i = 1, 2, \ldots, n$ and $j = 1, 2, \ldots, q$. This formulation of the problem can be stated in matrix form as

$$\mathbf{x} = \begin{bmatrix} x_1 \\ x_2 \\ \cdot \\ \cdot \\ \cdot \\ x_n \end{bmatrix} \quad \boldsymbol{\delta} = \begin{bmatrix} \delta_1 \\ \delta_2 \\ \cdot \\ \cdot \\ \cdot \\ \delta_n \end{bmatrix} \quad \text{and} \quad \mathbf{Z} = \begin{bmatrix} z_{11} & z_{12} & \cdots & z_{1q} \\ z_{21} & z_{22} & \cdots & z_{2q} \\ \cdot & \cdot & \cdot & \cdot \\ \cdot & \cdot & \cdot & \cdot \\ \cdot & \cdot & \cdot & \cdot \\ z_{n1} & z_{n2} & \cdots & z_{nq} \end{bmatrix}.$$

The matrix approach is useful since complicated systems of equations can be expressed compactly and operations on data sets can be performed efficiently by a computer. For parameter estimation, the survivor, density, hazard, and cumulative hazard functions now have an extra parameter $\mathbf{z}$ associated with them:

$$S(t, \mathbf{z}, \boldsymbol{\theta}, \boldsymbol{\beta}) \qquad f(t, \mathbf{z}, \boldsymbol{\theta}, \boldsymbol{\beta}) \qquad h(t, \mathbf{z}, \boldsymbol{\theta}, \boldsymbol{\beta}) \qquad H(t, \mathbf{z}, \boldsymbol{\theta}, \boldsymbol{\beta}),$$

where the vector of unknown parameters $\boldsymbol{\theta}$ consists of those associated with the baseline distribution, which must be estimated along with the regression coefficients $\boldsymbol{\beta}$. The likelihood function can now be written in the usual form:

$$L(\boldsymbol{\theta}, \boldsymbol{\beta}) = \prod_{i \in U} f(x_i, \mathbf{z}_i, \boldsymbol{\theta}, \boldsymbol{\beta}) \prod_{i \in C} S(x_i, \mathbf{z}_i, \boldsymbol{\theta}, \boldsymbol{\beta}).$$

The log likelihood function is

$$\log L(\boldsymbol{\theta}, \boldsymbol{\beta}) = \sum_{i \in U} \log f(x_i, \mathbf{z}_i, \boldsymbol{\theta}, \boldsymbol{\beta}) + \sum_{i \in C} \log S(x_i, \mathbf{z}_i, \boldsymbol{\theta}, \boldsymbol{\beta}),$$

or, equivalently,

$$\log L(\boldsymbol{\theta}, \boldsymbol{\beta}) = \sum_{i \in U} \log h(x_i, \mathbf{z}_i, \boldsymbol{\theta}, \boldsymbol{\beta}) - \sum_{i = 1}^{n} H(x_i, \mathbf{z}_i, \boldsymbol{\theta}, \boldsymbol{\beta}).$$

Two observations with respect to this model formulation are important. First, the maximum likelihood estimators for $\boldsymbol{\theta}$ and $\boldsymbol{\beta}$ for most of the models in this section cannot be expressed in closed form (as was the case for the exponential distribution in Chapter 8), so numerical methods often need to be used to find the values of the estimates. Second, the choice of whether to use a model of dependence or to examine each population separately is dependent on the number of unique covariate vectors $\mathbf{z}$ and the number of observations, n. If, for example, n is large and there is only a single binary covariate (that is, only two unique covariate vectors, $z_1 = 0$ and $z_1 = 1$), it is probably wiser to analyze each of the two populations separately by the techniques described in Chapter 8.

For simplicity and tractability, only the log linear form of the link function $\psi(\mathbf{z}) = e^{\boldsymbol{\beta}'\mathbf{z}}$ is considered here. This assumption is not necessary for some of the derivations, and many of the results apply to a wider range of link functions.

9.2   ACCELERATED LIFE

The accelerated life model

$$S(t, \mathbf{z}) = S_0(t \, \psi(\mathbf{z}))$$

is assumed to be an appropriate representation of the relationship between the covariates and the survival pattern of the items under consideration. Parameter estimation in the accelerated life model requires numerical methods for the exponential and Weibull baseline distributions, each of which will be considered separately.

Exponential Baseline Distribution

When the baseline distribution is exponential [$h_0(t) = \lambda$] and the link function assumes the log linear form [$\psi(\mathbf{z}) = e^{\boldsymbol{\beta}'\mathbf{z}}$], the hazard function associated with a covariate vector $\mathbf{z}$ is

$$h(t, \mathbf{z}, \lambda, \boldsymbol{\beta}) = \psi(\mathbf{z}) \, h_0(t\psi(\mathbf{z})) = \lambda \, e^{\boldsymbol{\beta}'\mathbf{z}}.$$

It is often more convenient notationally to define an additional covariate, $z_0 = 1$, in this case for all n items on test. This allows the baseline parameter $\lambda = e^{\beta_0 z_0}$ to be included in the vector of regression coefficients, rather than having to consider it separately. The baseline hazard function has been effectively absorbed into the link function. In this case, the hazard function can be expressed more compactly as

$$h(t, \mathbf{z}, \boldsymbol{\beta}) = e^{\boldsymbol{\beta}'\mathbf{z}},$$

where $\boldsymbol{\beta} = (\beta_0, \beta_1, \ldots, \beta_q)'$ and $\mathbf{z} = (z_0, z_1, \ldots, z_q)'$. The corresponding cumulative hazard function is

$$H(t, \mathbf{z}, \boldsymbol{\beta}) = t \, e^{\boldsymbol{\beta}'\mathbf{z}}.$$

Using this parameterization, the log likelihood function is

$$\log L(\boldsymbol{\beta}) = \sum_{i \in U} \log h(x_i, \mathbf{z}_i, \boldsymbol{\beta}) - \sum_{i=1}^{n} H(x_i, \mathbf{z}_i, \boldsymbol{\beta})$$

$$= \sum_{i \in U} \boldsymbol{\beta}'\mathbf{z}_i - \sum_{i=1}^{n} x_i \, e^{\boldsymbol{\beta}'\mathbf{z}_i}.$$

Differentiating this expression with respect to β_j yields the scores

$$\frac{\partial \log L(\boldsymbol{\beta})}{\partial \beta_j} = \sum_{i \in U} z_{ij} - \sum_{i=1}^{n} x_i \, z_{ij} \, e^{\boldsymbol{\beta}'\mathbf{z}_i}$$

for $j = 0, 1, \ldots, q$. When the scores are equated to zero, the resulting $(q+1) \times (q+1)$ set of nonlinear equations in $\boldsymbol{\beta}$ must be solved numerically. In the example that follows, there is a closed-form solution for this set of simultaneous equations when there is a single binary covariate, often referred to as the two-sample case.

To find the observed information matrix and the Fisher information matrix, a second partial derivative of the log likelihood function must be found:

$$-\frac{\partial^2 \log L(\boldsymbol{\beta})}{\partial \beta_j \partial \beta_k} = \sum_{i=1}^{n} x_i \, z_{ij} \, z_{ik} e^{\boldsymbol{\beta}'\mathbf{z}_i}$$

for $j = 0, 1, \ldots, q$ and $k = 0, 1, \ldots, q$. The observed information matrix can be determined by using the maximum likelihood estimate $\hat{\boldsymbol{\beta}}$ as an argument in this second partial derivative. Thus the (j, k) element of the observed information matrix is

$$\left[-\frac{\partial^2 \log L(\boldsymbol{\beta})}{\partial \beta_j \partial \beta_k} \right]_{\boldsymbol{\beta} = \hat{\boldsymbol{\beta}}} = \sum_{i=1}^{n} x_i \, z_{ij} \, z_{ik} e^{\hat{\boldsymbol{\beta}}'\mathbf{z}_i}$$

for $j = 0, 1, \ldots, q$ and $k = 0, 1, \ldots, q$. For computational purposes, this can be expressed in matrix form as

$$O(\hat{\boldsymbol{\beta}}) = \mathbf{Z}' \hat{\mathbf{B}} \, \mathbf{Z},$$

where $\hat{\mathbf{B}}$ is an $n \times n$ diagonal matrix whose elements are $x_1 e^{\hat{\boldsymbol{\beta}}'\mathbf{z}_1}, x_2 e^{\hat{\boldsymbol{\beta}}'\mathbf{z}_2}, \ldots, x_n e^{\hat{\boldsymbol{\beta}}'\mathbf{z}_n}.$

The Fisher information matrix is more difficult to calculate since it involves the expected value of the second partial derivative:

$$E\left[-\frac{\partial^2 \log L(\boldsymbol{\beta})}{\partial \beta_j \partial \beta_k}\right] = \sum_{i=1}^{n} z_{ij}\, z_{ik}\, e^{\boldsymbol{\beta}'\mathbf{z}_i}\, E[x_i]$$

for $j = 0, 1, \ldots, q$ and $k = 0, 1, \ldots, q$. Determining the value of $E[x_i]$ will be considered separately in the paragraphs that follow for uncensored ($r = n$) and censored ($r < n$) data sets.

For a complete data set, $E[x_i] = E[t_i]$, $i = 1, 2, \ldots, n$, because there is no censoring. Since the mean of the exponential distribution is the reciprocal of the failure rate and the ith item on test has failure rate $e^{\boldsymbol{\beta}'\mathbf{z}_i}$, $E[x_i] = e^{-\boldsymbol{\beta}'\mathbf{z}_i}$. Returning to the Fisher information matrix, the (j, k)th element is

$$E\left[-\frac{\partial^2 \log L(\boldsymbol{\beta})}{\partial \beta_j \partial \beta_k}\right] = \sum_{i=1}^{n} z_{ij}\, z_{ik}\, e^{\boldsymbol{\beta}'\mathbf{z}_i} e^{-\boldsymbol{\beta}'\mathbf{z}_i} = \sum_{i=1}^{n} z_{ij}\, z_{ik}$$

for $j = 0, 1, \ldots, q$ and $k = 0, 1, \ldots, q$. This result for the Fisher information matrix has a particularly tractable matrix representation

$$I(\boldsymbol{\beta}) = \mathbf{Z}'\mathbf{Z},$$

which is a function of the matrix of covariates only.

For a censored data set, the expression for $E[x_i]$ is a bit more complicated. Since the failure rate for the ith item on test is $e^{\boldsymbol{\beta}'\mathbf{z}_i}$,

$$E[x_i] = E[\min \{t_i, c_i\}]$$

$$= \int_0^{c_i} t_i f(t_i) dt_i + c_i\, P[t_i \geq c_i]$$

$$= \int_0^{c_i} t_i e^{\boldsymbol{\beta}'\mathbf{z}_i} e^{-e^{\boldsymbol{\beta}'\mathbf{z}_i} t_i} dt_i + c_i e^{-e^{\boldsymbol{\beta}'\mathbf{z}_i} c_i}$$

$$= e^{-\boldsymbol{\beta}'\mathbf{z}_i}(1 - e^{-e^{\boldsymbol{\beta}'\mathbf{z}_i} c_i})$$

for $i = 1, 2, \ldots, n$, by using integration by parts. This means that the (j, k)th element of the Fisher information matrix is

$$E\left[-\frac{\partial^2 \log L(\boldsymbol{\beta})}{\partial \beta_j \partial \beta_k}\right] = \sum_{i=1}^{n} z_{ij}\, z_{ik}\, e^{\boldsymbol{\beta}'\mathbf{z}_i} e^{-\boldsymbol{\beta}'\mathbf{z}_i}[1 - e^{-e^{\boldsymbol{\beta}'\mathbf{z}_i} c_i}] = \sum_{i=1}^{n} z_{ij}\, z_{ik}(1 - \gamma_i),$$

where $\gamma_i = e^{-e^{\boldsymbol{\beta}'\mathbf{z}_i} c_i}$ is the probability that the ith item on test is censored, for $i =$

$1, 2, \ldots, n$. Note that the potential censoring time for the ith item on test, c_i, must be known for each item in order to compute the Fisher information matrix, which is not always the case. Letting Γ be a diagonal matrix with elements $\gamma_1, \gamma_2, \ldots, \gamma_n$, this expression can also be written in matrix form

$$I(\boldsymbol{\beta}) = \mathbf{Z}'\,(I - \Gamma)\,\mathbf{Z},$$

which is independent of the failure times.

Before ending the discussion on the exponential baseline distribution, the two-sample case, where a binary covariate z_1 is used to differentiate between the control ($z_1 = 0$) and treatment ($z_1 = 1$) cases, is considered. This case is of interest because the maximum likelihood estimates can be expressed in closed form. The notation for the two-sample case is summarized in Table 9.1. As before, $z_0 = 1$ is included in the vector of covariates to account for the baseline distribution. The 2×2 set of nonlinear equations for finding the estimates of $\boldsymbol{\beta} = (\beta_0, \beta_1)'$ is

$$\sum_{i \in U} z_{i0} - \sum_{i=1}^{n} x_i\, z_{i0}\, e^{\beta_0 z_{i0} + \beta_1 z_{i1}} = 0,$$

$$\sum_{i \in U} z_{i1} - \sum_{i=1}^{n} x_i\, z_{i1}\, e^{\beta_0 z_{i0} + \beta_1 z_{i1}} = 0.$$

Let $r_0 > 0$ be the number of observed failures in the control group ($z_1 = 0$), and let $r_1 > 0$ be the number of observed failures in the treatment group ($z_1 = 1$). Since $z_0 = 1$ for all items on test, the equations reduce to

$$r_0 + r_1 - \sum_{i=1}^{n} x_i\, e^{\beta_0 + \beta_1 z_{i1}} = 0,$$

$$r_1 - \sum_{i=1}^{n} x_i\, z_{i1}\, e^{\beta_0 + \beta_1 z_{i1}} = 0.$$

These equations can be further simplified by partitioning the summations based on the value of z_1:

TABLE 9.1   TWO-SAMPLE ACCELERATED LIFE MODEL NOTATION

	Control Group	Treatment Group
Number of failures	r_0	r_1
Baseline covariate z_0	1	1
Binary covariate z_1	0	1

$$r_0 + r_1 - \sum_{i\,|\,z_{i1}=0} x_i e^{\beta_0} - \sum_{i\,|\,z_{i1}=1} x_i\, e^{\beta_0 + \beta_1} = 0,$$

$$r_1 - \sum_{i\,|\,z_{i1}=1} x_i\, e^{\beta_0 + \beta_1} = 0.$$

Letting $\lambda_0 = e^{\beta_0}$ be the failure rate in the control group ($z_1 = 0$) and letting $\lambda_1 = e^{\beta_0 + \beta_1}$ be the failure rate in the treatment group ($z_1 = 1$), the equations become

$$r_0 + r_1 - \lambda_0 \sum_{i\,|\,z_{i1}=0} x_i - \lambda_1 \sum_{i\,|\,z_{i1}=1} x_i = 0,$$

$$r_1 - \lambda_1 \sum_{i\,|\,z_{i1}=1} x_i = 0.$$

When these equations are solved simultaneously, the maximum likelihood estimates for λ_0 and λ_1 are the same as those for the exponential distribution with two separate populations:

$$\hat{\lambda}_0 = \frac{r_0}{\displaystyle\sum_{i\,|\,z_{i1}=0} x_i} \qquad \hat{\lambda}_1 = \frac{r_1}{\displaystyle\sum_{i\,|\,z_{i1}=1} x_i}.$$

Comparisons between the control and treatment groups can be made by using the F test from the previous chapter.

Example 9.1

The survival times in the 6-MP drug experiment are broken down into a control group that did not receive the drug ($z_1 = 0$) and a treatment group that did receive the drug ($z_1 = 1$). The remission times, in weeks, for the 21 individuals in the control group are

$$\begin{array}{cccccccccccc} 1 & 1 & 2 & 2 & 3 & 4 & 4 & 5 & 5 & 8 & 8 & 8 \\ 8 & 11 & 11 & 12 & 12 & 15 & 17 & 22 & 23. \end{array}$$

The remission times for the 21 individuals that received the drug are

$$\begin{array}{cccccccccccc} 6 & 6 & 6 & 6^* & 7 & 9^* & 10 & 10^* & 11^* & 13 & 16 & 17^* & 19^* \\ & 20^* & 22 & 23 & 25^* & 32^* & 32^* & 34^* & 35^*. \end{array}$$

There are a total of $n = 42$ individuals on test, and there are a total of $r = 30$ observed cancer recurrences, $r_0 = 21$ of which are in the control group and $r_1 = 9$ of which are in the treatment group. Placing the control group values first in the **x** vector, the values of **x**, **δ**, and **Z** are given in Figure 9.1. Note that for this analysis the *order* of the observations in the **x** vector is irrelevant. For tied values, the censored values have been placed last. The maximum likelihood estimates for the failure rates for the two populations are

$$\hat{\lambda}_0 = \frac{r_0}{\displaystyle\sum_{i\,|\,z_{i1}=0} x_i} = \frac{21}{182} = 0.115 \quad \text{and} \quad \hat{\lambda}_1 = \frac{r_1}{\displaystyle\sum_{i\,|\,z_{i1}=1} x_i} = \frac{9}{359} = 0.0251$$

$$
\mathbf{x} = \begin{bmatrix} 1 \\ 1 \\ 2 \\ 2 \\ 3 \\ 4 \\ 4 \\ 5 \\ 5 \\ 8 \\ 8 \\ 8 \\ 8 \\ 11 \\ 11 \\ 12 \\ 12 \\ 15 \\ 17 \\ 22 \\ 23 \\ 6 \\ 6 \\ 6 \\ 6 \\ 7 \\ 9 \\ 10 \\ 10 \\ 11 \\ 13 \\ 16 \\ 17 \\ 19 \\ 20 \\ 22 \\ 23 \\ 25 \\ 32 \\ 32 \\ 34 \\ 35 \end{bmatrix}
\qquad
\boldsymbol{\delta} = \begin{bmatrix} 1 \\ 1 \\ 1 \\ 1 \\ 1 \\ 1 \\ 1 \\ 1 \\ 1 \\ 1 \\ 1 \\ 1 \\ 1 \\ 1 \\ 1 \\ 1 \\ 1 \\ 1 \\ 1 \\ 1 \\ 1 \\ 1 \\ 1 \\ 1 \\ 0 \\ 1 \\ 0 \\ 1 \\ 0 \\ 0 \\ 1 \\ 1 \\ 0 \\ 0 \\ 0 \\ 1 \\ 1 \\ 0 \\ 0 \\ 0 \\ 0 \\ 0 \end{bmatrix}
\quad \text{and} \quad
\mathbf{Z} = \begin{bmatrix} 1 & 0 \\ 1 & 1 \\ 1 & 1 \end{bmatrix}
$$

Figure 9.1   Data values for the two-sample 6-MP experiment.

or, equivalently, the expected remission times of the control and treatment groups are $\frac{182}{21} =$ 8.67 weeks and $\frac{359}{9} = 39.9$ weeks, respectively. These estimates can be easily converted to the coefficients in the accelerated life model:

$$\hat{\beta}_0 = \log\left[\frac{21}{182}\right] = -2.16 \quad \text{and} \quad \hat{\beta}_1 = \log\left[\frac{(9)(182)}{(359)(21)}\right] = -1.53.$$

Confidence intervals can be determined separately for the two populations since the remission times in each are assumed to be exponentially distributed. Using the techniques based on the chi-square distribution from Chapter 8, an exact 95% confidence interval for λ_0 is

$$\frac{(0.115)(26.00)}{42} < \lambda_0 < \frac{(0.115)(61.78)}{42}$$

$$0.0714 < \lambda_0 < 0.170$$

using the chi-square distribution with 42 degrees of freedom. An approximate 95% confidence interval for λ_1 is

$$\frac{(0.0251)(8.23)}{18} < \lambda_1 < \frac{(0.0251)(31.53)}{18}$$

$$0.0115 < \lambda_1 < 0.0439$$

based on the chi-square distribution with 18 degrees of freedom. The first confidence interval is exact because the control group contains no censored observations, and the second confidence interval is approximate because the treatment group has randomly censored observations. Since these confidence intervals have no overlap, it can be concluded that 6-MP is effective in increasing remission times.

Since exact confidence intervals apply only to the two-sample case with exponential baseline distribution, no censored values, and Type II censoring, asymptotic intervals will also be calculated here to illustrate how they are developed in the general case. The Fisher information matrix cannot be calculated here since the observed data values do not have corresponding censoring times. The observed information matrix is easily calculated using the matrix formulation

$$O(\hat{\boldsymbol{\beta}}) = \mathbf{Z}'\hat{\mathbf{B}}\,\mathbf{Z} = \begin{bmatrix} 30 & 9 \\ 9 & 9 \end{bmatrix},$$

where $\hat{\mathbf{B}}$ is a 42×42 diagonal matrix whose elements are $x_1 e^{\hat{\boldsymbol{\beta}}'z_1}$, $x_2 e^{\hat{\boldsymbol{\beta}}'z_2}$, ..., $x_{42} e^{\hat{\boldsymbol{\beta}}'z_{42}}$. Since the determinant of this matrix is $(30)(9) - 9^2 = 189$, it has inverse

$$O^{-1}(\hat{\boldsymbol{\beta}}) = \begin{bmatrix} \dfrac{9}{189} & -\dfrac{9}{189} \\ -\dfrac{9}{189} & \dfrac{30}{189} \end{bmatrix},$$

which estimates the variance–covariance matrix of the maximum likelihood estimates. The negative elements on the off-diagonal positions indicate a negative correlation between β_0 and β_1. The square roots of the diagonal elements yield asymptotic estimates for the standard deviation of the regression parameter estimates. Thus the asymptotic estimated standard deviation of the estimate for β_0 is $\sqrt{\frac{9}{189}} = 0.218$, and the asymptotic estimated standard deviation of the estimate for β_1 is $\sqrt{\frac{30}{189}} = 0.398$. These values can be used in the usual fashion to obtain asymptotically valid confidence intervals and perform hypothesis testing with respect to the regression parameter estimates. Note that $\hat{\beta}_1 = -1.53$ is more than three standard deviation units away from 0, supporting the fact that there is a statistically significant difference between the patients that take 6-MP versus those that do not with respect to their remission times. Since the sign of $\hat{\beta}_1$ is negative, the drug prolongs the remission times. More specifically, since the accelerated life model is being used, a patient taking the 6-MP drug will "age," or move along the time axis, at a rate that is $e^{\hat{\beta}_1} = e^{-1.53} = 0.217$ times that of a patient who does not take the drug.

Weibull Baseline Distribution

When the baseline distribution is Weibull in the accelerated life model, the situation is more complicated mathematically, but the same principles apply. There are now two unknown parameters for the baseline distribution, the scale parameter λ and the shape parameter κ. Based on the accelerated life model assumption $H(t, \mathbf{z}) = H_0(t\,\psi(\mathbf{z}))$ and using the Weibull baseline cumulative hazard function $H_0(t) = (\lambda t)^\kappa$, the cumulative hazard function is

$$H(t, \mathbf{z}, \lambda, \kappa, \boldsymbol{\beta}) = H_0(t\psi(\mathbf{z})) = (\lambda\, e^{\boldsymbol{\beta}'\mathbf{z}} t)^\kappa \qquad t \geq 0,$$

where $\mathbf{z} = (z_1, \ldots, z_q)'$ and $\boldsymbol{\beta} = (\beta_1, \ldots, \beta_q)'$. The scale parameter in the baseline distribution can again be absorbed into the regression coefficient vector by defining an additional covariate, $z_0 = 1$ for all n items on test. As in the case of the exponential baseline, let $\lambda = e^{\beta_0 z_0}$. The cumulative hazard function can now be expressed more compactly as

$$H(t, \mathbf{z}, \kappa, \boldsymbol{\beta}) = (e^{\boldsymbol{\beta}'\mathbf{z}} t)^\kappa = e^{\kappa\boldsymbol{\beta}'\mathbf{z}} t^\kappa \qquad t \geq 0,$$

where $\mathbf{z} = (z_0, z_1, \ldots, z_q)'$ and $\boldsymbol{\beta} = (\beta_0, \beta_1, \ldots, \beta_q)'$. Since $h(t) = H'(t)$, the corresponding hazard function is

$$h(t, \mathbf{z}, \kappa, \boldsymbol{\beta}) = \kappa\, e^{\kappa\boldsymbol{\beta}'\mathbf{z}} t^{\kappa-1} \qquad t \geq 0.$$

The log likelihood function is

$$\log L(\kappa, \boldsymbol{\beta}) = \sum_{i \in U} \log h(x_i, \mathbf{z}_i, \kappa, \boldsymbol{\beta}) - \sum_{i=1}^{n} H(x_i, \mathbf{z}_i, \kappa, \boldsymbol{\beta})$$

$$= \sum_{i \in U} \left[\log \kappa + \kappa\boldsymbol{\beta}'\mathbf{z}_i + (\kappa - 1) \log x_i \right] - \sum_{i=1}^{n} e^{\kappa\boldsymbol{\beta}'\mathbf{z}_i} x_i^\kappa$$

$$= r \log \kappa + \kappa \sum_{i \in U} \boldsymbol{\beta}' \mathbf{z}_i + (\kappa - 1) \sum_{i \in U} \log x_i - \sum_{i=1}^{n} e^{\kappa \boldsymbol{\beta}' \mathbf{z}_i} x_i^{\kappa}.$$

This expression must be differentiated with respect to κ and β_j, $j = 0, 1, \ldots, q$ and the resulting equations set equal to zero and solved to obtain $\hat{\kappa}$ and $\hat{\boldsymbol{\beta}}$. This $(q+2) \times (q+2)$ set of nonlinear equations must be solved numerically. Asymptotically valid confidence intervals for the parameters can be obtained by calculating the inverse of the observed information matrix, which involves differentiating each element of the score vector.

9.3   PROPORTIONAL HAZARDS

Parameter estimation for the proportional hazards model can be divided into two cases: when the baseline distribution form is known and when it is unknown. When the baseline is known, the procedure follows along the same lines as in the previous section. The proportional hazards model assumptions are

$$h(t, \mathbf{z}, \boldsymbol{\theta}, \boldsymbol{\beta}) = \psi(\mathbf{z}) \, h_0(t) = e^{\boldsymbol{\beta}' \mathbf{z}} \, h_0(t)$$

and

$$H(t, \mathbf{z}, \boldsymbol{\theta}, \boldsymbol{\beta}) = \psi(\mathbf{z}) \, H_0(t) = e^{\boldsymbol{\beta}' \mathbf{z}} \, H_0(t),$$

where $\boldsymbol{\theta}$ is a vector of unknown parameters associated with the baseline distribution. The log likelihood function is

$$\log L(\boldsymbol{\theta}, \boldsymbol{\beta}) = \sum_{i \in U} \log h(x_i, \mathbf{z}_i, \boldsymbol{\theta}, \boldsymbol{\beta}) - \sum_{i=1}^{n} H(x_i, \mathbf{z}_i, \boldsymbol{\theta}, \boldsymbol{\beta})$$

$$= \sum_{i \in U} [\boldsymbol{\beta}' \mathbf{z}_i + \log h_0(x_i)] - \sum_{i=1}^{n} e^{\boldsymbol{\beta}' \mathbf{z}_i} \, H_0(x_i).$$

This expression can be differentiated with respect to all the unknown parameters to arrive at the score vector and then equated to zero and solved numerically to arrive at the maximum likelihood estimates. Since the accelerated life and proportional hazards coincide when the baseline distribution is assumed to be Weibull, the derivations in the previous section can be used for Weibull baselines in the proportional hazards case. The derivations for other baseline distributions unfold analogously, so further attention will be focused on cases for which the baseline distribution is unknown.

In many applications, the baseline distribution is not known. Furthermore, the modeler may not be interested in the baseline distribution, rather only in the influence of the covariates on survival. A technique has been developed for the proportional hazards model that allows the coefficient vector $\boldsymbol{\beta}$ to be estimated without knowledge of the parametric form of the baseline distribution. This type of analysis may be appropriate when the modeler wants to detect which covariates are significant, to determine which covariate is the most significant, or to analyze interactions among covariates. This technique is characteristic of nonparametric methods since it is impossible to misspecify the baseline distribution.

The focus of this estimation technique is on the *indexes* of the components on test, as will be seen in the derivation to follow. Since this procedure is very different from all previous estimation work, an example will be carried through the derivation to illustrate the notation and the method. The purpose in this small example is to determine whether light bulb wattage influences light bulb survival. In this example and the derivation, it is initially assumed that there is no censoring and there are no tied observations.

Example 9.2

A set of $n = 3$ light bulbs are placed on test. The first and second bulbs are 100-watt bulbs and the third bulb is a 60-watt bulb. A single ($q = 1$) covariate z_1 assumes the value 0 for a 60-watt bulb and 1 for a 100-watt bulb. The purpose of the test is to determine if the wattage has any influence on the survival distribution of the bulbs. The baseline distribution is unknown and unspecified, so there is only one parameter in the proportional hazards model, the regression coefficient β_1, that needs to be estimated. This small data set is used for illustrative purposes only, and we would obviously need to collect more than three data points to detect any statistically significant difference between the two wattages. Let $t_1 = 80$, $t_2 = 20$, and $t_3 = 50$ denote the lifetimes of the three bulbs. From the notation developed earlier in this chapter,

$$\mathbf{x} = \begin{bmatrix} 80 \\ 20 \\ 50 \end{bmatrix} \qquad \boldsymbol{\delta} = \begin{bmatrix} 1 \\ 1 \\ 1 \end{bmatrix} \qquad \mathbf{Z} = \begin{bmatrix} 1 \\ 1 \\ 0 \end{bmatrix}.$$

The order statistics are $t_{(1)} = 20$, $t_{(2)} = 50$, and $t_{(3)} = 80$. Figure 9.2 illustrates the definitions made thus far. The *risk set* $R(t)$, parameterized by the failure times, is defined as the set of indexes of bulbs at risk just prior to t. In this case

$$R(t_{(1)}) = R(t_2) = \{1, 2, 3\}$$

since all bulbs are at risk just prior to $t_{(1)}$. At time $t_{(2)}$, the risk set is

$$R(t_{(2)}) = R(t_3) = \{1, 3\}$$

since bulbs 1 and 3 are at risk just prior to $t_{(2)}$. Finally, at time $t_{(3)}$ the risk set is

$$R(t_{(3)}) = R(t_1) = \{1\}$$

since only bulb 1 is still on test just prior to $t_{(3)}$. Similar to the concept of a pointer array from computer science, a *rank vector* $\mathbf{r}$ is used here to simplify the notation. The ith element of the rank vector is the index of the item that fails at $t_{(i)}$, for $i = 1, 2, 3$. In this case

$$\mathbf{r} = \begin{bmatrix} 2 \\ 3 \\ 1 \end{bmatrix}$$

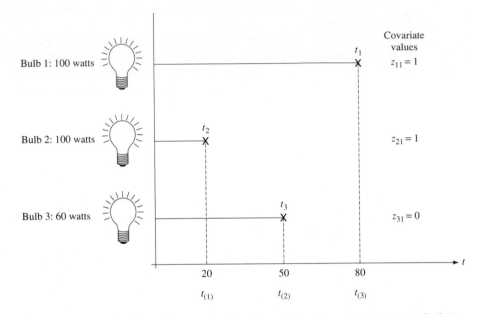

Figure 9.2 Proportional hazards parameter estimation notation. (*Source*: D. R. Cox and D. Oakes, *Analysis of Survival Data*, 1984. Adapted and reprinted by permission of Chapman and Hall.)

since bulb 2 fails first, bulb 3 fails next, and bulb 1 fails last. The failure times can thus be determined from the order statistics and the rank vector.

The notation defined in the example is easily extended from three items on test with a single, binary covariate to the general case. Let $t_1, t_2, \ldots, t_n$ be n distinct lifetimes and t_i has an associated $q \times 1$ vector of covariates $\mathbf{z}_i$, for $i = 1, 2, \ldots, n$. The ith-order statistic is given by $t_{(i)}$, $i = 1, 2, \ldots, n$, and the risk set $R(t_{(i)})$ is the set of indexes of all items that are at risk just prior to $t_{(i)}$. The ith element of the rank vector $\mathbf{r}$ is the index of the item that fails at $t_{(i)}$, for $i = 1, 2, \ldots, n$. The failure times and their associated indexes are equivalent to the order statistics and the rank vector. Now that the notation has been defined, the emphasis switches to determining the probability that a particular permutation of the indexes has appeared in the rank vector.

Example 9.3

The joint distribution of the elements of the rank vector, $f(r_1, r_2, r_3)$, is now considered for the data set containing three elements. In this case there are $3! = 6$ possible permutations of the ranks of the elements:

$$\begin{bmatrix} 1 \\ 2 \\ 3 \end{bmatrix} \begin{bmatrix} 1 \\ 3 \\ 2 \end{bmatrix} \begin{bmatrix} 2 \\ 1 \\ 3 \end{bmatrix} \begin{bmatrix} 2 \\ 3 \\ 1 \end{bmatrix} \begin{bmatrix} 3 \\ 1 \\ 2 \end{bmatrix} \begin{bmatrix} 3 \\ 2 \\ 1 \end{bmatrix}.$$

If the wattage of the light bulb had no influence on survival, then clearly $f(r_1, r_2, r_3) = \frac{1}{6}$ for all six permutations, since all three items are drawn from a homogeneous population with respect to survival. The mass function for the rank vector will be determined by finding the conditional probabilities associated with the ranks. For example, assume that a failure has just occurred at time $t_{(2)} = 50$, and the history up to time 50, that is, bulb 2 failed at time $t_{(1)} = 20$, is known. The bulb that fails at time 50 is either bulb 1 or bulb 3. For small Δt, the conditional probability that the bulb failing at time 50 is bulb 1 is

$$P[r_2 = 1 \mid t_{(1)} = 20, t_{(2)} = 50, r_1 = 2] = \frac{P[\text{bulb 1 fails at time 50}]}{P[\text{one item from } R(t_{(2)}) \text{ fails at time 50}]}$$

$$= \frac{h(50; z_{11}) \Delta t}{h(50; z_{11}) \Delta t + h(50; z_{13})\Delta t}$$

$$= \frac{h(50; z_{11})}{h(50; z_{11}) + h(50; z_{13})}$$

$$= \frac{\psi(z_{11})h_0(50)}{\psi(z_{11})h_0(50) + \psi(z_{13})h_0(50)}$$

$$= \frac{\psi(z_{11})}{\psi(z_{11}) + \psi(z_{13})}$$

$$= \frac{e^{\beta_1 z_{11}}}{e^{\beta_1 z_{11}} + e^{\beta_1 z_{13}}}$$

$$= \frac{e^{\beta_1}}{e^{\beta_1} + 1},$$

since the first bulb is 100 watts ($z_{11} = 1$) and the third bulb is 60 watts ($z_{13} = 0$). Note that the baseline hazard function has dropped out of this expression, so this probability will be the same regardless of the choice of $h_0(t)$. Also, the first two order statistics, $t_{(1)}$ and $t_{(2)}$, were not used in the calculation of this conditional probability. By similar reasoning, the conditional probability that the 60-watt bulb is the second to fail is

$$P[r_2 = 3 \mid t_{(1)} = 20, t_{(2)} = 50, r_1 = 2] = \frac{1}{e^{\beta_1} + 1}.$$

In the example, as well as in the general case, the conditional probability expression does not involve the failure times, making it possible to shorten $P[r_j = i \mid t_{(1)}, t_{(2)}, \ldots, t_{(j)}, r_1, r_2, \ldots, r_{j-1}]$ to $P[r_j = i \mid r_1, r_2, \ldots, r_{j-1}]$. The probability that the jth element of the rank vector will be equal to i, given $t_{(j)}$ and the failure history up to $t_{(j)}$, is

$$P[r_j = i \mid r_1, r_2, \ldots, r_{j-1}] = \frac{h(t_{(j)}; \mathbf{z}_i) \Delta t}{\displaystyle\sum_{k \in R(t_{(j)})} h(t_{(j)}; \mathbf{z}_k) \Delta t}$$

$$= \frac{h(t_{(j)}; \mathbf{z}_i)}{\displaystyle\sum_{k \in R(t_{(j)})} h(t_{(j)}; \mathbf{z}_k)}$$

$$= \frac{\psi(\mathbf{z}_i) h_0(t_{(j)})}{\displaystyle\sum_{k \in R(t_{(j)})} \psi(\mathbf{z}_k) h_0(t_{(j)})}$$

$$= \frac{\psi(\mathbf{z}_i)}{\displaystyle\sum_{k \in R(t_{(j)})} \psi(\mathbf{z}_k)}$$

$$= \frac{e^{\boldsymbol{\beta}' \mathbf{z}_i}}{\displaystyle\sum_{k \in R(t_{(j)})} e^{\boldsymbol{\beta}' \mathbf{z}_k}}.$$

Example 9.4

It is now a simple task to use this conditional probability to determine the probability mass function for the indexes. For the three light bulbs, this mass function is

$$f(r_1, r_2, r_3) = f(r_3 \mid r_1, r_2) \, f(r_1, r_2)$$

$$= f(r_3 \mid r_1, r_2) \, f(r_2 \mid r_1) \, f(r_1)$$

$$= f(r_1) \, f(r_2 \mid r_1) \, f(r_3 \mid r_1, r_2)$$

over all six permutations of the rank vector. Since the sequence that was observed for the rank vector was $(2, 3, 1)$, this becomes

$$f(2, 3, 1) = f(2) \, f(3 \mid 2) \, f(1 \mid 2, 3)$$

$$= \frac{\psi(z_{12})}{\psi(z_{11}) + \psi(z_{12}) + \psi(z_{13})} \frac{\psi(z_{13})}{\psi(z_{11}) + \psi(z_{13})} \frac{\psi(z_{11})}{\psi(z_{11})}$$

$$= \frac{e^{\beta_1 z_{12}}}{e^{\beta_1 z_{11}} + e^{\beta_1 z_{12}} + e^{\beta_1 z_{13}}} \frac{e^{\beta_1 z_{13}}}{e^{\beta_1 z_{11}} + e^{\beta_1 z_{13}}}$$

$$= \frac{e^{\beta_1}}{e^{\beta_1} + e^{\beta_1} + 1} \frac{1}{e^{\beta_1} + 1}$$

$$= \frac{e^{\beta_1}}{(2e^{\beta_1} + 1)(e^{\beta_1} + 1)}.$$

Treating this expression as a likelihood function $L(\beta_1)$, the problem reduces to determining the β_1 value that maximizes the log likelihood function

$$\log L(\beta_1) = \beta_1 - \log(2e^{\beta_1} + 1) - \log(e^{\beta_1} + 1).$$

The score statistic is

$$\frac{\partial \log L(\beta_1)}{\partial \beta_1} = 1 - \frac{2e^{\beta_1}}{2e^{\beta_1} + 1} - \frac{e^{\beta_1}}{e^{\beta_1} + 1}.$$

Solving for the maximum likelihood estimator using numerical methods, $\hat{\beta}_1 = -0.347$, indicating that there is lower risk for the 100-watt bulbs than for 60-watt bulbs. More specifically, the hazard function for 100-watt light bulbs is $e^{\hat{\beta}_1} = e^{-0.347} = 0.706$ times that of the baseline hazard function for 60-watt bulbs, regardless of what baseline distribution is considered. To see if this regression coefficient is statistically significant involves calculating the derivative of the score:

$$-\frac{\partial^2 \log L(\beta_1)}{\partial \beta_1^2} = \frac{2e^{\beta_1}}{(2e^{\beta_1} + 1)^2} + \frac{e^{\beta_1}}{(e^{\beta_1} + 1)^2}.$$

When this expression is evaluated at $\beta_1 = \hat{\beta}_1 = -0.347$, the observed information is 0.485, so the asymptotic estimate of the variance of β_1 is $1/0.485 = 2.06$, and the asymptotic estimate of the standard deviation of β_1 is $\sqrt{2.06} = 1.44$. Since $\hat{\beta}_1$ is only a fraction of a standard deviation away from 0, z_1 is not statistically significant. This result is not surprising considering the small sample size. Note that these values are only asymptotically correct and are obviously poor approximations when $n = 3$. In addition, only the order of the failure times and not their numerical values were used to find $\hat{\beta}_1$. This means, for example, that the failure time of the third bulb, t_3, could have fallen anywhere on the interval (20, 80), and the estimate would have been the same since the order of the observed failure times was not changed.

The procedure for estimating β_1 can be generalized from the example without any significant difficulties. The mass function for the indexes, or the likelihood function for $\boldsymbol{\beta}$, is now

$$L(\boldsymbol{\beta}) = f(r_1)\, f(r_2 \mid r_1) \ldots f(r_n \mid r_1, r_2, \ldots, r_{n-1})$$

$$= \prod_{j=1}^{n} \frac{\psi(\mathbf{z}_{r_j})}{\displaystyle\sum_{k \in R(t_{(j)})} \psi(\mathbf{z}_k)}$$

$$= \prod_{j=1}^{n} \frac{e^{\boldsymbol{\beta}'\mathbf{z}_{r_j}}}{\displaystyle\sum_{k \in R(t_{(j)})} e^{\boldsymbol{\beta}'\mathbf{z}_k}}.$$

The log likelihood is

$$\log L(\boldsymbol{\beta}) = \sum_{j=1}^{n} \left[\boldsymbol{\beta}'\mathbf{z}_{r_j} - \log \sum_{k \in R(t_{(j)})} e^{\boldsymbol{\beta}'\mathbf{z}_k} \right].$$

The score vector has sth component

$$\frac{\partial \log L(\boldsymbol{\beta})}{\partial \beta_s} = \sum_{j=1}^{n} \left[z_{sr_j} - \frac{\displaystyle\sum_{k \in R(t_{(j)})} z_{sk} e^{\boldsymbol{\beta}'\mathbf{z}_k}}{\displaystyle\sum_{k \in R(t_{(j)})} e^{\boldsymbol{\beta}'\mathbf{z}_k}} \right]$$

for $s = 1, 2, \ldots, q$. The vector of maximum likelihood estimators $\hat{\boldsymbol{\beta}}$ is obtained when the score vector is equated to zero and solved. To determine an estimate for the variance of $\hat{\boldsymbol{\beta}}$, the score vector must be differentiated, yielding the observed information matrix. The diagonal elements of the inverse of the observed information matrix are asymptotically valid estimates of the variance of $\hat{\boldsymbol{\beta}}$.

There are two approaches to handle right censoring that do not significantly complicate the derivation presented thus far. The first approach is to assume that right censoring occurs immediately after a failure occurs. This assumption is valid for a Type II censored data set, but will involve an approximation for more general right-censoring schemes. In this case the rank vector is shortened to only r elements, corresponding to the indexes of the observed failure times $t_{(1)}, t_{(2)}, \ldots, t_{(r)}$. The likelihood function is

$$L(\boldsymbol{\beta}) = \prod_{j=1}^{r} \frac{\psi(\mathbf{z}_{r_j})}{\sum\limits_{k \in R(t_{(j)})} \psi(\mathbf{z}_k)} = \prod_{j=1}^{r} \frac{e^{\boldsymbol{\beta}'\mathbf{z}_{r_j}}}{\sum\limits_{k \in R(t_{(j)})} e^{\boldsymbol{\beta}'\mathbf{z}_k}}.$$

The log likelihood function is

$$\log L(\boldsymbol{\beta}) = \sum_{j=1}^{r} \left[\boldsymbol{\beta}'\mathbf{z}_{r_j} - \log \sum_{k \in R(t_{(j)})} e^{\boldsymbol{\beta}'\mathbf{z}_k} \right].$$

The score vector has sth component

$$\frac{\partial \log L(\boldsymbol{\beta})}{\partial \beta_s} = \sum_{j=1}^{r} \left[z_{sr_j} - \frac{\sum\limits_{k \in R(t_{(j)})} z_{sk} e^{\boldsymbol{\beta}'\mathbf{z}_k}}{\sum\limits_{k \in R(t_{(j)})} e^{\boldsymbol{\beta}'\mathbf{z}_k}} \right]$$

for $s = 1, 2, \ldots, q$.

The second approach to censoring is to write the likelihood function as the sum of all likelihoods for complete data sets that are consistent with the censoring pattern. Fortunately, this second approach yields the same likelihood function as the first approach, as illustrated by the following example.

Example 9.5

In the previous example, the data set consisted of three observed failure times: 80, 20, 50. Now, if the situation changes to where the third light bulb is right censored at time 50, the data set is 80, 20, 50*. This situation is illustrated in Figure 9.3. Using the first approach, the observed rank vector is now $\mathbf{r} = (2, 1)$, and the likelihood function is

$$L(\beta_1) = \prod_{j=1}^{2} \frac{\psi(z_{r_j})}{\sum\limits_{k \in R(t_{(j)})} \psi(z_k)}$$

$$= \frac{\psi(z_{12})}{\psi(z_{11}) + \psi(z_{12}) + \psi(z_{13})} \frac{\psi(z_{11})}{\psi(z_{11})}$$

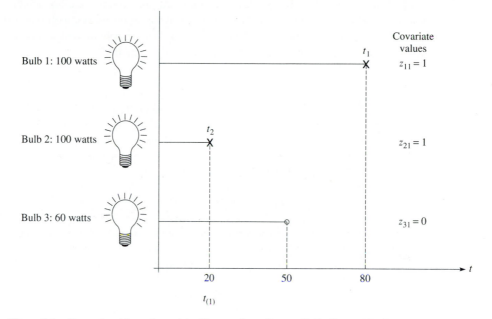

Figure 9.3   Proportional hazards model with censoring. (*Source*: D. R. Cox and D. Oakes, *Analysis of Survival Data*, 1984. Adapted and reprinted by permission of Chapman and Hall.)

$$= \frac{\psi(z_{12})}{\psi(z_{11}) + \psi(z_{12}) + \psi(z_{13})}.$$

For the second approach, there are two possibilities for the rank vector if there was no censoring: if the second bulb failed before time 80, the observed rank vector would be (2, 3, 1); if the second bulb failed after time 80, the observed rank vector would be (2, 1, 3). In the first case, the likelihood function would be that from the previous example:

$$\frac{\psi(z_{12})}{\psi(z_{11}) + \psi(z_{12}) + \psi(z_{13})} \frac{\psi(z_{13})}{\psi(z_{11}) + \psi(z_{13})} \frac{\psi(z_{11})}{\psi(z_{11})}.$$

In the second case, the likelihood function would be

$$\frac{\psi(z_{12})}{\psi(z_{11}) + \psi(z_{12}) + \psi(z_{13})} \frac{\psi(z_{11})}{\psi(z_{11}) + \psi(z_{13})} \frac{\psi(z_{13})}{\psi(z_{13})},$$

and the sum of these two likelihood functions is

$$\frac{\psi(z_{12})}{\psi(z_{11}) + \psi(z_{12}) + \psi(z_{13})},$$

which is the same result as in the first approach.

Tied values are typically handled by an approximation. When there are several failures at the same time value, each is assumed to contribute the same term to the likelihood function. Consequently, all the items with tied failure times are included in the risk set at the time of the tied observation. This approximation works well when there are not many tied observations in the data set and has been implemented in many software packages that estimate the vector of regression coefficients $\boldsymbol{\beta}$.

Example 9.6

Using the 6-MP drug experiment with a single binary covariate z_1 to denote the control $(z_1 = 0)$ and treatment $(z_1 = 1)$ cases, the maximum likelihood estimate for the single regression parameter is $\hat{\beta}_1 = -1.51$. This differs only slightly from the corresponding value in the accelerated life model in Example 9.1, where the values of the failure times were used. The value obtained in Example 9.1 was -1.53. The log likelihood function attains a value of -86.38 at the maximum likelihood value, the observed information matrix has a single value 5.962, and the inverse of the observed information matrix is $1/5.962 = 0.168$. This means that an asymptotic estimate of the standard deviation of the maximum likelihood estimate is $\sqrt{\hat{V}[\hat{\beta}_1]} = \sqrt{0.168} = 0.41$, which indicates that the maximum likelihood estimate is $1.51/0.41 = 3.7$ standard deviations units away from 0. It can be concluded, with a P-value less than 0.001, that the 6-MP drug is effective in increasing the remission times for leukemia patients, assuming that the proportional hazards model is appropriate here. Regardless of the baseline hazard function $h_0(t)$ chosen, the hazard function in the treatment case is $e^{\hat{\beta}_1} = e^{-0.151} = 0.221$ times that of the baseline hazard function for all time values. Note that no work has been done here to assess model adequacy, and all these conclusions have been based on the fact that the proportional hazards model adequately describes the situation.

The next example moves from the case of a single binary covariate to a single covariate that can assume a continuous range of values.

Example 9.7

Forty motorettes were placed on test at four different temperatures, 150°, 170°, 190°, and 220°C. The failure times are given in Example 8.4. This is an accelerated test, and the modeler is trying to determine how the motors will perform at the operating temperature of 130°C. The original authors used the single covariate $z_1 = 1000/(273.2 + °C)$, and eliminated the data at 150°C since there were no observed failures. In addition, failure times are treated as exact, even though interval censoring was evident by the way the data were collected. These assumptions are followed in the analysis performed here. Thus, at the temperatures 170°, 190°, and 220°C, the covariate z_1 assumes the values 2.26, 2.16, and 2.03. The maximum likelihood estimate for the regression parameter is $\hat{\beta}_1 = -13.8$. The log likelihood attains a value of -40.6 at the maximum likelihood value, the observed information matrix has a single value 0.031, and the inverse of the observed information matrix is $1/0.031 = 32.3$. This means that an asymptotic estimate of the standard deviation of the maximum likelihood estimate is $\sqrt{32.3} = 5.68$, which indicates that temperature does indeed influence survival. Assuming that the proportional hazards model is appropriate here for temperatures between 170° and 220°C, the fitted model is

$$h(t; z_1) = e^{-13.8z_1} h_0(t),$$

where $h_0(t)$ is any baseline distribution. To determine the lifetime distribution of the motorettes at the operating temperature of 130°C or, equivalently, $z_1 = 2.48$, the baseline distribution must be estimated. It must also be assumed that the model may be extrapolated beyond the range of the data values collected. The baseline distribution can be estimated parametrically conditioned on the values of the regression coefficients using the techniques from Chapter 8, or it can be estimated nonparametrically using the techniques introduced in Chapter 10.

Finally, the last example moves from the single covariate case to the case for which there are q covariates, and the analyst is attempting to determine which of the covariates significantly influences survival.

Example 9.8

The proportional hazards model has been used in diverse applications, such as recidivism, which considers the probability that an inmate will return to prison in the future after release. Recidivism can be predicted using survival models. Several factors related to inmate background that could affect an inmate's adjustment to society are potential screening variables. North Carolina collected recidivism data on $n = 1540$ prisoners in 1978. The lifetime of interest here is the time of release until the time of return to prison. Obviously, all inmates will not return to prison, so a more complicated *split model,* for which some of the lifetimes are assumed to be infinite, may also be used. In addition, there is significant censoring in the data set. The purpose of the study is to assess the impact of the $q = 15$ covariates. Table 9.2 presents the estimates of the regression coefficients and their standard deviations in order of their significance. The column labeled *Covariate* gives a short description of the covariate considered. The next two columns give the regression coefficient estimator and an asymptotic estimate of its standard deviation. The column labeled $\hat{\beta}/\sqrt{\hat{V}[\hat{\beta}]}$ gives a test statistic for testing H_0: $\beta_i = 0$ versus H_1: $\beta_i \neq 0$, for $i = 1, 2, \ldots, 15$. The column labeled *P-value* indicates the significance of the covariates. A value less than $\alpha = 0.05$ indicates that a covariate is a significant indicator of recidivism. Ten of the fifteen covariates are significant. The covariates are time served, age, number of prior convictions, number of rule violations in prison, education, race, gender, alcohol problems, drug problems, marital status, probationary period, participation in a work release program, type of crime, crime against person, and crime against property. Note that many of these covariates are indicator variables.

9.4   FURTHER READING

The model formulation and notation used here are similar to that used in Cox and Oakes (1984) and Kalbfleisch and Prentice (1980). Software packages for parameter estimation and model adequacy assessment are reviewed in Nelson (1990, pp. 238–239).

More details on the accelerated life and proportional hazards models are contained in Cox and Oakes (1984) and Lawless (1982). Kalbfleisch and Prentice (1980, pp. 52–54) give two additional significance tests for a single binary covariate in addition to the technique used in Example 9.1.

TABLE 9.2   NORTH CAROLINA RECIDIVISM MODEL

Name	Covariate	$\hat{\beta}$	$\sqrt{\hat{V}[\hat{\beta}]}$	$\dfrac{\hat{\beta}}{\sqrt{\hat{V}[\hat{\beta}]}}$	P-value	Significant
z_2	AGE	−3.3420	0.5195	−6.4328	0.0000	•
z_3	PRIORS	0.8355	0.1371	6.0957	0.0000	•
z_1	TSERVD	1.1666	0.1957	5.9616	0.0000	•
z_6	WHITE	−0.4444	0.0876	−5.0701	0.0000	•
z_8	ALCHY	0.4285	0.1043	4.1103	0.0000	•
z_{13}	FELON	−0.5782	0.1633	−3.5412	0.0002	•
z_9	JUNKY	0.2819	0.0970	2.9058	0.0018	•
z_7	MALE	0.6745	0.2423	2.7834	0.0027	•
z_{15}	PROPTY	0.3894	0.1578	2.4678	0.0068	•
z_4	RULE	3.0788	1.6890	1.8229	0.0342	•
z_{10}	MARRIED	−0.1532	0.1077	−1.4227	0.0774	
z_5	SCHOOL	−0.2507	0.1933	−1.2966	0.0974	
z_{12}	WORKREL	0.0865	0.0902	0.9587	0.1688	
z_{14}	PERSON	0.0737	0.2425	0.3039	0.3806	
z_{11}	SUPER	−0.0088	0.0966	−0.0914	0.4636	

Source: P. Schmidt and A. D. Witte, *Predicting Recidivism Using Survival Models*, 1988. Adapted and reprinted by permission of Springer-Verlag New York, Inc.

The original work on the proportional hazards models is from Cox (1972), and the derivation given here parallels that of Cox and Oakes (1984), where time-dependent covariates are considered. Figures 9.2 and 9.3 are similar to Figure 7.1 from Cox and Oakes (1984, p. 92). Ties in the data are treated by Peto (1972), where ratios corresponding to tied observations are simply multiplied together in the likelihood function. Cox and Oakes (1984, pp. 101–104) have a separate section on tied observations. Kalbfleisch and Prentice (1980, pp. 58–59) analyze the motorette data from Nelson and Hahn (1972) given in Example 9.7. The North Carolina recidivism data in Example 9.8 are from Schmidt and Witte (1988). They compared the results of fitting the proportional hazards model and other survival models to recidivism data. Schmidt and Witte (1988) concluded that the time to return for prisoners in North Carolina has a nonmonotonic hazard function and that survival models including covariates are most appropriate. Ellermann et al. (1992) give a new approach to analyzing recidivism data using the quantile residual life function and give a good recidivism literature review.

The models presented in this chapter have been used in applications as diverse as brake discs on high speed trains (Bendell et al., 1986), air conditioning compressors (Landers and Kolarik, 1987), computer systems (Drury et al., 1988), weapons systems (Gray et al., 1988), transmission equipment failures (Baxter et al., 1988), and machine tools (Mazzuchi and Soyer, 1989).

9.5   EXERCISES

9.1.   Lawless (1982, p. 286) considers survival data (see Table 9.3) on $n = 40$ advanced lung cancer patients, which is a subset of a larger body of data. The purpose of the study is to compare the effects of two chemotherapy treatments: standard and test. There are $q = 7$ covariates associated with survival: z_1, performance status; z_2, age; z_3, months from diagnosis to entry into the study; z_4, tumor type (1 squamous, 0 otherwise), z_5, tumor size (1 small, 0 otherwise); z_6, tumor type (1 adeno, 0 otherwise); and z_7, treatment (1 test, 0 standard). He gives the following parameter estimates for the regression coefficients in the accelerated life model with an exponential baseline distribution: $\hat{\beta}_0 = 4.722$, $\hat{\beta}_1 = 0.0544$, $\hat{\beta}_2 = 0.0085$, $\hat{\beta}_3 = 0.0034$, $\hat{\beta}_4 = 0.3448$, $\hat{\beta}_5 = -0.121$, $\hat{\beta}_6 = -0.8634$, and $\hat{\beta}_7 = -0.2778$. Using these estimated regression coefficients, find the value of the log likelihood function at the maximum likelihood estimators. Center the first three covariates about their means to avoid any roundoff error.

9.2.   For Example 9.1, calculate the Fisher information matrix assuming that all x_i values denote failure times (that is, there is no censoring).

9.3.   Show that the observed information matrix for the accelerated life model with exponential baseline distribution in the two-sample case is

$$\begin{bmatrix} r & r_1 \\ r_1 & r_1 \end{bmatrix}.$$

TABLE 9.3

x_i	δ_i	z_1	z_2	z_3	z_4	z_5	z_6	z_7
411	1	70	64	5	1	0	0	1
126	1	60	63	9	1	0	0	1
118	1	70	65	11	1	0	0	1
92	1	40	69	10	1	0	0	1
8	1	40	63	58	1	0	0	1
25	0	70	48	9	1	0	0	1
11	1	70	48	11	1	0	0	1
54	1	80	63	4	0	1	0	1
153	1	60	63	14	0	1	0	1
16	1	30	53	4	0	1	0	1
56	1	80	43	12	0	1	0	1
21	1	40	55	2	0	1	0	1
287	1	60	66	25	0	1	0	1
10	1	40	67	23	0	1	0	1
8	1	20	61	19	0	0	1	1
12	1	50	63	4	0	0	1	1
177	1	50	66	16	0	0	0	1
12	1	40	68	12	0	0	0	1
200	1	80	41	12	0	0	0	1
250	1	70	53	8	0	0	0	1
100	1	60	37	13	0	0	0	1
999	1	90	54	12	1	0	0	0
231	0	50	52	8	1	0	0	0
991	1	70	50	7	1	0	0	0
1	1	20	65	21	1	0	0	0
201	1	80	52	28	1	0	0	0
44	1	60	70	13	1	0	0	0
15	1	50	40	13	1	0	0	0
103	0	70	36	22	0	1	0	0
2	1	40	44	36	0	1	0	0
20	1	30	54	9	0	1	0	0
51	1	30	59	87	0	1	0	0
18	1	40	69	5	0	0	1	0
90	1	60	50	22	0	0	1	0
84	1	80	62	4	0	0	1	0
164	1	70	68	15	0	0	0	0
19	1	30	39	4	0	0	0	0
43	1	60	49	11	0	0	0	0
340	1	80	64	10	0	0	0	0
231	1	70	67	18	0	0	0	0

9.4. Compute the likelihood ratio statistic for the accelerated life model with an exponential baseline distribution for the 6-MP data set. Use this statistic to determine whether the value of z_1 significantly influences survival.

9.5. Find the elements of the score vector for the accelerated life model with a Weibull baseline distribution.

9.6. Find the elements of the score vector for the accelerated life model with a log logistic baseline distribution.

9.7. Consider a proportional hazards model with $n = 3$ items on test and distinct failure times t_1, t_2, t_3. Compute the joint mass value for the $3! = 6$ possible rank vectors, and show that they sum to 1.

9.8. For the data set in Example 9.2, if the second light bulb's failure time was censored at time 20 (rather than failing at time 20), show that the two approaches indicated for handling right censoring are equivalent.

9.9. A Cox proportional hazards model with unknown baseline distribution is fitted to a data set of drill bit failure times (in number of items drilled) with $q = 2$, for which the covariates denote the turning speed (revolutions per minute, rpm) and the hardness of the material (Brinell hardness number, bhn) being drilled. The turning speeds range from 2400 to 4800 rpm and the hardness of the materials ranges from 250 to 440 BHN. Interactions are not considered and the variables are not centered. The fitted model has estimated regression vector $\hat{\boldsymbol{\beta}} = (0.014 \quad 0.45)'$, and the inverse of the observed information matrix is

$$O^{-1}(\hat{\boldsymbol{\beta}}) = \begin{bmatrix} 0.000081 & 0.000016 \\ 0.000016 & 0.010000 \end{bmatrix}.$$

Write a paragraph interpreting these results.

9.10. Give the equations that must be solved in order to find the MLEs $\hat{\lambda}$, $\hat{\kappa}$, and $\hat{\boldsymbol{\beta}}$ for a proportional hazards model with log logistic baseline distribution and log linear link function. A random censoring scheme is used.

10

Nonparametric Methods and Model Adequacy

In the previous three chapters, the focus has been on fitting parametric models to a data set. The emphasis switches here to letting the data "speak for itself," rather than approximating the lifetime distribution by one of the parametric models. There are several reasons to take this approach. First, it is not always possible to find a parametric model that adequately describes the lifetime distribution. This is particularly true of data arising from populations with nonmonotonic hazard functions. The most popular parametric models, such as the exponential and Weibull, have monotonic hazard functions. A nonparametric analysis might provide more accurate estimates. Second, data sets are often so small that fitting a parametric model results in parameter estimators with confidence intervals that are so wide that they are of little use. Finally, obtaining raw data is not always possible, and some nonparametric methods may be used on grouped data.

The first section in this chapter addresses nonparametric estimates of the survivor function for raw data in the complete and right-censored cases. The second section considers *life tables*, which are used in situations for which grouped rather than raw data are available. Life tables are often used by actuaries to determine appropriate premiums for life and casualty insurance policies.

The last two sections concern assessing the adequacy of a parametric model to approximate a data set. Once a modeler has fitted a parametric model to a set of failure times, it is important to determine whether or not the model is a reasonable approximation to the data set. For simplicity, discussion here is limited to univariate lifetime distributions with no covariates. Since continuous models have been emphasized throughout the text, the Kolmogorov–Smirnov test is presented for complete, Type I, and Type II censored data sets, assuming that all the parameters are known a priori for the hypothesized distribution. The final section provides modifications of the

Kolmogorov–Smirnov test to accommodate a distribution with parameters estimated from sample data. There are many goodness-of-fit tests other than those presented here.

10.1   SURVIVOR FUNCTION ESTIMATION

Estimation of the survivor function from a set of raw data is considered in this section. Complete and right-censored data sets are considered separately. Using the ball bearing data set from Example 8.1, Figure 10.1 shows three survivor functions that illustrate one of the reasons that parametric analysis can lead to erroneous conclusions. A life test with $n = 23$ ball bearings placed on test is concluded when all the bearings fail. The highest survivor function on the graph denotes the population survivor function for the ball bearing lifetimes. The population survivor function represents the failure time distribution of all possible ball bearings from which the sample of $n = 23$ was drawn. This survivor function is typically unknown, of course, but if all the items in the population could be tested to failure under operating environmental conditions, a curve like this could be obtained. The second survivor function, which is a step function, is the nonparametric estimate from a sample of $n = 23$ ball bearing lifetimes sampled from the population. This particular nonparametric estimate of $S(t)$ is simply the number of bearings at risk at any time t, divided by n. This estimate takes jumps downward of size $1/n$ at each data point. Notice that, due to sampling error, this nonparametric estimate happens to lie below the true population survivor function for most time values, giving an overly pessimistic estimate of the survivor function. To make matters worse, the data

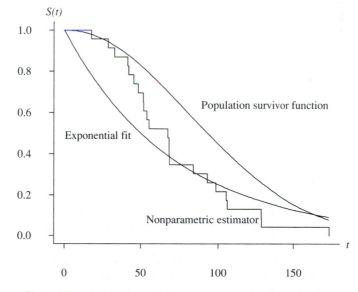

Figure 10.1   Parametric versus nonparametric survivor function estimates.

analyst is not careful and decides to fit an exponential distribution to this data set, which is clearly not appropriate here based on the shape of the step function. The third survivor function is the exponential fit to the data set using the usual estimate for the failure rate λ, the number of observed failures divided by the total time on test. Particularly for small t values, the fitted exponential survivor function is significantly lower than the population survivor function. Thus sampling error plus the use of an approximate model, the exponential, have taken their toll on this parametric estimate, and it clearly is a poor approximation of the population survivor function.

Consider the nonparametric estimation of the survivor function of a complete data set of n lifetimes with no ties. The function $R(t)$ introduced in Chapter 9, known as the risk set, contained the indexes of all items at risk just prior to time t. Let $n(t) = |R(t)|$ be the cardinality, or number of elements in $R(t)$. The simplest and most popular nonparametric estimate for the survivor function is

$$\hat{S}(t) = \frac{n(t)}{n} \qquad t \geq 0,$$

which is often referred to as the *empirical* survivor function. This step function has a downward step of $1/n$ at each observed lifetime. It is also the survivor function corresponding to a discrete distribution for which n mass values are equally likely. Ties are not difficult to adjust for since the formula for $\hat{S}(t)$ remains the same, and the function will take a downward step of d/n if there are d tied observations at a particular time value.

When there are no ties in the data set, determining asymptotically valid confidence intervals for the survivor function is based on the normal approximation to the binomial distribution. Recall that a binomial random variable X models the number of successes in n independent Bernoulli trials, each with probability of success p. The expected value and variance of the number of successes are $E[X] = np$ and $V[X] = np(1 - p)$. The fraction of successes, X / n, on the other hand, has expected value and variance $E[X / n] = p$ and $V[X / n] = p(1 - p)/n$.

Survival to time t can be considered a Bernoulli trial for each of the n items on test. Thus the number of items that survive to time t, or $n(t)$, has the binomial distribution with parameters n and probability of success $S(t)$, where success is defined to be survival to time t. The first survivor function estimate introduced, $\hat{S}(t) = n(t)/n$, is the fraction of successes having expected value $E[\hat{S}(t)] = S(t)$ and variance $V[\hat{S}(t)] = S(t)(1 - S(t))/n$. Furthermore, when the sample size n is large and $S(t)$ is not too close to 0 or 1, the binomial distribution assumes a shape that is closely approximated by a normal probability density function and thus can be used to find interval estimates for $S(t)$. Notice that these interval estimates are most accurate, in terms of coverage, around the median of the distribution, since the normal approximation to the binomial distribution works best when the probability of success is about $1/2$, where the binomial distribution is symmetric. Replacing $S(t)$ by $\hat{S}(t)$ in the variance formula, an asymptotically valid $100(1 - \alpha)\%$ confidence interval for the probability of survival to time t is

$$\hat{S}(t) - z_{\alpha/2}\sqrt{\frac{\hat{S}(t)(1-\hat{S}(t))}{n}} < S(t) < \hat{S}(t) + z_{\alpha/2}\sqrt{\frac{\hat{S}(t)(1-\hat{S}(t))}{n}}.$$

This confidence interval is also appropriate when there are tied observations, although it becomes more approximate as the number of ties increases. Confidence limits greater than 1 or less than 0 are typically truncated, as illustrated in the following example.

Example 10.1

> For the ball bearing data set from Example 8.1 with $n = 23$ bearings placed on test until failure, find a nonparametric survivor function estimator and a 95% confidence interval for the probability that a ball bearing will last 50,000,000 cycles.
>
> Recall that the ball bearing failure times in 10^6 revolutions are
>
> | | | | | | | | | |
> |-------|-------|-------|-------|-------|-------|-------|-------|-------|
> | 17.88 | 28.92 | 33.00 | 41.52 | 42.12 | 45.60 | 48.48 | 51.84 | 51.96 |
> | 54.12 | 55.56 | 67.80 | 68.64 | 68.64 | 68.88 | 84.12 | 93.12 | 98.64 |
> | | | 105.12 | 105.84 | 127.92 | 128.04 | 173.40. | | |

The nonparametric survivor function estimate $\hat{S}(t)$ is shown as the solid line in Figure 10.2. In this figure and others, the downward steps in $\hat{S}(t)$ have been connected by vertical lines. This is useful when visually comparing a nonparametric estimator of $S(t)$ to a fitted parametric model. The survivor function takes a downward step of 1/23 at each data value, with the exception of the tied value, 68.64, where it takes a downward step of 2/23. Some authors prefer to connect the survivor function estimates at the failure times with lines, although the step function (with risers) convention is adopted here. Since the data is given in 10^6 revolutions, a point estimate for the survivor function at $t = 50$ is $\hat{S}(50) =$

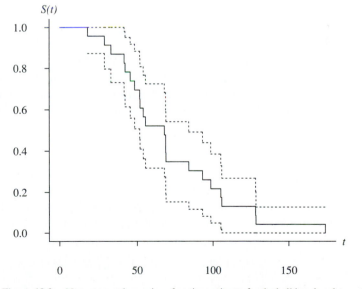

Figure 10.2   Nonparametric survivor function estimate for the ball bearing data set.

$16/23 = 0.696$, and a 95% confidence interval for the survivor function at $t = 50$ is

$$\hat{S}(50) - 1.96 \sqrt{\frac{\hat{S}(50)(1 - \hat{S}(50))}{23}} < S(50) < \hat{S}(50) + 1.96 \sqrt{\frac{\hat{S}(50)(1 - \hat{S}(50))}{23}},$$

which reduces to

$$0.508 < S(50) < 0.884.$$

This process can be done for all t values, yielding the 95% confidence bands for $S(t)$ given by the dashed lines in Figure 10.2. The confidence bands are truncated at 0 and 1. Also, the lower confidence band appears to be absent prior to the first observed failure at $t_{(1)} = 17.88$. This is due to the fact that $\hat{S}(t)$ is 1 for t values between 0 and the first failure time, so the upper and lower confidence limits are both equal to 1.

The general case for which there are both ties and right-censored values is now considered. Let $y_1 < y_2 < \cdots < y_k$ be the k distinct failure times, and let d_j denote the number of observed failures at y_j, $j = 1, 2, \ldots, k$. Let $n_j = n(y_j)$ denote the number of items on test just before time y_j, $j = 1, 2, \ldots, k$, and it is customary to include any values that are censored at y_j in this count. As usual, $R(y_j)$ is the set of all indexes of items that are at risk just before time y_j, $j = 1, 2, \ldots, k$.

The search for a survivor function estimator begins by assuming that the data arose from a discrete distribution with mass values at $y_1 < y_2 < \cdots < y_k$. For a discrete distribution, $h(y_j)$ is a conditional probability with interpretation $h(y_j) = P[T = y_j \mid T \geq y_j]$. As shown in Appendix F, the survivor function can be written in terms of the hazard function at the mass values:

$$S(t) = \prod_{j \in R(t)'} [1 - h(y_j)] \qquad t \geq 0,$$

where $R(t)'$ is the complement of the risk set at time t. Thus a reasonable estimator for $S(t)$ is $\prod_{j \in R(t)'} [1 - \hat{h}(y_j)]$, which reduces the problem of estimating the survivor function to that of estimating the hazard function at each mass value. An appropriate element for the likelihood function at mass value y_j is

$$h(y_j)^{d_j} [1 - h(y_j)]^{n_j - d_j}$$

for $j = 1, 2, \ldots, k$. The above expression is correct since d_j is the number of failures at y_j, $h(y_j)$ is the conditional probability of failure at y_j, $n_j - d_j$ is the number of items on test not failing at y_j, and $1 - h(y_j)$ is the probability of failing after time y_j conditioned on survival to time y_j. Thus the likelihood function for $h(y_1), h(y_2), \ldots, h(y_k)$ is

$$L(h(y_1), h(y_2), \ldots, h(y_k)) = \prod_{j=1}^{k} h(y_j)^{d_j} [1 - h(y_j)]^{n_j - d_j},$$

and the log likelihood function is

$$\log L(h(y_1), h(y_2), \ldots, h(y_k)) = \sum_{j=1}^{k} \left\{ d_j \log h(y_j) + (n_j - d_j) \log \left[1 - h(y_j) \right] \right\}.$$

The ith element of the score vector is

$$\frac{\partial \log L(h(y_1), h(y_2), \ldots, h(y_k))}{\partial h(y_i)} = \frac{d_i}{h(y_i)} - \frac{n_i - d_i}{1 - h(y_i)}$$

for $i = 1, 2, \ldots, k$. Equating this vector to zero and solving for $h(y_i)$ yields the maximum likelihood estimate:

$$\hat{h}(y_i) = \frac{d_i}{n_i}.$$

This estimate for $\hat{h}(y_i)$ is sensible, since d_i of the n_i items on test at time y_i fail, so the ratio of d_i to n_i is an appropriate estimate of the conditional probability of failure at time y_i. This derivation may strike a familiar chord since, at each time y_i, estimating $h(y_i)$ with d_i divided by n_i is equivalent to estimating the probability of "success," that is, failing at time y_i, for each of the n_i items on test. Thus this derivation is equivalent to finding the maximum likelihood estimators for the probability of success for k binomial random variables.

Using this particular estimate for the hazard function at y_i, the survivor function estimate becomes

$$\hat{S}(t) = \prod_{j \in R(t)'} [1 - \hat{h}(y_j)]$$

$$= \prod_{j \in R(t)'} \left[1 - \frac{d_j}{n_j} \right],$$

commonly known as the Kaplan–Meier or product-limit estimate. One problem that arises with the product-limit estimate is that it is not defined past the last observed failure time. The usual way to handle this problem is to cut the estimator off at the last observed failure time y_k. The following example illustrates the product-limit estimate.

Example 10.2

Find an estimate for $S(14)$ for the treatment group in the 6-MP experiment from Example 8.3.

The data set contains $n = 21$ patients on test, $r = 9$ observed failures, and $k = 7$ distinct failure times. The data values are

$$6 \quad 6 \quad 6 \quad 6* \quad 7 \quad 9* \quad 10 \quad 10* \quad 11* \quad 13 \quad 16$$
$$17* \quad 19* \quad 20* \quad 22 \quad 23 \quad 25* \quad 32* \quad 32* \quad 34* \quad 35*$$

and Table 10.1 gives the values of y_j, d_j, n_j, and $1 - d_j / n_j$ for $j = 1, 2, \ldots, 7$. In particular, the product-limit survivor function estimate at $t = 14$ weeks is

$$\hat{S}(14) = \prod_{j \in R(14)'} \left[1 - \frac{d_j}{n_j} \right]$$

TABLE 10.1   PRODUCT-LIMIT CALCULATIONS FOR
6-MP TREATMENT CASE

j	y_j	d_j	n_j	$1 - d_j/n_j$
1	6	3	21	$1 - \frac{3}{21}$
2	7	1	17	$1 - \frac{1}{17}$
3	10	1	15	$1 - \frac{1}{15}$
4	13	1	12	$1 - \frac{1}{12}$
5	16	1	11	$1 - \frac{1}{11}$
6	22	1	7	$1 - \frac{1}{7}$
7	23	1	6	$1 - \frac{1}{6}$

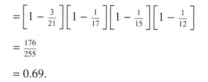

$$= \left[1 - \frac{3}{21}\right]\left[1 - \frac{1}{17}\right]\left[1 - \frac{1}{15}\right]\left[1 - \frac{1}{12}\right]$$

$$= \frac{176}{255}$$

$$= 0.69.$$

The product-limit survivor function estimate for all t values is plotted in Figure 10.3.
Downward steps occur only at observed failure times. The effect of censored

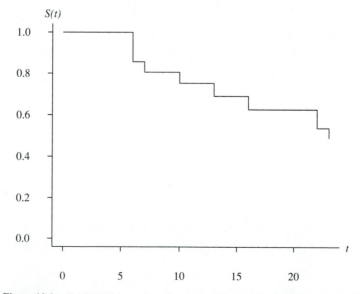

Figure 10.3   Product-limit survivor function estimate for the 6-MP treatment group.

observations in the survivor function estimate is a larger downward step at the next subsequent failure time. If there are ties between the observations and a censoring time, as there is at time 6, our convention of including the censored values in the risk set means that there will be a larger downward step following this tied value. Note that the estimate is truncated at time 23, since that is the last observed failure.

There is a second and perhaps more intuitive way of deriving the product-limit estimator. This derivation is based on the probability mass function and is illustrated on the 6-MP treatment group data set.

Example 10.3

For the $n = 21$ individuals in the treatment group for the 6-MP test, each failure/censoring time is initially given a mass value of $1/n$ as follows:

6	6	6	6 *	7	9 *	10	10 *	...
$\frac{1}{21}$	$\frac{1}{21}$	$\frac{1}{21}$	$\frac{1}{21}$	$\frac{1}{21}$	$\frac{1}{21}$	$\frac{1}{21}$	$\frac{1}{21}$	...

If there were no censored observations, the fractions would be the appropriate estimators for the probability mass function values. Combining the three tied observed failures at $t = 6$ yields

6	6 *	7	9 *	10	10 *	11 *	13	...
$\frac{1}{7}$	$\frac{1}{21}$	$\frac{1}{21}$	$\frac{1}{21}$	$\frac{1}{21}$	$\frac{1}{21}$	$\frac{1}{21}$	$\frac{1}{21}$	...

As indicated earlier, there are mass values in the product-limit estimator only at observed failure times. Since the random censoring model is assumed, the mass associated with the individual censored at 6 weeks can be split evenly among each of the 17 subsequent failure/censoring times:

6	6 *	7	9 *	10	10 *	11 *	13	...
$\frac{1}{7}$	0	$\frac{6}{119}$	$\frac{6}{119}$	$\frac{6}{119}$	$\frac{6}{119}$	$\frac{6}{119}$	$\frac{6}{119}$	...

since $\frac{1}{21} + \frac{1}{17}\frac{1}{21} = \frac{6}{119}$. The survivor function estimator at $t = 6$ and $t = 7$ has now been determined. The mass value $\frac{6}{119}$ associated with the individual censored at time 9 can be allocated among the 15 subsequent failure/censoring times as

6	6 *	7	9 *	10	10 *	11 *	13	...
$\frac{1}{7}$	0	$\frac{6}{119}$	0	$\frac{32}{595}$	$\frac{32}{595}$	$\frac{32}{595}$	$\frac{32}{595}$	...

since $\frac{6}{119} + \frac{1}{15}\frac{6}{119} = \frac{96}{1785} = \frac{32}{595}$. After allocating the mass at 10* to the subsequent 13 data values and the mass at 11* to the subsequent 12 data values, the estimator becomes

6	6 *	7	9 *	10	10 *	11 *	13	...
$\frac{1}{7}$	0	$\frac{6}{119}$	0	$\frac{32}{595}$	0	0	$\frac{16}{255}$	...

When this process is continued through all the observed failures, a mass function that corresponds to the product-limit estimator results. To check this for one specific time value, note that

$$\hat{S}(14) = 1 - \tfrac{1}{7} - \tfrac{6}{119} - \tfrac{32}{595} - \tfrac{16}{255} = \tfrac{176}{255} = 0.69,$$

which matches the result from the previous example.

To find an estimate for the variance of the product-limit estimate is significantly more difficult than for the uncensored case. The Fisher and observed information matrices require a derivative of the score vector:

$$-\frac{\partial^2 \log L(h(y_1), h(y_2), \ldots, h(y_k))}{\partial h(y_i)\, \partial h(y_j)} = \frac{d_i}{h(y_i)^2} + \frac{n_i - d_i}{(1 - h(y_i))^2},$$

when $i = j$ and 0 otherwise, for $i = 1, 2, \ldots, k$, $j = 1, 2, \ldots, k$. Both the Fisher and observed information matrices are diagonal. Replacing $h(y_i)$ by its maximum likelihood estimate, the diagonal elements of the observed information matrix are

$$\left[-\frac{\partial^2 \log L(h(y_1), h(y_2), \ldots, h(y_k))}{\partial h(y_i)^2} \right]_{h(y_i) = d_i/n_i} = \frac{n_i^3}{d_i(n_i - d_i)},$$

for $i = 1, 2, \ldots, k$. Using this fact and some approximations referenced at the end of the chapter, an estimate for the variance of the survivor function is

$$\hat{V}[\hat{S}(t)] = [\hat{S}(t)]^2 \sum_{j \in R(t)} \frac{d_j}{n_j(n_j - d_j)},$$

often known as Greenwood's formula. The formula can be used to find asymptotically valid confidence intervals for $S(t)$ by using the normal critical values as in the uncensored case:

$$\hat{S}(t) - z_{\alpha/2}\sqrt{\hat{V}[\hat{S}(t)]} < S(t) < \hat{S}(t) + z_{\alpha/2}\sqrt{\hat{V}[\hat{S}(t)]}.$$

Example 10.4

For the 6-MP treatment group in the previous example, give a 95% confidence interval for the probability of survival to time 14.

The point estimator for the probability of survival to time 14 from the previous example is $\hat{S}(14) = 0.69$. Greenwood's formula is used to estimate the variance of the survivor function estimator at time 14:

$$\hat{V}[\hat{S}(14)] = [\hat{S}(14)]^2 \sum_{j \in R(14)} \frac{d_j}{n_j(n_j - d_j)}$$

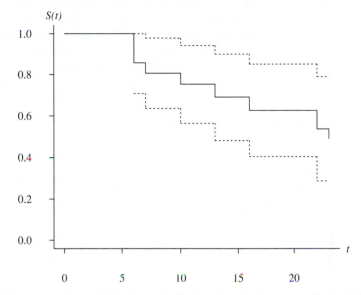

Figure 10.4   Confidence bands for the product-limit survivor function estimate for the 6-MP treatment group.

$$= (0.69)^2 \left[\frac{3}{21(21-3)} + \frac{1}{17(17-1)} + \frac{1}{15(15-1)} + \frac{1}{12(12-1)} \right]$$

$$= 0.011.$$

Thus an estimate for the standard deviation of the survivor function estimate is $\sqrt{0.011} = 0.11$ at $t = 14$. A 95% confidence interval for $S(14)$ is

$$\hat{S}(14) - z_{0.025}\sqrt{\hat{V}[\hat{S}(14)]} < S(14) < \hat{S}(14) + z_{0.025}\sqrt{\hat{V}[\hat{S}(14)]}$$

$$0.69 - 1.96\sqrt{0.011} < S(14) < 0.69 + 1.96\sqrt{0.011}$$

$$0.48 < S(14) < 0.90$$

Figure 10.4 shows the 95% confidence bands for the survivor function for all t values. These have also been cut off at the last observed failure time, $t = 23$. Note that the bounds are particularly wide since there are only $r = 9$ observed failure times.

10.2   LIFE TABLES

Life tables have historically been used by actuaries for estimating the survival distribution of humans, but apply equally well to reliability and biostatistical situations for which grouped data, rather than raw data, are available. Assume that the time axis is partitioned into k intervals $[a_0, a_1), [a_1, a_2), \ldots, [a_{k-1}, a_k)$. In actuarial applications, the intervals typically have the same width (1 year) since life insurance premiums vary by the age of the insured individual. The presentation here is more general, however, and the intervals do not necessarily have the same width. In this section, d_j denotes the number of failures in interval j, m_j denotes the number of items censored in interval j, and n_j denotes the number of items at risk just prior to interval j, $j = 1, 2, \ldots, k$. For an item that is functioning at the beginning of interval j, the conditional probability of failure during the interval could be estimated by d_j/n_j (if all censorings occur at the end of the interval) or by $d_j/(n_j - m_j)$ (if all censorings occur at the beginning of the interval). The usual convention is to estimate this conditional probability by $d_j/(n_j - m_j/2)$, which considers items that are censored during the interval to be at risk for only half of the interval. Analogous to the product-limit survivor function estimator, the life table survivor function estimator at a_j is

$$\hat{S}(a_j) = \prod_{i=1}^{j} \left(1 - \frac{d_i}{n_i - m_i/2} \right)$$

for $j = 1, 2, \ldots, k$. This survivor function estimator has step discontinuities at the interval boundaries and is constant over each interval. Greenwood's formula can be adapted to estimate the variance of this survivor function estimate. Replacing n_j with $n_i - m_i/2$ yields

$$\hat{V}[\hat{S}(a_j)] = [\hat{S}(a_j)]^2 \sum_{i=1}^{j} \frac{d_i}{(n_i - m_i/2)(n_i - m_i/2 - d_i)}.$$

for $j = 1, 2, \ldots, k$. The example that follows considers a grouped data set with right censoring and unequal interval widths, the most general case.

Example 10.5

The 6-MP treatment group is subdivided into $k = 5$ intervals of unequal width. The intervals, number of individuals at risk, number of observed cancer recurrences, and number of censorings during interval j are given in Table 10.2. As before, the survivor function estimator cuts off after the interval containing the last observed failure. Find a point estimator and 95% confidence interval for $S(14)$.

Note that $\hat{S}(12) = 0.75$ and $\hat{S}(18) = 0.62$. The grouping of the data has introduced a significant change in the estimator at $t = 14$ weeks, since $\hat{S}(14) = 0.75$ assumes that the survivor function estimator is constant throughout the interval $[12, 18)$. A 95% confidence interval for $S(14)$ is

$$0.75 - (1.96)(0.098) < S(14) < 0.75 + (1.96)(0.098)$$

$$0.56 < S(14) < 0.94$$

which is shifted to the right of the confidence interval for the raw data using Greenwood's formula.

TABLE 10.2   LIFE TABLE ESTIMATES FOR THE 6-MP TREATMENT GROUP

j	a_{j-1}	a_j	n_j	d_j	m_j	$\dfrac{d_j}{(n_j - m_j)/2}$	$\hat{S}(a_j)$	$\sqrt{\hat{V}[\hat{S}(a_j)]}$
1	0	8	21	4	1	$\dfrac{8}{41}$	0.80	0.088
2	8	12	16	1	3	$\dfrac{2}{29}$	0.75	0.098
3	12	18	12	2	1	$\dfrac{4}{23}$	0.62	0.12
4	18	24	9	2	2	$\dfrac{1}{4}$	0.46	0.13
5	24	36	5	0	5	0	$\cdot$	$\cdot$

Life tables have their genesis in actuarial science. When dealing with human populations, the sample sizes can be extremely large, resulting in very accurate survival estimates. Two types of life tables are used by actuaries: generational (or cohort) tables and current life tables.

A generational life table tracks the survival experience of a group (or cohort) of individuals born in the same year. All individuals born in this particular year are considered through consecutive years, and the generational life table reflects the mortality experience of all those individuals.

A current life table differs in the sense that it considers individuals of all ages during one particular year, say 1988. The survival pattern for all individuals is subject to the death rate during the year 1988. The factors that influence the death rate include medical advances, nutrition, environmental factors, and family life. Thus a current life table gives a snapshot of the mortality experience during one particular year. This type of table would certainly be useful to an actuary in determining the premium for a 1-year term life insurance policy for an individual. The next example illustrates how a current life table, referred to as a life table for brevity, is used.

Example 10.6

Life tables for the United States often use 100,000 births at $t = 0$. As seen in Table 10.3, this results in variance estimators that are significantly smaller than the life table in the previous example. Most life tables of this kind are further subdivided by gender and race. A life table of this type is appropriate for the *population,* but not necessarily for an individual. Genetic, occupational, and life-style factors will increase or decrease these survival probabilities for any given person. Infant mortality is apparent by looking at the numbers in the d_j column of the table.

TABLE 10.3   LIFE TABLE FOR THE UNITED STATES, 1988

j	a_{j-1}	a_j	n_j	d_j	m_j	$\hat{S}(a_j)$	$\sqrt{\hat{V}[\hat{S}(a_j)]}$
1	0	1	100,000	999	0	0.990	0.000314
2	1	5	99,001	128	0	0.989	0.000334
3	5	10	98,803	120	0	0.988	0.000351
4	10	15	98,683	134	0	0.986	0.000369
5	15	20	98,549	431	0	0.982	0.000422
6	20	25	98,118	565	0	0.976	0.000482
7	25	30	97,553	596	0	0.970	0.000537
8	30	35	96,957	717	0	0.963	0.000596
9	35	40	96,240	924	0	0.954	0.000664
10	40	45	95,316	1204	0	0.942	0.000741
11	45	50	94,112	1777	0	0.924	0.000838
12	50	55	92,335	2766	0	0.896	0.000964
13	55	60	89,569	4238	0	0.854	0.00112
14	60	65	85,331	6208	0	0.792	0.00128
15	65	70	79,123	8344	0	0.708	0.00144
16	70	75	70,779	11,096	0	0.597	0.00155
17	75	80	59,683	13,654	0	0.461	0.00158
18	80	85	46,029	15,858	0	0.302	0.00145
19	85	∞	30,171	30,171	0	0.000	$\cdot$

10.3 KOLMOGOROV–SMIRNOV TEST: ALL PARAMETERS KNOWN

Since there has been an emphasis on continuous lifetime distributions thus far in the text, the discussion here is limited to model adequacy tests for continuous distributions. The popular chi-square goodness-of-fit test can be applied to both continuous and discrete distributions, but suffers from the limitations of arbitrary interval widths and application only to large data sets. This chapter focuses on the Kolmogorov–Smirnov (K–S) goodness-of-fit test for assessing model adequacy.

A notational difficulty arises in presenting the K–S test. The survivor function $S(t)$ has been emphasized to this point in the text, but the cumulative distribution function, where $F(t) = P[T \leq t] = 1 - S(t)$ for continuous distributions, has traditionally been used to define the K–S test statistic. To keep with this tradition, $F(t)$ is used in the definitions in this chapter.

The K–S goodness-of-fit test is typically used to compare an empirical cumulative distribution function with a fitted or hypothesized parametric cumulative distribution function for a continuous model. The K–S test statistic is defined in the following subsection; then tables of critical values are given for the all-parameters-known case.

K–S Test Statistic

The K–S test statistic is the maximum difference between the empirical cumulative distribution function $\hat{F}(t)$ versus a hypothesized or fitted cumulative distribution function $F_0(t)$. The null and alternative hypotheses for the test are

$$H_0:\ F(t) = F_0(t)$$

$$H_1:\ F(t) \neq F_0(t)$$

where $F(t)$ is the underlying population cumulative distribution function. In other words, the null hypothesis is that the random lifetime T has cumulative distribution function $F_0(t)$. For a complete data set, the test statistic is

$$D_n = \sup_t |\hat{F}(t) - F_0(t)|,$$

where *sup* is an abbreviation for *supremum*. This test statistic has intuitive appeal since larger values of D_n indicate a greater difference between $\hat{F}(t)$ and $F_0(t)$ and hence a poorer fit. In addition, D_n is independent of the parametric form of $F_0(t)$ when the cumulative distribution function is hypothesized. From a practical standpoint, computing the K–S test statistic requires only a single loop through the n data values. This simplification occurs because $\hat{F}(t)$ is a nondecreasing step function and $F_0(t)$ is a nondecreasing continuous function, so the maximum difference must occur at a data value.

This section considers only hypothesized cumulative distribution functions $F_0(t)$. To illustrate the geometric aspects of the K–S test statistic D_n, however, a fitted exponential distribution is compared to the empirical cumulative distribution function. The first two figures show the difference between the use of the survivor function and the

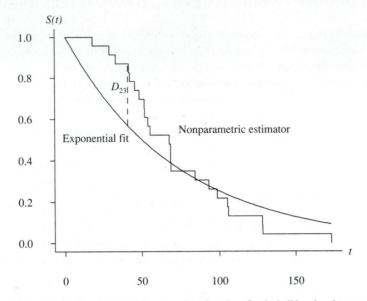

Figure 10.5   Empirical and fitted survivor functions for the ball bearing data set.

cumulative distribution function in computing D_n. Figure 10.5 shows the empirical step survivor function $\hat{S}(t)$ associated with the failure times of the $n = 23$ ball bearing failure times from Example 8.1, along with the exponential fit $S_0(t)$. The maximum difference between these two cumulative distribution functions occurs just to the left of

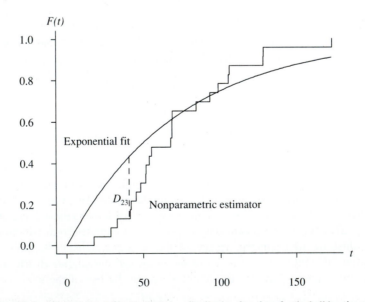

Figure 10.6   Empirical and fitted cumulative distribution functions for the ball bearing data set.

$t_{(4)} = 41.52$ and is $D_{23} = 0.301$ as indicated on the figure. Figure 10.6 is the complement of Figure 10.5 and considers the cumulative distribution function, rather than the survivor function. The maximum difference again occurs just to the left of $t_{(4)}$. To calculate D_{23}, it is necessary to loop through all 23 data points and consider the three cases outlined next.

The first case is shown in Figure 10.7, where $F(t)$ and $F_0(t)$ are shown around the data value $t_{(12)} = 67.80$. When $i = 12$, the fitted cumulative distribution function $F_0(t_{(i)})$ falls above $\hat{F}(t_{(i)})$; that is, $F_0(t_{(i)}) \geq \hat{F}(t_{(i)})$. As shown in the figure, the maximum difference between the two cumulative distribution functions in a neighborhood around $t_{(i)}$ occurs just to the left of $t_{(i)}$. This case indicates why sup, rather than max, is used in the definition of D_n. The difference between the empirical and fitted cumulative distribution functions at $t_{(i)}$ is $F_0(t_{(i)}) - \hat{F}(t_{(i-1)})$.

The second case is illustrated in Figure 10.8, where the fitted distribution $F_0(t)$ intersects the riser associated with the step in $\hat{F}(t)$ at $t_{(17)} = 93.12$. The condition associated with this case is $\hat{F}(t_{(i-1)}) < F_0(t_{(i)}) < \hat{F}(t_{(i)})$. The difference between the two cumulative distributions at $t_{(i)}$ depends on whether $F_0(t)$ intersects the top half or the bottom half of the riser at $t_{(i)}$.

The third case is shown in Figure 10.9, where $\hat{F}(t)$ and $F_0(t)$ are shown around the data value $t_{(19)} = 105.12$. In this case, the fitted cumulative distribution function at $t_{(i)}$ falls below $\hat{F}(t_{(i-1)})$; that is, $F_0(t_{(i)}) \leq \hat{F}(t_{(i-1)})$. The difference between the empirical and fitted cumulative distribution functions at $t_{(i)}$ is $\hat{F}(t_{(i)}) - F_0(t_{(i)})$.

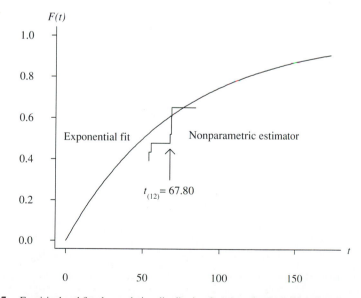

Figure 10.7   Empirical and fitted cumulative distribution functions for the ball bearing data set around $t_{(12)}$.

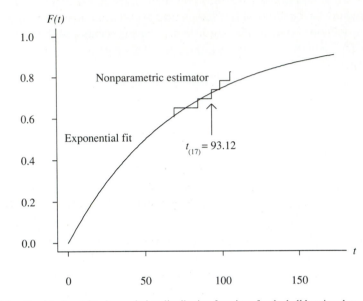

Figure 10.8   Empirical and fitted cumulative distribution functions for the ball bearing data set around $t_{(17)}$.

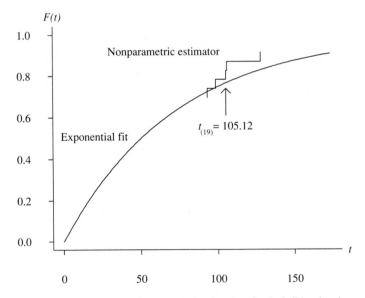

Figure 10.9   Empirical and fitted cumulative distribution functions for the ball bearing data set around $t_{(19)}$.

One computational method for determining D_n is to determine which of the above three cases each data value belongs to, compute the difference at each data value, and then take the maximum of the n values. A second method, used more often than the first, is to define

$$D_n^+ = \max_{i=1, 2, ..., n} \left(\frac{i}{n} - F_0(t_{(i)}) \right),$$

$$D_n^- = \max_{i=1, 2, ..., n} \left(F_0(t_{(i)}) - \frac{i-1}{n} \right),$$

and then let $D_n = \max\{D_n^+, D_n^-\}$. These are typically referred to as the *computational* formulas as opposed to the *defining* formula for D_n given earlier. The computational formulas are typically easier to translate into computer code for implementation.

K–S Critical Values (All Parameters Known)

The test statistic for the K–S test is nonparametric in the sense that it has the same distribution regardless of the distribution of the parent population under H_0 when all the parameters in the hypothesized distribution are known. The reason for this is that $F_0(t_{(1)})$, $F_0(t_{(2)})$, . . . , $F_0(t_{(n)})$ have the same joint distribution as U(0, 1)-order statistics under H_0 regardless of the functional form of F_0. These are often called *omnibus tests* since they are not tied to one particular distribution (for example, the Weibull) and apply equally well to any hypothesized distribution $F_0(t)$. This also means that fractiles of the distribution of D_n depend on n only. The next section considers the critical values for D_n when all the parameters in $F_0(t)$ are known (that is, not estimated from data).

The rows in Table 10.4 denote the sample sizes and the columns denote several levels of significance. The values in the table are estimates of the $1 - \alpha$ fractiles of the distribution of D_n under H_0 and have been determined by Monte Carlo simulation with 1,000,000 replications. Due to sampling variability, the table values are only good to two digits, rather than the three reported in the table. Not surprisingly, the fractiles are a decreasing function of n, since increased sample sizes will have lower sampling variability. Test statistics that exceed the appropriate critical value lead to rejecting H_0.

Example 10.7

Use the K–S test to determine whether the ball bearing data set from Example 8.1 was drawn from a Weibull population with $\lambda = 0.01$ and $\kappa = 2$. Run the test at $\alpha = 0.10$.

Note that the Weibull distribution in this example is a *hypothesized*, rather than *fitted* distribution, so the all-parameters-known case for determining critical values is appropriate. The goodness-of-fit test

$$H_0: \ F(t) = 1 - e^{-(0.01t)^2},$$

$$H_1: \ F(t) \neq 1 - e^{-(0.01t)^2},$$

TABLE 10.4   APPROXIMATE K–S CRITICAL
VALUES (ALL PARAMETERS KNOWN)

n	$1 - \alpha$			
	0.80	0.90	0.95	0.99
1	0.900	0.950	0.975	0.995
2	0.683	0.776	0.842	0.930
3	0.565	0.636	0.708	0.829
4	0.493	0.565	0.624	0.733
5	0.447	0.509	0.563	0.668
6	0.410	0.468	0.519	0.617
7	0.381	0.436	0.483	0.576
8	0.358	0.409	0.454	0.542
9	0.339	0.388	0.430	0.513
10	0.323	0.369	0.409	0.489
11	0.308	0.352	0.391	0.468
12	0.296	0.338	0.376	0.449
13	0.285	0.325	0.361	0.433
14	0.275	0.314	0.349	0.418
15	0.266	0.304	0.338	0.404
16	0.258	0.295	0.327	0.392
17	0.250	0.286	0.318	0.381
18	0.243	0.278	0.309	0.370
19	0.237	0.271	0.302	0.361
20	0.232	0.265	0.294	0.352
21	0.226	0.259	0.287	0.345
22	0.221	0.253	0.281	0.337
23	0.217	0.248	0.275	0.330
24	0.212	0.242	0.269	0.323
25	0.208	0.237	0.264	0.317
30	0.190	0.218	0.242	0.290
35	0.176	0.202	0.224	0.269
40	0.165	0.189	0.210	0.253
45	0.156	0.179	0.199	0.238
50	0.148	0.170	0.189	0.227

does not involve any parameters estimated from data. The test statistic is $D_{23} = 0.274$. The empirical cumulative distribution function, the Weibull(0.01, 2) cumulative distribution function and the maximum difference between the two [which occurs at $t_{(15)} = 68.88$] are shown in Figure 10.10. At $\alpha = 0.10$, the critical value is 0.248, so H_0 is rejected. In this case, the test statistic is very close to the critical value for $\alpha = 0.05$, so the attained P-value for the test is approximately $p = 0.05$.

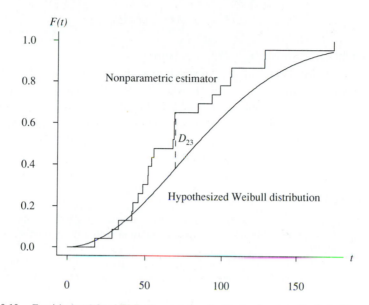

Figure 10.10   Empirical and fitted Weibull cumulative distribution functions for the ball bearing data set.

Approximate critical values for sample sizes that are not in the table are given by references at the end of the chapter.

Right-censored Data Sets

The K–S test is easily adapted to the cases of Type I and Type II right censoring. The situation is more complex for randomly right-censored data sets. For Type II censored data sets, the defining formula for the K–S test statistic is

$$D_{n,r} = \sup_{0 \le t \le t_{(r)}} |\hat{F}(t) - F_0(t)|,$$

where $t_{(1)}, t_{(2)}, \ldots, t_{(r)}$ are the ordered observed lifetimes. For Type I censored data sets, the defining formula for the K–S test statistic is

$$D_{n,p} = \sup_{0 \le t \le c} |\hat{F}(t) - F_0(t)|,$$

where c is the time that the test is terminated and $p = F_0(c)$ is the expected fraction censored under H_0. The computational formulas for these test statistics are modified in a straightforward fashion. In the case of Type II censoring, for example,

$$D_{n,r}^+ = \max_{i=1, 2, \ldots, r} \left(\frac{i}{n} - F_0(t_{(i)}) \right),$$

$$D_{n,r}^- = \max_{i=1,2,\dots,r} \left(F_0(t_{(i)}) - \frac{i-1}{n} \right).$$

Then let $D_{n,r} = \max \{ D_{n,r}^+, D_{n,r}^- \}$ as before.

The distribution of $D_{n,r}$ depends only on n and r and the distribution of $D_{n,p}$ depends only on n and p under H_0 when $F_0(t)$ is the hypothesized cumulative distribution function. Unfortunately, the tables of critical values in these situations are overwhelming due to the many possible combinations of n, r and n, p. Thus a single example is considered, and the critical values for one particular combination of n and r are determined by Monte Carlo methods.

Example 10.8

Use the K–S test to determine whether the automotive a/c switch data set given in Example 8.2 was drawn from an exponential population with a mean number of cycles to failure of 100,000. Run the test at $\alpha = 0.10$.

Recall that the automotive a/c switch data set was Type II right censored with $n = 15$ and $r = 5$. The ordered observed failure times measured in number of cycles are

$$1410 \quad 1872 \quad 3138 \quad 4218 \quad 6971.$$

Note again that the exponential distribution in this example is a hypothesized, rather than fitted distribution, so the all-parameters-known case for determining critical values is appropriate. The goodness-of-fit test with $\lambda = 1/100,000 = 0.00001$ is

$$H_0: \ F(t) = 1 - e^{-0.00001t},$$

$$H_1: \ F(t) \neq 1 - e^{-0.00001t}$$

and does not involve any parameters estimated from data. The critical values for the test have been determined by Monte Carlo simulation with 500,000 samples and are shown in Table 10.5. The test statistic is $D_{15,5} = 0.266$. The maximum difference between the two cumulative distribution functions [which occurs at $t_{(5)} = 6971$] is shown in Figure 10.11, and the hypothesized distribution does not appear to follow the sample data. At $\alpha = 0.10$, the critical value is 0.244, so H_0 is rejected.

TABLE 10.5   APPROXIMATE K–S CRITICAL VALUES FOR TYPE II CENSORING WITH $n = 15$ AND $r = 5$ (ALL PARAMETERS KNOWN)

		$1 - \alpha$			
n	r	0.80	0.90	0.95	0.99
15	5	0.204	0.244	0.283	0.366

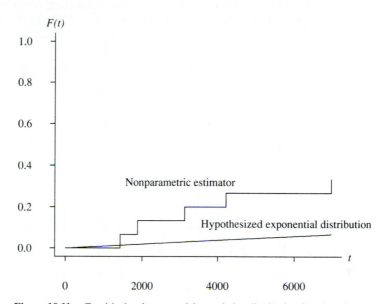

Figure 10.11   Empirical and exponential cumulative distribution functions for the automotive a/c switch data set.

10.4   KOLMOGOROV–SMIRNOV TEST: PARAMETERS ESTIMATED FROM DATA

Unfortunately, most of the applications of the K–S test occur in the case where the distribution parameters are estimated from data. This results in critical values that depend on the distribution under consideration. Only the exponential is considered here in order to illustrate the critical values for the test.

The K–S test statistic is first computed in the usual fashion, comparing the empirical cumulative distribution function with the fitted exponential cumulative distribution having failure rate $\hat{\lambda}$. Table 10.6 shows the critical values associated with this test. They have also been determined by Monte Carlo simulation with 500,000 replications. Fortunately, these critical values are appropriate for all values of $\hat{\lambda}$. These critical values are significantly different from those in Table 10.4, so using the all-parameters-known table when comparing a data set to a fitted distribution will yield an incorrect level of significance.

Example 10.9

Determine whether the ball bearing data can be considered a random sample from an exponential population with failure rate $\hat{\lambda} = 0.0138$, the maximum likelihood estimator. Use $\alpha = 0.10$.

TABLE 10.6   APPROXIMATE K–S CRITICAL VALUES FOR A FITTED
EXPONENTIAL DISTRIBUTION (PARAMETERS ESTIMATED FROM DATA).

	$1 - \alpha$			
n	0.80	0.90	0.95	0.99
2	0.550	0.593	0.613	0.628
3	0.451	0.511	0.551	0.600
4	0.401	0.444	0.484	0.557
5	0.360	0.405	0.442	0.512
6	0.332	0.373	0.409	0.476
7	0.310	0.348	0.381	0.446
8	0.291	0.328	0.359	0.421
9	0.276	0.310	0.341	0.400
10	0.262	0.295	0.325	0.381
11	0.251	0.283	0.311	0.365
12	0.241	0.271	0.298	0.352
13	0.232	0.261	0.287	0.338
14	0.224	0.253	0.278	0.328
15	0.217	0.244	0.268	0.317
16	0.211	0.237	0.261	0.308
17	0.205	0.230	0.253	0.299
18	0.199	0.224	0.246	0.291
19	0.194	0.218	0.240	0.284
20	0.189	0.213	0.234	0.277
21	0.185	0.208	0.229	0.271
22	0.181	0.204	0.224	0.265
23	0.177	0.199	0.219	0.259
24	0.173	0.196	0.215	0.254
25	0.170	0.192	0.211	0.249
30	0.156	0.176	0.193	0.229
35	0.145	0.163	0.179	0.213
40	0.136	0.153	0.168	0.199
45	0.128	0.144	0.159	0.188
50	0.122	0.137	0.151	0.179

The hypothesis test is

$$H_0: \ F(t) = 1 - e^{-0.0138t},$$

$$H_1: \ F(t) \neq 1 - e^{-0.0138t}.$$

As shown earlier in Figures 10.5 and 10.6, there is a significant difference between the empirical and fitted cumulative distribution functions, resulting in a large test statistic $D_{23} = 0.301$. Comparing this statistic with the tabled critical value 0.199 at $\alpha = 0.10$

leads to rejecting the null hypothesis. The same conclusion is drawn as that in Chapter 8, where the Weibull distribution was chosen over the exponential distribution for modeling the ball bearing lifetimes. There is additional statistical evidence here indicating that the population of ball bearings is indeed wearing out, and an exponential model is not appropriate.

A similar pattern continues for conducting the K–S test for other population distributions when the parameters are estimated from the data. The previous discussion for complete data sets does not easily generalize to the case of random right censoring. Unfortunately, the distribution of the test statistic becomes more complicated in the case of random right censoring. Many researchers have devised approximate methods for determining the critical values for the K–S test with random right censoring and parameters estimated from data. This chapter has emphasized Monte Carlo methods for determining P-values for the K–S test, which applies to all types of censoring.

10.5   FURTHER READING

Books with a separate chapter on nonparametric methods include Cox and Oakes (1984), David and Moeschberger (1978), Elandt-Johnson and Johnson (1980), Hinkley et al. (1991), Lawless (1982), Lee (1992), Padgett (1988), and Zacks (1992). An exact confidence interval for $S(t)$ for a complete data set is given by Leemis and Trivedi (1994). The computations required to compute this confidence interval require numerical methods. In the case of a complete data set, the survivor function estimator introduced in this chapter, $\hat{S}(t)$, has bias problems for small sample sizes; hence some competitors have been developed over the years. The first is

$$\hat{S}_2(t) = \frac{n(t) + 1}{n + 1} \qquad t \geq 0,$$

which has downward steps of $1/(n + 1)$, but suffers from the limitation that $\lim_{t \to \infty} S(t) = 1/(n + 1)$, so the estimator is not symmetric. The second uses the following estimate over the range of the data values:

$$\hat{S}_3(t) = \frac{n(t) - 1/2}{n - 1} \qquad t_{(1)} < t \leq t_{(n)}$$

and is 1 for t values less than or equal to $t_{(1)}$ and is 0 for t values greater than $t_{(n)}$. This estimator is symmetric and has downward steps of $1/(n - 1)$ at all data points except for the first and the last, where it has downward steps of $1/[2(n - 1)]$. Still another survivor function estimate is given in Martz and Waller (1982, p. 105):

$$\hat{S}_4(t) = \frac{n(t) - 1 + 0.625}{n + 0.25} \qquad t \geq 0.$$

Kaplan and Meier (1958) first introduced the product-limit estimate, and the estimate of the variance of the survivor function is given by Greenwood (1926). Some authors (for example, Lee, 1992, p. 23, or Lewis, 1987, p. 133) prefer to connect the survivor function estimators at the failure times by lines, as opposed to the step function (with risers) convention that has been adopted here. The development of the product-limit estimator based on the probability mass function illustrated in Example 10.3 is known as the "redistribute-to-the-right" algorithm and is referenced in Miller (1981, p. 52). The approximations that are used for Greenwood's formula are given in Cox and Oakes (1984, p. 50) and Kalbfleisch and Prentice (1980, p. 11).

The life table notation used here is similar to that used in Cox and Oakes (1984), Kalbfleisch and Prentice (1980), and Lawless (1982). The approximations to $\hat{S}(t)$ and $\hat{V}[\hat{S}(t)]$ are the same as those in Kalbfleisch and Prentice (1980, pp. 15–16) for life tables. The United States current life table data are from DHHS (1991).

The presentation of the K–S goodness-of-fit test here follows Lawless (1982). Stephens (1974) compares the K–S test statistic with other goodness-of-fit statistics for the all-parameters-known case, the exponential fit case, and the normal fit case. Barr and Davidson (1973), Koziol and Byar (1975), and Dufour and Maag (1978) consider the distribution of the K–S statistic for censored data sets.

Gail and Gastwirth (1978) consider a goodness-of-fit test for a fitted exponential model based on Gini's statistic. Goodness-of-fit tests for other distributions include the exponential (Durbin, 1975 and Margolin and Maurer, 1976), Weibull (Chandra et al., 1981), inverse Gaussian (Pavur et al., 1992), Pareto (Porter et al., 1992), and discrete distributions and grouped data (Pettitt and Stephens, 1977). In the case of the proportional hazards model, goodness of fit is considered by Lin (1991). For repairable systems, goodness-of-fit tests for a power law process are considered by Park and Kim (1992) and Aubrey and Rigdon (1993).

10.6 EXERCISES

10.1. (Zacks, 1992, p. 101) Twenty electric generators were placed on an accelerated life test. The failure times of the $n = r = 20$ generators (in hours) are

> 7.5   121.5   279.8   592.1   711.5   848.2   1051.7   1425.5   1657.2
> 1883.6   2311.1   2951.2   5296.6   5637.9   6054.3   6303.9   6853.7
> 7201.9   9068.5   10,609.7

(a) Assuming that the population at the accelerated conditions is exponential, find a point and 95% confidence interval estimate for the probability of survival to 6000 hours.

(b) Using nonparametric methods, find a point and 95% confidence interval estimate for the probability of survival to 6000 hours under the accelerated conditions.

10.2. Show that the product-limit estimate reduces to the survivor function estimate for a complete data set when the failure times are distinct.

10.3. Show that the diagonal elements of the observed information matrix associated with the product-limit estimate are

$$\left[-\frac{\partial^2 \log L(h(y_1), h(y_2), \ldots, h(y_k))}{\partial h(y_i)^2} \right]_{h(y_i) = d_i/n_i} = \frac{n_i^3}{d_i(n_i - d_i)}$$

for $i = 1, 2, \ldots, k$.

10.4. Find a point and 95% confidence interval estimate for the probability of survival to 20 weeks for the control group and treatment groups of the 6-MP data set from Example 8.3. Draw any conclusions that may be appropriate about the drug 6-MP's influence on survival to 20 weeks.

10.5. (Lawless, 1982, p. 73) Plot the product-limit survivor function estimator for the control and treatment groups in the 6-MP data set from Example 8.3.

10.6. (Mann and Fertig, 1973) Thirteen aircraft components are placed on a life test that is discontinued after the tenth failure. The failure times, in hours, are

$$0.22 \quad 0.50 \quad 0.88 \quad 1.00 \quad 1.32 \quad 1.33 \quad 1.54 \quad 1.76 \quad 2.50 \quad 3.00$$

See also Crowder et al. (1991, p. 43).

(a) Assuming that the population is exponential, find a point and 95% confidence interval estimate for the probability of survival to 1.6 hours.
(b) Using nonparametric methods, find a point and 95% confidence interval estimate for the probability of survival to 1.6 hours.

10.7. Use Table 10.3 to estimate the probability that a 35 year old will survive to age 40 assuming that the conditions (for example, medical care) are constant for the next 5 years.

10.8. Write a computer program to verify the numbers in the last two columns of Table 10.3.

10.9. Use Monte Carlo simulation to estimate the K–S fractiles shown in Table 10.4 for the case when $F_0(t)$ is hypothesized and the data set is complete.

10.10. Find the distribution of the K–S test statistic when $n = 1$ in the all-parameters-known case. [*Hint:* Since D_1 is independent of the population distribution, it may be helpful to consider a U(0, 1) population.]

10.11. Use Monte Carlo simulation to estimate the K–S fractiles shown in Table 10.5 for the case when $F_0(t)$ is hypothesized and the data set is Type II right censored with $n = 15$ and $r = 2, \ldots, 15$.

10.12. Use Monte Carlo simulation to estimate the K–S fractiles shown in Table 10.6 for the case when $F_0(t)$ is the fitted exponential cumulative distribution function and the data set is complete.

10.13. (Lawless, 1982, p. 433) For a complete data set, the Cramer–von Mises goodness-of-fit statistic is

$$W_n^2 = n \int_0^\infty [\hat{F}(t) - F_0(t)]^2 dF_0(t)$$

and the Anderson–Darling statistic is

$$A_n^2 = n \int_0^\infty \frac{[\hat{F}(t) - F_0(t)]^2}{F_0(t)[1 - F_0(t)]} dF_0(t).$$

The computational formulas for these statistics are

$$W_n^2 = \sum_{i=1}^{n} \left(F_0(t_{(i)}) - \frac{i-0.5}{n} \right)^2 + \frac{1}{12n}$$

and

$$A_n^2 = -\sum_{i=1}^{n} \frac{2i-1}{n} \left(\log[F_0(t_{(i)})] + \log[1 - F_0(t_{(n+1-i)})] \right) - n.$$

Compute these test statistics for the ball bearing data set fitted to the exponential distribution.

10.14. Write a program suitable for complete or Type II censored data sets that will print out (in columns) the distribution name (include exponential and Weibull only), the estimation technique (consider maximum likelihood for exponential and both maximum likelihood and regression for the Weibull), the parameter estimates, the K–S goodness-of-fit statistics, and the P-value for the K–S test. Illustrate that the goodness-of-fit portion of your program is working correctly by testing the complete data set 1, 2, 6 by hand and by your program.

Appendix A: Exponential Distribution Properties

Assume that T is a random variable having the exponential distribution with survivor function

$$S(t) = e^{-\lambda t} \qquad t \geq 0.$$

The properties stated in Section 4.2 are proved in this appendix.

Property 4.1 (memoryless property) If $T \sim$ exponential(λ), then

$$P[T \geq t] = P[T \geq t + h \,|\, T \geq h] \qquad t \geq 0; h \geq 0.$$

Proof The conditional probability of surviving to $t + h$ is

$$
\begin{aligned}
P[T \geq t + h \,|\, T \geq h] &= \frac{P[T \geq t + h]}{P[T \geq h]} \\
&= \frac{S(t + h)}{S(h)} \\
&= \frac{e^{-\lambda(t + h)}}{e^{-\lambda h}} \\
&= e^{-\lambda t} \\
&= S(t) \\
&= P[T \geq t].
\end{aligned}
$$

Property 4.2   The exponential distribution is the only continuous distribution with the memoryless property.

Proof (Ross, 1993, p. 203) Since T is memoryless,

$$S(t + h) = S(t)S(h) \qquad \text{for all } t \geq 0, \, h \geq 0.$$

It needs to be shown that this property implies that $S(t) = e^{-\lambda t}$. For any two positive integers m and n, $S(m/n) = [S(1/n)]^m$ since

$$S\left(\frac{m}{n}\right) = S\left(\frac{m-1}{n}\right)S\left(\frac{1}{n}\right) = S\left(\frac{m-2}{n}\right)S\left(\frac{1}{n}\right)S\left(\frac{1}{n}\right) = \cdots = \left[S\left(\frac{1}{n}\right)\right]^m.$$

When $m = n$, this yields $S(1) = [S(1/n)]^n$ or, equivalently $S(1/n) = [S(1)]^{1/n}$. Substituting this expression into the previous expression for $S(m/n)$ yields

$$S\left(\frac{m}{n}\right) = [S(1)]^{m/n}.$$

Since $S(t)$ is a continuous function, m/n can be replaced by t:

$$S(t) = [S(1)]^t.$$

For $S(t)$ to be a legitimate survivor function, $S(1)$ must be chosen so that $S(t)$ is nonincreasing, $S(0) = 1$, and $\lim_{t \to \infty} S(t) = 0$. Therefore, $0 < S(1) < 1$. Equivalently, some $\lambda > 0$ may be chosen so that $S(1) = e^{-\lambda}$, and

$$S(t) = e^{-\lambda t} \qquad t \geq 0.$$

Property 4.3   If $T \sim \text{exponential}(\lambda)$, then $\lambda T \sim \text{exponential}(1)$.

Proof The survivor function for λT is

$$P[\lambda T \geq t] = P[T \geq t / \lambda]$$

$$= e^{-\lambda(t/\lambda)}$$

$$= e^{-t} \qquad t \geq 0,$$

so λT has survivor function e^{-t}, which is exponential(1).

Property 4.4   If T is a continuous nonnegative random variable with cumulative hazard function $H(t)$, then $H(T) \sim \text{exponential}(1)$.

Proof The survivor function for $H(T)$ is

$$P[H(T) \geq t] = P[-\log S(T) \geq t]$$

$$= P[S(T) < e^{-t}]$$
$$= P[U < e^{-t}]$$
$$= e^{-t},$$

where $U = S(T)$ is uniformly distributed between 0 and 1 by the probability integral transformation, so $H(T) \sim$ exponential(1) since it has survivor function e^{-t}.

Property 4.5 If $T \sim$ exponential(λ) then $E[T^s] = \lambda^{-s}\Gamma(s + 1)$, for $s > -1$.

Proof The expected value of T^s is

$$E[T^s] = \int_0^\infty t^s \lambda e^{-\lambda t} dt$$

$$= \lambda^{-s} \int_0^\infty x^s e^{-x} dx \qquad \text{(substituting } x = \lambda t)$$

$$= \lambda^{-s}\Gamma(s + 1) \qquad s > -1.$$

Property 4.6 (self-reproducing) If T_1, T_2, $\ldots$, T_n are independent, $T_i \sim$ exponential(λ_i), for $i = 1, 2, \ldots, n$, and $T = \min\{T_1, T_2, \ldots, T_n\}$, then $T \sim$ exponential($\sum_{i=1}^n \lambda_i$).

Proof The survivor function for T is

$$S_T(t) = P[T \geq t]$$

$$= P[\min\{T_1, T_2, \ldots, T_n\} \geq t]$$

$$= P[T_1 \geq t, T_2 \geq t, \ldots, T_n \geq t]$$

$$= P[T_1 \geq t] P[T_2 \geq t] \ldots P[T_n \geq t]$$

$$= e^{-\lambda_1 t} e^{-\lambda_2 t} \ldots e^{-\lambda_n t}$$

$$= e^{-\sum_{i=1}^n \lambda_i t}$$

so that $T \sim$ exponential($\sum_{i=1}^n \lambda_i$).

Property 4.7 If $T_1, T_2, \ldots, T_n$ are independent and identically distributed exponential random variables with parameter λ, then $2\lambda \sum_{i=1}^n T_i \sim \chi^2(2n)$.

Proof Since $T_1, T_2, \ldots, T_n$ are independent and identically distributed exponential(λ),

$$\sum_{i=1}^{n} T_i \sim \text{Erlang}(\lambda, n)$$

$$\lambda \sum_{i=1}^{n} T_i \sim \text{Erlang}(1, n)$$

$$2\lambda \sum_{i=1}^{n} T_i \sim \chi^2(2n).$$

Property 4.8   If $T_1, T_2, \ldots, T_n$ are independent and identically distributed exponential(λ) random variables, $T_{(1)}, T_{(2)}, \ldots, T_{(n)}$ are the corresponding order statistics, and the kth gap is defined to be $G_k = T_{(k)} - T_{(k-1)}$ for $k = 1, 2, \ldots, n$, and $T_{(0)} = 0$, then

(a) $P[G_k \geq t] = e^{-(n-k+1)\lambda t}$ $t \geq 0; \ k = 1, 2, \ldots, n.$

(b) $G_1, G_2, \ldots, G_n$ are independent.

Proof (Barlow and Proschan, 1981, p. 59)
(a) Since G_1 is the minimum of n exponential random variables,

$$P[G_1 \geq t] = e^{-n\lambda t}   t \geq 0.$$

Since G_2 is the minimum of $n-1$ exponential random variables,

$$P[G_2 \geq t] = e^{-(n-1)\lambda t}   t \geq 0.$$

In general, since G_k is the minimum of $n-k+1$ exponential random variables,

$$P[G_k \geq t] = e^{-(n-k+1)\lambda t}   t \geq 0, \ k = 1, 2, \ldots, n.$$

(b) We need to show that

$$f_{G_1, G_2, \ldots, G_n}(g_1, g_2, \ldots, g_n) = f_{G_1}(g_1) \, f_{G_2}(g_2) \cdots f_{G_n}(g_n).$$

The joint probability density function of $T_{(1)}, T_{(2)}, \ldots, T_{(n)}$ is

$$f_{T_{(1)}, T_{(2)}, \ldots, T_{(n)}}(t_1, t_2, \ldots, t_n) = n! \lambda e^{-\lambda t_1} \lambda e^{-\lambda t_2} \ldots \lambda e^{-\lambda t_n}   0 \leq t_1 \leq \cdots \leq t_n.$$

The transformation ϕ maps $T_{(1)}, T_{(2)}, \ldots, T_{(n)}$ to $G_1, G_2, \ldots, G_n$:

$$\phi: \quad
\begin{aligned}
G_1 &= & & T_{(1)} \\
G_2 &= & & T_{(2)} - T_{(1)} \\
G_3 &= & & T_{(3)} - T_{(2)} \\
&\ \ \vdots & & \qquad \vdots \\
G_n &= T_{(n)} - T_{(n-1)}
\end{aligned}
\qquad
\phi^{-1}: \quad
\begin{aligned}
T_{(1)} &= & & G_1 \\
T_{(2)} &= & & G_2 + G_1 \\
T_{(3)} &= & & G_3 + G_2 + G_1 \\
&\ \ \vdots & & \qquad \vdots \\
T_{(n)} &= G_n + G_{n-1} + \cdots + G_1
\end{aligned}$$

and is a 1–1 transformation from $A = \{T_{(1)}, \ldots, T_{(n)} \mid 0 \leq T_{(1)} \leq \cdots \leq T_{(n)}\}$ to $B = \{G_1, \ldots, G_n \mid G_i \geq 0; \ i = 1, 2, \ldots, n\}$ with Jacobian $|J| = 1$, so that

$$f_{G_1, G_2, \ldots, G_n}(g_1, g_2, \ldots, g_n) = f_{T_{(1)}, T_{(2)}, \ldots, T_{(n)}}(\phi^{-1}(g_1, g_2, \ldots, g_n))|J|$$

$$= n! \, \lambda^n e^{-\lambda g_1} e^{-\lambda(g_1 + g_2)} \ldots e^{-\lambda(g_1 + g_2 + \cdots + g_n)}$$

$$= n! \, \lambda^n e^{-\lambda(ng_1 + (n-1)g_2 + \cdots + g_n)}$$

$$= (n\lambda e^{-n\lambda g_1})((n-1)\lambda e^{-(n-1)\lambda g_2}) \ldots (\lambda e^{-\lambda g_n})$$

$$= f_{G_1}(g_1)f_{G_2}(g_2) \ldots f_{G_n}(g_n)$$

for $g_i \geq 0$, $i = 1, 2, \ldots, n$, so that $G_1, G_2, \ldots, G_n$ are independent.

Property 4.9   If $T_1, T_2, \ldots, T_n$ are independent and identically distributed exponential(λ) and $T_{(r)}$ is the rth order statistic, then

$$E[T_{(r)}] = \sum_{k=1}^{r} \frac{1}{(n-k+1)\lambda}$$

$$V[T_{(r)}] = \sum_{k=1}^{r} \frac{1}{[(n-k+1)\lambda]^2} \, .$$

Proof The gaps $G_1, G_2, \ldots, G_n$ defined in Property 4.8 have survivor functions

$$P[G_k \geq t] = e^{-(n-k+1)\lambda t} \qquad t \geq 0; \, k = 1, 2, \ldots, n$$

so

$$E[G_k] = \frac{1}{(n-k+1)\lambda} \qquad k = 1, 2, \ldots, n$$

$$V[G_k] = \frac{1}{[(n-k+1)\lambda]^2} \qquad k = 1, 2, \ldots, n.$$

Since $T_{(r)} = \sum_{k=1}^{r} G_i$,

$$E[T_{(r)}] = E\left[\sum_{k=1}^{r} G_k \right]$$

$$= \sum_{k=1}^{r} E[G_k]$$

$$= \sum_{k=1}^{r} \frac{1}{(n-k+1)\lambda}$$

and

$$V [T_{(r)}] = V \left[\sum_{k=1}^{r} G_k \right]$$

$$= \sum_{k=1}^{r} V[G_k]$$

$$= \sum_{k=1}^{r} \frac{1}{[(n-k+1)\lambda]^2} .$$

Property 4.10   If $T_1, T_2, \ldots$ are independent and identically distributed exponential(λ) random variables denoting the interevent times for a point process, then the *number* of events in the interval $(0, t]$ has the Poisson distribution with parameter λt.

Proof Since the first event occurs at time T_1, the second at time $T_1 + T_2$, and so on, the time of the nth event, $T_1 + T_2 + \cdots + T_n$, has an Erlang (λ, n) distribution with probability density function

$$f_{T_1 + T_2 + \cdots + T_n}(t) = \frac{(\lambda t)^{n-1}}{(n-1)!} \lambda e^{-\lambda t} \qquad t \geq 0$$

and survivor function

$$S_{T_1 + T_2 + \cdots + T_n}(t) = \sum_{k=0}^{n-1} \frac{(\lambda t)^k}{k!} e^{-\lambda t} \qquad t \geq 0.$$

If N is the number of events in $[0, t)$, then

$$P[N = n] = P[T_1 + T_2 + \cdots + T_n < t \leq T_1 + T_2 + \cdots + T_n + T_{n+1}]$$

$$= P[T_1 + T_2 + \cdots + T_n + T_{n+1} \geq t] - P[T_1 + T_2 + \cdots + T_n > t]$$

$$= \sum_{k=0}^{n} \frac{(\lambda t)^k}{k!} e^{-\lambda t} - \sum_{k=0}^{n-1} \frac{(\lambda t)^k}{k!} e^{-\lambda t}$$

$$= \frac{(\lambda t)^n}{n!} e^{-\lambda t} \qquad n = 0, 1, 2, \ldots,$$

which is Poisson(λ).

Property 4.11   If $T \sim$ exponential(1), then $Y = \log T$ has an extreme value distribution with survivor function

$$S_Y (y) = e^{-e^y} \qquad -\infty < y < \infty.$$

Proof If $S_T(t)$ is the survivor function for T, then the survivor function for Y is

$$S_Y(y) = P[Y \geq y]$$
$$= P[\log T \geq y]$$
$$= P[T \geq e^y]$$
$$= S_T(e^y)$$
$$= e^{-e^y} \qquad -\infty < y < \infty.$$

Appendix B: Gamma and Incomplete Gamma Functions

The *gamma function* arises in modeling lifetimes with the Weibull and gamma distributions. It is defined by

$$\Gamma(\alpha) = \int_0^\infty y^{\alpha-1} e^{-y} dy \qquad \alpha > 0.$$

When α is an integer, $\Gamma(\alpha) = (\alpha - 1)!$, so the factorials are effectively smoothed by the gamma function, as indicated in Figure B.1. Some other useful results concerning the gamma function are

$$\Gamma(\alpha + 1) = \alpha \Gamma(\alpha) \qquad \alpha > 0$$

and

$$\Gamma\left(\frac{1}{2}\right) = \sqrt{\pi}.$$

References for computing the gamma function numerically are given in Crowder et al. (1991, p. 17).

The *incomplete gamma function* is defined by

$$I(\alpha, x) = \frac{1}{\Gamma(\alpha)} \int_0^x y^{\alpha-1} e^{-y} dy \qquad \alpha > 0; \ x > 0.$$

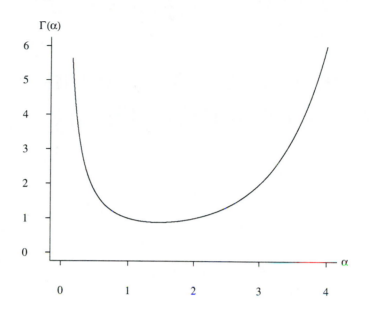

Figure B.1 Gamma function.

It can be recognized that, ignoring the scaling factor in front of the integral, the incomplete gamma function is a generalization of the gamma function, with an upper limit of x rather than ∞. Since $\lim_{x \to \infty} I(\alpha, x) = 1$, the incomplete gamma function always assumes values between zero and one. The incomplete gamma function is also the cumulative distribution function for the gamma distribution when the shape parameter is 1 ($\kappa = 1$) and the scale parameter is α. Many software packages have subprograms that compute the gamma and incomplete gamma functions.

Appendix C: A Result in Competing Risks Theory

The result from competing risks theory from Section 5.1,

$$h_{X_j}(t) = \frac{\pi_j \, f_{Y_j}(t)}{\sum\limits_{i=1}^{k} \pi_i \, S_{Y_i}(t)} \qquad t \geq 0, \qquad\qquad (\text{C.1})$$

for $j = 1, 2, \ldots, k$, is proved in this appendix. This result allows a modeler to determine the distribution of the net lives, given the distribution of the crude lives and the probabilities of failure from the various risks. The net lives are assumed to be independent random variables.

Assuming that $\pi_j = P[J = j]$ and $S_{Y_j}(t)$ are known for $j = 1, 2, \ldots, k$, define

$$P_{Y_j}(t) = P[T \geq t, J = j] = \pi_j S_{Y_j}(t) \qquad t \geq 0, \qquad\qquad (\text{C.2})$$

for $j = 1, 2, \ldots, k$, as the probability of survival to time t, and j is the cause of failure. The result may then be stated in terms of P_{Y_j} as

$$h_{X_j}(t) = -\frac{\dfrac{d}{dt} P_{Y_j}(t)}{\sum\limits_{i=1}^{k} P_{Y_i}(t)} \qquad t \geq 0 \qquad\qquad (\text{C.3})$$

for $j = 1, 2, \ldots, k$. The following lemma (Birnbaum, 1979) is required in order to prove the more general result.

Lemma   The derivative of $P_{Y_j}(t)$ is

$$\frac{d}{dt} P_{Y_j}(t) = \left[\frac{\partial}{\partial x_j} S(x_1, \ldots, x_k) \right]_{x_1 = \cdots = x_k = t} \tag{C.4}$$

for $j = 1, 2, \ldots, k$.

Proof Consider the left-hand side of the result first. Without loss of generality, consider $j = 1$. By definition,

$$P_{Y_1}(t) = P[T \geq t, J = 1]$$

$$= P[X_1 \geq t, X_1 < X_i \text{ for } i \neq 1]$$

$$= \int_t^\infty \int_{x_1}^\infty \cdots \int_{x_1}^\infty f(x_1, \tau_2, \ldots, \tau_k) \, d\tau_k \ldots d\tau_2 dx_1$$

for $t \geq 0$. Thus

$$\frac{d}{dt} P_{Y_1}(t) = - \int_t^\infty \int_t^\infty \cdots \int_t^\infty f(t, \tau_2, \ldots, \tau_k) \, d\tau_k \ldots d\tau_2.$$

The focus now shifts to the right-hand side of equation (C.4). Consider the joint survivor function for the net lives

$$S(x_1, \ldots, x_k) = P[X_1 \geq x_1, \ldots, X_k \geq x_k] = \int_{x_1}^\infty \cdots \int_{x_k}^\infty f(t_1, \ldots, t_k) \, dt_k \ldots dt_1.$$

Taking the partial derivative with respect to x_1 and evaluating at t yields

$$\left[\frac{\partial}{\partial x_1} S(x_1, \ldots, x_k) \right]_{x_1 = \cdots = x_k = t} = - \left[\int_{x_2}^\infty \cdots \int_{x_k}^\infty f(x_1, \tau_2, \ldots, \tau_k) \, d\tau_k \ldots d\tau_2 \right]_{x_1 = \cdots = x_k = t}$$

$$= - \int_t^\infty \cdots \int_t^\infty f(t, \tau_2, \ldots, \tau_k) \, d\tau_k \ldots d\tau_2,$$

which completes the proof of the lemma since the left- and right-hand sides of equation (C.4) are equal to the same quantity.

Returning to the proof of the original result, since the net lives are assumed to be independent,

$$S(x_1, \ldots, x_k) = \prod_{i=1}^{k} S_i(x_i).$$

Differentiating with respect to x_j,

$$\frac{\partial}{\partial x_j} S(x_1, \ldots, x_k) = -h_{X_j}(x_j) S(x_1, \ldots, x_k).$$

So, by equation (C.4)

$$\frac{d}{dt} P_{Y_j}(t) = -h_{X_j}(t) S(t, t, \ldots, t) \tag{C.5}$$

for $j = 1, 2, \ldots, k$. Now,

$$S(t, t, \ldots, t) = \prod_{i=1}^{k} S_{X_i}(t) = e^{-\sum_{i=1}^{k} H_{X_i}(t)}$$

and equation (C.5) becomes

$$\frac{d}{dt} P_{Y_j}(t) = -h_{X_j}(t) e^{-\sum_{i=1}^{k} H_{X_i}(t)} \tag{C.6}$$

for $j = 1, 2, \ldots, k$. Summing over j

$$\frac{d}{dt} \sum_{j=1}^{k} P_{Y_j}(t) = -\sum_{j=1}^{k} h_{X_j}(t) e^{-\sum_{i=1}^{k} H_{X_i}(t)},$$

and integrating with respect to t yields

$$\sum_{j=1}^{k} P_{Y_j}(t) = e^{-\sum_{j=1}^{k} H_{X_j}(t)} + c,$$

where c is the constant of integration. The constant c is zero since $\sum_{j=1}^{k} P_{Y_j}(0) = 1$ and $\sum_{j=1}^{k} H_j(0) = 0$, so equation (C.6) can be solved for the hazard function for the net life X_j:

$$h_{X_j}(t) = -\frac{\dfrac{d}{dt} P_{Y_j}(t)}{\displaystyle\sum_{i=1}^{k} P_{Y_i}(t)}, \qquad t \geq 0, \tag{C.7}$$

for $j = 1, 2, \ldots, k$, which is equivalent to equation (C.3).

Appendix D: Weibull Distribution Initial Parameter Estimation

The Weibull distribution does not have closed-form maximum likelihood estimators for its parameters. As indicated in Section 8.3, the equation

$$g(\kappa) = \frac{r}{\kappa} + \sum_{i \in U} \log x_i - \frac{r \sum_{i=1}^{n} x_i^{\kappa} \log x_i}{\sum_{i=1}^{n} x_i^{\kappa}} = 0$$

must be solved iteratively to determine $\hat{\kappa}$ for complete, Type II, Type I, and randomly right-censored data sets. The scale parameter estimator $\hat{\lambda}$ is easily determined once $\hat{\kappa}$ has been determined. The Newton–Raphson technique is often used to find the roots of this equation. This technique requires an initial estimate for κ_0 since the algorithm is recursive. The case of a complete data set is considered first.

Complete Data Sets

When a data set is complete, a closed-form expression for an initial shape parameter κ_0 has been given by Menon (1963):

$$\kappa_0 = \left\{ \frac{6}{(n-1)\pi^2} \left[\frac{\sum_{i=1}^{n} (\log t_i)^2 - \left(\sum_{i=1}^{n} \log t_i \right)^2}{n} \right] \right\}^{-1/2}.$$

This initial estimator should be reasonably close to the maximum likelihood estimator $\hat{\kappa}$ and allows the algorithm to converge to the desired accuracy in just a few iterations.

Example D.1

Consider the $n = 23$ ball bearings failure times given in Example 8.1 and analyzed in Example 8.16. The initial estimate for the Weibull shape parameter is

$$\kappa_0 = \left\{ \frac{6}{22\pi^2} \left[\frac{\sum\limits_{i=1}^{23} (\log t_i)^2 - \left(\sum\limits_{i=1}^{23} \log t_i \right)^2}{23} \right] \right\}^{-1/2} = 2.40,$$

which is close to the maximum likelihood estimator $\hat{\kappa} = 2.10$.

Complete and Censored Data Sets

A least squares technique to find an initial shape parameter estimator κ_0 can be applied to any complete or right-censored data set where $r \geq 2$ failures are observed. The estimator for κ_0 has a bonus: it can be used for assessing model adequacy. The derivation for this estimator is based on the survivor function for the Weibull distribution

$$S(t) = e^{-(\lambda t)^\kappa} \qquad t \geq 0.$$

Taking the logarithms of both sides of this equation yields

$$\log S(t) = -(\lambda t)^\kappa \qquad t \geq 0.$$

Negating and taking another logarithm yields

$$\log[-\log S(t)] = \kappa \log \lambda + \kappa \log t.$$

This equation is valid for all $t > 0$, and simple linear regression can be used to estimate the slope (κ) and intercept ($\kappa \log \lambda$). In addition, if the Weibull distribution is an appropriate model for the data, then a plot of $\log t$ versus $\log[-\log S(t)]$ should fall in a line. More specifically, for any index $i \in U$ (that is, for all observed failures),

$$\log \left[\log \frac{1}{S(x_i)} \right] = \kappa \log \lambda + \kappa \log x_i.$$

The only problem that remains is to determine an appropriate estimator for $S(x_i)$. Let the risk set $R(t)$ be the indexes of items that are at risk just prior to time t, and let $n(t) = |R(t)|$ be the number of indexes in $R(t)$ at time t. In other words, $n(t)$ is the number of items on test just prior to time t. Two estimators that are often used to estimate $S(t)$ are $n(t)/n$ and $n(t)/(n + 1)$. The second choice will be used here since it avoids getting a survivor function estimate of 1, resulting in logarithm difficulties in the regression equation. Thus

$$\hat{S}(t) = \frac{n(t)}{n + 1},$$

resulting in the regression equation

$$\log\left[\log\frac{n+1}{n(x_i)}\right] = \kappa\log\lambda + \kappa\log x_i$$

for any index $i \in U$. Since the focus of this appendix is only on determining an initial estimate for the shape parameter κ, the estimate for λ is ignored. The least squares estimate for the slope parameter is given by (Neter et al., 1989, p. 42)

$$\kappa_0 = \frac{\displaystyle\sum_{i \in U}(X_i - \bar{X})(Y_i - \bar{Y})}{\displaystyle\sum_{i \in U}(X_i - \bar{X})^2}$$

where $X_i = \log x_i$ and $Y_i = \log[\log((n+1)/n(x_i))]$ for any index $i \in U$, and $\bar{X}$ and $\bar{Y}$ are the corresponding sample means.

Example D.2

Consider the ball bearing data again. There are $n = 23$ values used in the regression. The initial estimator for κ is $\kappa_0 = 2.04$, which is also quite close to the maximum likelihood estimator $\hat{\kappa} = 2.10$. Figure D.1 shows a plot of the X_i and Y_i pairs for $i = 1, 2, \ldots, n$, along with the regression line. Only 22 points are plotted because of the tied observations (68.64), but all 23 points are used in determining the regression line. Since the relationship between the pairs appears to be linear, the Weibull distribution is a reasonable model for the ball bearings.

Prior to the widespread use of computers for reliability analysis, "Weibull paper" was used to determine if the Weibull distribution was an appropriate model for a data set. The paper saved the analyst the trouble of taking all the logarithms used in the derivation.

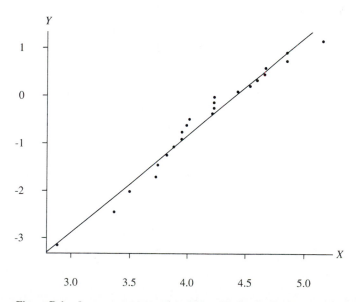

Figure D.1 Least squares regression estimator for κ_0 for ball bearing data.

Appendix E: Extreme Value Distribution Parameter Estimation

The probability density function for the Weibull distribution is

$$f(t; \lambda, \kappa) = \kappa \lambda^{\kappa} t^{\kappa - 1} e^{-(\lambda t)^{\kappa}} \qquad t \geq 0,$$

where $\lambda > 0$ and $\kappa > 0$ are the scale and shape parameters of the distribution, respectively. The survival function is

$$S(t; \lambda, \kappa) = e^{-(\lambda t)^{\kappa}} \qquad t \geq 0.$$

The parameters λ and κ may be estimated by the maximum likelihood estimation technique for a complete ($r = n$) or Type II censored data set ($r < n$), where r is the number of observed failures and n is the number of items on test (see Section 8.3). The extreme value distribution is often fitted to the data for numerical stability. Only complete data sets and Type II right-censored data sets are considered here to illustrate the technique. Let $t_1 \leq t_2 \leq \cdots \leq t_r$ be the observed lifetimes from the Weibull distribution, and let $y_1 \leq y_2 \leq \cdots \leq y_r$ be the corresponding extreme value lifetimes, where $y_i = \log t_i, i = 1, 2, \ldots, r$.

The probability density function and survival function for the extreme value distribution are (Lawless, 1982, pp. 141–143)

$$f(y; u, b) = \frac{1}{b} e^{\left(\frac{y - u}{b}\right)} e^{-e^{\left(\frac{y - u}{b}\right)}} \qquad -\infty < y < \infty$$

and

$$S(y; u, b) = e^{-e^{\left(\frac{y-u}{b}\right)}} \qquad -\infty < y < \infty$$

where $u = \log(1/\lambda)$ and $b = 1/\kappa$ are location and scale parameters, respectively. The joint probability density function of $y_1, \ldots, y_r$ is

$$\frac{n!}{(n-r)!}\left[\prod_{i=1}^{r}\frac{1}{b}e^{\left(\frac{y_i-u}{b}\right)}e^{-e^{\left(\frac{y_i-u}{b}\right)}}\right]\left[e^{-e^{\left(\frac{y_r-u}{b}\right)}}\right]^{n-r}.$$

The likelihood function for complete or Type II censored lifetimes (where U is the set of indexes of the uncensored values and C is the set of indexes of the censored values) is

$$L(u, b) = \prod_{i \in U} f(y_i) \prod_{i \in C} S(y_i)$$

$$= \frac{1}{b^r}\, e^{\sum_{i=1}^{r}\left(\frac{y_i-u}{b}\right)} e^{-\sum_{i=1}^{r}e^{\left(\frac{y_i-u}{b}\right)}} e^{-(n-r)e^{\left(\frac{y_r-u}{b}\right)}}$$

$$= \frac{1}{b^r}\, e^{\sum_{i=1}^{r}\left(\frac{y_i-u}{b}\right) - \sum_{i=1}^{r}e^{\left(\frac{y_i-u}{b}\right)} - (n-r)e^{\left(\frac{y_r-u}{b}\right)}}.$$

So the log likelihood is

$$\log L(u, b) = -r \log b + \sum_{i=1}^{r}\left(\frac{y_i-u}{b}\right) - \sum_{i=1}^{r}e^{\left(\frac{y_i-u}{b}\right)} - (n-r)e^{\left(\frac{y_r-u}{b}\right)}.$$

The partial derivatives with respect to u and b are

$$\frac{\partial \log L(u, b)}{\partial u} = -\frac{r}{b} + \frac{1}{b}\sum_{i=1}^{r}e^{\left(\frac{y_i-u}{b}\right)} + \frac{n-r}{b}e^{\left(\frac{y_r-u}{b}\right)}$$

and

$$\frac{\partial \log L(u, b)}{\partial b} = -\frac{r}{b} - \frac{1}{b}\sum_{i=1}^{r}\left(\frac{y_i-u}{b}\right) + \frac{1}{b}\sum_{i=1}^{r}\left(\frac{y_i-u}{b}\right)e^{\left(\frac{y_i-u}{b}\right)}$$

$$+ \frac{n-r}{b}\left(\frac{y_r-u}{b}\right)e^{\left(\frac{y_r-u}{b}\right)}.$$

The maximum likelihood estimates $\hat{u}$ and $\hat{b}$ can be obtained by solving

$$\frac{\partial \log L(u, b)}{\partial u} = 0 \quad \text{and} \quad \frac{\partial \log L(u, b)}{\partial b} = 0$$

simultaneously. Since no closed-form solution exists, numerical methods are required to compute $\hat{u}$ and $\hat{b}$. Fortunately, the first equation can be solved for $\hat{u}$ in terms of $\hat{b}$. Simplifying the first equation

$$-\frac{r}{\hat{b}} + \frac{1}{\hat{b}}\, e^{-\hat{u}/\hat{b}} \sum_{i=1}^{r} e^{y_i/\hat{b}} + \frac{n-r}{\hat{b}}\, e^{-\hat{u}/\hat{b}}\, e^{y_r/\hat{b}} = 0$$

and solving for $\hat{u}$ yields

$$\hat{u} = \hat{b} \log\left[\frac{1}{r} \sum_{i=1}^{r} e^{y_i/\hat{b}} + \left(\frac{n-r}{r}\right) e^{y_r/\hat{b}} \right].$$

Substituting this into

$$\frac{\partial \log L(u, b)}{\partial b} = 0$$

yields

$$f(\hat{b}) = -\hat{b} - \frac{1}{r}\sum_{i=1}^{r} y_i + \frac{\displaystyle\sum_{i=1}^{r} y_i e^{y_i/\hat{b}} + (n-r)y_r e^{y_r/\hat{b}}}{\displaystyle\sum_{i=1}^{r} e^{y_i/\hat{b}} + (n-r)e^{y_r/\hat{b}}} = 0$$

after a bit of algebra. This equation must be solved iteratively for $\hat{b}$. Using the Newton–Raphson technique,

$$\hat{b}_i = \hat{b}_{i-1} - \frac{f(\hat{b}_{i-1})}{f'(\hat{b}_{i-1})}, \qquad i = 1, 2, \ldots,$$

where

$$f'(b) = -1 - \frac{\left(\displaystyle\sum_{i=1}^{r} e^{y_i/b} + (n-r)e^{y_r/b}\right)\left(\displaystyle\sum_{i=1}^{r} y_i^2 e^{y_i/b} + (n-r)y_r^2 e^{y_r/b}\right) - \left(\displaystyle\sum_{i=1}^{r} y_i e^{y_i/b} + (n-r)y_r e^{y_r/b}\right)^2}{b^2 \left(\displaystyle\sum_{i=1}^{r} e^{y_i/b} + (n-r)e^{y_r/b}\right)^2}.$$

Appendix F: A Result for Discrete Lifetime Distributions

This appendix considers the result

$$S(t) = \prod_{j \in R(t)'} [1 - h(t_j)] \qquad t \geq 0,$$

where $S(t) = P[T \geq t]$ is the survivor function, $h(t)$ is the hazard function, $R(t)$ is the risk set containing the indexes of all items at risk just prior to time t, and T is a discrete lifetime with mass values at $t_1 < t_2 < t_3 \cdots$. This result is used in constructing the Kaplan–Meier product-limit estimator for the survivor function derived in Section 10.1.

The proof of the result begins by considering the definition of the probability mass function

$$f(t_i) = P[T = t_i]$$

for $i = 1, 2, \ldots$. The survivor function is

$$S(t) = P[T \geq t] = \sum_{j \in R(t)} f(t_j)$$

for $t \geq 0$. Since the survivor function is a step function, the probability mass function can be written in terms of the survivor function as

$$f(t_i) = S(t_i) - S(t_{i+1})$$

for $i = 1, 2, \ldots$. By definition, the hazard function at the mass values is

$$h(t_i) = P[T = t_i \mid T \geq t_i] = \frac{f(t_i)}{S(t_i)}$$

for $i = 1, 2, \ldots$. The hazard function can be rewritten as

$$h(t_i) = \frac{f(t_i)}{S(t_i)} = \frac{S(t_i) - S(t_{i+1})}{S(t_i)} = 1 - \frac{S(t_{i+1})}{S(t_i)}$$

for $i = 1, 2, \ldots$. Solving for $S(t_{i+1})$ yields a recursive equation for determining the survivor function at the mass values:

$$S(t_{i+1}) = S(t_i)[1 - h(t_i)]$$

for $i = 1, 2, \ldots$. By definition, $S(t_1) = 1$ and

$$S(t_2) = S(t_1)[1 - h(t_1)] = [1 - h(t_1)],$$

$$S(t_3) = S(t_2)[1 - h(t_2)] = [1 - h(t_1)][1 - h(t_2)],$$

and so on. A general version of this relationship is

$$S(t_i) = \prod_{j \in R(t_i)'} [1 - h(t_j)] \qquad t \geq 0$$

for $i = 1, 2, \ldots$. Since the survivor function is constant between mass values, this can be generalized to

$$S(t) = \prod_{j \in R(t)'} [1 - h(t_j)] \qquad t \geq 0,$$

which is the result of interest.

References

Abouammoh, A.M., "On the Criteria of the Mean Remaining Life," *Statistics and Probability Letters,* Vol. 6, No. 4, pp. 205–211, 1988.

Allison, P.D., *Event History Analysis: Regression for Longitudinal Event Data,* Sage Publications, Beverly Hills, Calif., 1984.

Ascher, H., and Feingold, H., *Repairable Systems Reliability,* Marcel Dekker, Inc., New York, 1984.

Aubrey, D., and Rigdon, S., "Goodness-of-Fit Tests for the Power-Law Process" in *Advances in Reliability*, A. Basu, ed., North-Holland, New York, pp. 21–28, 1993.

Bain, L.J., and Engelhardt, M., *Statistical Analysis of Reliability and Life-testing Models: Theory and Methods,* 2nd ed., Marcel Dekker, Inc., New York, 1991.

Balanda, K.P., and MacGillivray, H.L., "Kurtosis: A Critical Review," *The American Statistician,* Vol. 42, No. 2, pp. 111–119, 1988.

Ball, M.O., and Provan, J.S., "Bounds on the Reliability Polynomial for Shellable Independence Systems," *SIAM Journal on Algebraic and Discrete Methods,* Vol. 3, No. 2, pp. 166–181, 1982.

Barlow, R.E., "Geometry of the Total Time on Test Transform," *Naval Research Logistics Quarterly,* Vol. 26, No. 3, pp. 393–402, 1979.

Barlow, R.E., and Proschan, F., *Statistical Theory of Reliability and Life Testing: Probability Models,* To Begin With, Silver Springs, Md., 1981.

Barlow, R.E., and Wu, A.S., "Coherent Systems with Multistate Components," *Mathematics of Operations Research,* Vol. 3, No. 4, pp. 275–281, 1978.

Barr, D.R., and Davidson, T., "A Kolmogorov–Smirnov Test for Censored Samples," *Technometrics,* Vol. 15, No. 4, pp. 739–757, 1973.

Baxter, L.A., "Continuum Structures I," *Journal of Applied Probability,* Vol. 21, No. 4, pp. 802–815, 1984.

Baxter, M.J., Bendell, A., Manning, P.T., and Ryan, S.G., "Proportional Hazards Modelling of Transmission Equipment Failures," *Reliability Engineering and System Safety,* Vol. 21, No. 2, pp. 129–144, 1988.

Bendell, A., Walley, M., Wightman, D.W., and Wood, L.M., "Proportional Hazards Modelling in Reliability Analysis—An Application to Brake Discs on High Speed Trains," *Quality and Reliability Engineering International,* Vol. 2, pp. 45–52, 1986.

Billinton, R., and Allan, R., *Reliability Evaluation of Engineering Systems,* Pittman Advanced Publishing Program, Boston, 1985.

Birnbaum, Z.W., "On the Mathematics of Competing Risks," Vital and Health Statistics: Series 2, No. 77, U.S. Department of Health, Education and Welfare, Washington, D.C., pp. 1–58, 1979.

Birnbaum, Z.W., Esary, J.D., and Saunders, S.C., "Multi-Component Systems and Structures and Their Reliability," *Technometrics,* Vol. 3, No. 1, pp. 55–77, 1961.

Birolini, A., *On the Use of Stochastic Processes in Modeling Reliability Problems,* Springer-Verlag, Inc., New York, 1985.

Block, H.W., and Savits, T.H., "Continuous Multistate Structure Functions," *Operations Research,* Vol. 32, No. 3, pp. 703–714, 1984.

Boedigheimer, R.A., *Customer-driven Reliability Models for Multistate Coherent Systems,* Ph.D. Dissertation, School of Industrial Engineering, University of Oklahoma, Norman, 1992.

Bogdanoff, J.L., and Kozin, F., "On Nonstationary Cumulative Damage Models," *Journal of Applied Mechanics,* Vol. 49, No. 1, pp. 37–42, 1982.

Bowman, K.O., and Shenton, L.R., *Properties of Estimators for the Gamma Distribution,* Marcel Dekker, Inc., New York, 1988.

Chan, F., Chan, L.K., and Lin, G.D., "On Consecutive-*k*-out-of-*n*: F Systems," *European Journal of Operational Research,* Vol. 36, No. 2, pp. 207–216, 1988.

Chan, W., and Rueda, N.G., "Nonexistence of the Maximum Likelihood Estimates in the Weibull Process," *Naval Research Logistics,* Vol. 39, No. 3, pp. 359–368, 1992.

Chandra, M., Singpurwalla, N.D., and Stephens, M.A., "Kolmogorov–Smirnov Statistics for Tests of Fit for the Extreme-value and Weibull Distributions," *Journal of the American Statistical Association,* Vol. 76, No. 375, pp. 729–731, 1981.

Chhikara, R.S., and Folks, L.S., *The Inverse Gaussian Distribution: Theory, Methodology and Applications,* Marcel Dekker, Inc., New York, 1989.

Cinlar, E., *Introduction to Stochastic Processes,* Prentice Hall, Englewood Cliffs, N.J., 1975.

Cohen, A.C., and Whitten, B.J., *Parameter Estimation in Reliability and Life Span Models,* Marcel Dekker, Inc., New York, 1988.

Colbourn, C.J., *The Combinatorics of Network Reliability,* Oxford University Press, New York, 1987.

Condra, L.W., *Reliability Improvement with Design of Experiments,* Marcel Dekker, Inc., New York, 1993.

Cox, D.R., "Regression Models and Life-Tables" (with discussion), *Journal of the Royal Statistical Society B,* Vol. 34, No. 2, pp. 187–220, 1972.

Cox, D.R., and Hinkley, D.V., *Theoretical Statistics,* Chapman and Hall, New York, 1974.

Cox, D.R., and Isham, V., *Point Processes,* Chapman and Hall, New York, 1980.

Cox, D.R., and Oakes, D., *Analysis of Survival Data,* Chapman and Hall, New York, 1984.

Crow, L.H., "Confidence Interval Procedures for the Weibull Process with Applications to Reliability Growth," *Technometrics,* Vol. 24, No. 1, pp. 67–72, 1982.

Crowder, M.J., Kimber, A.C., Smith, R.L., and Sweeting, T.J., *Statistical Analysis of Reliability Data,* Chapman and Hall, New York, 1991.

Crowell, J.I., and Sen, P.K., "Estimating an Optimal Block Replacement Policy Using Stochastic Approximation" in *Advances in Reliability*, A. Basu, ed., North-Holland, New York, pp. 75–87, 1993.

Csorgo, M., Csorgo, S., and Horvath, L., *An Asymptotic Theory for Empirical Reliability and Concentration Processes,* Springer-Verlag, Inc., New York, 1986.

Dalal, S.R., Fowlkes, E.B., and Hoadley, B., "Risk Analysis of the Space Shuttle: Pre-Challenger Prediction of Failure," *Journal of the American Statistical Association,* Vol. 84, No. 408, pp. 945–957, 1989.

David, H.A., and Moeschberger, M.L., *The Theory of Competing Risks,* Macmillan, Inc., New York, 1978.

Davis, H.T., and Feldstein, M.L., "The Generalized Pareto Law as a Model for Progressively Censored Survival Data," *Biometrika,* Vol. 66, No. 2, pp. 299–306, 1979.

DHHS, *Vital Statistics of the United States,* Vol. II—Mortality, Part A, U.S. Department of Health and Human Services, Public Health Service, Centers for Disease Control, National Center for Health Statistics, Hyattsville, Md., 1991.

Dhillon, B.S., *Reliability Engineering in Systems Design and Operation,* Van Nostrand Reinhold, Inc., New York, 1983.

Dhillon, B.S., *Quality Control, Reliability and Engineering Design,* Marcel Dekker, Inc., New York, 1984.

Dodson, B.T., *Weibull Analysis,* ASQC Quality Press, Milwaukee, Wisc., 1995.

Doty, L.A., *Reliability for the Technologies,* Industrial Press, Inc., New York, 1985.

Dovich, R.A., *Reliability Statistics,* ASQC Quality Press, Milwaukee, Wisc., 1990.

Drury, M.R., Walker, E.V., Wightman, D.W., and Bendell, A., "Proportional Hazards Modelling in the Analysis of Computer Systems Reliability," *Reliability Engineering and System Safety,* Vol. 21, No. 3, pp. 197–214, 1988.

Duane, J.T., "Learning Curve Approach to Reliability Monitoring," *IEEE Transactions on Aerospace,* Vol. 2, No. 2, pp. 563–566, 1964.

Dufour, R., and Maag, U.R., "Distribution Results for Modified Kolmogorov–Smirnov Statistics for Truncated or Censored Samples," *Technometrics,* Vol. 20, No. 1, pp. 29–32, 1978.

Dummer, G.W.A., and Winton, R.C., *An Elementary Guide to Reliability,* 4th ed., Pergamon Press, New York, 1990.

Durbin, J., "Kolmogorov–Smirnov Tests When Parameters Are Estimated with Applications to Tests of Exponentiality and Tests on Spacings," *Biometrika,* Vol. 62, No. 1, pp. 5–22, 1975.

Edgeman, R.L., "Assessing the Inverse Gaussian Distribution Assumption," *IEEE Transactions on Reliability,* Vol. 39, No. 3, pp. 352–355, 1990.

Elandt-Johnson, R.C., and Johnson, N., *Survival Models and Data Analysis,* John Wiley & Sons, Inc., New York, 1980.

Ellermann, R., Sullo, P., and Tien, J.M., "An Alternative Approach to Modeling Recidivism Using Quantile Residual Life Functions," *Operations Research,* Vol. 40, No. 3, pp. 485–504, 1992.

El-Neweihi, E., Proschan, F., and Sethuraman, J., "Multistate Coherent Systems," *Journal of Applied Probability,* Vol. 15, No. 4, pp. 675–688, 1978.

Enrick, N.L., *Quality, Reliability and Process Improvement,* 8th ed., Industrial Press, Inc., New York, 1985.

Epstein, B., and Sobel, M., "Life Testing," *Journal of the American Statistical Association,* Vol. 48, No. 263, pp. 486–502, 1953.

Epstein, B., and Sobel, M., "Sequential Life Tests in the Exponential Case," *Annals of Mathematical Statistics,* Vol. 26, No. 1, pp. 82–93, 1955.

Everitt, B.S., and Hand, D.J., *Finite Mixture Distributions,* Chapman and Hall, New York, 1981.

Fisher, R.A., and Tippett, L.H.C., "Limiting Forms of the Frequency Distribution of the Largest or Smallest Member of a Sample," *Proceedings of the Cambridge Philosophical Society,* Vol. 24, pp. 180–190, 1928.

Fleming, T.R., and Harrington, D.P., *Counting Processes and Survival Analysis,* John Wiley & Sons, Inc., New York, 1991.

Foster, J.W., Phillips, D.T., and Rogers, T.R., *Reliability, Availability and Maintainability,* M/A Press, Beaverton, Ore., 1981.

Freund, J.E., "A Bivariate Extension of the Exponential Distribution," *Journal of the American Statistical Association,* Vol. 56, No. 296, pp. 971–977, 1961.

Fuqua, N.B., *Reliability Engineering for Electronic Design,* Marcel Dekker, Inc., New York, 1987.

Gail, M.H., and Gastwirth, J.L., "A Scale-free Goodness-of-fit Test for the Exponential Distribution based on the Gini Statistic," *Journal of the Royal Statistical Society: B,* Vol. 40, No. 3, pp. 350–357, 1978.

Galambos, J., *The Asymptotic Theory of Extreme Order Statistics,* John Wiley & Sons, Inc., New York, 1978.

Gaver, D.P., and Acar, M., "Analytical Hazard Representations for Using Reliability, Mortality and Simulation Studies," *Communications in Statistics—Simulation and Computation,* Vol. B8, No. 2, pp. 91–111, 1979.

Gehan, E.A., "A Generalized Wilcoxon Test for Comparing Arbitrarily Singly-censored Samples," *Biometrika,* Vol. 52, Parts 1 and 2, pp. 203–223, 1965.

Gentleman, R., and Crowley, J., "Graphical Methods for Censored Data," *Journal of the American Statistical Association,* Vol. 86, No. 415, pp. 678–683, 1991.

Gertsbakh, I.B., *Statistical Reliability Theory,* Marcel Dekker, Inc., New York, 1989.

Goldberg, H., *Extending the Limits of Reliability Theory,* John Wiley & Sons, Inc., New York, 1981.

Gray, C., Harris, N., Bendell, A., and Walker, E.V., "The Reliability Analysis of Weapon Systems," *Reliability Engineering and System Safety,* Vol. 21, No. 4, pp. 245–269, 1988.

Greenwood, M., "The Natural Duration of Cancer," *Reports on Public Health and Medical Subjects,* Her Majesty's Stationery Office, London, Vol. 33, pp. 1–26, 1926.

Grosh, D.L., *A Primer of Reliability Theory,* John Wiley & Sons, Inc., New York, 1989.

Halpern, S., *The Assurance Sciences: An Introduction to Quality Control and Reliability,* Prentice Hall, Englewood Cliffs, N.J., 1978.

Harr, M.E., *Reliability-based Design in Civil Engineering,* McGraw-Hill, Inc., New York, 1987.

Henley, E.J., and Kumamoto, H., *Reliability Engineering and Risk Assessment,* Prentice Hall, Englewood Cliffs, N.J., 1981.

Henley, E.J., and Kumamoto, H., *Designing for Reliability and Safety Control,* Prentice Hall, Englewood Cliffs, N.J., 1985.

Hinkley, D.V., Reid, N., and Snell, E.J., *Statistical Theory and Modeling,* Chapman and Hall, New York, 1991.

Hjorth, U., "A Reliability Distribution with Increasing, Decreasing, Constant and Bathtub-shaped Failure Rates," *Technometrics,* Vol. 22, No. 1, pp. 99–107, 1980.

Hogg, R.E., and Craig, A.T., *Introduction to Mathematical Statistics,* 5th ed., Prentice Hall, Englewood Cliffs, N.J., 1995.

Hogg, R.E., and Ledolter, J., *Applied Statistics for Engineers and Physical Scientists,* 2nd ed., Macmillan, Inc., New York, 1992.

Hudson, J.C., and Kapur, K.C., "Reliability Analysis for Multistate Systems with Multistate Components," *IIE Transactions,* Vol. 15, No. 2, pp. 127–135, 1983.

Iyer, S., "The Barlow-Proschan Importance and Its Generalizations with Dependent Components," *Stochastic Processes and Their Applications,* Vol. 42, No. 2, pp. 353–359, 1992.

Jensen, F., and Petersen, N.E., *Burn-in: An Engineering Approach to the Design and Analysis of Burn-in Procedures,* John Wiley & Sons, Inc., New York, 1982.

Johnson, M.A., "Selecting Parameters of Phase Distributions: Combining Nonlinear Programming, Heuristics, and Erlang Distributions," *ORSA Journal on Computing,* Vol. 5, No. 1, pp. 69–83, 1993.

Johnson, N.L., and Kotz, S., *Distribution in Statistics: Continuous Univariate Distributions,* Vols. I and II, John Wiley & Sons, Inc., New York, 1970.

Jones, J.V., *Engineering Design: Reliability, Maintainability and Testability,* Tab Professional and Reference Books, Blue Ridge Summit, Pa., 1988.

Jordan, C.W., *Life Contingencies,* Society of Actuaries, Chicago, 1967.

Kalbfleisch, J.D., and Prentice, R.L., *The Statistical Analysis of Failure Time Data,* John Wiley & Sons, Inc., New York, 1980.

Kang, K., and Schmeiser, B., "Graphical Methods for Evaluating and Comparing Confidence-interval Procedures," *Operations Research,* Vol. 38, No. 3, pp. 546–553, 1990.

Kaplan, E.L., and Meier, P., "Nonparametric Estimation from Incomplete Observations," *Journal of the American Statistical Association,* Vol. 53, No. 282, pp. 457–481, 1958.

Kapur, K.C., and Lamberson, L.R., *Reliability in Engineering Design,* John Wiley & Sons, Inc., New York, 1977.

Kaufmann, A., Grouchko, D., and Croun, R., *Mathematical Models for the Study of the Reliability of Systems,* Academic Press, Inc., New York, 1977.

Kececioglu, D., *Reliability Engineering Handbook,* Vols. 1 and 2, Prentice Hall, Englewood Cliffs, N.J., 1991.

Klaassen, K.B., and van Peppen, J.C.L., *System Reliability: Concepts and Applications,* Edward Arnold, New York, 1989.

Klinger, D.J., Nakada, Y., and Menendez, M.A., *AT&T Reliability Manual,* Van Nostrand Reinhold, Inc., New York, 1990.

Koziol, J.A., and Byar, D.P., "Percentage Points of the Asymptotic Distributions of One and Two Sample K–S Statistics for Truncated or Censored Data," *Technometrics,* Vol. 17, No. 4, pp. 507–510, 1975.

Krishnamoorthi, K.S., *Reliability Methods for Engineers,* ASQC Quality Press, Milwaukee, Wisc., 1992.

Landers, T.L., and Kolarik, W.J., "Proportional Hazards Analysis of Field Warranty Data," *Reliability Engineering,* Vol. 18, No. 2, pp. 131–139, 1987.

Larsen, R.J., and Marx, M.J., *An Introduction to Mathematical Statistics and its Applications,* 2nd ed., Prentice Hall, Englewood Cliffs, N.J., 1986.

Law, A.M., and Kelton, W.D., *Simulation Modeling and Analysis,* 2nd ed., McGraw-Hill, Inc., New York, 1991.

Lawless, J.F., *Statistical Models and Methods for Lifetime Data,* John Wiley & Sons, Inc., New York, 1982.

Lee, E., *Statistical Methods for Survival Data Analysis,* 2nd ed., John Wiley & Sons, Inc., New York, 1992.

Lee, M.T., "Mixtures of Lifetime Distributions" in *Advances in Reliability*, A. Basu, ed., North-Holland, New York, pp. 231–245, 1993.

Lee, S., Wilson, J.R., and Crawford, M.M., "Modeling and Simulation of a Nonhomogeneous Poisson Process with Cyclic Features," *Communications in Statistics—Simulation and Computation,* Vol. 20, Nos. 2 and 3, pp. 777–809, 1991.

Leemis, L.M., "Relationships Among Common Univariate Distributions," *The American Statistician,* Vol. 40, No. 2, pp. 143–146, 1986.

Leemis, L.M., "Variate Generation for Accelerated Life and Proportional Hazards Models," *Operations Research,* Vol. 35, No. 6, pp. 892–894, 1987.

Leemis, L.M., "Nonparametric Estimation of the Cumulative Intensity Function for a Nonhomogeneous Poisson Process," *Management Science,* Vol. 37, No. 7, pp. 886–900, 1991.

Leemis, L.M., and Shih, L., "Exponential Parameter Estimation for Data Sets Containing Left and Right Censored Observations," *Communications in Statistics—Simulation,* Vol. 18, No. 3, pp. 1077–1085, 1989.

Leemis, L.M., and Trivedi, K., "A Comparison of Approximate Interval Estimators for the Bernoulli Parameter," Technical Report, Department of Mathematics, College of William and Mary, Williamsburg, Va., 1994.

Leiderman, F.H., Babu, B., Kagia, J., Kraemer, H., and Leiderman, G., "African Infant Precocity and Some Social Influences During the First Year," *Nature,* Vol. 242, No. 6, pp. 247–249, 1973.

Lewis, E.E., *Introduction to Reliability Engineering,* John Wiley & Sons, Inc., New York, 1987.

Lieblein, J., and Zelen, M., "Statistical Investigation of the Fatigue Life of Deep-groove Ball Bearings," *Journal of Research of the National Bureau of Standards,* Vol. 57, No. 5, pp. 273–316, 1956.

Lin, D.Y., "Goodness-of-Fit Analysis for the Cox Regression Model Based on a Class of Parameter Estimators," *Journal of the American Statistical Association,* Vol. 86, No. 415, pp. 725–728, 1991.

Lloyd, D.K., and Lipow, M., *Reliability: Management, Methods, and Mathematics,* 2nd ed., American Society for Quality Control, Milwaukee, Wisc., 1984.

Loh, W., "A New Generalization of the Class of NBU Distributions," *IEEE Transactions on Reliability,* Vol. R-33, No. 5, pp. 419–422, 1984.

Mann, N.R., and Fertig, K.W., "Tables for Obtaining Weibull Confidence Bounds and Tolerance Bounds Based on Best Linear Invariant Estimates of Parameters of the Extreme-value Distribution," *Technometrics,* Vol. 15, No. 1, pp. 87–101, 1973.

Mann, N.R., Schafer, R.E., and Singpurwalla, N.D., *Methods for Statistical Analysis of Reliability and Life Data,* John Wiley & Sons, Inc., New York, 1974.

Margolin, B.H., and Maurer, W., "Tests of the Kolmogorov–Smirnov Type for Exponential Data with Unknown Scale, and Related Problems," *Biometrika,* Vol. 63, No. 1, pp. 149–160, 1976.

Marshall, A.W., and Olkin, I., "A Multivariate Exponential Distribution," *Journal of the American Statistical Association,* Vol. 62, No. 317, pp. 30–44, 1967.

Martz, H.F., and Waller, R.A., *Bayesian Reliability Analysis,* John Wiley & Sons, Inc., New York, 1982.

Martz, H.F., and Zimmer, W.J., "The Risk of Catastrophic Failure of the Solid Rocket Boosters on the Space Shuttle," *The American Statistician,* Vol. 46, No. 1, pp. 42–47, 1992.

Mazzuchi, T.A., and Soyer, R., "Assessment of Machine Tool Reliability Using a Proportional Hazards Model," *Naval Research Logistics,* Vol. 36, No. 3, pp. 765–777, 1989.

Meeker, W.Q., and Hahn, G.J., *How to Plan an Accelerated Life Test,* American Society for Quality Control, Milwaukee, Wisc., 1985.

Menon, M.V., "Estimation of the Shape and Scale Parameters of the Weibull Distribution," *Technometrics,* Vol. 5, No. 2, pp. 175–182, 1963.

Miller, R., *Survival Analysis,* John Wiley & Sons, Inc., New York, 1981.

MIL-HDBK-217F, *Military Handbook: Reliability Prediction of Electronic Equipment,* Department of Defense, Washington, D.C., 1992.

Modarres, M., *What Every Engineer Should Know about Reliability and Risk Analysis,* Marcel Dekker, Inc., New York, 1993.

Moore, E.F., and Shannon, C.E., "Reliable Circuits Using Less Reliable Relays," *Journal of the Franklin Institute,* Vol. 262, Part I, pp. 191–208; Vol. 263, Part II, pp. 281–297, 1956.

Moschopoulos, P.G., "A General Procedure for Deriving Distributions," *Communications in Statistics—Theoretical Methods,* Vol. 12, No. 17, pp. 2005–2015, 1983.

Moss, M., *Designing for Minimal Maintenance Expense,* Marcel Dekker, Inc., New York, 1985.

Moura, E.C., *How to Determine Sample Size and Estimate Failure Rate in Life Testing,* ASQC Quality Press, Milwaukee, Wisc., 1991.

Musa, J., Iannino, A., and Okumoto, K., *Software Reliability: Measurement, Prediction, Application,* McGraw-Hill, Inc., New York, 1987.

Muth, E.J., "Reliability Models with Positive Memory Derived from the Mean Residual Life Function" in *The Theory and Applications of Reliability*, C. P. Tsokos and I. Shimi, eds., Academic Press, Inc., New York, pp. 401–435, 1977.

Nelson, W., *Applied Life Data Analysis,* John Wiley & Sons, Inc., New York, 1982.

Nelson, W., *Accelerated Testing: Statistical Models, Test Plans and Data Analysis,* John Wiley & Sons, Inc., New York, 1990.

Nelson, W., and Hahn, G.J., "Linear Estimation of a Regression Relationship from Censored Data: Part I—Simple Methods and Their Application," *Technometrics,* Vol. 14, No. 2, pp. 247–269, 1972.

Neter, J., Wasserman, W., and Kutner, M.H., *Applied Linear Regression Models,* 2nd ed., Richard D. Irwin, Inc., Homewood, Ill., 1989.

Neufelder, A.M., *Ensuring Software Reliability,* Marcel Dekker, Inc., 1993.

Neuts, M.F., *Matrix-Geometric Solutions in Stochastic Models,* Johns Hopkins University Press, Baltimore, Md., 1981.

O'Connor, P.D.T., *Practical Reliability Engineering,* 3rd ed., John Wiley & Sons, Inc., New York, 1991.

Padgett, W.J., "Nonparametric Estimation of Density and Hazard Rate Functions When Samples Are Censored" in *Handbook of Statistics 7: Quality Control and Reliability*, P.R. Krishnaiah and C.R. Rao, eds., North-Holland, New York, pp. 313–332, 1988.

Park, W.J., and Kim, Y.G., "Goodness-of-Fit Tests for the Power-law Process," *IEEE Transactions on Reliability,* Vol. 41, No. 1, pp. 107–111, 1992.

Parzen, E., "Nonparametric Statistical Data Modeling," *Journal of the American Statistical Association,* Vol. 74, No. 365, pp. 105–131, 1979.

Pavur, R.J., Edgeman, R.L., and Scott, R.C., "Quadratic Statistics for the Goodness-of-Fit Test of the Inverse Gaussian Distribution," *IEEE Transactions on Reliability,* Vol. 41, No. 1, pp. 118–123, 1992.

Peto, R., Contribution to the Discussion of Professor Cox's Paper, *Journal of the Royal Statistical Society B,* Vol. 34, No. 2, pp. 205–207, 1972.

Pettitt, A.N., and Stephens, M.A., "The Kolmogorov–Smirnov Goodness-of-Fit Statistic with Discrete and Grouped Data," *Technometrics,* Vol. 19, No. 2, pp. 205–210, 1977.

Porter, J.E., Coleman, J.W., and Moore, A.H., "Modified KS, AD, and C-vM Tests for the Pareto Distribution with Unknown Location and Scale Parameters," *IEEE Transactions on Reliability,* Vol. 41, No. 1, pp. 112–117, 1992.

Prentice, R.L., "Discrimination among Some Parametric Models," *Biometrika,* Vol. 62, No. 3, pp. 607–619, 1975.

Proschan, F., "Theoretical Explanation of Observed Decreasing Failure Rate," *Technometrics,* Vol. 5, No. 3, pp. 375–383, 1963.

Ramakumar, R., *Engineering Reliability: Fundamentals and Applications,* Prentice Hall, Englewood Cliffs, N.J., 1993.

Rao, S.S., *Reliability Based Design,* McGraw-Hill, Inc., New York, 1992.

Rigdon, S.E., and Basu, A.P., "Mean Squared Errors of Estimators of the Intensity Function of a Nonhomogeneous Poisson Process," *Statistics and Probability Letters,* Vol. 8, No. 5, pp. 445–449, 1989.

Ross, S.M., "Multivalued State Component Systems," *Annals of Probability,* Vol. 7, No. 2, pp. 379–383, 1979.

Ross, S.M., *Introduction to Probability Models,* 5th ed., Academic Press, Inc., Boston, 1993.

Sander, P., and Badoux, R., eds., *Bayesian Methods in Reliability,* Kluwer Academic Publishers, Boston, 1991.

Sarhan, A.E., and Greenberg, B.G., *Contributions to Order Statistics,* John Wiley & Sons, Inc., New York, 1962.

Schmeiser, B.W., Personal communication, 1984.

Schmidt, P., and Witte, A.D., *Predicting Recidivism Using Survival Models,* Springer-Verlag, Inc., New York, 1988.

Schwarz, C.J., and Samanta, M., "An Inductive Proof of the Sampling Distributions for the MLE's of the Parameters in an Inverse Gaussian Distribution," *The American Statistician,* Vol. 45, No. 3, pp. 223–225, 1991.

Shaked, M., and Shanthikumar, J.G., "Reliability and Maintainability" in *Handbooks in OR and MS,* Vol. 2, D.P. Heyman and M.J. Sobel, eds., Elsevier Science Publishers B.V. (North-Holland), New York, 653–713, 1990.

Shier, D., *Network Reliability and Algebraic Structures,* Oxford University Press, New York, 1991.

Shih, L., The Nonhomogeneous Poisson Process with Covariate Effects, Ph.D. dissertation, School of Industrial Engineering, University of Oklahoma, Norman, 1991.

Shooman, M.L., *Probabilistic Reliability: An Engineering Approach,* McGraw-Hill, Inc., New York, 1968.

Sinha, S.K., *Reliability and Life Testing,* John Wiley & Sons, Inc., New York, 1986.

Smith, C.O., *Introduction to Reliability in Design,* McGraw-Hill, Inc., New York, 1976.

Smith, R.M., and Bain, L.J., "An Exponential Power Life-testing Distribution," *Communications in Statistics,* Vol. 4, No. 5, pp. 469–481, 1975.

Stacy, E.W., "A Generalization of the Gamma Distribution," *Annals of Mathematical Statistics,* Vol. 33, No. 3, pp. 1187–1192, 1962.

Stephens, M.A., "EDF Statistics for Goodness of Fit and Some Comparisons," *Journal of the American Statistical Association,* Vol. 69, No. 347, pp. 730–737, 1974.

Sundararajan, C.R., *Guide to Reliability Engineering: Data, Analysis, Applications, Implementation, and Management,* Van Nostrand Reinhold, Inc., New York, 1991.

Swartz, G.B., "The Mean Residual Life Function," *IEEE Transactions on Reliability,* Vol. R-22, No. 2, pp. 108–109, 1973.

Sweet, A.L., "On the Hazard Rate of the Lognormal Distribution," *IEEE Transactions on Reliability,* Vol. 39, No. 3, pp. 325–328, 1990.

Syski, R., *Random Processes,* Marcel Dekker, Inc., New York, 1979.

Thompson, W.A., *Point Process Models with Applications to Safety and Reliability,* Chapman and Hall, New York, 1988.

Tobias, P.A., and Trindade, D., *Applied Reliability,* Van Nostrand Reinhold, Inc., New York, 1986.

Trivedi, K.S., *Probability and Statistics with Reliability, Queuing and Computer Science Applications,* Prentice Hall, Englewood Cliffs, N.J., 1982.

Ushakov, I.A., and Harrison, R.A., *Handbook of Reliability Engineering,* John Wiley & Sons, Inc., New York, 1994.

von Alven, W.H., *Reliability Engineering,* ARINC Research Corporation, Prentice Hall, Englewood Cliffs, N.J., 1964.

Weibull, W., "A Statistical Theory of the Strength of Materials," *Ingeniors Vetenskaps Akademien Handlingar,* No. 153, 1939.

Weibull, W., "A Statistical Distribution Function of Wide Applicability," *Journal of Applied Mechanics,* Vol. 18, pp. 293–297, 1951.

Wilson, J.G., "Group Replacement Policies That Incorporate Statistical Learning" in *Advances in Reliability* A. Basu, ed., North-Holland, New York, pp. 445–457, 1993.

Zacks, S., *Introduction to Reliability Analysis: Probabilistic Models and Statistical Methods,* Springer-Verlag, Inc., New York, 1992.

Index

Page numbers are *italicized* in this index to indicate the definition or main source of information about an entry. Entries are *italicized* to indicate that an entire chapter, section, subsection, or appendix is devoted to the entry.

A

a/c switches, *see* automotive a/c switch failure times
accelerated life model, 9, 11–12, *121–124*, 131–132, *230–238*
    application, 234–237, 249–251
    with a binary covariate, 122, 126–128, 231–237, 249
    comparison with proportional hazards model, *126–128*, 228–229
    covariates in, 14, 121–122
    distribution representations, 123–124, 126
    exponential baseline distribution, *230–237*, 249–250
    generalizations of, 129
    likelihood function, 229
    link function, 122–128, 228–229
    log likelihood function, 230–232
    log-linear link function, 122–126, 128, 131–132, 229–238, 241–251
    parameter estimation, 11–12, *230–238*
    relation to a regression model, 123
    stratification, 129
    Weibull baseline distribution, *124*, 127–128, *237–238*, 251
accelerated life testing, 128, 214, 246–247, 276, *see also* accelerated life model; motorette failure times
actuarial science, 1–2, 12, 109, 252, 261
    applications, 46, 52, 97, 119–120, 181, 187, 263–264
actuaries, *see* actuarial science
age replacement policy, *134–135*, 158, *see also* replacement policies
age-specific death rate, *see* hazard function
Air Force, United States, 157
airplane propellers, 18–19
alternating renewal process, *151*, 158
alternative hypothesis, 201, *see also* hypothesis testing
Anderson–Darling statistic, 277–278
applications, *see* actuarial science; data sets; system design applications
approximate confidence interval, 168, *see also* interval estimation
asymptotic properties, *see also* interval estimation; point estimation
    among distributions, 99
    of the likelihood function, 172, *179–181*, 187, 205–208, *see also* likelihood theory
    of a point estimator, 165–166
asymptotically exact confidence interval, 168

automotive a/c switch failure times, *190*, 220
    comparing two populations under exponential assumption, 210
    exponential fit, 199–200, 223
    goodness-of-fit test, 272–273
    hypothesis testing under exponential assumption, 201–202
    Weibull fit, 226
automobile
    brake systems, 17, 56
    engine, 17
    lug nuts, 31, 38
    tires, 4
availability, 9–10, *147–154*, 157
    availability function, 10
    definition, 148–150
average availability, *150–153*, 157

B

ball bearing failure times, *190*, 220
    confidence intervals under exponential assumption, 196–197
    exponential fit, *194–197*, 219, 223
    goodness-of-fit test, 265–271, 273–275, 278
    nonparametric survivor function estimator, 195–196, *255–256*
    population versus fitted survivor functions, 253
    Weibull fit, *217–220*, 222, 226, 292–293
baseline model, 122, *see also* accelerated life model; proportional hazards model
bathtub-shaped hazard function, 8, *51–52*, 65, 94, 97, 100, 108–110, 220
    applied to human lifetimes, 8, 52
    applied to human performance, 52, 71, 80
Bayesian model, 101, *120–121*, 128, 214–215, *see also* continuous mixture model
Bernoulli, Daniel, 109
Bernoulli distribution, 57, 254
best linear unbiased estimate, 223
bimodal failure, 38, *43–44*, 86, 109
binary assumption (for coherent systems), *see* binary model
binary covariate, *122*, 126–128, 131, 189–190, 231–237, 239–251
binary model, 3, 16, 34, 37–38

binomial distribution, 254, 257
biostatisticians, *see* biostatistics
biostatistics, *1–2*, 187, 205
birth-death models, 101, *154–156*, 157
    application, 155–156
    expected transition time, 155–156
bivariate distributions, *see* multivariate distributions
bivariate exponential distribution, 101, 106–107
block diagram, 7–8, *17*, 24–26, 39–41, *see also* system
        configurations
    for airplane propellers, 18–19
    for O–rings, 5
    relationship to electrical wiring diagram, 17
    repeated components in, 18–20
block replacement policy, *134–135*, 158, *see also*
        replacement policies
bounds, *see* reliability bounds
bridge structure, 19–20, *see also* system configurations
BT (bathtub-shaped) hazard function, *see* bathtub-shaped
        hazard function
burn-in, *52*, 75, 104, 124, *136–138*
Burr distribution, 101

C

cancer, *see* leukemia remission times; lung cancer data
case study, *5–7*, 13, *see also Challenger* accident
casualty insurance application, 119–120
censored data, *see* censoring
censoring, 10–13, 160, *181–186*, *see also* exponential
        distribution; Weibull distribution
    graphical methods for, 187
    left, 183–184
    left and right, *183*, 222–223
    in life tables, 262–264
    likelihood function, 184–186, 229
    notation, 184–186, 229
    potential censoring times, 233
    probabilistic approaches to, 184
    progressive Type II, 187
    random, *183–184*, 190, 205–208, 215–220, 259, 275
    Type I, *182–184*, 203–205, 221, 223–225, 271–273
    Type II, *182*, 184, 188, 190, 197–203, 211–213,
        222–226, 271–273
    value in obtaining exact failure times, 181
central limit theorem, 8, 81, 172, 179
Challenger accident, 1, *5–7*, 9, 13
    system design, 5, 7
    temperature as a covariate, 6, 9
characteristic function, 45
characteristic life, *89*, 97, 104
Chebyshev's inequality, 69
chi-square distribution, 94
    as a limiting distribution, 179–181
    as a special case of the gamma distribution, 94
    use in confidence intervals for exponential data, 86,
        166–168, 170–172, 194–196, 198, 204–206, 209,
        213, 221, 223, 236, 281–282
    nonsymmetry of, 167, 195
CIS, *see* confidence interval scatterplot

classes of distributions, *see* distribution classes
closure, 65–66
coefficient of variation, *60*, 69, 85, 89, 93, 105–106, 141
coherent systems analysis, 20–44
    component versus system redundancy, *20–22*, 39, 43
    definition of a coherent system, 20
    examples of noncoherent systems, 20
    minimal cut sets, results for, 26–27, 36–37
    minimal path sets, results for, 25–27, 36–37
    minimal path sets and minimal cut sets, 23–27
    reliability importance, *35*, 42, 104
    results for coherent systems, 20–21, 25–27, 36–38,
        66–68, 76
    structural importance, 21–23, 35, 40, 42
    structure function for, 7, *15–32*, 37–43
    system reliability, *see* system reliability calculations
cohort life table, 263
cold standby systems, *see* standby systems
common-cause failures, 28
comparison of distributions
    in the accelerated life model, 234–237
    exponential populations, 208–210
    in proportional hazards models, 246
    univariate distributions, 99
comparison of survivor functions, 46–47, 253–254
competing risks, 9–10, *109–117*, 128–130, 147, 155
    crude lifetimes, *110–117*, 129–130, 288–290
    distribution of crude lifetimes, 116–117
    distribution of net lifetimes from crude lifetimes,
        116–117, *288–290*
    and finite mixtures, 119–120
    general formulas for, 114–115
    identifiability in, 117, 129
    independence in, 111–117, 129–130, 288–290
    net lifetimes, *110–117*, 129–130, 288–290
    probability of failure from risk j, 111, 113–117,
        129–130
    risk removal, 129–130, 225
complete data sets, *181–182*, 184, 189, 192–197,
        265–271, *see also* censoring
complex arrangement of components, 18–20, *see also*
        system configurations
component redundancy, *20–22*, 39, 43
component reliability, 28, *see also* system reliability
        calculations
component versus system redundancy, *20–22*, 39, 43
component versus system reliability, 29–31, 36–37
compound distributions, 118
computer program
    reliability of, 52, 56, *see also* system design
        applications
    for lifetime data analysis, 222
concomitant variable, *see* covariate
conditional distribution, 120, 241–243
conditional likelihood, 241–246
conditional survivor function, 46–47, 91
conditioning argument, 33
confidence bands, *see* confidence limits
confidence interval, 166–172, *see also* interval estimation
confidence intervals for quantities other than the failure
        rate, 196–197

confidence interval scatterplot (CIS), 169–172, *see also* interval estimation
    effect of changing α on, 172
    rotating a, 172
confidence level, 201, *see also* hypothesis testing; interval estimation
confidence limits
    for a confidence interval, 12–13, *166–172*
    for a survivor function estimate, 255–256, 260–261
confidence region, 11, *218–219*, 226–227
consecutive *k*-out-of-*n* system, 38, *see also* *k*-out-of-*n* system
consistency, 165–166, 177
consumer's risk, 210–213, 225–226, *see also* life testing
continuous mixture model, 117–118, *120–121*, 128, 130–131
    in life testing, 214–215
continuous systems, 34, 38
continuous-time Markov process, 154–157
control group, 122, 190, 193, 233–237, 246, *see also* leukemia remission times
convolution property, 81
corrective maintenance, 135
correlation, 107, 168, 237
cost optimization, 102, 202–203, 213
counting process, 137–138, *see also* point process models
covariance, 174, *see also* variance-covariance matrix
covariate, 2, 9, 11–12, *121–122*, 131–132
    examples, 103, 108, 117, 122, 129, 190–191, 233–237, 246–248
Cox model, *see* proportional hazards model
Cramer–Rao inequality, 163–164, 186, *see also* point estimation
Cramer–von Mises statistic, 277–278
crude lifetimes, *110–117*, 129–130, 288–290, *see also* competing risks
crude probabilities, 110–117, *see also* competing risks
cumulative damage model, 101
cumulative distribution function
    definition, 46
    relationship with probability density function, 48
    role in goodness-of-fit tests, 265–275
cumulative hazard function, 8, *53*, 56–58
    aliases, 53
    applications, 53
    definition, 53
    for discrete distributions, 56–58
    existence properties, 53
    relation to other functions, *54–55*, 72
    role in the log likelihood function, 186, 230
cumulative intensity function, 138–139, *145–146*, 158
current life table, 263–264
cut vector, 24, 32–33, 40
cut vector technique, *32–33*, *see also* system reliability calculations

D

data sets, *189–191*
    aircraft components, 277

automotive a/c switches, *190*, 220, *see also* automotive a/c switch failure times
ball bearings, *190*, 220, *see also* ball bearing failure times
burn-in, 223
electric generators, 276
leukemia remission times, *190*, 220, *see also* leukemia remission times
light bulbs, 204–205, 239–245
lung cancer, 249–250
motorette failure times, *191*, 220, *see also* motorette failure times
recidivism, 247–249
United States mortality data, *263–264*, 276
decomposition technique, *33–34*, *see also* system reliability calculations
deep-groove ball bearings, *see* ball bearing failure times
definition technique, *28–29*, *see also* system reliability calculations
delta-star technique, 38, *see also* system reliability calculations
density quantile function, 68
dependent components, 34, 38
design applications, *see* system design applications
design considerations, *see* system design considerations
deteriorating item, *136–138*, 144–147
DFR (decreasing failure rate), 51–52, *65–69*, 79, 98, 100, 137, *see also* distribution classes
DFRA (decreasing failure rate on the average), 65, 68–69, *see also* distribution classes
discrete lifetime distributions, *55–59*, 68, 73–74, 256–257, 276, *297–298*
distributions (failure time), *78–107*
    Bernoulli, 57, 254
    binomial, 254, 257
    bivariate exponential, 101, 106–107
    Burr, 101
    chi-square, 94, *see also* chi-square distribution
    Erlang, 93–94, *see also* Erlang distribution
    exponential, *81–88*, *191–215*, *see also* exponential distribution
    exponential power, 97, 99–101, 105–106, 131–132, 220, 226
    extreme value, 88, 91, 99, 217, 284–285, *294–296*
    F, *209–210*, 225
    gamma, 91–96, *see also* gamma distribution
    generalized F, 101
    generalized gamma, 101
    generalized Pareto, 98–101
    geometric, *57–58*, 73–74, 84
    Gompertz, 97, 99–101
    hyperexponential, 98–101, 119
    hypoexponential, 98–101
    IDB, 97, 99–101, 106
    inverse Gaussian, *96–97*, 99–101, 177–179, 186, 222, 276
    log gamma, 99
    logistic, 99, 106
    log logistic, *96*, 99–100, 105–106, 120, 124, 130–131, 226, 251
    log normal, *95–96*, 99–101, 105–106, 187, 222, 226

Makeham, 97, 99–101
Muth, 95, 99–101
normal, 8, 43, 79, 81, 88, 95, 99, 170–172, 179–180, 205, 208, 223, 260
Pareto, 72–73, 97, 99–101, 105, 158, 188, 276
Poisson, 121, *139–140*, 145, 284
Rayleigh, *88*, 97, 99
t, 170, 187
truncated normal, 101
uniform, 72, 75–76, *95*, 99–100, 105, 119, 269
Weibull, *88–91*, *215–221*, *see also* Weibull distribution
distribution classes, *64–68*, 80, 100
   DFR (decreasing failure rate), 51–52, *65–69*, 79, 98, 100, 137
   DFRA (decreasing failure rate on the average), 65, 68–69
   DMRL (decreasing mean residual life), 69
   HNBUE (harmonic new better than used in expectation), 69
   HNWUE (harmonic new worse than used in expectation), 69
   IFR (increasing failure rate), 51, *65–69*, 76–77, 79, 91, 100, 137, 196
   IFRA (increasing failure rate on the average), *68–69*, 77
   IMRL (increasing mean residual life), 68–69
   NBAFR (new better than used average failure rate), 69
   NBU (new better than used), 69, 77
   NBUE (new better than used in expectation), 69, 77
   NWU (new worse than used), 69
   NWAFR (new worse than used average failure rate), 69
   NWUE (new worse than used in expectation), 69
distribution function, *see* cumulative distribution function
DMRL (decreasing mean residual life), 69, *see also* distribution classes
drift (electrical components), 16
drill bit, 3, 12, 251, *see also* system design applications
dual system, 40
dynamic reliability calculations, 8, *27–35*, *see also* system lifetime distribution; system reliability calculations

E

efficiency, 162–163, *see also* point estimation
electrical wiring diagrams, 17, *see also* block diagrams
electronic component failure rates, 160
empirical survivor function, 11, 195–196, 200, *253–264*
engineering design, *see* system design considerations
engineering design applications, *see* system design applications
engineering design considerations, *see* system design considerations
environmental conditions, 2, 4, 6–7, 122, 124, 132, 136, 208, 246–247
epoch, 2, *see also* point process models
Erlang distribution, 93–94
   shifted, 180–181

as sum of exponentials, *94*, 140, 142–143, 162, 166, 168, 180, 282, 284
   survivor function, 93, 105
event trees, 38
exact confidence interval, *167–168*, 194–200, 209–210, *see also* interval estimation
exact failure times, *see* raw data
expectation, 59, *see also* moments
expectation technique, 30–32, *see also* system reliability calculations
expected value, *see* expectation
explanatory variable, 121–122, *see also* covariate
exponential distribution, *81–88*, *191–215*
   applications, 43, 70, 72–76, 102–106, 277
   as baseline in accelerated life model, 230–237, 249–250
   asymptotic properties of the score vector, 180–181
   in the bivariate exponential distribution, 101, 106–107
   ceiling of an exponential random variable, 74
   coefficient of variation, *85*, 103, 105, 223
   comparing two populations, 208–210
   in competing risks, 111–113, 115–117, 129–130
   complete data sets, 192–197
   confidence intervals for λ, 86, 194–199, 204–210
   confidence intervals for $S(t)$, 196–197
   confidence intervals for θ, 166–168, 170–172, 223
   curve shapes, 82
   definition, 54, 81–82, 95
   distribution classes, 65, 100, 103
   exact confidence intervals, 167–168, 170–172, 194–195, 209–210, 223
   estimation techniques, *161–173*, 175–177, 180–181, *191–215*, 221–223
   fractiles, 61
   generalizations, 95, 99, 103
   goodness-of-fit test, 265–278
   information matrix, 177, 187, 193–195, 198–199, 203, 206, 208, 225
   kurtosis, *85*, 102, 105, 223
   left and right censoring, 222–223
   in *life testing*, 202–203, *210–215*, 221, 223–225
   likelihood function, 175, 192
   log likelihood function, 175, 192, 198, 203, 205
   maximum likelihood estimator of λ, 192–199, 204–205
   maximum likelihood estimator of θ, 172–173, 197, 199
   mean, 61, 85, 161, 223
   median, 225
   memoryless property, 8–9, *82–84*, 87, 103, 141, 214, 279–280
   minimum of exponential random variables, 66–68, *86*, 103, 282–283
   in mixture distributions, 66–68, *118–120*
   for modeling lifetimes of electrical components, 9, 160
   moments, 85, 281
   order statistics, *86–87*, 198, 202–203, 213
   parameters, 79, 81, 191
   parametric methods for, 175–181, 191–215
   Poisson process, relationship with, *87*, 140, 142–143, 203, 214, 284
   probabilistic properties, 82–88, *279–285*
   with random parameter, 120

(exponential distribution, cont'd)
   randomly right-censored data sets, 205–208
   references, 101, 220–221
   relationships to other distributions, 88, 99, 104
   in renewal processes, 142–143
   in repairable systems, 150–156, 158
   score, 175, 187, 192, 203
   self-reproducing property, 86, 281
   skewness, 61, *85*, 102, 105, 223
   system reliability with exponential components, 63–64,
      75–76, 102–103
   test for exponentiality, 85, 217–220, 222, 265–276
   total time on test transform for, 73
   Type I censored data sets, 203–205, 221
   Type II censored data sets, 197–203, 211–213,
      222–223
   unit exponential distribution, 84, 88, 95, 224, 280
   variance, 61, 85, 161
   variate generation, 84
exponential power distribution, *97*, 99–101, 105–106,
   131–132, 220, 226
extreme value distribution, 88, 91, 99, 217, 284–285,
   294–296

F

F distribution, *209–210*, 225
failure modes and effects analysis (FMEA), 38
failure physics, 196
failure replacement policy, 134–135, *see also*
   replacement policies
failure time distributions, *see* distributions
fault trees, 38
field joint rotation, 5–6, *see also Challenger* accident
finite mixture model, 117–120, *see also* mixture
   distribution
Fisher information matrix, 174–179, 188
   for the accelerated life model, 231–233, 249
   for the exponential distribution, 187, 193–194, 198,
      203, 205
   for the inverse Gaussian distribution, 179
   for the Weibull distribution, 217, 219
5-out-of-10 system, 203
force of decrement, 49, *see also* hazard function
force of mortality, 49, *see also* hazard function
forgetfulness property, *see* memoryless property
fractiles, 59–62
fuse, 3, 56, 59, 83, 102, *see also* system design
   applications

G

gamma distribution, 91–96
   coefficient of variation, 93, 105
   curve shapes, 93
   definition, 92
   distribution classes, 92, 100
   kurtosis, 93, 105
   life testing, 227

   mean, 93
   moments, 92–93
   parameter estimation, 222
   parameters, 79, 92
   properties, 104, 287
   references, 101, 222
   relationships with other distributions, 93–95, 99, 162
   in renewal processes, 143–144
   in repairable systems, 157–158
   skewness, 93, 105
   special cases, 92–94, 162
   in stochastic parameter models, 121, 130
   tail behavior, 92
   variance, 93
gamma function, 85, 89–91, 102, 104, *286–287*
gamma-Poisson distribution, 121
gap statistics, 87, 282–284
generalized F distribution, 101
generalized gamma distribution, 101
generalized Pareto distribution, 98–101
generational life table, 263
geometric distribution, *57–58*, 73–74, 84
Gini's statistic, 276
Gompertz distribution, 97, 99–101
goodness-of-fit test, 12, 195–196
   chi-square, 265
   Kolmogorov–Smirnov, all parameters known, 265–273
   Kolmogorov–Smirnov, parameters estimated from data,
      273–275
   Kolmogorov–Smirnov, test statistic, 265–269
Greenwood's formula, 260–263, 276
grouped failure times, 160, 252, 262, 276, *see also* life
   tables
guarantee parameter, 79

H

hazard function, 8, *49–58*
   age-specific death rate, 49
   aliases, 49
   bathtub-shaped, 8, *51–52*, 65, 71, 80, 94, 97, 100,
      108–110, 220
   definition, 49
   for discrete distributions, 56–58
   existence conditions, *50*, 71
   intensity function, 49, 145
   interpretation of, 49–53
   Mill's ratio, 49, 97
   rate function, 49
   relation to a nonhomogeneous Poisson process, 49,
      136–137
   relation to other functions, *54–55*, 70, 72
   role in the log likelihood function, 186, 230
   units on, 51
hazard rate, *see* hazard function
HNBUE (harmonic new better than used in expectation),
   69, *see also* distribution classes
HNWUE (harmonic new worse than used in expectation),
   69, *see also* distribution classes

homogeneous Poisson process, 139–140, 146, *see also* Poisson process
human performance tasks, 52, 71, 80
hump-shaped hazard function, *see* UBT hazard function
hyperexponential distribution, 98–101, 119
   relationship with exponential, 98
hypoexponential distribution, 98–101
   relationship with Erlang, 98
hypothesis testing, 180, *200–202*
   applications, 201–202, 209–215, 225–226, 246–248, 265–275
   definitions, 200–201
   errors associated with, 201

I

IDB distribution, *97*, 99–101, 106
identifiability
   in competing risks, 117, 129
   in mixtures, 119
IFR (increasing failure rate), 51, *65–69*, 76–77, 79, 91, 100, 137, 196, *see also* distribution classes
IFRA (increasing failure rate on the average), 68–69, 77, *see also* distribution classes
IFRA closure theorem, 68–69, *see also* distribution classes
importance
   reliability, *35*, 42, 104
   structural, *21–23*, 35, 40, 42
improving item, *136–138*, 144–147
IMRL (increasing mean residual life), 68–69, *see also* distribution classes
incomplete gamma function, 89, 92, 104–105, 144, *286–287*
increasing failure rate, *see* IFR
increasing (improving) system reliability, 5, 20–23, 35, *see also* reliability growth
independence assumption, 3, 6, *27–28*, 34, 37–38
independent increments, 138–139, 145
infant mortality, 52
infinitesimal generator, 150–151, 154–156
information matrix, *see* Fisher information matrix; observed information matrix
insurance companies, *see* actuarial science
integrated hazard function, *see* cumulative hazard function
intensity function, 136–138, 145–147, *see also* nonhomogeneous Poisson process
interval censoring, 184, *see also* censoring
interval estimation, 11–13, 160, *166–172*, 180, 186
   in the accelerated life model, 231–233, 236–238
   applied to the exponential distribution, 166–168, 170–172, 194–199, 204–210, 220–221, 223–225
   applied to the Weibull distribution, 217–220
   approximate confidence interval, *168*, 170–171, 204–208
   asymptotically exact confidence interval, *168*, 204–208, 254–256, 260–264
   confidence interval scatterplot, 169–172
   exact confidence interval, *167–168*, 194–200, 209–210

expected interval width, 169, 172
   for the exponential distribution, 86, 166–168, 170–172, 194–199, 204–208
   interval width, 169, 172
   joint distribution of the upper and lower limits, 168–169, 186
   scatterplot, 169–172
   stated coverage, 166
   typical choices for α, 166
   variance of the interval width, 169, 172
interval estimator, *see* interval estimation
invariance property for maximum likelihood estimators, 176, 196–197
inverse cumulative distribution function technique, 77, 84, *see also* Monte Carlo simulation
inverse cumulative hazard function technique, 84–85, *see also* Monte Carlo simulation
inverse Gaussian distribution, *96–97*, 99–101, 177–179, 186, 222, 276
irrelevant component, 20

J

Jacobian, 282
joint probability density function of L and U, *167–172*, 186, *see also* interval estimation
joint probability density function of order statistics in Type II censoring, 187, 282–283
joint survivor function in competing risks, 114–115, 289

K

k-out-of-n system, *17*, 18, 38
   applications, 17, 40, 42
   5-out-of-10 system, 203
   relationship to series and parallel systems, 17
   2-out-of-3 system, 18, 32, 41–42, 102
   2-out-of-4 system, 40, 43
Kaplan–Meier estimator, *see* product-limit estimator
key component, 33–34
Kolmogorov–Smirnov test, 12, *265–275*
   all parameters known, 265–273
   critical values, 269–275
   parameters estimated from data, 273–275
   test statistic, 265–269
kurtosis, 60
   definition, 60
   for the exponential distribution, *85*, 102, 105, 223
   for the gamma distribution, 93, 105
   for other parametric distributions, 105
   references, 69
   for the Weibull distribution, *89–90*, 104–105

L

Laplace transformation, 144
large sample properties, *see* asymptotic properties of the log likelihood function

law of diminishing returns, *30–31*, 64, *see also* parallel system
least squares, 216–217, 292–293
left and right censoring in a single data set, *183*, 222–223
left censoring, 183–184, *see also* censoring
leukemia remission times, *190*, 220
   accelerated life model fit, 234–237, 249
   confidence intervals for survivor function estimate for treatment group, 260–261
   exponential fit to control group, 193
   exponential fit to treatment group, 205–208, 225
   life table estimate for survivor function, 262–263
   product-limit survivor function estimate for treatment group, 257–261, 277
   proportional hazards model fit, 246
   Weibull fit to treatment group, 226
life table, 1–2, 12, *261–264*
life testing, 86–87, *210–215*, 221, 223–226
   with replacement, 188, 203, 223–224
   without replacement, 188, 203, 223, 225–227
lifetime data analysis, 2, 9–10, *160–188*, *see also* data sets; interval estimation; point estimation
lifetime distribution representations, 8, *45–59*, *see also* cumulative hazard function; hazard function; mean residual life function; probability density function; probability mass function; survivor function
   continuous distributions, 45–55
   discrete distributions, 55–59
   relationships between, 54–55
lifetime distributions, *see* distributions
light bulb, *see* system design applications
likelihood function, 172–179, *see also* likelihood theory
likelihood ratio statistic, 180, 207–208, 217–219
   in accelerated life model with exponential baseline, 249
likelihood theory, 160, *172–179*, *see also* exponential distribution; Weibull distribution
   asymptotic properties, 172, *179–181*, 187, 205–208
   censored data, 181–186
   Fisher information matrix, 174–179, 193–195, 203, 205, *see also* Fisher information matrix
   invariance property of the maximum likelihood estimator, 176–177, 196–197
   likelihood function, 172, 175, 192, 242, 244–245, 256, 295
   log likelihood function, 172, 175, 192, 198, 203, 205–208, 215–219, 230–232, 237–238, 242–251, 256–257, 295–296
   maximum likelihood estimator, 172, 174–179, 192–199, 203–205, 215–221, 230–251, 257–261, 295–296
   observed information matrix, 177–179, 194–195, 198–199, 203–206, 208, 217, 219–220, 231, 236–238, 243–244, 246–249, 251, 260, 276–277
   one-parameter model application, 175–177, 191–208
   score vector definition, 174–175, *see also* score vector
   two-parameter model application 177–179, 215–220
limiting availability, 150–153, *see also* availability
limiting average availability, 150–153, *see also* availability
limiting distributions, 98–99, 101

link function, 122, 131–132, *see also* accelerated lifetime model; proportional hazards model
   log-linear form, 122, 124–126, 131–132, 228–229, 251
   other forms, 122, 128
link vector, *see* path vector
location parameter, 78–79
log gamma distribution, 99
logistic distribution, 99, 106
log likelihood function, 178–179, *see also* likelihood theory
log-linear link function, 122, *see also* accelerated life model; proportional hazards model
log logistic distribution, *96*, 99–100, 105–106, 120, 124, 130–131, 226, 251
log normal distribution, *95–96*, 99–101, 105–106, 187, 222, 226
lung cancer data, 249–250

M

m-out-of-*n* system, *see* *k*-out-of-*n* system
maintainability, 37, 157, *see also* availability
maintenance models, 133–136
Makeham distribution, 97, 99–101
Markov inequality, 69
Markov models, 101, 154–157
maximum likelihood estimator, 11–12, *172*, 175–179, 187–188, 192–199, 203–205, 215–227, 230–251, *see also* likelihood theory
mean, 59–60, 85, 89, 93, 106, 161, 175–176, *see also* moments
mean residual life function, 8, *53–54*, 57–58, 68, 72–73
   definition, 54
   for discrete distributions, 57–58
   existence conditions, 54, 72
   interpretation, 53–54
   relation to other functions, 54–55, 71–72
mean squared error, 164–165, *see also* point estimation
mean time between failures (MTBF), 60
mean time to failure (MTTF), 60, 151
mean time to repair (MTTR), 151
mechanical component failure rates, 160
median, 60, 72, 75, 88, 104, 161, 225, 254
Mellin transform, 45, 68, 72
memoryless property, 57–58, 82–84
   applied to the exponential distribution, 8–9, 67, *82–84*, 87, 103, 131–132, 141, 214, 279–280
   applied to the geometric distribution, 57–58, 73, 84
   misapplications, 83
mercaptopurine, *see* leukemia remission times
MIL-HDBK-217, 103, 160, 186
Mill's ratio, 49, 97, *see also* hazard function
minimal cut sets, *24–27*, 36–38, 40–41
minimal cut vectors, 24
minimal path sets, 19, *24–27*, 36–38, 40–41
minimal path vectors, *24*, 40
minimum life parameter, 79
minimum of exponential random variables, 66–67, *86*, 103, 281–283
minimum of Weibull random variables, 91

minimum-variance unbiased estimator, 163–164, *see also* point estimation
mix parameters, 118
mixed discrete-continuous distribution, 59, 68, *74–75*
mixture distribution, 9, 65–66, *117–121*, 128, 130–131
    and competing risks, 119–120
    continuous, 120–121, 130–131
    of exponential distributions, 67
    finite, 117–120, 130
mode, 70, 104, 131
model adequacy, *see* goodness-of-fit test
modes of failure, *see* bimodal failure
modular decomposition technique, 38, *see also* system reliability calculations
moment generating function, 45, 68, 143–144, 188
moments, *59–62*, 69, 77, 79, 92, 161
    definition, 59
    exponential distribution, 61, 85, 102, 105, 161
    gamma distribution, 93, 105
    mean, variance, skewness, kurtosis definitions, 59–60
    Weibull distribution, 89–90, 104–105
monotonic hazard function, 9
Monte Carlo simulation
    applications, 77, 95–97, 105, 107, 131–132, 223–224, 269–270, 272–275, 277
    in competing risks, 113
    generating Weibull variates, 84
    in repairable systems, 150, 158, 222
motorette failure times, *191*, 220
    proportional hazards fit, 246–247
MTBF (mean time between failures), 60
MTTF (mean time to failure), 60, 151
MTTR (mean time to repair), 151
multiple decrements, *see* competing risks
multiple regression model, 123
multiple Type I and Type II censoring, 187, *see also* censoring
multistate systems, 34, 38
multivariate distributions, 101
    bivariate exponential distribution, 101, 106–107
Muth distribution, 95, 99–101

N

NBAFR (new better than used average failure rate), 69, *see also* distribution classes
NBU (new better than used), 69, 77, *see also* distribution classes
NBUE (new better than used in expectation), 69, 77, *see also* distribution classes
negative exponential distribution, *see* exponential distribution
net lifetimes, 110–117, 129–130, 288–290, *see also* competing risks
net probabilities, 110–117, *see also* competing risks
Newton–Raphson technique, 216–217, 221–222, 296
NHPP, *see* nonhomogeneous Poisson process
nominal coverage (confidence interval), *see* stated coverage

nonhomogeneous Poisson process, 49, *144–147*
    application, 158, 222, 227
    intensity function, 136–137, 145–147
    notation, 137–138
    references, 157
nonmonotonic hazard function, 9, *see also* BT; UBT
nonparametric methods, 12–13, 239, *252–264*
    life tables, 261–264
    survivor function estimation, 253–261
nonrepairable assumption, 27
normal distribution, 8, 43, 79, 81, 88, 95, 99, 170–172, 179–180, 205, 208, 223, 260
null hypothesis, 201, *see also* hypothesis testing
number on test, 11, 161, *182*, 197–198, *210–214*, 221, 229
NWAFR (new worse than used average failure rate), 69, *see also* distribution classes
NWU (new worse than used), 69, *see also* distribution classes
NWUE (new worse than used in expectation), 69, *see also* distribution classes

O

O–rings, 5–7, 9, *see also Challenger* accident
observed information matrix, *177*, 179, 276–277
    for the accelerated life model, 231, 236–238
    for the exponential distribution, 177, 194–195, 198–199, 203, 206, 208, 225
    for the inverse Gaussian distribution, 177–179
    for the proportional hazards model, 243–244, 246–249, 251, 260
    for the Weibull distribution, 217, 219–220
omnibus tests, 269
on/off cycling, 3–4, 13, *see also* system design considerations
open and short failure, 38, 43, 86, 109
operating characteristic curve, 211
optimal block replacement policy, 157, *see also* replacement policies
order statistic censoring, *see* Type II censoring
order statistics, 75, 161, 186–188, 241
    exponential distribution, 86–87, 198, 213, 222, 282–283
overdispersed, 141–142, 157

P

P-value, 201, *see also* hypothesis testing
parallel-series system, 27, 38, 42
parallel system, 7, *17–18*, 21, 30, 66–68
    applications, 40–43, 76, 103, 106, 203
    applied to O–rings, 5
    block diagram for, 18
    definition, 17–18
    law of diminishing returns, *30–31*, 64
    relationship with k-out-of-n system, 17
    shared-parallel system, 31
    standby system, 31

(parallel system, *cont'd*)
　　system reliability, 30, 64, 103
parameter estimation, 189–251, see also accelerated life
　　　model; exponential distribution; proportional
　　　hazards model; Weibull distribution
parameter transformation, 186
parameters, 91
　　location, *78–79*
　　scale, 11, *79*
　　shape, 11, *79*
Pareto distribution, 72–73, 97, 99–101, 105, 158, 188,
　　276
path vector, 23–24, 40
path vector technique, 31–32, see also system reliability
　　calculations
percentiles, 59, *see also* fractiles
phase-type distribution, 101
physics of failure, 196
point availability, 150–153
point estimation, 11, 161–166
　　in the accelerated life model, 228–238
　　applied to the exponential distribution, 161–164,
　　　172–173, 192, 194, 197–198, 203–205, 220–221,
　　　223–225
　　applied to the Weibull distribution, 215–221, 226
　　bias versus variability trade-off, 164–165
　　consistency, 165–166, 177
　　Cramer–Rao inequality, 163–164, 186
　　efficiency, 162–163
　　mean squared error, 164–165
　　minimum-variance unbiased estimator, 163–164
　　in the proportional hazards model, 238–249, 251
　　relationship to interval estimators, 161, 166
　　unbiased estimator, 161–166, 221–223, 225
　　variance of point estimates, 161–164
point estimator, 161–166, *see also* point estimation
point process applications in safety and reliability, 157
point process models, 133, 136–147, 157
　　nonhomogeneous Poisson, 49, 137–138, *144–147*,
　　　157–158, 227
　　notation, 137–138
　　parameter estimation, 157, 227
　　Poisson, 87, 94, *137–140*, 142–147, 157, 203, 214
　　realization, 138–139
　　renewal, 137–138, *140–144*, 157
　　terminology from the literature, 2
Poisson distribution, 121, *139–140*, 145, 284
Poisson process, 139–140, 146, 157
　　notation, 137–138
　　relation with exponential distribution, 87, 94, 140,
　　　142–147, 203, 214
population versus individual, 52
power function, 211–213
power law process, 146, 158, 227, 276
power (of a hypothesis test), 201, *see also* hypothesis
　　testing
preventive maintenance, 4, 135
prior distribution, 101, 120, 128, 214, *see also* Bayesian
　　model
probabilistic models for coherent systems, *see* coherent
　　systems analysis

probability density function, 8, 48
　　definition, 48
　　existence properties, 48
　　interpretation, 48
　　relation to other functions, 48, *54–55*, 71–72
　　role in the likelihood function, 185, 229
probability integral transformation, 84, 281, *see also*
　　Monte Carlo simulation
probability of failure from risk *j*, 111, 113–117, 129–130,
　　see also competing risks
probability mass function, 56–58, 73–75, 242–243,
　　297–298
probability models, *see* coherent systems analysis;
　　distributions; reliability calculations; repairable
　　systems; specialized models
producer's risk, 210–213, 225–226, *see also* life testing
product-limit estimator, 12–13, 257–261, 276–277, 297
　　confidence limits for, 12–13, 260–261
progressive Type I and Type II censoring, 187, *see also*
　　censoring
proportional hazards model, 9, 11–13, 121–122,
　　125–128, 131–132, *238–249*, 251
　　applications, 246–251
　　with a binary covariate, 122, 126–128, 239–251
　　comparison with accelerated life model, *126–128,*
　　　228–229
　　covariates in, 14, 121–122
　　distribution representations, 125–126
　　generalizations of, 129
　　goodness-of-fit test, 276
　　link function, 122–128, 228–229
　　maximum likelihood, 11–12, 238–249, 251
　　parameter estimation, 11–12, *238–247*
　　stratification, 129
　　Weibull baseline distribution, 125–128, 132

Q

quality control, 1, 4
quantiles, *see* fractiles

R

random censoring, *183–184*, 190, 205–208, 215–220,
　　259, 275
random sample, 191–192
random variate generation, *see* Monte Carlo simulation
randomly right-censored data set, 189–190
　　exponential distribution, 205–208
　　Weibull distribution, 215–220
rank vector, 239–243
rate of occurrence of failures, 138, 140
raw data (exact failure times), 160, 181, 252–253
Rayleigh distribution, *88*, 97, 99
Reagan, Ronald, 6
recidivism, 247–249
redistribute to the right algorithm, 259–260, 276
redundancy allocation problem, 134

redundancy in system design, 5, *see also* parallel system
redundant-series system, *see* parallel-series system
regression coefficients, 122–123, 131–132
regression model, 122–123, 128, *see also* accelerated life model; proportional hazards model
  interaction terms, 123, 238
  nonlinear relationships, 123
  regression coefficients, 122–123, 246–249
  stepwise selection of covariates, 123
  Weibull regression parameter estimation, 292–293
regressor variables, *see* covariates
relationships among lifetime distributions, 98–99, 101
relative efficiency, *see* point estimation
reliability
  adequate performance in definition, 2–3
  alternative definitions of time in, 3
  applications, *see* system design applications
  binary model in, 3, 16, 34, 37–38
  boundary in definition, 3
  calculation of, *see* system reliability calculations
  component, 28
  continuous operation versus on/off cycling, 3–4, 13
  definition, 2–4
  environmental conditions associated with, 2, 4, 6–7, 122, 124, 132, 136, 208, 246–247
  inconsistencies in the literature, 2
  misconceptions, 4, 14
  purpose in definition, 2–3
  relationship with quality, 4
  standards for, 3
  time units, 3, 28
Reliability and Maintainability 2000 Program, 157
reliability bounds, 36–37, 39, 43
reliability calculations, *see* system reliability calculations
reliability engineers, 1, *see also* system design considerations
reliability function, 8, 27–35, 36–39, 41–43, 62–64, *see also* system reliability calculations
reliability growth, 8, 69, 157
reliability importance, *35*, 42, 104
reliability literature, 2
reliability textbooks, 12–13
reliability vector, 28
renewal equation, 144, 157–158
renewal process, 140–144, 157–158
  distribution of the number of failures by time t, 142–144
  distribution of the time of the nth failure, 142–144
  notation, 137–138
repair models, 133, 136
repair time, 147–149
  definition, 147
  partitioning, 148
repairable system, 9–11, *133–159*, *see also* availability; birth-death models; point process models
  differences between repairable and nonrepairable, 136–138
  system state, 148
  terminology, 136–138, 157
repeated components in block diagrams, 18–20, *see also* block diagrams

replacement models, 133–135, *see also* replacement policies
replacement policies, 72, *134–135*
  age, 134–135, 158
  block, 134–135, 158
  failure, 134–135
residual property, 81
right censoring, 11–13, 182–191, 197–227, 244–251, *see also* censoring
risk set, 239–247
Rogers Commission, 5–6, 13, *see also Challenger* accident
rule of elimination, 33

S

sample size, 11, *see also* number on test
sampling distribution, 161
scale parameter, 79
score statistic, 175, 187, 192, 203, 205, 242–243, *see also* score vector
score vector, 173–181, 187, 215, 231, 243–244, 251, 257
self-reproducing property, 81, 86, 91, 103, 281–283
sequential sampling, 214, 226, *see also* life testing
series system, 7–8, 16–17, 29, 158
  applications, 40–41, 43, 75–76, 103, 106
  applied to O–rings, 5
  block diagram for, 7, *17*
  in competing risks, 109
  definition, 16–17
  relationship with k-out-of-n, 17
  reliability importance of components, 35
  in repairable systems, 155–156, 158
  system reliability, 29, 63–64, 86
  weakest link property, 29, 35
series-parallel system, 27, 38, 42, 102
series-redundant systems, *see* series-parallel systems
service industry, 14
shape parameter, 79
shared-load system, 38
shared-parallel system, 31, *see also* parallel system
shift parameter, 79
shock models, 87, 106
significance level, 201, *see also* hypothesis testing
significant digits, 195
single binary covariate, *see* binary covariate
6-MP (6–mercaptopurine) experiment, *see* leukemia remission times
skewness, 60–61
  definition, 60
  for the exponential distribution, 61, *85*, 102, 105, 223
  for the gamma distribution, 93, 105
  for other parametric distributions, 105
  references, 69
  for the Weibull distribution, *89*, 104–105
smallpox, 109
social science applications, 136, 156
socket model, 134, 140–142, 158
software reliability, 52, 56
space shuttle, *see Challenger* accident

spares, 102, 141
specialized models, 108–132, *see also* accelerated life
    model; competing risks; mixture distribution;
    proportional hazards model
split model, 247
standard deviation, 60, *see also* moments
standby systems, 31, 38, 105, 155–156, 159, *see also*
    parallel system; system design applications
standard error, 219
static reliability calculations, *see* system reliability
    calculations
stated coverage (confidence interval), 166, *see also*
    interval estimation
state vector, *see* system state vector
static reliability calculations, 8, *see also* system reliability
    calculations
stationarity, 138, 140, 145
stochastic parameter model, 117, *see* continuous mixture
    model
stochastic parameters, *see* Bayesian model
stress-strength model, 43
structural importance, *21–23*, 35, 40, 42, *see also*
    coherent systems analysis
structure function, 7, *15–32*, 37–43, *see also* coherent
    systems analysis
student *t* distribution, *see t* distribution
subsystems, 5, 19, 23, 25–27, 40–41
superadditive, 77
superpositioning, 146–147
survival distributions, *see* distributions
survivor function, 8, *46–47*, 56–58, 265–266
    aliases, 46
    applications, 91
    comparison of, 46–47
    confidence interval for, 254–256, 260–261
    definition, 46
    for discrete distributions, 56–58
    empirical estimation of, 11, 195–196, 200, *253–264*,
        274, 276–277
    existence properties, 46
    interpretation, 46
    parametric estimation of, 11, 189–227
    relation to other functions, *54–55*, 71–72
    role in determining system reliability, 62–64, 69,
        75–76
    role in the likelihood function, 185, 229
switch, 56, *see also* automotive a/c switch failure times
switching, *see* standby systems
system, definition, 7
system configurations
    bridge, 19–20
    complex, 18–20
    k-out-of-*n*, 18–19, *see also k*-out-of-*n* system
    parallel, 17–18, *see also* parallel system
    series, 16–17, *see also* series system
system design applications, *see also* system
    configurations
    aircraft, 9–10, 135–136, 150
    airline industry, 14, 71
    airplane propellers, 18–19
    automobile, 3, 4, 14–15, 17, 135–136

automobile brakes, 17, 56
automobile engine, 17
automobile tires, 4
automobile wheel lug nuts, 31, 38
ball bearings, 3, 83, 135, *see also* ball bearing failure
    times
battery, 79, 83, 135
bicycle wheel spokes, 17
calculator, 9–10, 17, 111–113
candle, 83
Christmas tree lights, 29
communication network, 26
computer program, 52, 56
computer terminal, 2
diodes, 103
drill, 3
drill bit, 3, 11, 251
fuse, 3, 56, 59, 83, 102
grenade, 4
hospital power sources, 31
kidneys, 17
light bulb, 10–12, 14, 74, 79, 134, 136, 140, 142–143,
    184, 239–246
light switch, 3
nuclear power plant, 1
overnight package delivery, 14
person, 14, 122, *see also* actuarial science
service industry, 14
sociological events, 136, 156
space shuttle, *see Challenger* accident
spare tire, 31
spring, 90–91
switch, 31, 56
suspension bridge, 17, 28
television set, 14
transistor, 103
system design considerations
    availability, 9–10, *147–154*
    component versus system redundancy, 20–22, 39, 43
    continuous operation versus on/off cycling, 3–4, 13
    environmental factors, 2, 4, 6–7, 122, 124, 132, 136,
        208, 246–247
    independence of components, 3, 6, *27–28*, 34, 37–38
    maintainability, 133–136
    reliability importance, 35, 42, 104
    structural importance, 21–23, 35, 40, 42
system lifetime distribution, 62–64, 69, 75–76
system redundancy, *20–22*, 39, 43
system reliability calculations, 8, *27–35*, *see also* system
    lifetime distribution
    cut vector technique, 32–33
    decomposition technique, 33–34
    definition technique, 28–29
    delta-star technique, 38
    expectation technique, 30–32
    modular decomposition, 38
    path vector technique, 31–32
system reliability bounds, *see* reliability bounds
system state (repairable item), 148
system state vector (deterministic), 16
    inequality in, 23

system state vector (random), 28
system unreliability, 31
systems of components, *see* system configurations

T

t distribution, 170, 187
threshold parameter, 79
tie set, *see* path set
tie vector, *see* path vector
tied observations, 234, 245–246, 255–256, 259, 293
time censoring, *see* Type I censoring
time-dependent covariates, 129, 249
time persistent statistic, 157
total time on test transform, 68, 73
total time on test, 198–199, 203–205, 220, 254
transition matrix (for a Markov process), 150, 154, 156
traveling psychiatrist, 183, 187
treatment group, 122, 190, 205–208, 226, 233–237, 246, 257–263, *see also* leukemia remission times
trivial bounds, 36
truncated life test, 214, *see also* life testing
truncated normal distribution, 101
2-out-of-3 system, 18, 32, 41–42, 102
2-out-of-4 system, 40, 43
Type I censoring, *182–184*, 203–205, 221, 223–225, 271–273, *see also* censoring
Type I error, 201, *see also* hypothesis testing
Type I right-censored data set, 189, 191, *see also* motorette failure times
Type II censoring, *182*, 184, 188, 190, 197–203, 211–213, 222–226, 271–273, *see also* censoring
Type II error, 201, *see also* hypothesis testing
Type II right-censored data set, 189–190, *see also* automotive a/c switch failure times

U

UBT (upside-down bathtub-shaped) hazard function, 95–96, 100
unavailability, 153
unbiased estimator, 161–166, 221–223, 225
uncensored data sets, *see* complete data sets
underdispersed, 141–142, 157
uniform distribution, 72, 75–76, *95*, 99–100, 105, 119, 269
unit exponential distribution, *see* exponential distribution
unreliability (system), 31

V

variance, *60–61*, 72, 75, 85, 89, 93, 142, 161–166, 176, 181, 188

variance-covariance matrix, 174–176, 179–181, 219, 237, *see also* Fisher information matrix; observed information matrix
variate generation, 131–132, *see also* Monte Carlo simulation

W

Wald distribution, *see* inverse Gaussian distribution
warranty period, 52, 62–63, 79
weakest link property (for series systems), 29, 35
wear (mechanical components), 16
wear-out failures, 52, 136–138
Weibull distribution, *88–91*, *215–221*
 applications, 62, 69–72, 76–77, 102–105
 as baseline in accelerated life model, 124, *237–238*, 251
 as baseline in proportional hazards model, 125–126, 127–128
 characteristic life, 89, 104
 coefficient of variation, 89, 105
 in competing risks, 130
 conditional survivor function, 69–71, 91
 confidence region for λ and κ, 11, *218–219*
 curve shapes, 90
 definition, 50, 55, *88–91*, 95–96
 distribution classes, 88, 100
 goodness-of-fit test, 269–270, 276, 278
 information matrix, 217, 219–220
 initial estimator for κ, 216–217, 221–222, *291–293*
 kurtosis, *89–90*, 104–105
 least-squares parameter estimates, 291–293
 log likelihood function, 215, 217–219
 maximum likelihood estimates, 11–12, 215–222, 226
 mean, 89
 median, 88, 104
 mode, 88, 104
 moments, 89–90
 in a nonhomogeneous Poisson process, 146, 158
 in a renewal process, 158
 parameter estimation, *215–221*, 226, *294–296*
 parameters, 11, 88, 102, 226
 probabilistic properties, 88–91
 references, 101, 221–222
 regression estimators, 291–293
 relationship to the power law process, 146, *see also* power law process
 relationships to other distributions, 91, 94, 99, 103
 in renewal processes, 158
 self-reproducing property, 91
 skewness, *89*, 104–105
 special cases, 88
 system reliability with Weibull components, 76–77
 variance, 89
 variate generation, 84–85
Weibull paper, 293

Chapter 6   Repairable Systems

c	Time between replacements
$T_1, T_2, \ldots$	Failure times
$X_1, X_2, \ldots$	Times between failures
$N(t)$	Number of failures on $(0, t]$
$\Lambda(t)$	Cumulative intensity function
$\lambda(t)$	Intensity function
$R_1, R_2, \ldots$	Repair times
$X(t)$	State of the system at time t
$A(t)$	Point availability at time t
A	Limiting availability
A_c	Average availability on $[0, c)$
A_∞	Limiting average availability
λ_0, λ_1	Failure and repair rates

Chapter 7   Lifetime Data Analysis

n	Number of items on test (sample size)
$t_1, \ldots, t_n$	Data set of lifetimes
$t_{(1)}, \ldots, t_{(n)}$	Order statistics
θ	Mean of the exponential distribution
$\hat{\theta}$	Maximum likelihood estimator of θ
α	Significance level
L	Confidence interval lower limit
U	Confidence interval upper limit
W	Confidence interval width
θ_0	True value of a parameter
p	Number of unknown parameters
$\boldsymbol{\theta}$	$p \times 1$ Vector of unknown parameters
$L(\mathbf{t}, \boldsymbol{\theta})$	Likelihood function
$\hat{\boldsymbol{\theta}}$	$p \times 1$ Maximum likelihood estimator of θ
$\mathbf{U}(\boldsymbol{\theta})$	$p \times 1$ Score vector
$I(\boldsymbol{\theta})$	$p \times p$ Fisher information matrix
$O(\hat{\boldsymbol{\theta}})$	$p \times p$ Observed information matrix
r	Number of observed failures
$c_1, \ldots, c_n$	Right censoring times
U	Index set of uncensored observations
C	Index set of censored observations
$\delta_1, \ldots, \delta_n$	Censoring indicator variables
$x_1, \ldots, x_n$	Minimums of failure times and censoring times
*	Denotes a right-censored observation